BRINGING THE LAW BACK IN

Bringing the Law Back In

Essays in Land, Law and Development

PATRICK McAUSLAN
Professor of Law; MBE; BA, BCL
Birkbeck College

Routledge
Taylor & Francis Group
LONDON AND NEW YORK

First published 2003 by Ashgate Publishing

Reissued 2019 by Routledge
2 Park Square, Milton Park, Abingdon, Oxon, OXl 4 4RN
52 Vanderbilt Avenue, New York, NY 10017

Routledge is an imprint of the Taylor & Francis Group, an informa business

A Library of Congress record exists under LC control number:

ISBN 13: 978-1-138-72543-0 (hbk)
ISBN 13: 978-1-138-72541-6 (pbk)
ISBN 13: 978-1-315-19188-1 (ebk)

Contents

Preface and acknowledgements

This collection of papers attempts to offer a coherent view of the work I have undertaken in the area of land law in developing countries over the last 20 years. The collection is in two parts, Opinions and Operations, the essays in the first part being or attempting to be more reflective and discursive, more academic or policy-orientated, while those in the second part are derived from or reflect on specific operations that I have been involved in over that period. With one exception (Stren, 1995 and Fernandes and Varley, 1998) these papers represent my principal non-consultation report writing in the area of land law and development over the last two decades.

I have been studying, teaching and working as a consultant in the area of land law in developing countries for over 35 years. I started my career as a lecturer in the then University College, Dar es Salaam in 1961 and began teaching land law there in 1965. I wrote my first paper on land law in East Africa in 1966 (Sawyerr, 1967). I continued writing on the subject from an academic observer's position (*e.g.* Ghai and McAuslan, 1970; Kanyeihamba and McAuslan, 1978) until I undertook my first consultancy in 1977 – a UN consultancy to the Capital Development Authority in Dodoma, Tanzania – discussed, amongst other cases, in Chapter 7 of this book.

From then on, I have tended in my writings to combine my practical experiences in the field (or more accurately in the city for I have usually been working with Ministries in central governments located in the capital rather than with the owners and occupiers of land in rural areas) with my academic interests and perspectives to try and give some broad general overviews of the role of law in the development and reform of land policy and management in those countries that I have been involved in. The title of the book sums up my overall stance: there is an important role for law in development generally and in land reform in particular and it is, in my view, wholly beneficial that after almost three decades of virtually ignoring the role of law in development (which, by definition, continued to be used for that purpose in developing countries) international financial institutions, aid agencies and scholars in the West are beginning to appreciate and re-affirm both its centrality to development in practice and its centrality to understanding the process of development and change in societies in developing countries.

I have always considered that trying to give some wider publicity to one's work as a consultant is part of the duties of a consultant. We need to let people know what we are doing and we need feedback on what we are doing from independent critics. Too often, consultants' reports are deemed to be confidential or where they are available for circulation, do not in practice receive wide publicity and so do not circulate outside a very restricted circle. Writing about my work and publishing in journals and books has been an attempt to put my views about publicity into practice. The papers in this book are scattered about in various publications and it seemed worthwhile in the year that I reach the silver jubilee of my role as a consultant to bring them together so that there is an opportunity for those interested in the subject to assess my contribution to the field.

At the same time, this book provides me with an opportunity to pay tribute to all those persons – national officials, lawyers, academics, members of NGOs, international civil servants, fellow consultants, politicians, aid agencies and their staffs, and secretaries – with whom I have been privileged to work over the four decades of my involvement in land issues and law in development and from whom I have learned so much. It would be invidious to single out any one person from the many I have worked with: I would like to thank them all equally for their patience, understanding, goodwill, good humour and what they have taught me. It is important too to make the point very strongly that in every country that I have worked in – now over 30 – and in every agency I have worked in or with, I have found the people I have worked with to be hard working and committed to their work. We have not always agreed – that will be clear from some of the chapters in the book – but I have found the disagreements to be as productive of positive developments in my own thinking and actions as the agreements. I have always enjoyed working with my colleagues of all disciplines; they have always given me great support. This book could not have been written without their contributions.

In view of the provenance of this work, I must make absolutely clear that the views expressed therein are mine and mine alone and must not in any way be assumed to be or represent the views or opinions or ideas or attitudes of any of the agencies, governments, firms or colleagues I have worked for or with in connection with any of the consultancies which form the basis of any of the chapters of this book.

I would like to acknowledge and thank all those publishers and editors who agreed to my re-publishing papers that first appeared in their journals or books. After careful consideration, apart from correcting misprints, and factual mistakes, I have left most of the papers as they were originally published. They were my views at the time; they influenced what I had done then and thereafter so it seems to be best to let them be considered now in the context in which they were written.

I must thank all those in Ashgate Publishing and outside for their help with the preparation of the typescript. Without their contributions, this book would never have seen the light of day.

PART I: OPINIONS

1 Land policy: a framework for analysis and action*

Introduction

There are few more important aspects to the life of any society than land and the relations between land and human kind. Economists recognise land as being one of the three economic fundamentals of society along with labour and capital. It is no accident that anthropologists have, in investigating traditional societies, spent a great deal of energy in probing those societies' rules and practices about land since they know that that will tell them much about those societies both in the pre-colonial and in the colonial era. The ownership of land has, throughout the ages and in all societies, been a major factor in determining class structures and relations and in the allocation and exercise of political power. Equally the many and often conflicting uses to which land – sometimes the same plot of land – can be put have given rise both to complex laws and serious disputes in many societies.

The scramble for Africa, the carve up of the Pacific, the settlement of Australasia were, at bottom, organised, governmentally sanctioned and ultimately directed, land grabbing exercises and the constant disputes between colonisers and colonised all over the world could time and again be traced back to unequal agreements, if they could be dignified by that name, about land. The tensions about land carried over into the negotiations for independence and the final settlement enshrined in a constitution and an independence aid package. In Kenya and Zimbabwe for instance, both constitutions and aid packages were constructed to take account of the need both to placate settler fears and meet African aspirations over prime agricultural land. In many of the new island states of the South Pacific, provisions on land rights are enshrined in the constitutions and are designed to restore or confirm to the indigenous inhabitants of those states their traditional rights over land (Ghai, 1987). Even more significant, we may think, is that the Governments of Australia (Peterson, 1985), Canada (Lysyk, 1973) and the USA (Coulter and Tulberg, 1985) are, belatedly, trying to make amends for the way they have in the past treated and to some extent still do treat the indigenous inhabitants of those countries by reallocating land and land rights to them, a clear recognition of the importance that land has for those people and of the inequitable way that they were treated in the past in respect of their land.

To complete the picture of the central importance of land in virtually all societies, I must too refer to the fact of famine and poverty and the reaction of aid and development agencies. There seems to be one constant theme in the approach of these agencies, whether official like the World Bank (Falloux, 1987) or unofficial like Oxfam; the need to make more effective use of land in both urban and rural sectors; the need for land reform, the need to prevent degradation of the land (Blaikie, 1985), the need for efficient and equitable methods of land allocation. Whether one adopts a basic human needs strategy of development or a more market orientated strategy to overcome problems of poverty and underdevelopment, the central place of land in the development process is acknowledged on all sides.

We can all agree then that land is of central importance in any society. But what follows from that? It is this question that I address in this chapter by asking and trying to answer four questions: first, what is the most useful or relevant way to approach the whole issue of land, land relations and rights and land law in a developing society? Second, what are the essential national interests in land that would justify a national land policy; third what matters should feature in such a policy; and fourth, what models are available and appropriate for the implementation of a national land policy? My aim then is to lay out the ground, to clear away some of the misconceptions about land and highlight some of the issues which need to be considered. I am not trying to formulate a land policy for anywhere in particular for that would be presumptuous but I hope that the approach adopted here might contribute to a better understanding of the strengths and weaknesses of existing policies and the development of new policies in the future.

What is the best way to approach land?

In the brief introduction to the central importance of land in society, attention was drawn to the economic, the anthropological, the political and the developmental aspects of land. This was deliberate: the first lesson to be learned about land is that it cannot be treated in policy terms as if it had only one aspect or dimension. It is multi-dimensional. Too often, policy has focused on one aspect of land to the exclusion of other aspects and, not surprisingly, such a policy has failed to achieve its goals, because it failed to take account of the multi-dimensional nature of land. Consider the issue of title to and marketability of land, a policy much favoured by the World Bank and some governments who consider that modernisation involves a sweeping away of laws which prevent the operation of a market for land, *i.e.* customary law. Marketability of land is however only one aspect of land, an aspect moreover which is grounded in a particular theory or ideology about, or approach to society, which may not accord with the approach to society adopted by others in that society.

We can in fact isolate two broad approaches to land in society; one of which sees land as basically part of the social relations between people and society, the other of which sees land as basically part of the economic relations between persons and persons in society. The former in turn is based on an approach to society which does not differentiate between economic and social relations in society; economic are part of social and social relations are all important. Traditional societies governed by customary laws provide examples of such an approach to land. Modern societies on the other hand are dominated by the market where economic and social relations are kept strictly apart and land is viewed as a commodity and a factor of production. Modern statutory land law is designed to facilitate the operation of the market and so advance this approach to society and land. But the older approach cannot be abolished at the stroke of a pen, so a new statutory regime of land as commodity begins after a time to be infiltrated by the older notion of land as an aspect of social relations with consequent difficulties for those administering or indeed learning the law.

This is a particular problem in societies where customary land law, and the approach to land and society, of which it is the outward sign, exists alongside statutory land law and the approach to land and society it personifies, and I will come back to that later, but I want first to stress that this latent conflict between two approaches to land exists in other societies and their laws as well. English land law may be taken as an example. In England the evidence of social history and current practice shows that there is a broad difference of approach between those who stress the importance of protecting the users and occupiers of land and those who stress the importance of maintaining the marketability of land. The reforms to the land law of 1925 were designed to enshrine the philosophy of alienability in the law, the triumph of the commodity approach to land in the market economy. But what has happened? Slowly bit by bit, another philosophy is making itself felt in the land law through the decisions of the courts as much as through the activities of the legislature. This philosophy is based on the ideas thought to be overthrown by statute in 1925 – the protection of users and occupiers. If we look at the post-World War Two development of the licence, of equitable estoppel, of constructive trusts, of the deserted wife's equity and the family home, of the freeing of the law of restrictive covenants of some of its limiting rules, of the generous interpretation given to the concept of "actual occupation" in the Land Registration Act, 1925, of the protection of the interests of the mortgagor in arrears, they can all be explained by reference to this older philosophy of protection of the user, a philosophy with roots going back hundreds of years. So it is no surprise that English land law is or is thought to be complicated; what we see is the working out in the cases and in the statutes of contrasting philosophies and the difficulties of reconciling them – *a fortiori*, when this law forms the basis of statutory land law in so many countries in the Commonwealth where it exists alongside customary law.

If English land law today exhibits a certain amount of schizophrenia when English society is generally dominated by a market economy, it is not to be wondered at that states which still retain strong elements of traditional approaches to land in society, the social approach as opposed to the modern economic approach, have great difficulty in formulating coherent land policies or developing national and universal systems of land law. Unless some recognition is given to both approaches to land, land policy and land law reform are unlikely to be effective.

How can this recognition be given to two such opposed approaches? The first step is to understand their existence and as an aid to this I advance an analysis which may be called the three circuits of land in society. This notion of circuits is taken from the Brazilian geographer Milton Santos who formulated the notion of the two circuits of the urban economy in his book *The Shared Space* (1979). His two circuits are interrelated and overlapping. He describes them as follows (p. 8):

> The upper circuit is the direct result of technological progress and its most representative elements are the monopolies. Most of its relations take place outside the city and surrounding area and operate in a national or international framework. The lower circuit consists of small-scale activities and is almost exclusively for the poor. Unlike the upper circuit, the lower circuit is well entrenched in the city and enjoys privileged relations with its environment.

He advances his approach as a way of making sense of the urban economy of cities in developing societies and so arriving at policy prescriptions which are likely to have more success in tackling the problems of those cities. His fundamental point is that there are two very different economies co-existing and overlapping in the same space, the city; both have a role to play in the city and policy must recognise that.

His approach is very illuminating and can be adapted to our concern with land. It is suggested that there are three circuits of land relations in many developing states, certainly in the majority of states in Africa and the Pacific and several states too Asia, Latin America and the Caribbean as well. These circuits too are overlapping and share the same space and must be taken account of by policy makers.

The circuits are: (i) customary land and its regulation via traditional processes – its space is principally but not exclusively in rural society; (ii) an unofficial market in land regulated by custom and practice – its space is principally urban and peri-urban but it is growing in the rural society; and (iii) the modern official land market regulated by statutory codes of law interpreted and applied by professionals and state officials – its space is both urban and rural. Using Santos's terms, it could be said that the modern official land market is the upper circuit in both rural and urban sectors; customary land is the lower circuit in the rural, and unofficial markets the lower circuit in the urban sector, and where customary and unofficial markets exist in the same space both are lower to the upper modern circuit. All the circuits are however essential not only to the general health and functioning of society but to each other; that is, there is a place for all of them in any society and any attempt to ignore or, worse, peremptorily to abolish or eliminate one circuit, is likely to have unforeseen deleterious consequences on the other circuits.

This notion of circuits in shared space replaces the notion of discrete sectors of the economy which has been the language hitherto used in discussions of land and land policy; the former directs attention to economy *and* society, the interaction between them and the interrelationship between the different land relations. The latter stresses only economy and implies that there is a sharp divide between the modern and traditional sectors, a divide which statute law has been used to give official sanction to but which, since it is not reflected in land relations in society at large, fails to provide support for efficient land management.

Let us begin then our attempts to understand the place of land in society by recognising that there exist three overlapping and interrelated sets of land relations in society, and by land relations is meant social and economic relations between people and land. These sets of relations or circuits overlap in two senses; first, people move between the circuits both in terms of their actual relationship to land and the transactions they engage in – a person may both own and deal in land in the upper circuit in town and have rights and duties in respect of customary land in the lower circuit in his or her village of origin – and in terms of their assumptions about relationships to land; a formal transaction in the upper circuit may be infused with notions about or contain elements of rights and duties derived from the lower circuit.

Second, it may be difficult to determine whether a particular piece of land is within a particular circuit; it may well be within more than one circuit, each circuit giving rise to its own sets of rights and duties. This would often be the case with squatter settlements or popular housing where urban land in the upper or third circuit is occupied and dealt with according to the norms of and so brought within the lower or second circuit. It does not have to be squatter settlements however. Land compulsorily acquired by the state may formally pass into the third circuit but for its erstwhile customary occupiers, it may remain in the lower first circuit if lower circuit rules and practices are not followed at the time of dispossession. In Malawi and Lesotho, real problems are caused by land on the outskirts of towns being developed with housing by permission of the local chief. Under customary law this is a legitimate activity; under statutory planning and land law it is illegal. In the eyes of the Aborigines in Australia, large parts of Australia still remain in "their" lower circuit notwithstanding that according to formal statutory Australian law, it is owned and occupied in accordance with laws of the upper circuit. Thus too, and the land revolution in Australia over the last decade or so testifies to this, it is vitally important to appreciate that each circuit is, in the eyes of its users, legitimate; each circuit is an integral part of the whole society and one cannot make assumptions about the legality or illegality, legitimacy or illegitimacy of any circuit.

What are the essential national interests in land?

What are the essential national interests in land which would or can justify national intervention into land relations in the form of a land policy and formal institutions of land management? This fundamental question is too often ignored or dismissed by pointing to the undeniable fact that virtually all countries have some sort of national land policy or a variety of instruments and mechanisms available to influence, guide or regulate land relations which, if carefully examined, point to some sort of national view on land relations. One can in other words have a national land policy without having formally to articulate it in the shape of a document as the Japanese do in an annual report on the Use of National Land produced in accordance with section 3 of the National Land Use Planning Act, 1968 (OECD, 1986).

The fact that all countries, East, West, North, South, capitalist or socialist, have national land policies does not answer the question posed at the beginning of this section. Yet clearly we must answer it for unless each state has sorted out what the purpose or purposes of its land policy is or are, it is likely to be difficult to justify or explain particular laws or practices, and to be vunerable to national and international pressures to adopt measures in relation to land which may harm the national interest. What then are the components of a national interest in land? The following are put forward as being the basic building blocks of any national land policy: efficiency; equity; certainty; safeguarding the state and the national patrimony; recognising the legitimacy of difference.

Efficiency

In any society land is a scarce resource. It may be scarce because of population pressure; because little of it is habitable or usable; because the resources of capital necessary to make it habitable or usable are themselves unavailable; because certain practices make extravagant uses of land; or because too much land is owned or under the control of people who prefer the land to lie idle than to be brought into productive or socially beneficial use. Whatever the reason, intervention by national, state, or local agencies – no assumptions are being made about where intervention powers should be located – in order to ensure the efficient allocation and use of land is justifiable in the national interest. At this point too, no assumptions are being made about the most appropriate tools or mechanisms for achieving efficiency in land allocation or land use and in particular, no choice is being made between use of the market and use of public regulation to achieve efficiency. The point here is that efficiency in the allocation and use of a scarce resource like land is a sufficiently important goal for any society to aim for to provide a justification for the governmental organs of that society to have policies about it and to seek to implement those policies.

Equity

Efficiency is a goal with which few people can disagree though they may very well disagree about the policies and means needed to achieve that goal. Equity is a more overt value judgement and so likely to give rise to disagreement as a goal. But it may be argued that on several grounds, equity is a necessary goal for any form of land policy. By equity is meant no more than that a fair and reasonable proportion of the resources of society, in this case land, be made available to all members of society and that as a corollory of that, steps be taken to ensure that this is done and that the position is maintained.

Why should this be so? First, equity can itself be regarded as an aspect of efficiency. A labour force which is badly housed in overcrowded, poor environmental conditions is likely to be unhealthy and hence inefficient; better housing, more open space for recreation, a pollution-free environment is both more equitable and more efficient. The same point can be made for rural society. If, as is beginning to happen in some countries in Africa, more and more land is turned over to agribusiness – estates growing export crops run by multinational corporations – then the amount and quality of land available for food crops shrinks; the rural population can no longer adequately feed itself let alone produce a surplus for urban populations; such land as it can use is degraded through overuse with further falls in food production and a vicious circle sets in; malnutrition, further migration to urban centres, foreign exchange having to be spent on the import of food for the urban population and local funds used to subsidise food prices. An equitable distribution of land between peasants for food crops and cash crops, and agribusiness would achieve a more efficient use of national resources although it might reduce some private profits.

But equity can be justified on grounds other than efficiency. Leaving aside the comparatively few states in the world where the sole aim of the rulers appears to be to enrich themselves irrespective of the damage done to the resources or citizens of the state or a state such as Israel where state policy is to deny resources to citizens and those persons whose land it is illegally occupying on racial grounds, we find that most states recognise the need for the institutions of government to be regarded as legitimate by the citizenry, and legitimacy is in turn greatly assisted if the citizenry feel that they have a stake in society or gain some benefits from the institutions of government. In a state where the vast majority of the population live in rural areas, that stake in society is obtained through occupation and use of land. Even in urban centres, there is much evidence to indicate that the urban poor will commit more of their meagre resources to their homes if they have security of tenure – a stake in the city – and so are much less likely to be the raw material for revolutionary or terrorist activity. Equity in land policy then focuses in part on the importance of ensuring that the citizenry feel that they have a stake in society, that the society of which they are a part is worth supporting if not actively in the sense of participating in government then at least passively to the extent of not becoming involved in trying to overthrow the institutions of government. Equity in land policy is an aspect of democracy one might say; a good in its own right and a good in its contribution towards social and political stability.

Certainty

Efficiency and equity may be seen as economic and social aspects of land policy. Certainty is much more of an administrative and legal aspect. It is not difficult to think of statements in cases when judges have stressed the importance of certainty in property relations as a reason for denying a party a claim to which in fairness and justice, it might be thought he or she is entitled. In England one of the most striking examples is *Green's case* (1981) where old farmer Green gave his son an option to purchase his farm for a very reasonable sum. The son's solicitors omitted to register the option under the Land Charges Act; the father fell out with the son and, knowing of the failure to register the option, sold the farm, now worth £40,000, to his wife for £500. The House of Lords, reversing a Court of Appeal presided over by Lord Denning, held unanimously that the sale was good; the law was clear and it was imperative that certainty was preserved: if you registered a registrable interest you were protected; if you did not, you were not protected against a sale for money or money's worth, and the courts could not enter into an investigation of whether a price was fair, or reasonable.

We may think that this case goes too far, though we should remember that Green had a remedy against his negligent solicitors, but it makes the point that for this aspect of land policy to be effective, it is not enough to aim for certainty in the abstract; one has also to ensure that the citizenry have knowledge of their rights, duties, obligations and privileges in respect of land, and knowledge of the mechanisms available to them through which disputes about these interests, whether between citizen and citizen, or citizen and state can be resolved and a final decision given. As with efficiency so here; one is not concerned with the kind of mechanism available to resolve disputes, and achieve certainty: customary law enforced in traditional courts, statutes enforced in High Courts, administrative decisions reviewed and sanctioned by administrative tribunals, even wholly informal and unofficial dispute settling bodies in squatter settlements are all capable of resolving disputes and providing certainty and so should not be ruled out in advance.

A further point must be made: just as equity may be seen as an aspect of efficiency, so certainty may be seen as contributing to both efficiency and equity. A system of land relations could not be regarded either as efficient or equitable if the interests of people in the land were constantly likely to be disturbed; if redress were impossible to obtain from any provided agency so that one had to resort to self-help, and there was a general lack of knowledge about who had what claims to what land. All societies whatever their level of sophistication realise that a failure to provide effective mechanisms for establishing an element of certainty in land relations will quickly lead to a breakdown of social and political relations. Certainty can make a reality of efficiency and equity.

Safeguarding the state and the national patrimony

The first three components of a national interest in land relations embrace economic, social and administrative/legal aspects of land policy. The last two components are concerned more with political aspects and are not perhaps so self-evident from their title as the first three. Recall the colonial era and the land-grabbing activities of the colonialists and settlers; their exploitation of the land and natural resources of the state with little regard for the present or future generations of the indigenous population. Recall too the concern at independence in states with large settler populations or large foreign owned natural resource – Kenya, Zimbabwe, Zambia, in Africa; Papua New Guinea, Vanuatu in the South Pacific; Jamaica in the Caribbean – that independent governments would not have the power and the money to buy out foreign owned land and natural resources. That seems to me a perfectly proper aspect of a national land policy and that is part of what is meant by safeguarding the state and the national patrimony. Where the wealth of a country consists of and is bound up with the efficient and equitable use of land, it is very much a matter of national concern that that land does not pass into the hands of aliens, particularly foreign corporations acting as absentee landlords concerned with short-term high profit projects only, rather than long-term lower profit projects combined with ecologically sound management and renewal of the land.

One can instance here the awful story of the Banabans on Ocean Island in the South Pacific recounted by Megarry V.C. in the famous case of *Tito v. Waddell* (1977). By a combination of chicanery, threats and force the Banabans in effect handed over their island, in pursuance of an agreement, to the British Phosphate Commissioners, a body consisting of representatives of the UK, Australian and New Zealand Governments, in return for derisory royalties obtained from the working and winning of phosphate, and a promise to restore their island after use. The Commissioners totally destroyed the island, declined to restore it and when the Banabans went to court they were told that there was no redress for them in the English courts since there was no enforceable legal agreement or fiduciary relationship between them and the British Government. In the face of decisions like that, a Government would be acting irresponsibly if it did not seek to control and regulate the foreign ownership of its land. I think that here too there is a definite link with equity; the importance of citizens having a stake in society through the opportunity to use and occupy land. If the best land has been acquired by foreign interests so that the indigenous people find themselves reduced to the status of tenants, licencees or squatters, they may cease to feel any loyalty to the institutions of a state which permits so inequitable a state of affairs to occur. The struggle for independence in Kenya is a good example of the close relationship between the stability of the state and inequitable land policies (Rosberg and Nottingham, 1966).

A further important aspect of protection of the national patrimony is the environmental and ecological dimension. Indeed some might argue that this should be seen a separate national interest in land policy, so important is it now seen to be. But the aim and purpose of an environmental aspect to land policy is to protect and enhance the quality and usefulness of land by discouraging bad and encouraging good land use practices. The time has long passed when environmental considerations were seen as inimical to development; now it is widely recognised that not to take account of environmental considerations in planning and executing development projects is inimical to development (WCED, 1987; Redclift; 1984). This is so whether one is concerned with major infrastructural development such as dams, power stations or airports, or projects to increase peasant farmer agricultural productivity. In all cases the environmental effect on the land to be used for the project, on neighbouring land, and on the national balance of land uses needs to be considered and this can be achieved by ensuring that there is an environmental dimension to land policy.

The recognition of differences

The last component of a national land policy may seem rather strange and is likely, as with questions of equity, to be contested. This component refers to the points made when the three circuits of land relations were first advanced – the existence of different but equally valid approaches to land relations in many states and societies in the developing world, the need to recognise those differences and frame policies accordingly. In many states in Africa (James, 1987; Ega, 1987) and the South Pacific, a major issue in land policy is the place of customary law. Great pressures from funding agencies such as the World Bank have been brought to bear on governments to move away from – get rid of would be more accurate – customary law and place all land and land relations on a modern statutory footing. This may be the preferred route which governments will wish to travel but this component of land policy is put in to ensure, or at least increase the possibility that different approaches to land relations are not lost sight of; and that there is a recognition that altering the legal framework of land relations will not automatically result in an altered approach to land relations.

It cannot be too often stressed that there are relevant values and practices in all the three circuits and an alternative and maybe better approach to land reform is to build on the three circuits, rather than trying to eliminate one or two of them, and create new frameworks which will allow the circuits to develop and interrelate in an evolutionary way. All the four previous components of land policy will be strengthened by this fifth component. There is no conclusive evidence that a wholesale sweeping away of customary land law and its replacement by a statutory regime has resulted in a marked increase in efficient allocation and use of land: it often leads to a marked increase in law suits and its external costs, which are thrown on to society and the state at large, often increased landlessness and urban drift, represent an inefficient use of human resources. Equally, a fundamental change in the legal framework of land relations causes great inequity; those with knowledge or access to knowledge of the new legal regime and finance can rapidly acquire land at the expense of those who suddenly find that they have no recognised interests in the land any more. Certainty for them disappears along with equity and the basis is laid for a dissaffected, landless peasantry and an unemployed urban proletariat, hardly a recipe for a stable society.

These five components then are closely linked to each other. Together they provide a sound rationale for the involvement of the institutions of government in the three circuits of land relations in society; they provide the principles by which to judge any formulation of national land policy and any implementation.

What should be the contents of a national land policy?

So far, this chapter has concentrated on two fundamental matters; first, a method of understanding the real world of land relations in most developing countries; and second, a set of principles which provide the justification for any state to have a national land policy. The concern now shifts to what may be called a second level question: given the circuits, given the justification for state involvement in the circuits, what should be the content of that involvement? What should be the components of a national land policy? Let us then consider policy in connection with the first circuit, customary land and its regulation via traditional processes.

Land policy in circuit one

It has already been suggested that a land policy based in the five components discussed earlier would be unlikely to include measures to sweep away customary land law and the social relations which are part of customary land, and that insofar as it did include such measures, they would be likely at the least to give rise to as many problems as they purported to solve. But one should not therefore go to the other extreme and suggest that customary land and law should be left in a ghetto of neglect. We need to remember that the overwhelming majority of the inhabitants of countries in the Third World are peasant farmers or pastoralists in Africa, the South Pacific and parts of Asia; their relationship to the land is governed by customary laws and practices – this is so, though to a lesser extent, in parts of Central and South America as well – so a land policy based on the suggested five components could not just ignore this circuit. The recognition of difference component points us towards accepting the continued existence of customary land relations; efficiency and equity point us towards devising policies which assist in the more beneficial use of customary land so as to increase its economic worth (its productive output) and its social utility (more persons to have a stake in society via a stake in the land).

It is not possible here to do more than sketch out the main points of such a land policy. If we ask what are the main deficiencies of land management and use in respect of customary land, the answer will focus on overuse and degradation of land, lack of capital input into land, uncertainty about rights in the land, and a lack of flexibility in land allocation which tends to be based too much on ethnic considerations. The aims of policy then should be to tackle these deficiencies. Policies could include: first, the encouragement of cooperatives and group rights in the land so as to assist in the availability of capital for the land. Second, the grafting on to customary law of some of the ideas from the lease and licence to make more palatable people from one ethnic group occupying and using land traditionally considered to belong to another ethnic group. Third, the investigation and recordation of customary land law to assist in its application by administrators and courts. Fourth, the establishment of mechanisms to enable people to transfer land and to ensure that those with power over land under customary law do not abuse their powers.

All these suggestions can in fact be found in operation – not necessarily all together – in different countries especially in East and Southern Africa. The deficiency which often afflicts them however is that they are operated in isolation from other policies on *e.g.* finance for agricultural development, for extension services, or alternatively those programmes are directed at "progressive" farmers who are assumed to be those willing to leave customary land – circuit one – and farm on land with a statutory registered title – circuit three. Such an approach is a self-fulfilling prophecy: starved of funds, in receipt of inappropriate technical advice and little governmental commitment, it is not surprising that land in circuit one becomes over-used and degraded. Policies must be accompanied by commitment, and a realisation that land and land relations in circuit one provides both a living and a way of life for many millions of people and cannot therefore be neglected or relegated to the status of second class.

There is one further point to be made on land policies in circuit one and since it applies equally to policies in circuit two it provides a convenient bridge between the two circuits. It is an aspect of equity, the pursuit of just and fair land policies. Policies cannot, if they are to aspire to fairness and justice, be laid down from on high; there must be a commitment to work with people in circuits one and two; policy making must be a cooperative effort with the knowledge, enthusiasm and experience of the people living within circuits one and two being used and harnessed to the different skills and experiences of professionals and experts from outside those circuits to produce land policies which have more chance of being effective because they have support from those who will be implementing them. In sum, the desirable approach to land policies in circuit one is that they must be developed in a way similar to and indeed must be a major part of integrated agricultural development plans, whose purpose is to revive and transform the agricultural and rural community by a concerted programme of development on all fronts – economic, social, agricultural, rural industry, the role of women, customary law and practices etc. So too with land policies in circuit one; starting from the reality of land relations as part of social relations, the aim must be to work with rather than against the grain, to develop land relations from the bottom up and from within rather than from the top down and from without, recognising the validity and usefulness of much of what occurs now, rather than assuming that it has no merit and needs to be swept away.

Land policy in circuit two

Circuit two is the intermediate circuit, it straddles both rural and urban society and it contains within itself aspects both of circuit one – customary rights in land – and circuit three – market relations. I am familiar with this circuit in connection with urbanisation but there is considerable evidence that it exists in rural society as well. Indeed one of the best examples of this phenomenon comes from rural society in Jamaica, not a country one associates with customary law. This example can be used to illustrate both the nature of the circuit and the pros and cons of possible land policy approaches to it.

Rural Jamaica has many thousand smallholder farmers, peasant farmers on plots of less than five acres going down to half and quarter acre plots. The policy of successive Jamaican governments stretching back over 40 years has been to break up large estates and allocate land from those estates to smallholders who have to pay for the land and ultimately will obtain a full legal title to the land. Policy is one thing; implementation is another. For reasons that need not be rehearsed here but which include an over-complicated land law and mechanisms for administering it, land has been allocated to farmers but the follow-up paper work has fallen way behind the land allocations. The result is that now there are upwards of 40,000 land titles outstanding, that is persons are on 40,000 plots[1] who are in varying stages paying for those plots but the evidence of whether they have paid, and if not, how much more they have to pay, whether they have adhered to conditions on the grant, whether they are still on the plots, whether the boundaries of the plots are still in place, is in a state of disarray. Official knowledge about the state of affairs on the ground is slight. Inevitably over the period of 40 years, an unofficial market in those plots has developed; land is bought and sold, sub-divided, occupied under agreements, left in wills, pledged for loans without reference to official Jamaican land law or the system of land registration. This is a classic circuit two situation where a market in land exists yet official laws governing land markets are ignored, not out of any deliberate policy of flouting that law but because it just does not cater for the needs of people within circuit two. Hence the other main examples of circuit two in operation are squatter settlements or unauthorised or popular housing in Third World cities where almost by definition official urban land law cannot apply – for by that law the housing development is illegal – yet people within the development engage in transactions in respect of "their" land.

The situation confronting land policy-makers in circuit two therefore is very different from that which confronts them in circuit one or three. The situation is basically one of formal illegality, land relations permeating throughout a defined group in society giving rise to mutual rights and obligations within that group yet unsupported by the formal legal and governmental system. Which way should land policy go, to recognise and work *with* the "illegal" land occupiers or to assert the formal legal system *against* the squatters? In the Jamaican example already outlined, the Government took the view that it must recognise reality. It embarked upon a major and very expensive long-term programme to upgrade its agencies and departments dealing with land (the Lands Office which allocates land and collects fees, the Survey Department which demarcates land and fixes boundaries, the Registrar of Titles which issues titles, and agricultural agencies which supply funds and extension services); to investigate the actual position of farmers on the ground and on the basis of the facts mount an accelerated programme to issue titles and supply funds to allow for the more efficient use of all the agricultural plots at present not fully utilised. In a sense the Government had no alternative but to adopt such a policy; it was not the fault of the farmers that they were on land without clear formal legal title and so a policy of dispossession would have been neither equitable nor efficient and would likely have given rise to a great deal of rural unrest, a prospect no elected government was likely to welcome.

The approach of the Jamaican Government is the only realistic one. Questions of "fault" or "illegality" are beside the point and indeed the concept of the three circuits, each equally entitled to be judged on its merits by the organs of the state, is aimed to get that point across in respect of both rural and urban society. The reality is that people are using land for homes, for food production, for industrial or commercial enterprise, as a source of income, often as a substitute for a state-operated social security system and where it is found that the land relations involved in all these activities are in the second circuit, that fact has to be accepted and policies devised which will make that circuit more efficient and equitable for those people and thus for the wider society. Just as the Jamaican Government did for its rural small holders, so other governments must do for their rural and urban small holders; adapt and reform the formal institutions and laws so that they can be of more use to the vast numbers of people in the second circuit rather than try to force the people from the second circuit to comply with laws, institutions, practices from the third circuit which have demonstrably failed in the past to cater for second circuit needs (McAuslan, 1985).

The thrust of policies towards the second circuit can be summed up as the provision of support – expertise, materials, a relevant and understandable legal and administrative framework, finance and land – for the initiative and enterprise already being shown by the people of the second circuit. Get right away from the crude stereotype of squatter settlements as being hotbeds of vice, crime, disease and incipient revolution. Policy based on such a stereotype may become a self-fulfilling prophecy here too as with policies based on an assumption that customary land is beyond redemption. Squatter settlements are in reality full of people on the make, who have made the immensely difficult psychological break with rural life to try their luck in the city, people who work long hours both in paid employment and in building their own shelters, people in other words trying to put down roots in the city and obtain a stake in city life. What they need is security of tenure for their homes; financial assistance to upgrade their homes and get started in business, and fewer or none of the host of licensing provisions on their commercial enterprises which criminalise their activities with no discernible benefits to the city or its administration. Where there are to be major policy initiatives on the part of government, then here, as in the first circuit, they must be developed in partnership with the people of the second circuit and must adopt the integrated approach, a concerned programme of urban development designed to affect and improve all aspects of the lives of the people of the second circuit (McAuslan, 1986). Appropriate land policies of the kind touched on here form part of such a programme.

Land policy in circuit three

The third circuit is the modern circuit, with which most administrators, lawyers, land professionals, aid agencies and governments are familiar. Land here is regulated by Acts of Parliament or their equivalent, Acts of Congress, or of the National Assembly, Decrees, Regulations, judicial decisions, administrative determinations and advice. In many developing countries, land within this circuit does not extend much beyond the boundaries of the cities and some large scale agricultural estates: beyond that, and the third circuit begins to shade into the second circuit. Kenya provides a good example of that where land reform carried out in the 1950s and 1960s with land transferred from customary to statutory titles and thereafter regulated by the Registered Land Act, 1963 is now either passing from smallholders to large land owners or slowly slipping back into a quasi-customary regime as traditional patterns of succession to land and dispute-settlement begin to reassert themselves. The amount of land involved is small therefore; however, its economic and social importance is very great. Just as in colonial times when the large landowners had disproportionate political power, derived from their economic power and vice versa, so now large landowners in the city and the countryside can drive up the price of land, of food, of shelter, use their landholdings to enhance their political and economic power and throw on to the community the costs of their abuse of their rights.

The aims and content of land policy then are different here to those for the first and second circuits. There, the aim and content is to guide and support, and to provide facilities for the better use of land. Here there is a need to have a policy which, while not inhibiting the profitable use and development of land, ensures that the externalities of that profitable use and development are properly considered before development commences; that is that the social and community costs and benefits are weighed as well as the private costs and benefits to the developer. It must be stressed that this policy needs to be applied to all developments in the third circuit, not just those being funded by private capital. Developments by public sector bodies – dams, hydro-electric schemes, roads, power stations, airports, new towns and capitals (Lawal, 1984), industrial estates – have their costs and benefits and often involve the compulsory acquisition of land and the compulsory movement of people in the first and second circuit. The costs to those people, the need for sensitive policies of relocation and support thereafter, the need to justify the acquisition and relocation in the first place are as necessary from an equity and efficiency perspective for public as for private sector development, more so in some respects if governments are to retain the support of the dispossessed citizens. So laws and policies regulating compulsory acquisition of land, the compulsory transfer of land from first or second to third circuit need to be reviewed in most states to ensure that proper consideration is given to these wider social factors involved in such transactions (Yahya, 1985; Kitay, 1987).

In addition to compulsory acquisition laws and practices, there is a place for some kind of planning and development control policy and practice. Cities in the developing world do not benefit from the kind of detailed planning control which town and country planning legislation provides for in the UK, and even in the UK there are those who would doubt the efficiency of such detailed control on development, but there is a strong case, from an efficiency and equity perspective, and where foreign involvement in development is present, from a safeguarding perspective as well,[2] for prior consideration to be given to proposals for significant developments, whether public or private which are going to consume large amounts of resources – *e.g.* foreign exchange for building materials, prime land and skilled workers and which are inevitably going to have spill over effects on surrounding land or the city generally. Land policy must provide for that, whether by planning legislation or by legislation requiring environmental impact assessment.

Policies discussed so far focus on the *ius utendi* – the right to use land in the third circuit. Modern land tenure also provides for the right to obtain the fruits of land and the right to dispose of land. Land policy should impact on those sets of rights as well, since they too can give rise to relations of exploitation between persons interested in land. The *ius fruendi* is at the heart of the landlord/tenant relationship and few societies have found it possible to ignore the implications from the equity perspective of the inequalities inherent in that relationship whether in the agricultural or the urban sector. Policy should focus on ensuring that bargains between landlord and tenant are fair and provide, within a framework of certainty, for the efficient and equitable use of land. An analogous relationship to landlord and tenant is that of mortgagee and mortgagor, analogous because of the inequality of bargaining power between the supplier of the desired commodity – land in the case of a landlord, finance in the case of a mortgagee – and the would-be consumer. So here too, policy needs to focus on ensuring that mortgage bargains are fair, a task the courts of equity in England took upon themselves from as far back as the seventeenth century.

Finally, what of the *ius abutendi*, the right to dispose of land. Traditionally, this has tended not to be the subject of as much regulation as the other two rights. Policy on this has focused on the need for efficiency and certainty in the operation of the market for land. Systems of registration of title are a good example of that and such systems can be useful. If land can be bought and sold and otherwise dealt with, as a factor of production, then there is a strong case for a clear, simple and straightforward framework of law and administration to facilitate such transactions.

But it may be argued that market factors in the third circuit have to operate within and be conditioned by the existence of the first and second circuits, and in particular by the different perceptions of people within the different circuits about land. Take for instance the thorny problem of sale by a chief or traditional land holder of land which in accordance with customary law he has no right to sell. Third circuit land policy concerned to uphold the market might adopt the position that the chief held the proceeds of the sale on trust for the people entitled to occupy the land and would further allow those people to trace that trust property. But people in the first circuit want the land, their land, and will not be satisfied with money or necessarily with land elsewhere. Here efficiency of markets and certainty of transactions clashes with equity and the recognition of differences. A solution to the problem must face up to these conflicts and not ignore them in the interest of the market. Such a solution would be to hand the land back to those lawfully occupying it under customary law and compensate the buyer with land elsewhere.

A similar issue of conflict between efficiency and equity in transaction policy arises in the cases of limitations on land holdings and restrictions on transfer based on ethnic grounds. There is little doubt that the operation of a bureaucracy to control the amount of land any one person may have is fraught with difficulty and in the countries where such a bureaucracy exists the law does not work at all well. Nigeria (James, 1987; Omotola, 1984) and India (Bhargava, 1983) are probably the two best recent examples, although Kenya (Salter, 1982) has had land control legislation for over 30 years directed to policing transactions on, *inter alia*, amount grounds. Transaction costs are increased but little public benefit seems to accrue. Similarly with inter-ethnic transactions, a feature of statutory land law in colonial Tanzania and Uganda and still operative in independent Fiji and New Zcaland. Strong feelings are aroused by such transactions and where controls exist, it may be impractical to argue for their complete removal but land policy in both cases must be directed to reconciling as far as possible the two components of efficiency and equity and not brushing over the conflict or downgrading the arguments of equity in the presumed higher interests of efficiency of markets.

What models of implementation should be used?

The fourth question is one of institutions and machinery. Given the existence of a national land policy which takes account of the three circuits of land relations, how should this policy or these policies be implemented; what should be the mix between involvement by agencies of central government, or local government, regulation by courts or tribunals; initiative left to private persons or taken by public officials; reliance on traditional mechanisms or modern statutory machinery? The possibilities are very great and again all that may be done here is to set out some guidelines and possible principles which should be taken account of in deciding on the "how" question – how to implement policy.

Rather than approach this in the way that was done in considering question three, by examining policy prescriptions in respect of each circuit, the approach here is to discuss possible models of implementation in terms of a continuum and points along the continuum. At one end we have complete public ownership and control, public ownership of all land and hence public regulation of all aspects of land relations, the public ownership model. At the other end we have no regulation at all, a complete free market in land with parties left to their own bargains and to decide for themselves how and in what manner they will use state facilities like courts to settle disputes. If parties prefer arbitration, domestic tribunals, traditional dispute settlement machinery, even self-help provided it does not disturb the public peace, then so be it. In other words the opposite end of the continuum to the model of complete public ownership and control is the model of complete privatisation and freedom from state control. In between these two is a wide variety of possibilities but they can be classified as: (i) a regulatory model where public agencies regulate one, two or all three of the three fundamental rights of ownership-use, income gathering and disposition and (ii) a facilitative model where public agencies exist and may or sometimes must be used to facilitate the exercise of the three rights.

Complete public ownership and control of land is commonly thought of as a socialist land policy. In fact that is not necessarily so. It was a feature of many colonial land regimes and so we find former colonies with land regimes modelled on the former colonial pattern. It is also a feature of strict Islamic land regimes. A feature of these land regimes is that freehold ownership of land is not permissible; private individuals may obtain land from the state but only for limited periods, and limited interests and the terms on which the land is obtained allow the state wide rights of re-entry if those terms and conditions of development are not complied with. The state uses its residuary rights of ownership, its reversionary rights in effect, to ensure development and to control the use which is made of the land; transactions which might be undertaken in respect of the land; and via rent payments and rent review clauses, obtains a share in the profits derived from the land. Even in the customary system where such exists, persons on the land derive their rights to be there not from a traditional source but from the state (Omotola, 1982). The arguments in favour of such an approach come down to this: that land is too important a resource to the state to allow private individuals to own it. If it is legitimate for the state to have a national land policy then it is logical and indeed necessary for the state to ensure that it can implement its policy. Implementation is most effective through ownership and control.

The arguments against such an approach are equally to the point: the disadvantages of large-scale governmental involvement in land relations far outweigh the presumed advantages. They include expense, corruption; misallocation of resources; inappropriate solutions to problems and agency capture. All these disadvantages can be shown to have happened somewhere – they are not a particularly Third World phenomenon. Agency capture for instance – the *de facto* control exerted by persons and organisations over a public agency established to control and regulate those very persons and organisations is a phenomenon much discussed and researched into in the USA and is as likely to affect land control agencies as any other. For example the involvement of estate agents and small builders as members of local planning authorities in the UK is well known. The inappropriate solutions and misallocation of resources in connection with low income housing – vast high rise blocks of flats – are as prevalent in Europe and N. America as they are in Africa and parts of Asia. So too is corruption in land transactions. It is not being argued here that public administration in respect of land relations is inevitably inefficient and corrupt. The point that is being made is that , in deciding whether to adopt this particular model of policy implementation, one must not be starry eyed about the benefits of public ownership and control. At its best (Singapore is a good example (Ricquier, 1985)) it can work and meet all the fundamental components of a land policy, but a realistic assessment of this model, looking at its plusses and minusses in practice around the world, would suggest that states should think carefully before adopting it; and that where such a model is or has been adopted, constant monitoring is necessary to ensure that it works to carry through the land policies implicit in it and does not impede them.

What then of the model of privatisation, of no state control, of a completely free market both in land and in dispute settlement about land. This model is much favoured in certain circles in Western Europe and North America – deregulation is the catchword – and so inevitably it is becoming the policy of the World Bank and the IMF. Give free rein to initiative and enterprise, the argument runs, and while in the short run there may be some disadvantages – the poor dispossessed of their land and homes, the rich misallocating resources on conspicious land consumption, disruption of traditional customs – in the long run the market will work, land will be allocated via the market to its highest and best use and through that, general prosperity will produce increased jobs, and income and so the wherewithal to obtain homes for the poor.

This too is a theoretical rather than an actual scenario. It really is impossible to point to any state where there is a perfect free market in land producing perfect Pareto optimal solutions: no one is made worse off by any changes. Rather, the evidence tends to suggest that a totally unregulated market in land produces land hoarding and speculation; a loss of land rights by the poor; a depletion of natural resources; and the external costs of land development – pollution, public health problems, degradation of land, transport costs – passed on to the public sector to deal with, and, particularly in countries where the three circuits of land relations are present, conflicts which may not be easily resolved. The free market in land is not costless and, as the UK has found, the costs of exerting control over a virtually totally free and unregulated market in land which existed in the eighteenth and early nineteenth centuries have been very great and are in effect still being paid today (Ashworth, 1954). Whatever the theorists of an unregulated land market might be able to prove via elegant equations, reality would suggest that here too this approach is not a practical proposition, as its actual costs to society would far outweigh its presumed benefits.

This brings us then to the variety of solutions somewhere along the continuum, all of which assume that there will be a mix of public and private inputs into the implementation of land policy and all of which can be workable in the three circuits. Take first the regulatory model closest to complete public ownership and control, private ownership with public regulation of all the three rights of use, income and disposition, a model which in effect embraces the alternative of selective regulation. We find that the vast majority of states in the world – capitalist as well as socialist, developed as well as underdeveloped – have mechanisms to control the private use of land: town and country planning laws, zoning laws, environmental impact assessment. Almost as many states have mechanisms to control aspects of the obtaining of an income from the land. Rent control legislation, mortgage protection legislation, control of eviction legislation are the commonest examples. Fewer countries try to regulate disposition *inter vivos* as opposed to making it easier to accomplish, but many seek to control disposition on death.

There is too a remarkable similarity in the mechanisms used: control of land use tends to be operated by bodies which mix professional with lay people, planners who advise local lay people on the decision to take. The lay people may be elected or appointed. This perhaps reflects the feeling that there should be an input from ordinary people about how or whether their environment is to be changed. To prevent local prejudice or ignorance from stopping development which might be in the national interest or, alternatively, to prevent development which is undesirable from a national perspective from being sanctioned by local people in respect of whom illegal methods may have been used to obtain a favourable decision, we usually find an appellate or reviewing mechanism provided on top of the local decision-making body and that appellate or reviewing body tends to be a professional body: lawyers, planners or a mixture of the two.

With control over the *ius fruendi* (obtaining an income from the land) we find that there is usually a more professional-dominated mechanism. Control is itself often more legalistic and technical and despite the best endeavours of those who would prefer that lawyers were not involved in these matters, we tend to find too that lawyers are more involved both in deciding cases and in presenting the arguments to the deciding body. The fact that there is here too a considerable element of discretion in determining *e.g.* rent levels, is reflected in the use of tribunals, boards, committees etc. rather than courts, with a composition of persons not all of whom may be lawyers. Similar sorts of controlling devices to these exist in those comparatively few countries where there is regulation of disposition of land *inter vivos*.

A characteristic of this model is that the decision of a public agency is needed before some action in respect of land can be taken and failure to obtain that decision usually results in the action, if it is nonetheless taken, being illegal or unauthorised, and subject to official sanction. Thus development of land without permission may lead to the service of an enforcement notice and official demolition of what was erected without permission. Failure to obtain permission before putting up rents or evicting tenants may, as a matter of law, lead to fines, repayment of excess rents, and possibly in some jurisdictions, compulsory acquisition of the landlord's interest. Failure to obtain permission to sell or purchase land usually results in the transaction being held void with often the corollary that no action is maintainable for the return of deposits etc.

Widespread though this model is, it has two major deficiencies in respect of developing countries. First it is on the whole inappropriate in the first and particularly in the second circuit, and secondly, it does not work at all well in the third circuit. I speak with some confidence about this as my knowledge is derived both from my work on planning housing and land matters in developing countries in Africa, Asia and the Caribbean and from students from those countries who come, year after year with first hand knowledge from having lived and often worked in the real world of land relations in all circuits.

In the third circuit the laws are often ignored with impunity. They are either based on out-dated metropolitan models or, where localised, backed up by too few resources or have still paid too little attention to local conditions. In the second circuit the laws are ignored by the land users; to do otherwise would often be to go without homes or land to use to obtain food, or an income; or are used spasmodically and oppressively by officials to dispossess squatters, bulldoze their houses and other erections and destroy their crops. Second circuit land users, even if willing to comply with the regulatory model, cannot afford the professionals and fees needed to do so. In the first circuit, regulations are likewise ignored, where they apply at all, as not paying sufficient attention to traditional models of regulation which indeed they are often designed to replace. In short, the standard regulatory model, beloved of western and western trained administrators and lawyers, and I include myself in that category, does not work in respect of land relations in the developing world. We have to think of something rather different.

What then of the facilitative model? A facilitative model of land policy implementation creates certain arrangements and mechanisms for facilitating actions and decisions in respect of land, provides that these mechanisms if used, will produce the desired results, but if not used, will not produce the desired results and may lead to future difficulties when further actions in respect of land are undertaken. Financial benefits too may flow from using the facilities, financial penalties may result from not using the facilities. The criminal law is not used as a sanction; self interest is the driving force. A typical example of a facilitative mechanism is a system of land title registration. If titles are registered, transactions in land become easier and cheaper to undertake than if they are not; or should be; and title registration can only work effectively if all transactions have to be registered. Jamaica is the awful example of a system of title registration so slow and bureaucratised that it is a positive invitation to move land relations from circuit three to circuit two. The compulsion to do so is not or should not be the sanction of the criminal law but self interest; those with interests in registered land cannot deal with them if they are not registered and those whose task it is to register interests would be liable in negligence if through failure to register, clients suffered loss.

This is the alternative which lawyers and administrators in the Third World and indeed consultants and others from elsewhere should develop as the principal model of implementing national land policy in the three circuits of land relations. Rather than criminalising failure to seek permissions, this is a model which could be developed so as to reward compliance and impose penalties of a fiscal or financial kind of non-compliance. Thus to register a land transaction would create the conditions for a loan at favourable interest rates, for reduced land tax liability and for increased assistance in complying with the necessary regulations governing land development. If registration is in fact a simpler, cheaper way to manage land, this should be reflected in reduced costs of public administration. Compliance with regulations on land development could likewise be tied in with loan facilities, tax liabilities and further permissions on alternative uses.

One may go further. It might be argued that there are regulatory aspects to land policy that are not appropriate for this treatment. What incentive could you give a landlord not illegally to raise rents when all the evidence points to his being able to do so with impunity, and probably avoid tax on his income as well? Why bother to seek permission to develop land or put up buildings in order to gain certain benefits when a bribe can ensure those benefits more easily? A suggestion here is to facilitate private enforcement of the law rather than rely on inefficient, over-worked or occasionally venal public servants. Provide mechanisms for allowing private citizens, tenants, neighbours, even amenity groups, to utilise the law against those who are not complying with it and thereby causing public or private harm. If the public bureaucracy will not or cannot act, why should the general public have to stand by and put up with the disadvantages caused by illegal activity, or activity contrary to the public interest, on land. In the third circuit, there are many legal doctrines which are available to those wishing to use them against anti-social or careless land users: nuisance, negligence, trespass, the rule in *Rylands v. Fletcher* to name but four from the common law world. I suggest that a way forward is to facilitate the use of these doctrines suitably adapted and extended if need be and available for use in small claims courts or their equivalent, to enforce necessary regulatory regimes at the behest of private citizens. If this results in some legal harassment of land developers, landlords or land owners, their remedy is simple; buy off the complainants and comply with the law. An *ex gratia* payment made to a private citizen in lieu of damages awarded by a court is much preferable to a bribe paid to an official in lieu of a fine levied by a court.

This may seem a novel, even an outrageous approach to adopt. It clearly could not be a complete substitute for publicly enforced regulations of some aspects of land relations and one would have to grapple with the inevitable problems; first, the private land developer or landlord who prefers the illegal use of force as a method of settlement out of court, and second, the public authority which ignores the regulations and then harasses complainants. But these problems already exist. They would not be caused by the proposals put forward here, and in any event the fact that some persons or organisations might find ways to avoid the application of a law is not necessarily a good reason for not proceeding with the introduction of the law.

But more important than that, to reiterate the point made earlier; traditional Weberian public administration and regulation does not, by and large, work well in any of the circuits of land relations in the Third World. If we accept the case for national land policies based on the five fundamental components discussed earlier, we have to confront the fact that policies with no means or extremely ineffective means of implementing them are useless; one might as well have no policies at all. The argument here is that a facilitative model of policy implementation offers a greater possibility then any of the other three models, that policies might actually be implemented in all the three circuits as the model seeks to harness the self interests of land users to the public interest in implementation rather than, as with the other models, set them at loggerheads with each other.

Conclusions

What is proposed here is a new mode of analysis of the business of creating a land policy for developing countries, in the hope that the mode will itself make the arriving at solutions that much more possible. One or two final general points may be made here.

Land is the foundation of shelter, food, work and a sense of nationhood. Land is therefore inseparable from the concept of a civil society and it is inseparable from social and economic relationships within that society. Policies about land are policies about society; how it shall be organised, and governed and what relationships there shall be between the different groups and people in society. Land policies then must be all-embracing and cannot be based on any assumption that some land relations are of little or no account and others are the "correct" ones because this is tantamount to saying some groups or people are of little or no account and others are the preferred ones. Such policies tended to be formulated during the colonial period particularly in respect of customary and statutory land relations but countries would be well advised to be extremely cautious before either continuing or adopting under international aid pressures, similar policies now.

Equally, it must be said, land policy cannot be allowed to go by default; a national land policy is at least as important as a national foreign or defence policy. In putting forward the three circuits of land relations and developing via those circuits, the principles, contents, and models of implementation of land policies, what is offered here is a comprehensive approach for the development of land polices in Third World countries which will recognise the worth and contribution to society of each circuits of land relations, a fundamental precondition to an effective national land policy.

---

*A revised text of a lecture given at the Faculty of Law, University of Lagos, as part of the Faculty's 25th anniversary celebrations, April 1987. First published in 1988, *Journal of African Law*, Vol. 31 (1 & 2), London.

Notes

[1] That was the official figure in the mid-1980s. There may well be more arising out of unofficial unrecorded land transactions.

[2] This was one of the main rationales for the proposed introduction of a detailed town and country planning law into the Turks and Caicos Islands where absentee N. American land speculators were buying up the choicer sites on the Islands, leaving too little for planned land developments which were in the national interest.

2 The urban land question*

The urban land question addresses the plight of the urban poor in, principally, Third World cities. Concern with this issue is not new but discussing it in terms of urban land policy – the title of the Habit International Council (HIC) paper – or the urban land question is a fairly recent development, so it may be worth devoting some space to trying to clarify what is embraced in these terms. Principal protagonists of looking at urban issues in terms of land policies, focus on the role of governments and public authorities in ensuring that land is planned and supplied at the right time, in the right place, and at the right price for the right sort of development – a description which begs all sorts of questions. But it does give direct attention to three crucial matters – public power over land, the market for land, and institutional structures for decision-making in respect of land. By public power over land we would include planning, development control, compulsory purchase, public development of all kinds and land taxation of all kinds. By the market for land we would include the legal and fiscal framework for the buying and selling, leasing, mortgaging and other commercial transactions relating to land and the professions involved in such activities. By institutional structures we would include public authorities, both central and local, their powers and the general legal framework for decision-making in the field of urban land.

So described, urban land policy or the urban land question is a vast field yet still excludes matters which have an effect on the use or misuse of urban land – rural and urban migration, agricultural policies, political influences particularly the political influences of large landowners, general national economic policies, the role of outside consultants, and international organisations such as the United Nations Centre for Human Settlements (UNCHS) (Habitat) and the World Bank. While these matters cannot be fully drawn into the urban land question, nor can they be completely ignored and what follows will refer to them where necessary.

Given the vast field one cannot hope to provide a full survey of the area. What I intend to do, however, is to try and highlight some of the current practices and problems and some of the legacies of past practices and problems in respect of the urban land question and then turn and consider the kinds of solutions to the problems now being argued for. The perspective will be that of a lawyer not a sociologist or geographer, though one who has some first-hand knowledge of the Third World, principally African countries – gained through living and working there, in the role of an educator, a consultant on planning, housing and allied legal matters, a UNCHS (Habitat) official and a full-time DFID technical adviser to a land reform project. I should also say that what follows will not be particularly original, for the issues, problems and possible solutions have been extensively discussed but rarely implemented.

The current situation

I would single out six past and present practices which are major contributory factors to the current situation of the urban poor in the Third World: the present political and economic framework; the colonial urban legacy; the multiplicity and lack of adequate urban governmental authorities, the inappropriate and out-of-date laws governing land tenure and land use; the over-grandiose master or original plans produced by the ton; and the role of consultants. I will deal briefly with all of these.

The political and economic framework

With very few exceptions, governments in the Third World are, through a variety of factors by no means all of their own making, not orientated to deal with the issues of the urban poor. Their economies are geared to produce primary products for sale, at disadvantageous prices, on the world market; what surplus such sales generate is too often misspent on armaments – with the enthusiastic cooperation of developed countries – or on prestige civil urban developments – airports, air traffic control systems, eight-lane highways, hotels etc. – which bring a good deal more benefit to foreign contractors than the local populace. They are, in short, locked into a world economic system which sees the Third World as an area for capitalist exploitation rather than as an equal partner in equitable development.

Such an economic framework cannot but have a deleterious effect on political institutions and philosophies of governance. Stability, however achieved, is more highly regarded by external and therefore more highly prized by internal rulers than democracy; military rulers or governments which owe their existence to military goodwill rather than the ballot-box do not have as a high priority a social welfare approach to urban governance. Even those governments trying to adopt policies directed to alleviating urban poverty and providing for the basic human needs of the urban poor are often defeated by a combination of external economic factors, internal political opposition, administrative inefficiencies, and the sheer scale of the problems which have to be tackled. Nor do they start with a *tabula rasa.*

The colonial legacy

In few areas of policy-making is the colonial legacy so persistent as in that of urban land policy. And for obvious reasons. The colonial legacy is the existing built environment, infrastructure, transport patterns, and usually legal frameworks. The built environment and the existing arrangements of services such as sewerage, water, electricity, roads, cannot be altered for the most part and continue to exert a powerful influence on urban investment and planning. The division of towns and cities into zones which used to correspond to ethnic and racial separation still exists but now corresponds more to economic class separation. Even where new urban communities are planned the implicit assumptions are usually those of the old; the central business district and low-density high cost housing are seen as a higher priority than housing for the urban majority. There is a natural and perfectly understandable reluctance to allow a city to "rundown" or to devote too great a proportion of public resources to urban development – many development economists would say too much already goes in that direction – but the result of these twin pressures is that much urban investment goes towards maintaining what is in the way it is rather than any form of radical restructuring of the built environment or re-allocation of investment priorities.

Urban government

In too many countries, urban government is under-financed, divided between a multiplicity of authorities – *ad hoc,* local, parastatal, national – and suffers from lack of adequately trained staff. Local government is either mistrusted for political reasons – it might become an alternative power base for opposition politicians – or is so hedged about with restrictions on spending or on the exercise of power by a central government ministry that it can achieve little by way of positive action or policies. Increasingly, one finds urban development corporations, by whatever name called, being established to take over the urban development and planning role of local governments, but the resulting division and conflicts of authority between local government and public corporation often outweigh any benefit that might in theory be gained by a single-purpose development authority. I would not say that there is never any case for the establishment of an urban development corporation, but too often establishment has not gone hand-in-hand with the fitting of the new body into the existing structures so that bureaucratic infighting predominates over action on the ground.

Multiplicity of government institutions also results from a city's expansion on the ground not being matched by a revision of the local government jurisdictional boundaries, so that what is a unified urban area in fact might as a matter of law be governed by two or twenty or more local authorities. Even if they all nominally belong to the same party, or to no party, they may well have different policies on planning and development which are uncoordinated by any superior authority.

It is, however, lack of finance which is the greatest handicap for local urban governments in the Third World. Some have no independent sources of finance, being wholly dependent on grants from central government; some have local sources – property or sales tax – which are inefficiently collected or based on out-of-date valuations or limited as to the amount that may be raised so that without central government grants (rarely available without strings) major urban developments cannot be mounted. We are, in the UK, only too well aware from our own experience of the most intractable problems involved in any reform of existing or introduction of new local taxation, especially property taxation, and increasingly aware also of the problems of collecting rents for accommodation from people who are sinking further and further below the poverty line, so that failure to grapple with these matters might be more sympathetically understood than in the past. But that does not alter the fact that continued lack of local sources of finance cannot but affect the capacity of local governments to serve the urban majority.

Inappropriate laws

As a lawyer I have a particular concern with this blockage to better urban land policies and a concern too that this blockage is too often underrated or ignored by international agencies and consultants. Over the whole field of urban land policy, in country after country, we find varieties of the following: former colonial laws often 60 or more years old still in place governing land tenure, land transactions, public health and housing;

piecemeal unrelated reforms altering one part of a total *corpus* of law without regard to its impact on other parts of the *corpus;* "reforms" which are in fact imports from a metropolitan power being sold to the Third World government as the latest and most up-to-date model without much regard to its local applicability or any associated need for handbooks, training etc. to give the new law at least an outside chance of undergoing a successful transplant; total ignoring (not ignorance) of local or any other laws by outside consultants and local officials' finally, reforms which are shied away from because their political implications are too great, or are enacted but not enforced for the same reason.

We must all be careful not to elevate our own discipline into the central position in any survey of issues and their possible solutions in urban land policy. But I would suggest that a legal framework that does not address itself to meeting the needs of the urban poor is an important deficiency in current urban land policy. Housing laws which have the effect of illegalising 80% of the residential accommodation in a city, by fixing standards beyond the financial and technological means of the urban majority, increase the difficulties of that majority in obtaining official recognition and assistance. Planning laws that are so complex and time-consuming that one cannot comply with them without professional help compound the problems faced by the urban poor in trying to find somewhere to live.

Similarly, with land transactions and land registration laws: the pursuit of perfection in the law, the absence of sufficient officials to administer the law, the official documents and official language in which the law is enshrined – often a language the urban majority do not speak, let alone read and write – increase the gulf between the government and the urban majority. It should be said here that, contrary to what is often assumed to be the case, countries where freehold or private ownership of land has been officially abolished are little different to those where private ownership of urban land is still permitted; official "foreign" laws still apply to land tenure and use, housing, building and rent control and are still remote from the urban poor. Law in the Third World cities is, in short, a weapon in the political struggle for adequate resources, so law reforms and implementation become an important touchstone in gauging any meaningful policy change.

Over-grandiose plans

I am not here decrying the relevance of land-use planning or of planning that seeks to bring together land use and socio-economic factors. But there must be a large question-mark set against many of the multi-volumed studies that thud so often on to the desks of bewildered public servants in many Third World countries. Often the plans overlap; a sub-regional study done by one group covers the same area as a regional study done by another group; or one plan is in effect a comment – usually a critical comment – on another plan produced just two or three years back for the same area. The plans use the latest scientific techniques and jargon and pretend to an accuracy that is quite impossible to achieve, given the absence of a full range of official statistics. Reading through these plans, prepared without the burdensome necessary of any form of public participation, one has to pinch oneself to be reminded that these are meant to be about the future living and working conditions of people whose yearly income would not be sufficient to purchase one copy of the plan – not that they are often on sale. Grandiose plans have three important harmful side-effects; first, they are too often regarded as a substitute for action and as an excuse for non-action; second, they help in the process of deflecting attention away from the needs of the urban poor who too rarely feature as the central issue in such plans; and third, too often, they provide a spurious justification for taking action against the urban poor in the name of "implementing the Master Plan".

Consultants and planners

I act as a consultant so I feel free to criticise consultants. I recognise that there are firms and individuals who would probably share some of my views and are playing a notable role in trying to shift governments towards paying more attention to the needs of the urban poor. But there are too many consultants who are not of that ilk; whose plans are of the grandiose kind likely to win awards as plans but achieve nothing permanent on the ground; and who pay no attention at all to the urban majority beyond passing references to the need to deal with, *i.e.* get rid of, uncontrolled and illegal settlements which stand in the way of new roads, airports and modern housing estates. Too many foreign planning consultants do not spend much time in the countries they are meant to be creating plans for and in my experience do not seem to like the countries all that much. How one can make a useful and relevant plan for a country or a city which one does not like and for people for whom one does not have much regard and does not mix with very much is a mystery to me, but that might explain why so many plans concentrate on impersonal physical developments rather than on measures to alleviate urban poverty. Another defect of much consultancy is that it does little to strengthen the institutional capacity of the country or urban government concerned; officials are required to service the consultants and inevitably are distracted from their normal work; there is too little integration between work-systems of consultants and of local administrators. Above all, consultants strengthen the "top-down" approach to planning and development, whereas a "bottom-up" approach is a necessary first step in planning to tackle urban poverty.

So much then for the agenda of current defects in respect of urban land policies. Between them they add up to a formidable list of obstacles to overcome if more humane and relevant policies are to be adopted. What are some of the principal aspects of a new approach to urban land policy?

Aspects of the new approach

I would list six key factors: the adoption of a basic human needs strategy; the adoption of a participatory "bottom-up" planning system; the closer linking of employment opportunities with residential development; the development of greater institutional capacity; the creation of financial arrangements and institutions to serve the low-income sector of the urban population; and the revision, up-dating and localising of urban laws.

A basic human needs strategy

Much has been written about the basic human needs and what a strategy focusing on them will entail. Rather than add to a plethora of individual descriptions I will adopt the description contained in the influential ILO publication of 1977, *The Basic Needs Approach to Development.* After making the fundamental point that the approach is designed to meet "the basic needs of the poor masses within the shortest possible period", requires redistribution of income and wealth and accords a key role to public services in the implementation of the approach, the publication goes on to list some elements to basic needs:

First certain minimum requirements of a family for private consumption, adequate food, shelter and clothing, certain household equipment and furniture. Second they include essential services provided by and for the community at large, such as safe drinking water, sanitation, public transport and health and educational facilities. A basic-needs oriented policy implies the participation of the people in making the decisions which affect them ... The satisfaction of an absolute level of basic needs as so defined should be placed within a broader frame-work – namely the fulfilment of basic human rights, which are not only ends in themselves but also contribute to the attainment of other goals. In all countries employment enters into a basic needs strategy ...

Adoption of such strategies in practice as well as in the literature of planning would have a dramatic effect on urban land policy. Plans would take as their principal focus the needs of the urban majority and how to satisfy them; discussion and decision-making would cease to be in terms of what to do about slums, uncontrolled urban settlements, squatters, illegal development – all pejorative terms which assume that in some way the urban majority are the aberration, the departure from the norm – and would instead begin to concentrate on how to provide facilities for citizens, to enable them to live a decent life. Action would concentrate on providing land with secure title, and with basic facilities to enable people to become urban dwellers rather than urban transients. New roles for officials would be created; instead of the land rangers or enforcement officers whose job is to demolish illegal developments, community workers would be employed to assist newcomers to towns and cities to adapt to urban ways; building inspectors would concentrate on assistance and advice to self-builders rather than harass them for failure to comply with the regulations. Basic human needs then is an approach to policy and action as well as a set of prescriptions for action; inevitably rather general, the specifics come through in the other five aspects of the new approach.

Participatory planning

In Western liberal democracies, participation refers to the people discussing draft plans and proposals for development when they are still at the formative stage, in the hope of influencing official decisions and actions. That sort of participation cannot be ignored in Third World cities, though it must be pointed out that in many cities the prior step of involving local councillors and local politicians in planning has yet to be fully accepted. But much more important and relevant is participation by action: the harnessing of the creative energies of the urban majority to develop their own environments and build their own homes in, as far as possible, the places they have chosen. In terms of programmes, this means site-and-service, and squatter upgrading schemes are to be preferred to public housing schemes modelled on, *e.g.* the English pattern. But even within these preferred schemes, the emphasis should be on: "bottom-up" administration; discovering what facilities the communities want, in what order of priority and where; allocating some funds for community-directed disbursement – and accepting the possible waste or misallocation of funds which may result, it will be a lot less than that involved in public housing schemes which never pay their way or in allocating the money to be disbursed to officials which won't get much further than those officials – and helping build up community-based governing institutions which will perform an essential self-management role in the schemes.

Participatory planning is small-scale planning. There may be a role for a national urban policy and its inevitable concomitant, regional plans and master plans for the major cities, but planners – both local and imported – should cease to give the illusion that such plans are a *sine qua non* of a relevant urban land policy for the urban majority. Too often, whatever the good intentions, such plans become ends in themselves and because there is no public participation involved in their making, they do not in fact sufficiently address the real issues in urban development. Small-scale plans are both easier to grasp and likely to be within the capacity of administrators and ordinary people to follow.

Employment

The linking of employment with massive urban settlement is a key component of basic human needs. Just as large-scale public housing programmes do not meet the needs of the urban majority, so too large-scale industrial developments of the import substitution type are of questionable benefit, particularly where they are capital rather than labour-intensive. What needs to be created, at least as an additional element in an employment strategy, is more small-scale light industry, located within high-density developments so as to reduce transport costs for workers and increase employment and income possibilities for women. Additionally, there needs to be more tolerance of, indeed more facilitation of, the informal economy – which provides a good deal of employment too often stigmatised as "illegal" because some licence has not been obtained or some regulation not complied with. Without increased opportunities for employment, which the official economy can in no way meet, the likelihood of the urban majority being able or willing to take advantage of a changed approach to urban land policy and land development is remote. Place the creation of employment opportunities in the forefront of a basic human needs strategy and many of the less desirable features of existing policies – relocation of squatters on the outskirts of towns or even further afield, creation of massive low-cost housing estates with no nearby employment existing or planned, large-scale office and commercial developments in city centres displacing residential accommodation and small kiosks and shops, rigid zoning of uses replacing the natural evolution of mixed development and uses – would have to be altered.

Institutional capacity

A major contribution to a more equitable urban land policy more equitably applied would be better urban government. What is meant by "better" here?

First, a clear allocation of responsibilities, powers and duties to local government and other authorities given roles in urban development.

Second, a greater effort to provide some consistency and stability in the financing of local government. This is easier to state in these general terms than to achieve in practice. Local taxes have to be easy to assess and collect and not easily avoidable, by fair means or foul. They have too to be related to the capacity of people to pay – a flat rate poll tax, beloved by colonial administrators is relatively easy to collect but is highly regressive. If there is to be a formula by which central government allocates grants to local government, then it should be relatively simple, related to needs and performance in meeting those needs. Where the finances include rents and charges from low-cost developments – for leases or services such as water and sewerage – then it may be necessary to develop novel forms of administration to encourage payments and keep arrears down.

Third, staff need to be re-trained – or in many cases trained – to implement a basic human needs strategy, and new skills need to be drawn into the public service. A basic human needs strategy cannot be imposed by remote officials who do not leave their desks; it may be assisted by officials who are seen to be participating in the programmes for which they are responsible.

Fourth is the issue of the redress of grievances: it is too much to expect that every official will be imbued with the spirit of dedication and self-sacrifice that a basic human needs strategy implies; an unreasonable decision, an overbearing attitude, the suspicion of corruption and a good programme in theory becomes a resented one in practice. Participation may reduce but it will not eliminate these practices so effective mechanisms for redress of grievances is an essential part of better institutional capacity. Education and training have an important part to play in bringing about the necessary changed approach to urban administration and this is an area where cooperation between Third World countries, UNCHS (Habitat) and institutions specialising in such training in developed countries has a valuable role to perform. Above all, it should be realised that there will nearly always be too few staff, so administrative systems must be kept straightforward.

Fifth, the role of consultants may briefly be mentioned. The practices of the best should become the norm. One is in a country to build up not ignore local institutions; to work with not against local counterparts; to provide advice and assistance relevant to the needs of the area one is concerned with however unconventional or uncomfortable such advice may be when judged against the latest trends and fashions of one's country of origin, or, in the final analysis, the prevailing beliefs of the consulting country. Consultants should endeavour to leave tracks, that is, modes of working, ideas, practices, guides which can be built on and used by the local officials whose job it will be to implement the advice or plan or law left behind. It may be that serious consideration should be given to the drawing up of a code of practice for international planning consultants to raise the general level of responsibility and conduct.

Financial institutions

Too often, financial institutions established to assist home-ownership or industrial development in Third World countries are those of the West from which they have often derived their inspiration, law and administration. But building societies, however useful a mode of extending home-ownership in the United Kingdom, are of limited use in a society where barely 10% of the population can afford the kind of house a society is willing to lend money on; indeed, such an institution is positively harmful, for it channels the small savings of the majority towards housing provision for the minority. Micro-finance institutions need to be established with the specific duty of catering for the needs of the urban majority; loans should be of a limited size and at a subsidised rate and should not require a formal freehold or leasehold title as security; loans to housing cooperatives should be encouraged and loans could take the form of materials with the repayments to be in cash. The offices of such institutions need to be located in the low-income areas of a city; to have an imposing head office in the central business district is unnecessary and wasteful of funds. The application forms which such institutions require to be filled in must be kept simple; forms based on the kind of project documents that international financial agencies require when contemplating a major international loan – and I have seen such forms – are a positive disincentive to borrow. As with local authorities, so here; sensitive handling of arrears problems will be an important aspect of the work of such institutions. So too will monitoring the performance of the institutions for there are examples of financial institutions set up for the purpose of aiding the urban majority being quickly captured and their purposes subverted by the minority.

Revised and relevant urban laws

Inadequate and irrelevant laws reflect and legitimise an inadequate and irrelevant urban land policy. It by no means follows, however, that relevant carefully drafted laws will lead to relevant carefully administered policies; laws after all are not the only determinants and guides to behaviour. Laws can just as easily be weapons of propaganda as they can be tools of progress. However, given attempts to introduce a basic human needs strategy into urban land policy, it would clearly be giving a very large hostage to fortune to leave intact the old legal framework which was used to illegitimise so much of the activity of the urban majority and to sanction the unequal distribution of resources in favour of the urban minority. But here, more than anywhere, the contradictions of a basic human needs strategy are shown up, for it is the urban minority who are to be invited to agree to a change in the legal framework the aim of which is to lessen their privileges and increase the rights of the majority. Nowhere is this more obvious than in legislation designed to restrict the amount of land any one person may own or hold in the urban areas and to tax the betterment value of land allocated for profitable urban development. Several such laws exist in the Third World; how many are consistently and fairly implemented?

One has therefore to set one's sights at a fairly modest level, but even at this level, there is much to be done. The granting of security of tenure to squatters and the recording of their rights in a simple system of registration;

the enactment of a straightforward building code geared to the capacities of the urban majority and the repeal of laws which render their homes unauthorised structures and therefore illegal – such laws should also lay far more emphasis on the use of local materials and local traditional designs for house-building; the enactment of a planning law which allows for participation in plan-making and a more flexible system of development control replacing the rigid zoning and universal control which tends to be the pattern at present. Indeed, the revised law could very well release from planning controls a great deal of minor development in high-density areas which is theoretically subject to control now but in practice is not, the only effect of the law at present being to give rise to petty corruption and harassment. Rules governing compensation for compulsory acquisition of land need to be revised to increase amounts payable and speed up the process though it must be noted that in many cases this matter is governed by the Constitution.

Outside laws on urban land *stricto sensu,* there is a need for a drastic pruning of trading and business licence laws and the creation of relevant laws dealing with the partnerships, cooperatives, small industries and their regulation and financing. An important issue here is the possible abuse of the rights created by a more up-to-date and relevant code of urban land law and the ways in which this can be prevented. Squatters who are given rights in the land might be persuaded to sell land to speculators; a swifter, cheaper compulsory purchase procedure might be used to dispossess small businesses to make way for large office blocks rather than to acquire land from large landowners holding on to under-used land to allow low-cost urban development to take place; and a flexible planning law will likely be exploited by the commercial property developer rather than the householder wishing to start a business in his backyard. Abuse by officials and landowners with professional knowledge and advice at their disposal is unavoidable – it happens in all countries – and lame though the conclusion is, all one can say is that the education and training has a role here too and the ultimate question is not "how can we devise an abuse-free legal and administrative system to implement basic human needs strategy in respect of urban land policy?" but "can we devise a system which on balance is more likely than not to advance such a strategy?"

At the risk of dwelling too long on the law, I would like finally to comment on a recently made recommendation coming from a UNCHS (Habitat) conference concerning the collection and dissemination of laws and regulations on urban land to assist countries confronted with rapid urbanisation. I would very strongly endorse this recommendation. Even allowing for the fact that laws are culture-specific, countries can learn a great deal from what their neighbours and others with similar social and legal systems are doing by way of legal change and reform and it is often astonishing how little in fact filters across national boundaries – indeed in federations, sometimes state boundaries. I would go further however than the mere collection and dissemination of laws; there is a need for the articulation of principles and the commenting on existing laws – a handbook or manual similar to that produced by UNEP on Environmental Legislation in 1979. I would regard this as a very high priority – a major and relatively inexpensive way of improving both institutional capacity and relevant law-making.

Conclusion

Much of this paper is inevitably general; there is neither the space nor time to set out a detailed programme for reform of urban land policies, complete with draft laws, administrative systems and financial implications. Even if that had been possible, there is the prior need to discuss and clarify the principles on which such programmes of reform are to be based. It is this that I have tried to concentrate on and in doing so have sought to highlight some of the wider contexts in which urban land policy must be considered. Most of the matters discussed here were discussed with greater eloquence and force by Barbara Ward in *The Home of Man* in 1976, but the principles on which action should be based are still not generally agreed and in some respects there has been a regression from the mid-1970s, particularly amongst some aid donors. Hence the importance of constant reiteration of the basic principles both by the Habitat International Coalition and Habitat itself to which this paper has hopefully been a useful contribution.

---

*First published in (1982) *Habitat International*, p. 545.

3 Law and urban development: impediments to reform*

Introduction

There is widespread agreement that law has a major role to play in managing the urban environment and hence in managing growth in the urban environment. It is highly significant that the Rio Declaration on Environment and Development adopted at the Earth Summit in June 1992 laid considerable emphasis on the role of law in creating the appropriate framework for sustainable development. There is, however, a good deal less agreement on what exactly the law should contribute. In the past, great emphasis was laid on control of development and in many countries around the world there are codes of law in place whose *raison d'être* is to stop development. Their practical effect is to criminalise the efforts of many thousands of people, usually the urban poor, to house themselves, and to work where they live, in this case, usually women.

While thinking and writing have now moved on from this approach to law (*e.g.* Farvacque and McAuslan, 1992; McAuslan, 1993) it is regrettably the case that far too many officials in the cities of the developing world still believe that with a vigorous use of the law, they can rid "their" city of "slums" and unauthorised developments. It is an uphill battle to convince such people that working with the urban poor and using the law to facilitate their development is a more productive and effective use of their time than working against them and using the law to destroy their environment and remove them from cities. Not the least of the difficulties in the way of altering official policies and practices on the law relating to urban development is that the laws which officially permit the removal of unauthorised developments free up the land for more lucrative developments and the urban elite control both access to the land and to the use of the law. In such circumstances, intellectual argument is no match for individual acquisition and legal procedures give way to political power.

Does this mean that attempts to use the law to bring about change or reform in urban land management are futile? This is certainly a position which has been adopted by some commentators and aid practitioners in the past but here too attitudes are changing. Law is being seen as a crucial variable in the moves towards liberalisation now being urged upon the developing world and the transitional countries in Eastern Europe by the multilateral lending agencies, UN agencies and most bilateral aid agencies. Programmes of law reform and legal system reform have been instituted recently in China, Uganda, Vietnam and Venezuela, and reforms are in the process of being put together in Tanzania. This is merely the tip of the iceberg: in the interests of good governance, we may expect to see many more such programmes being developed over the next few years. It is, however, likely that the same naïve and ill-informed enthusiasm that aid agencies bring to "new" solutions to old problems, often caused by the application of the earlier "new" solutions to the problems, will affect the use of law as a solution to problems of good governance. We need to temper the enthusiasms with some down to earth realities. This chapter attempts to do this by reference to the role of law in urban land reform.

Contextual conditions for urban land and legal reform

I would argue that institutional and legal reforms must be placed in a wider context of, on the one hand, political development and change, and, on the other, socioeconomic development. To try to abstract law from these matters, to import legal developments from one society and impose them on another does not work, although this is not to say that one society cannot learn from the legal experience of another and cannot adapt laws from another to its own use. Thoughtful adaptation is, however, very different from unthinking imposition. The only occasion when this might not apply is in connection with a violent social upheaval following defeat in war or a revolution when legal niceties are usually the last issue on anybody's mind.

To turn from the general to the particular, I want to suggest what might be the pre-conditions for successful urban land reform and the role law might play or has played in such success that there has been. I turn first to issues of political change and development. First and foremost, there must be in place a government which has a collective belief in the benefits of an efficient and effective state and at the least a passive acceptance on the part of the citizenry that such a state exists. The government must, in other words, be legitimate. While legitimacy is customarily taken to be evidenced by a government elected to power by popular vote, the idea behind good governance is that there is more to legitimacy than the support of a majority in the legislature. Accountability, transparency, probity, equity and efficiency are all embraced in the notion of good governance, as is the assumption that if all these attributes are present in government, society as a whole will enjoy the benefits of economic and social progress. In those circumstances, reforms can be introduced and are likely to be acceptable to the citizenry. It is not necessary that all the above attributes be present in full measure all the time; it is a question of balance: over the long haul a government should show most of the attributes of good governance for much of the time. To expect more than that would be unrealistic.

When this essentially modest standard is applied to governments in Africa, it is easy to see why urban land reform has hitherto been conspicuous by its absence and/or failure. With the exception of Botswana, few governments can claim to meet the standards of good governance and, with the exception of Botswana, few governments can boast any carefully thought-out and executed programme of land reform (Bruce, 1987). Let us leave aside those states that to all intents and purposes have either no governments or governments whose whole effort is taken with staying where they are – Angola, Liberia, Congo, Sierra Leone, Somalia – and concentrate on some which have attempted some land reform, including urban land reform, and which have used law for this purpose.

Role of land in selected sub-Saharan African and Asian countries

Tanzania has an enviable record of stability and concern for the poor; it is also famous for its Ujamaa policies and its villagisation programme, designed to bring the benefits of health, education and minimal social welfare provisions to the rural peasants. The urban poor too were meant to profit from Ujamaa policies. A recently published report on land policies in Tanzania (*Report of the Presidential Commission*, 1994), put together on the basis of the most exhaustive study of land practices in the country based on evidence obtained from the ordinary people provides a deeply depressing insight into the reality of land policies over the last 25 years. The peasants were pushed about by high-handed petty bureaucrats, their land was seized without compensation, the urban poor were by a legal sleight of hand deprived of the land on which they might have lived for years, they received no or derisory compensation and no alternative land on which to build another house.

Throughout all this, the evidence time and again records a quite amazing faith in government and a belief that if only someone somewhere knew what was happening, matters would be put to rights. Unfortunately, what is happening now is that with the World Bank and IMF supported liberalisation policies in full flow, land grabbing by the elites is the order of the day so the peasants and urban poor are worse off under a land market regime than they were under a state land administration regime. Clearly, in the former regime, law provided no safeguard against abuse of state power; in a regime of market forces, the same law provides no safeguards against abuse of market power.

Tanzania is not alone in this failure to develop good governance in urban land policies and practices. Nigeria introduced laws in 1976 to promote, via state action, more equitable urban land allocation. The laws are constantly flouted by those whose job it is to enforce them (James, 1987). Kenya has a thriving urban land market and laws to enable it to function. This has not stopped abuse of the urban planning laws; political allocations of land and funds to develop land and constant harassment of the urban poor in their unauthorised settlements in order to obtain land for urban development. Zimbabwe has a well organised urban planning system and land market but rigid application of planning and building codes has left the urban poor little alternative to over-crowding and squatting (Pons and Mutambirwa, 1991). A similar picture exists in Francophone Africa (Farvacque, 1989; Durrand Lasserve, 1989).

This brings us to the second matter, socioeconomic change. Whether laws put in place a state administered land allocation system or a market allocation system, neither is likely to work as the laws provide if the social conditions are not in place. Any legal framework for urban land management, or indeed urban governance in general, assumes the existence of both a system of public administration and a civil society, *i.e.* persons with some familiarity with modern government and market processes, institutions with financial independence, the range of professions needed to operate land management processes, a variety of media outlets where matters of concern to the public can be openly discussed and information disseminated, and, as a consequence, governments which recognise some social limitations on their powers.

These social pre-conditions for the operation of a good governance urban land management system do not exist in most African cities. Governments are all powerful, even in market-oriented countries like Kenya with a growing middle class but civil societies are weak. The law can therefore be manipulated by governments for the benefit of its supporters and against its opponents. There is another matter. In few, if any, African states is there any alternative to land or political power as a means to become wealthy. There is no industry to speak of, the large-scale commercial enterprises are either owned by overseas companies or by non-indigenous citizens, and the stock markets which are now slowly coming into being are too small to be seen as a serious competitor to land as a source of wealth. Thus, those with political power may introduce laws which read as if a transparent market economy is being introduced, but they will be unlikely to allow them to operate in a way which might threaten their hold on either power or the traditional source of wealth – land.

Contrast with this picture the position in some Asian countries. First, in Japan, South Korea (Amsden, 1989), Taiwan (Wade, 1990) and China, fundamental land reform was imposed on society in the 1940s. The power of large landlords was broken. If wealth was to be acquired it had to be via industrial or commercial development. Similarly in Singapore, there was to all intents and purposes no land and what there was, was acquired at almost expropriation rates by the government to house the mass of the citizens (Lim, 1983; Motha and Yuen, 1989). In Malaysia, although the entrepreneurial group in society, the Chinese, could acquire land, they found a better outlet for the rapid acquisition of wealth by dominating trade and commerce. In these countries, governments presided over rapid economic development, displaying a considerable degree of efficiency and effectiveness in so doing, even if other indices of good governance were not always present, and as a consequence, civil society developed and land became of lesser importance as a means of acquiring wealth. Land was perceived by the urban citizen and government alike as a means to an end; housing, employment, recreation (although not too much of that) and via roads, a means of communication. This is not to say that urban development was not seen as a means of amassing wealth or that governments did not manipulate the land market to enable the favoured few to benefit from development. However, in all these societies, it is undeniable that rapid urban development has taken place, the vast majority of urban inhabitants are housed in legal housing, laws exist to enable a land market to operate and, while by no means without its problems, the market does operate.

In those Asian countries where land is still an important means of amassing wealth, the position is similar to that in Africa. Laws may exist which appear to provide a framework for the operation of either a land market or of a system for the public allocation of land but, as numerous studies have shown, these laws are ignored or manipulated to enable political and social elites to acquire land. Constant attempts at urban land reform in both Bangladesh (Islam and Chowdhury, 1992) and the Philippines (Mendiola, 1983) have come to naught for instance.

The position in India and Sri Lanka is more interesting, for in both those societies there are more of the indices of good governance present (in Sri Lanka, admittedly, the civil war has taken its toll on some of these indices) and a significant civil society. In India too there are many ways of amassing wealth apart from land acquisition and development. Hence, in these societies serious attempts have been made to bring about urban land reform and use the law to this end. These attempts have relied on the use of public power and have not been particularly successful, but this is as much because of the sluggish pace of bureaucracy and the opposition of civil society – which can take the form of legal and political challenges to government policies – as because governing elites are paying only lip-service to the reforms.

In some respects, Thailand is the most interesting country to examine from the perspectives of this paper. Hailed in some quarters as a new Asian "tiger" because of its very rapid economic growth, I would regard it more as a transitional country moving from the African/South Asian socioeconomic and governance positions to the East and South-East Asian positions. So too with urban land management; Thailand has long been held out as an example of a successful operative land market which has managed to deliver urban housing, via the private sector, to quite substantial numbers of lower-middle-income and low-income urban dwellers. Even where slums and squatter settlements still exist, and they do, Thailand has developed indigenous ways of reconciling low-income use needs with elite commercial development demands via such means as land sharing. It is important not to overexaggerate the success of Thailand's urban land policies: the urban poor still suffer from land shortages and a very poor urban environment, the urban elites still see land as a means of obtaining wealth and are eager to acquire it by any means, but there are other avenues to wealth and, to a greater extent than is the case in most African states, there are avenues available to the urban poor to obtain land (Tanphiphat and Simapichaicheth, 1991; Williamson, 1989; van Mehren and Sawers, 1992).

Overall, I would argue that there is a correlation between on the one hand good governance and on the other the socioeconomic pre-conditions for the existence of a market economy and the likelihood of successful efficient and effective urban land policies developed through the medium of law. Without the former, there is not much hope for the latter.

Good and ineffective ways of reforming land law

Let us assume, contrary to the earlier assessment that those countries in Africa and South and South-East Asia that do not at present seem either to be moving towards good governance or to be developing the necessary pre-conditions for a market economy do begin to move in the right direction on both those fronts. What other factors need to be present for the successful use of the law in bringing about change in urban land matters? First and foremost is the whole problem of indigenous versus imposed law. It is highly significant that the successful, in relative terms, countries in terms of urban land reform via law are those which have or have created out of disparate sources of law an indigenous legal framework for urban land management. In Botswana, for instance, urban land reform via law has taken the form of a careful, controlled engrafting of common law concepts and ideas on to customary land tenure and the use of authorities which again blend customary and modern elective and appointed officers. In Thailand, many observers have pointed to the skilful way that successive governments have taken ideas and concepts from various Western legal systems and moulded them to fit the needs, circumstances and culture of Thailand. Malaysia too has over the years "indigenised" its National Land Code which started life over 100 years ago as a colonial law designed to facilitate the acquisition of land from Malaysians by the colonial rubber plantations and settlers (Ahmad and Sihombing, 1989). Japan, South Korea and Taiwan began their modern post 1945 land management with a heavy dose of US law, but their laws too are now indigenised.

In contrast, most Anglophone African countries are still operating a dual system of land law; customary law and statutory law, which is basically English land law as it was prior to the reforms which took place in England in 1925. Some countries, of which Kenya is probably the best example, have made some efforts to develop out of English land law a more local version – *viz.* the Registered Land Act, 1963 and the various land adjudication laws – and, as we have already noted, Kenya has in place the legal framework necessary to enable a land market to function (Onalo, 1986).

Tanzania, on the other hand, has as its basic legislation on title registration, a law made in 1953 which in the words of its draftsman "had borrowed freely from the English Land Registration Act 1925", an act that in turn is intimately interrelated to substantive English land law and is increasingly acknowledged in its own country to be in need of a thorough overhaul in the light of changed social economic and legal developments since its enactment 70 years ago. It has to be said too that the Presidential Commission referred to earlier did not really get to grips with the need to develop a national Tanzanian land law, partly because of a deep ambivalence about individual and communal land tenure and how far one or the other should be encouraged and or facilitated.

Tanzania is not the only country which was very slow to emancipate itself from its English legal traditions or to begin the process of developing a national land law; Zambia was shown the way by a report on its land delivery system in 1988 but has not acted upon it (Halcrow Fox, 1989). Lesotho had a basically English system of land law imposed upon it in 1979 and not surprisingly has been most reluctant to implement it. Uganda has a mixture of Australian (Victorian) land registration law and pre-1925 English land law. If anything, the Francophone countries in Africa have been more wedded to metropolitan law than have the Anglophone ones.

The same English legal straitjacket affects legal developments in the Indian subcontinent. There is a mass of indigenous legislation on land, but the basic legislation covering land transactions and land use planning is founded on English models and there have been remarkably few attempts to develop truly indigenous land titling and transaction legislation in any country on the subcontinent. There are in other words no indigenous laws derived from a mixture of judicious and eclectic borrowing from abroad and national home-grown laws as in Thailand and other countries in East Asia. The extreme conservatism of the legal profession does not help either.

This last point leads onto another important factor. There have to be in existence in any country contemplating land law reform land-related professions sufficiently self-confident and intellectually curious to be able and willing to take the lead in developing proposals for reform. Just as laws cannot be imposed from the outside, the drive for reform cannot come from the outside. Outsiders – consultants, visiting academics, the fruits of an international conference – can all be helpful but only as contributors to a national effort. The National Land Code of Malaysia was developed by Malaysians, although as noted earlier it was based on a colonial land code and no doubt with contributions from non-Malaysians. It was enacted in 1965 and is now the basic land law of Malaysia. The major land law reforms carried out in Trinidad and Tobago in 1978–82 (Wylie, 1986) were undertaken by an international consultant, working closely with the Law Commission. Though enacted into law, they have yet to be brought into effect: the national land related professions do not have a sense of ownership of the project.

A subcategory of this point merits separate treatment. There has to be in existence, or at least developing, a national legal literature of some intellectual depth and maturity. A country cannot hope to produce lawyers and other land-based professionals with an understanding of the national land laws and the relationship between those laws and economic and social development if there is not a literature on the subject and if teaching of courses on land law consists of exegeses of foreign textbooks and casebooks trying thereby to localise them. The term "national legal literature" is used deliberately; it is not enough that law books on, for example, Nigerian land law reproduce the style, format and content of books on English Land Law while substituting Nigerian for English Land Law. What is needed is literature which addresses Nigerian land problems and the way the law is attempting to meet those problems. While one can point to individual examples in many developing countries of such books, it is more difficult to point to any national legal literature of the required kind. Too much legal literature, at least in the Anglophone developing world, apes English legal literature and within that genre, books on land law are probably the most intellectually narrow, eschewing reference to other disciplines or addressing the social or economic issues behind the law.

A fourth point concerns the time-scale of reform. At this point, it is not irrelevant to refer to the English experience of reforms of the land laws. Three characteristics stand out. First, the time it took. Reform of the land laws is generally considered to have culminated in the package of reforms known as the 1925 Property Law reform legislation. The reform process is generally thought to have been initiated by a speech on the need for law reform made by Lord Brougham in 1833, although he drew on ideas put forward by Bentham. So land law reform stretched over nearly a century. Nor is it ended yet, for the Law Commission is constantly coming forward with proposals for reform in that part of the land laws covered by the 1925 reforms, to say nothing of more "political" reforms in the land law which affects housing, *e.g.* landlord and tenant law, mortgage law and leasehold enfranchisement.

Land law reform in England has always been seen as highly political (Ofner, 1981; Anderson, 1992). Up until the early years of the twentieth century, the large landowners, dominant in the House of Lords, had to be convinced. The lawyers were constantly at odds with each other and with successive governments and there needed to be some common ground found within the profession between barristers and solicitors, northern and southern solicitors and rival solicitors' professional bodies. Successive Houses of Commons had to be convinced that land law reform merited the time being given to it. As the century of reform wore on, new actors entered the field, particularly the building society movement and these interests had to be accommodated. The upshot was, inevitably, compromise. The ideology of land law literature has always portrayed the reforms of 1925 as a seamless web of intellectual coherence. They were not, although they did and do hang together pretty well, and they met the principal aim of the reforms, which was to make land transactions simpler and cheaper.

Following on from this last point, the reforms over the century of reforms proceeded by fits and starts with some false starts along the way. Take title registration, which in many respects sparked off the most acrimonious debates within the legal profession and caused much heart-searching among the land owners who saw the spectre of public knowledge of their holdings becoming a reality (they need not have worried, it was not until 1990 that the Land Registry became open to the public). There were two legislative attempts at title registration in the nineteenth century – in 1862 and 1897 – before the current law of 1925 was enacted. The law of 1925 learned from the errors of the two previous attemps but the errors were not just technical errors but political ones as well, including the need to bring the legal profession on board as well as to create a viable and technically workable system.

Thus any programme of land law reform has to prepare for the long haul and cannot start off on the basis that reform is all just a question of technicalities which should be left to technical experts. This poses problems for reform programmes driven or at least encouraged by donors, technical aid and financial assistance. Such programmes must be able to produce results within a measurable span of time; very few donors or lending agencies are going to be satisfied to be told: "we're in the midst of a highly political exercise; come back in 50 years to judge whether it has been successful." However, if we take the major land and land law reform programme started in Kenya in 1956, admittedly under very special circumstances and still going on in the sense that adjudication of titles continues and land tenure is continuing to be converted from customary to statutory systems, can we say that it is successful and what do we mean by "successful"? What can be said is that if the programme had been pulled up by the roots every five years or so to assess its progress, a lot less would have been achieved than has been. I would argue too that there has been a consistent programme of continuous incremental reform in Malaysia in respect of land law over a very long period of time and equally in Indonesia, after a major reform in 1960, reform has been within the parameters set down by that reform (MacAndrews, 1986). However one measures success, therefore, an element of length of time must be built into the assessment process.

A fifth point makes explicit what is implicit in much of what has gone before. Land law reform is not a one-off process. It never ends. Even a major piece of legislation will need constant adjustments and it should not be seen as a mark of failure that reform needs reform. One year after the Law of Property Act, 1925 was passed, a Law of Property (Amendment) Act was passed to correct mistakes in the 1925 Act. The National Land Code of Malaysia was enacted in 1965; it has been amended 24 times since, some amendments being quite significant and adding to the Code. Arguably, one of the problems of the development and implementation of the basic land law in Kenya, enacted in 1963, is that it has not been subjected to continuous review and revision. Similarly too with the land ceiling legislation in India and Nigeria; it does not work and it has not been revised.

Even worse is the position with respect to town and country planning legislation: in most Anglophone African countries, this is regarded almost as if it were part of the law of the Medes and Persians; once enacted, never revised unless to incorporate some "reform" already introduced into the English town and country planning laws. In India too while the town and country laws might be changed, the underlying philosophy and basic structure of the laws remains English. It will be argued that land law must be stable and cannot be subject to constant changes as this will disturb the expectations of investors. What investors look for is a stable framework which can nonetheless respond to changing social and economic circumstances as occurs in Malaysia; they do not favour a legal framework which appears to have the stability of the dead.

Conclusions

Where does all this leave the role of law in urban land reform, and how should one proceed in respect of urban land law reform? Land law reform must be seen as an integral part of land reform rather than apart from it or a substitute for it. Policies on land must therefore be developed with lawyers as part of the policy team before law reform can be proceeded with. The fears of those who feel they might lose out by reform must be taken on board but not to the extent that no reform in practice occurs, as was the case in the Philippines with urban land reform during the Aquino Presidency. Those committed to reform need to articulate their goals clearly and build up a constituency for the process. Relevant laws, practices and processes of reform from other countries will need to be assessed and the process of adaptation for national use put in hand. There is no need to wait for official sanction before drafting and publishing for discussion draft land reform laws; these draft laws themselves are part of the process of public education and debate, not least among the legal profession, most of whom do not think about law reform.

While it will always be a minority who take the lead in pressing for reform, the need to persuade the majority must not be forgotten. It may be argued indeed that it might be counterproductive to try to "sell" land reform and its attendant laws by stressing the need to facilitate access by the urban poor to land. The aim should be to facilitate access by all to land, by making access and transaction processes cheaper and simpler; by developing appropriate mortgage institutions, facilities and laws; and by reducing the scope of and simplifying town and country planning and building control laws. In the course of creating such a legal framework, some special provisions may be introduced of particular relevance to lower-income groups – *e.g.* mortgage guarantee provisions, a much reduced land and building control regime for single storey houses below a certain cubic content, a special title registration regime for converting unauthorised to legal settlements – but these provisions will then be seen as part of the whole and will be available to all citizens.

The starting point of this chapter may be returned to: land reform, both urban and rural, and its attendant reform laws, to the extent that they are designed to facilitate access by all citizens to land and provide land for all citizens to have access to, are part and parcel of the process of democratisation of which good governance and wider socioeconomic reform are also part. Governments committed to the latter are more likely to make genuine efforts to go forward in the former than those not committed to democratisation, but even those governments committed to democracy will have difficulty in proceeding with land reform where elites, especially urban elites, cannot be offered any alternative sources of wealth accumulation. In such countries, reform of land laws, whatever its intent will be used to facilitate elite land accumulation. This will not be the fault of the laws, nor would any alternative set of laws prevent such elite accumulation. There is then a definite limit both to land reform and to laws to implement them; they can be used only as an aid to and not as a substitute for appropriate international and national economic and social policies designed to bring about sustainable and equitable development in developing countries.

---

*First published in 1994, *Cities*, Vol. 11, pp. 402–08.

4 Only the name of the country changes: the diaspora of "European" land law in Commonwealth Africa*

Introduction

This chapter will attempt a survey and assessment of the impact of "European"[1] land law on policy-making and legal reforms on land tenure in Commonwealth Africa. It will tend to concentrate on the impact of what I intend to call "old" English land law (this will be explained below) on Anglophone countries in the Commonwealth for that is where most of my practical and intellectual experience has been, especially in eastern and central African states – Kenya, Tanzania, Uganda, Malawi and Zambia – but the paper will also look at the Roman-Dutch experience in Southern Africa, drawing on the extensive South African scholarship on this topic and my work on aspects of land law in South Africa, Namibia, Swaziland, Lesotho and Zimbabwe when I have had to get to grips with Roman-Dutch law. My knowledge of developments in civil law Commonwealth states in Africa – Cameroon and Mozambique – and other civil law countries in Africa is less extensive and will have to rely on second hand sources but I think that some of the general points I shall be making are as applicable to those countries as to common law countries.

Issues which will be addressed will include:

- the effect that concepts and ideas drawn from English and other European land law had and continue to have on perceptions of who owns and controls land in traditional African societies;
- the effect of old English land law generally as an impediment to innovative approaches to land management in Africa and as a subsidiary issue here, the relationship between the conservatism of the legal and other land related professions in Africa on land issues and the continuance of English land law;

- the impact of the introduction of social control of land use (town and country planning law) on land tenure especially in urban areas;
- the divorce between the people's land law (customary tenure) and state land law (European-based land law) and the effect this has on land management;
- the way forward; the future of European land law in Africa; lessons and ideas from other parts of the common law world.

In the last decade, a considerable amount of work has been done and published on the legal culture clash between Roman-Dutch land law and customary tenures in South Africa and the ways forward towards integration but too little work has been done by legal writers on the clash between English land law and customary tenure in Anglophone Africa and the effect that the dominant position of English land law – dominant by virtue of its state backing – has had on systems of land management in African states, Charnock (1991) being a notable exception. This chapter is an attempt to fill this gap and it is hoped that it will contribute to a better understanding of the constraints and opportunities involved in the use of law as one of the principle tools of developing new approaches to securing land rights and managing the land resource in Africa on a sustainable basis.[2]

The reception clause

Every story has a beginning, a middle and an end, and this one is no exception. The beginning is the reception clause, a legal phenomenon well-known to lawyers in Anglophone Africa. It is perhaps less well known to non-lawyers but since it provides the foundation for the application of English-derived and Roman-Dutch law in those countries – and there are equivalent legislative provisions in civil law countries in Africa – it is necessary to explain it at the outset of this paper.

Throughout colonial Anglophone Africa, the reception clause provided that, as from a specified date, the common law, the doctrines of equity and statutes of general application applying in England[3] as on that specified date would apply in the particular country named in the reception clause. In the Southern African dependencies – now Botswana, Lesotho, Swaziland and Zimbabwe – the "received" law as it was called, was Roman-Dutch law from South Africa, which was applied also in Namibia after 1919.

Different reception dates applied to different colonial dependencies. The details of these dates and attendant footnotes explaining some points about them are set out in column 2 of the table contained in the Appendix to this chapter.

All these reception clauses have survived and indeed were confirmed at independence either in the independence Constitution or in an Act passed at the same time as the independence Constitution came into force. They have continued to survive and have been reconfirmed in every constitutional change which has taken place in every country since independence. Thus for periods varying from 80 years (Tanzania) to over 100 years in many other cases, the basic principles of old English Land Law (the land law applicable in England prior to the fundamental reforms of 1925) have been applied to some or all of the land in many Anglophone African countries outside the Roman-Dutch sphere. In very few of these countries has this basic received law been replaced in its entirety by a new country-specific basic law, although in most countries there have been piecemeal reforms. Similarly with the reception of Roman-Dutch law; the basic principles as developed in South Africa have continued to apply to the Southern African states where Roman-Dutch law is the received law. Likewise with the two civil law countries in the Commonwealth: Mozambique and the Francophone half of Cameroon.[4]

In the common law and Roman-Dutch legal systems, the development of the law relies very heavily on judicial precedent – the decisions of the judges of the higher courts which are fully reported in law reports and are then used in later cases to support and justify those later decisions. The effect of the reception clauses allied to the doctrine of judicial precedent has been to import into the legal and land systems of Anglophone Africa not just the law of England or South Africa as it was on the date of reception but, to some extent, as it continues to be interpreted and developed by judges in England and South Africa. Thus for good or ill – and this chapter is directed to that issue – English and South African land law as it is developed in those two countries – less so in respect of English land law for reasons to be explained below – continues to have a major influence via judicial decisions on the development of national land laws and thus on national land policies and practices. In some respects indeed, the influence has grown since independence; with the collapse in so many countries of a system of national law reports, judges rely on precedents from English and South Africa law reports which continue to be received in the law court libraries in lieu of anything else. This is a major difference to the position in civil law countries where judicial precedents are not nearly so important.

The basic concepts and presuppositions of "European" land law

Land law derived from the colonial powers of Europe is based on certain philosophical principles, uses certain concepts, ideas and techniques which are derived from the specific historical evolution of those European countries (and "white" South Africa and its European antecedents). In order to show what effect these laws have had on the evolution of land law and policy in African states, it is necessary to have some understanding of what these basic principles and concepts are. The case of English land law will be concentrated on.

English land law has always been based on the two fundamental principles of divided rights of ownership and the separation of what is owned from the physical substance of the land itself. In the common law countries – basically the Commonwealth, the USA and Ireland – which still base their land law on the English system, what is owned is not land but an *estate* or *interest* in the land; a bundle of rights which at its highest and best confer on the owner of the estate all the powers over a piece of land which a lay person would associate with someone who "owned" the land. Now, this bundle of rights may be thought of as a bundle of sticks and like a bundle of sticks, it can be split up into lesser bundles all of which can be owned. So, at any point in time, English land law may recognise several people as having different degrees of rights of ownership or rights of property in the same piece of land. The owner of the land in England is the Crown; subjects own estates in the land held from the Crown.

The historical reasons for this development which go back to the eleventh century are not entirely irrelevant to the story of the imposition of English land law in Africa. Briefly, William the Conqueror declared all land forfeited to him when he invaded and conquered England in 1066. He drew no distinction between conquest of a country and acquisition of the land of that country. To reward his supporters, he doled out land to them but consistent with the notion that conquest and land ownership were inseparable, his supporters did not get ownership of the land; they held their land from him in a form of tenure (Latin, *tenere* = to hold) and what they owned was an estate – an abstract concept – in that land.

By the time of the late nineteenth century when reception clauses began to be applied to British colonial dependencies, English land law had evolved into an immensely complex body of law with a huge variety of estates which people could own in the land; not just the freehold and leasehold estates which most lay people know of but future estates, estates for a life or lives, estates that could spring up in the future or shift to another person on the happening of a future event, legal estates and equitable estates based on the concept of the trust. The reason for all this complexity was the desire of the land-owning classes in England to keep land in the family; to make it as hard as possible for land to be sold or taken away from the family.

During the nineteenth century, a "long wave" of land law reform began which had as its aim the freeing of land from the family fetters and the facilitation of a market for land through the simplification of the law, the introduction of a system of title registration and the elimination and reorganisation of the rights of family members to block commercial transactions in land. Shades of land tenure reform in Africa at the commencement of the twenty-first century? Significant reforms took place in 1882 which however left substantial powers in the hands of traditional landowners and the basic rules of land law unchanged. The major reforms which totally altered both the legal framework, and, more important, the whole philosophical basis of the land law did not take place until 1925. The philosophical basis changed from a land law geared to protecting the interests of large landowners to a land law geared to facilitating a market in land; indeed commentators have suggested that the total *corpus* of land law enacted by the reforming legislation of 1925 can be seen as one large Vendor and Purchaser Act.

Thus, without exception, the English land law that was imposed on countries in Africa via the reception clause was *and, with very few exceptions remains*, old pre-1925 reform land law; in a few cases in West Africa indeed, pre-1882 land law; complex and wholly geared to English social and economic class relations in existence in late Victorian England but at the same time, a law that was in the process of being reformed to become more market-orientated. In no case was any attempt made to tailor the received land or any other law to the circumstances of the place to which it was to be applied.

The imposition of Roman-Dutch and civil law was in essence no different. The law that was imposed was the law of late nineteenth-century France and "European" South Africa – in the latter case, a law which was itself an imposed law and geared to supporting the carving out of large estates from African occupied land; the major difference in conceptual terms was and remains that both those systems of law reject any notion of divided rights of ownership and in philosophical or methodological terms, that while the English common law has developed casuistically on a case by case basis, the civil law develops largely on a strict deductive and syllogistic logic applied within a conceptualist framework. In relation to property, this approach leads to one and only one basic right of ownership – *dominium* – with other lesser rights being either limited real rights, acknowledged in Roman-Dutch law or purely personal rights. The matter is put thus by van der Walt (1996, p. 177):

> Ownership and only ownership is conceived in terms of the traditional definition of *dominium*, and therefore becomes the most important and valuable property right in terms of which all other rights (both personal rights and limited real rights) are defined and evaluated. Personal and limited real rights are described in terms of how far they fall short of ownership, thereby subjecting them to ownership as concepts and as rights.

On the basis of this admittedly very limited introduction to the basics of the imposed land laws, we may now turn to consider the ways in which they have been used on traditional societies and within states in Africa and the impact they have had and still have on indigenous land relations and land law.

The five phases of the use of received land law

The argument to be advanced here is that, taking the imposition of English land law as the model, we can see five interlocking phases – rather like Olympic circles – of relations between received and indigenous land law. An alternative analysis would be to see the phases as representing a layering of the law; one approach to law being laid on top of another approach rather than displacing it so that what looks at first sight like a new approach to the law might be disrupted at any time by an older approach breaking through. This is particularly likely to occur with the English common law and Roman-Dutch law where judicial precedents from one phase or layer may be used to subvert or displace another phase or layer.

The five phases are: *acquisition*; *destruction*; *reconstruction*; *substitution*; and *integration*. They will be discussed *seriatim*.

Acquisition

The phase of acquisition commenced in the nineteenth century. It involved, in effect, the reversion back to the feudal approach to land law; acquisition of territory involved acquisition of the land of which the territory consisted and its availability thereafter to be allocated to supporters of the new sovereign. Purists of British colonial constitutional law will protest that this analysis overlooks the careful and subtle gradations which existed in that law between conquered colonial territories, ceded colonial territories, protectorates and protected states in all of which the law about what law applied in the dependency, how much of existing law continued, what rights to land survived the transition to dependency was different and as the records show, exercised the minds of learned lawyers in the Colonial Office over many years (Hall, 1894; Lindley, 1926).

I would argue however that on the ground in colonial Africa, the subtleties of colonial constitutional law were not of great moment and to the extent that some officials at some point in time thought that the powers of the British Government were limited in some dependencies, their doubts were overcome by later interpretations of the law which offered more robust advice. Thus, without exception, and this included the Mandated Territory of Tanganyika, allocated to British rule by the League of Nations in 1920, the British colonial authorities assumed full rights to legislate about land over all land in every dependency. All existing customary land laws were subordinated to the received law and so all existing rights in land were at the mercy of the incoming power.

The courts played their part in this charade of disguising the exercise of political power as the objective application of rules of land law. Commentators have drawn attention to the key decisions of the Judicial Committee of the Privy Council – the final court of appeal for the Empire – in the first two decades of the twentieth century which culminated in the decision of *Sobhuza II v. Miller and others* in 1926,[5] the key sentence of which is worth quoting (p. 525):

> The true character of native title to land throughout the Empire including South and West Africa with local variations the principle is a uniform one … The notion of individual ownership is foreign to native ideas. Land belongs to the community not to the individual … The title of the native community generally takes the form of a usufructuary right … Obviously such a usufructuary right, however difficult to get rid of by ordinary means of conveyancing *may be*

extinguished by the action of a paramount power which assumes possession of the entire control of the land [italics added].

Conceptually, the view that "the true character of native title to land" did not embrace individual ownership was aided by the fact that freehold title as developed by the common law did not appear to exist in Africa (or Oceania or Asia for that matter) but could readily be introduced once the new legal regime was in place; the Crown as the allodial owner of the land, as in England, with its subjects able to obtain freehold estates from the Crown. Naturally those whose legal systems did not know freehold could not obtain it unless they left the system as some did in the dependencies in West Africa and in the very special case of Buganda in Uganda. In other parts of Africa, and this included the Roman-Dutch dependencies and South Africa, the lands were divided up into those available for settlement via freehold or leasehold or ownership and those set aside for Africans where customary law applied, but applied only by virtue of the fact that it was allowed to apply by the "paramount power".

The notion that the received land law as a superior law permits and justifies the unrestricted acquisition of land held by customary law dies hard. It was at the root of the Tanzanian case of *Akonaay v. A-G* in 1994 where the government argued that those holding land under customary tenure did not own any property and therefore were not entitled to compensation, when in pursuance of Operation Vijiji – the policy of villagisation – they were forcibly removed from their land and made to settle elsewhere, their land being allocated to others. As the Chief Justice remarked, such a proposition involved the notion that most Tanzanians were squatters in their own country. The Government's argument was rejected. This is indeed exactly the position that the colonial approach to customary land law involved. A further illustration is provided by a draft Communal Land Tenure Bill prepared by consultants for Namibia in 1995 which perpetuated the notion that those occupying land under communal (customary) tenure did so only by permission of the Government and could be moved off their land with minimal notice at any time. Constitutional rights to security of property applied apparently only to those holding land under Roman-Dutch tenure.

Destruction

Destruction followed naturally from acquisition. Acquisition involved the displacement of indigenous law by the received law so as to facilitate the displacement of indigenous landowners by incoming landowners as in East, Central and Southern Africa and as many commentators from the countries concerned have pointed out, in West Africa so as to facilitate the growth of a market in land, an essential aspect of the growth of a cash economy based on cash crops grown for export.

Destruction involved the denial that the rules and practices which appeared to govern land rights amongst Africans were in fact law at all. They certainly weren't law in the Austinian sense of "orders backed by threats" which was the foundation of the colonial system of law and denying the status of law to rules of customary tenure made it much easier to set the rules aside and so set the people living under those rules aside or at least accord them a lesser status in respect of their land rights. Here too the Privy Council cases noted earlier were relevant but statutory examples of asserting the superiority of received land law over customary land law abound. There are the obvious examples from what might be called the settler colonies of Eastern and Southern Africa but it is the less obvious examples which are perhaps the more telling.

Thus, in Uganda, outside the mailo land in Buganda, all land was declared to be Crown land and as such available for allocation via freehold or leasehold. Those actually occupying Crown land under customary tenure, *i.e.* all Ugandans except those on mailo land could be moved off any such land when it was leased, *i.e.* received law trumped customary law with Ugandans becoming tenants at will of the state. This position was retained after independence and in fact the position of customary land-holders worsened after the passage of the Land Reform Decree of 1975. It was only with the enactment of the Constitution of 1995 that those occupying land under customary tenure were accorded equal status in law with those occupying land under freehold, leasehold and mailo tenure – this last being a variant of freehold tenure.[6]

In Tanganyika as it then was, it required the intervention of the League of Nations in the 1920s to ensure that customary rights of occupancy were given the same legislative status as statutory rights of occupancy – the basic land-holding right in Tanzania to this day and governed by the received law – but as numerous commentators have pointed out, the position in practice has always been to accord the customary right of occupancy a lower status

(Twaib, 1996). Nowhere is this more overt than in the case of urban rights of occupancy where the extension of the Town and Country Planning Ordinance to areas governed by customary law instantly imposes development standards geared to English planning standards which customary occupiers cannot meet. The consequence is that their occupation becomes illegal. In rural areas too the independent Government of Tanzania continued the colonial approach to customary land tenure; purporting to abolish it and replace it by statutory laws on several occasions in the 1970s and 1980s.

Another area where customary law was set aside – effectively overthrown – was in relation to vacant and unoccupied lands. Colonial authorities everywhere in Africa claimed a right to such land – Bentsi-Enchill (1975) refers to it as a prerogative entitlement and goes on (p. 69): "The claim was everywhere met with the counter-assertion by indigenous peoples that there was no land without an owner." But that was to pose notions of customary tenure against the common law and the civil law and in that contest there could be only one winner. Bentsi-Enchill (p. 69) defends the colonial expropriation of "vacant land" as being in reality a "legislative device for preventing land from being unduly alienated to foreigners [a.k.a Europeans] and thus ensuring its use to local people. The model for this kind of legislation was the Land and Native Rights Ordinance 1916 of Nigeria", reproduced elsewhere in West African dependencies. It has to be said that it is a rather odd form of reasoning that justifies a government of foreigners imposing its own law on land occupied by Africans so that the land becomes subject to the superior power of that government so as to prevent those Africans from disposing of their land to those same foreigners. It can only be understood if it is realised that to the foreign governments, their law did not *replace* customary law; it applied law where there was none before. Bentsi-Enchill further states (p. 70):

> The colonial powers took surprisingly few positive steps to reform or modernise these systems of law ... The noteworthy fact is that very little legislative assistance was given during the colonial period to the necessary process of adapting and modifying the indigenous systems of land tenure to enable them to cope more efficiently with changing circumstances.

The fact is only noteworthy if it is assumed that the colonial powers saw these as systems of *law* which could be and should be reformed by legislative means. On the contrary, if there was a policy at all, it was one of benign neglect. Customary law was a stage in the evolutionary process; it would gradually be replaced by the received law. In civil law Africa, this was to be hastened by *immatriculation,* a formal process whereby a person could opt out of customary law and become subject to the received law. In common law Africa, it was left to market forces and judicial decisions in West Africa where freehold tenure slowly began to make headway over customary tenure and customary tenure itself began to be overlaid with concepts from the common law. In East, Central and Southern Africa, on the other hand, customary land tenure was increasingly used as a tool of governance – a matter taken up in the third phase.

I would argue however that there was another reason why land law reform via legislation, at least in common law Africa and in the early decades of the twentieth century, was not considered to be a possible way forward. Old English land law was perfectly suited to the circumstances of colonial society certainly in East, Central and Southern Africa and could readily be adapted to the hierarchies of traditional societies in West Africa: its social basis was small numbers of large landowners able to tie their land up in ways to prevent others, *e.g.* governments and "the people" getting their hands on it, with large numbers of people with no security of title to their land occupation and so available for work on terms fixed by the large landowners. This was precisely the social basis of colonialism. The thrust of land law reform in England – and during colonial times, only law reform in England was considered as relevant to the circumstances of the colonies – was, in very broad terms, in a democratic direction: a new land law to reflect and assist into being a new society where it would become easier for ordinary people of limited means to acquire land with secure tenure. This was not an approach favoured either by colonial authorities or the new (common law) landowners.

Reconstruction

The use of the term "reconstruction" here may not be quite apt but it is designed to draw attention to the "new scholarship" on law in Africa which seeks to show how colonial officials used and adapted customary law to their own ends; how customary law in fact long ago ceased to be part of traditional society – a bulwark against the colonial authorities – and became, instead, part of the colonial apparatus of rule. This was particularly the case with customary tenure; indeed arguably, the general case is made on the basis of the reconstruction of customary tenure.

Here it must be admitted that it is not so much the specific rules of received land law which were an operative factor as what might be called the public law face of land law. There has always been a close connection between land law and public law in Europe not less than in Africa as the rules which regulate the manner in which people may acquire, deal with, use and lose land greatly affect political stability in any state and therefore must be of prime concern to governments. This connection between land law and political stability was made an important basis for the system of indirect rule or rule through chiefs which characterised British colonial rule in Africa and was not entirely absent from other colonial systems. In areas set aside for Africans in British dependencies in East, Central and Southern Africa, traditional authorities were accorded significant powers over the allocation of land and these powers could be and were used to police and control populations.

Essentially, what was at issue here was the question of rights versus administrative discretions. Received land law dealt with rights and in particular the rights of individuals to own and deal with *their* land as they saw fit, subject to some fairly general common law restrictions such as nuisance and trespass and some few statutory restrictions. As the American legal philosopher, Cohen, put it in a famous piece written in the 1920s (I paraphrase), ownership of land enables one to put up a sign at the boundary of one's land addressed to the world: "Keep off." But it was precisely that attitude to the world which it was quite impermissible for Africans to have to colonial authority. Thus, not only were the benefits of received land law denied to the majority of inhabitants in colonial dependencies but strenuous efforts were also made to prevent the growth or infiltration of ideas from received land law into customary tenure.

Charnock summarises the position as follows (pp. 68, 71):

> The question of how to respond to the growing assertion of individual rights and especially to the sale of land, became the crucial terrain of conflict over customary tenure. For it seemed fairly plain that this was not customary behaviour and therefore not legitimate for Africans to engage in. It appeared to be against both the legal and the socio-political regimes of colonialism and against the views of African social institutions sanctioned by both conservative administrators and liberal anthropologists ... This process of assertion of individual rights has also generally been reproved by historians. Typical is Boahen's summation: "the commercialisation of land ... led to illegal sale of communal land by unscrupulous family heads."

> [There were] fundamental concerns of colonial governments about [developments in the areas of leasing, mortgage and sale]: a fear of social dislocation, often cast in a protective framework of concern over the creation of an indebted peasantry and a landless class ... Extensive legal intervention by the state was consistently proved to be necessary to maintain the customary regime. Native authorities and district officers were given wide powers to check dispositions of interests in land.

The reconstructive approach to customary tenure was the dominant approach in what might be called the middle era of colonialism: the 1920s to the 1950s. This reconstruction of customary tenure by, *inter alia*, the deliberate suppression of any cross-fertilisation from the received land law and the imposition of administrative controls on the operation of customary tenure has had a profound effect on approaches to land tenure and land law reform in the era of independence, at least until very recently. In virtually all countries in Anglophone Africa, the dominant approach to land tenure was one of the maintenance of the dual system and the imposition of tight administrative controls on the customary system. In some countries, *e.g.* Tanzania in the 1960s and Zambia in 1975, controls were based on the principle that customary tenure did not recognise a market in land and that such an imported excrescence must be prevented from developing. In Nigeria, a more or less unrestricted land market in the Southern part of the country was subjected to the administrative controls long imposed on land tenure in the Northern part of the country via the Land Use Decree of 1978. In Swaziland, one of the bases of the King's coup in 1973 was to reassert full politico-administrative control over the land and use that power the better to assert control over the population. Even where, as we will see in more detail in the next section, a land market was accepted and provided for, it was on the basis that customary law had to be replaced.

Substitution

The era of substitution may be dated from the mid 1950s and a defining document was the report of the Royal Commission on East Africa (1955) with its firm espousal of a rapid move towards security of tenure based on freehold tenure for the indigenous populations of the three East African countries of Kenya, Tanganyika (as it then was) and Uganda. Kenya was the first country to take such a step, impelled as much by political factors associated with Mau Mau as by the economic factors which lay behind the Royal Commission's recommendations. Kenya's policies and laws, developed in the 1950s and refined via the Registered Land Act, 1962 and the Land Adjudication Act, 1968 remain the benchmark for why to do it, what to do, how to do it, and why it has/hasn't worked for the rest of Anglophone Africa.

The aim of these laws is to record the customary rights and interests in land which exist, metamorphose them into "equivalent" rights and interests recognised by the common law, register them and provide a legal framework for the operation of a market in these newly minted rights and interests. The legal framework created in Kenya – the Registered Land Act – was the first piece of land legislation in Anglophone Africa which consciously and deliberately was modelled on the "new" 1925 English land law, suitable adapted and simplified for the circumstances of Kenya, with the same broad social aims in view as the original legislation had in England – to facilitate the growth of a property owning democracy via a simplification of the process of acquiring and dealing in land.

These aims may now, some 40 years on and with the advantage of hindsight and our knowledge of the imperfections of the land market in Kenya, seem naïve, but they have influenced and continue to influence policies elsewhere. Malawi provided for adjudication and conversion of customary tenure as far back as 1967. Zanzibar, from 1964 in the aftermath of the Revolution, a practitioner of strict administrative controls over land, has, in a series of major reforming laws in the early 1990s, gone most of the way down the Kenyan route, though not to the extent of permitting freehold tenure (Jones, 1996). The Tanzanian National Land Policy, following the recommendations of the Presidential Commission on Land Matters committed the Government to permit persons holding land under customary tenure to obtain, via a process akin to adjudication, a customary right of occupation of indefinite duration – the dreaded "f" word not being politically correct in Tanzania – and the Land Act, 1999 and Village Land Act, 1999 provides for this. Uganda's Land Act, 1998 too provides adjudicatory mechanisms for the acquisition of individual customary titles and the conversion of these titles to freehold, governed thereafter by the received law. Zambia's Land Act, 1995 provides for the conversion of customary use and occupation rights into leases of 99 years, also governed thereafter by the received law.

There are some differences between the Kenyan model and the more recent developments. The Ugandan Land Act and the Tanzanian laws make more attempt than did the Kenyan law to assimilate customary law and the received law and so come closer to the integration model discussed below.

But to the extent that they adopt the fundamental principle that the overall aim of the reforms is to move towards individual ownership of land or rights in land, that that is, in a sense, to be the norm of the future, I would argue that their's too is a substitution approach. Another difference between the Kenyan model and the Ugandan and Zambian model is that the latter two countries have, to date, retained much of the old English land law rather then developing a more country-specific land law.[7]

An alternative variant to the Kenyan model has been what might be called the *immatriculation* model, although it is to be doubted whether there has been any conscious borrowing from civil law countries when this model has been introduced in Anglophone Africa. Under this model, the received law is "opened up" to the whole population so that those who want to can obtain land under, *e.g.* a lease or right of occupancy without any restrictions and this land could be land which was hitherto governed by customary tenure. Thus, the Land Act, 1979 of Lesotho introduced leasehold as the main statutory system of land-holding in Lesotho and it is clear from the Act that this system of land-holding was designed to replace customary tenure at least in the urban areas of Lesotho. No formal system of adjudication was established however and the Act has proved unpopular and virtually unworkable since its enactment, as it was perceived as an attempt to cut the chiefs out of the land allocation process and to facilitate foreign (a.k.a. South African) acquisition of land in Lesotho (Franklin, 1995).

Another example of this model is the Agriculture (Commercial Land Reform) Act, 1995 of Namibia which sets up a programme for the resettlement of Namibians from the overcrowded communal lands in the north of the country to the sparsely populated ranch lands in the south. Those who move will be governed by Roman-Dutch law as the basic land law modified by strict ministerial controls on transactions. No allowance is made in the Act for the application of customary law at all.

It is perhaps appropriate to mention here the matter of registration of title. Title registration is an integral part of the Kenyan model of substitution and as such finds a central place in the new Zanzibari laws. But provisions for the registration of title have long been a part of the received law all over Africa and it must be admitted fit rather uneasily into the framework of analysis offered here. They were mainly concerned to provide for the registration of non-African owned land, but not exclusively so. Where they had a wider remit, they can be seen as an early form of the substitution layer. A good example of this is the Registration of Title Act of

Uganda passed in 1922 and a strong contender for the title of the worst drafted statute on land law in Anglophone Africa (West, 1966, pp. 166 *et seq.* for a splendid critique of same). Based on the registration statute of the State of Victoria enacted there in 1916, it provides for the registration of, *inter alia*, mailo land in Uganda with dealings thereafter having to comply with the statutory code rather than customary rules. Kenya too in 1908 introduced a registration law designed to bring order to the chaos, as it was perceived to be, of titles in the coastal strip – the old and original Protectorate of Kenya, leased from the Sultan of Zanzibar. More than 90 years on, there is still confusion on titles at the coast.

The history of registration in Ghana is quite instructive in this respect (Woodman, 1988; Agbosu, 1990). Registration was first introduced into the Gold Coast (as Ghana then was) in 1883. The Land Registration Ordinance of that year and its successor Land Registry Ordinance of 1895 were basically deeds rather than title registration laws and were introduced to try and bring about some order and security of title in the rapidly growing land market which was developing in the southern parts of the Gold Coast via an amalgam of customary and common law. As successive Commissions over the years testified, the Ordinances were gravely deficient and did little to lessen land disputes or increase security of title. The Land Registry Act, 1962 did little to rectify matters. In Agbosu's words (pp. 120–21):

> The Land Registry Act inherits substantially the same defects from which its predecessors suffered. The Act retains the deeds registration system which falls short of a title registration system … It falls short of making the attachment of accurate plans to registrable instruments a *conditio sine qua non* for their acceptance for registration … The Act makes no positive provision for the establishment of an adjudication tribunal and its supporting staff for the purpose of final determination of title to land.

The Law of 1986 however made a decisive break with the past. It provides for the registration of titles and as a corollary, for processes of adjudication. Unlike the Kenyan model however, the Law provides for the registration of existing customary rights in the land without any changes to the nature or content of those rights. As Woodman points out, this marks this system off from those, argued for consistently and strongly by Simpson (1976), a former Land Tenure Adviser to the British Ministry of Overseas Development, and his successor Lawrence that title registration must in effect be seen as part and parcel of tenure reform, in particular, the replacement of customary tenure by English-type tenure. This approach to title registration causes Woodman to see the Law as neutral in its effect on possible future developments in tenure whereas Agbosu (p. 124) argues that:

> The introduction of a system of title registration at this time is not motivated simply by a desire to secure titles so as to prevent costly litigation. It is intended to satisfy the demands of the business community by confirming, consolidating and crystallising in legal form the private landed rights acquired in the last hundred years through the commercialisation, usurpation and privatisation of communal land ...

Agbosu sees the introduction and use of English land law and doctrines of contract over the same period as being directed to the same end. Thus, he would argue that the maintenance of the *form* of customary tenure in the Law of 1986 should not blind one to the fact that the Law is part and parcel of a policy of changing the *substance* of the law to facilitate the operation of the market economy – the same *raison d'être* of the Kenyan model.

Integration

The Ghana case study makes an appropriate lead into the fifth phase of the use of received law and its relationship with customary tenure. Integration – perhaps reformulation would be an equally appropriate term – refers to the attempts to develop a new common land law of a particular country from the disparate parts of the existing law – received law, customary law, statute law. The basis for this approach is a rejection of any notion of a hierarchy of land laws within a country; there is just one land law derived from different sources and it is the function of the legislature and in particular of the judiciary to fashion from these diverse sources, based on different philosophies one law based on one philosophy which can apply to all land and all people.

In terms both of articulating this approach intellectually and applying it in practice, the land reform programme of South Africa leads the way here, though this programme is by no means the first attempt at this approach. That must be accorded to Botswana and its pioneering Tribal Land Act of 1968 (Frimpong, 1986; Ng'ong'ola, 1992). This law aimed at modernising customary land tenure by democratising the process of allocation of land through the establishment of land boards which make the allocations on the basis of applications for land, developing a more formal approach both to allocation and cancellation of a grant and providing for the possibility that boards may, instead of making grants of customary rights in land, grant leases and freeholds which would be governed by the received Roman-Dutch law, subject to the overriding powers of the land boards as lessors of the land. Integration here was to be a function more of administration than of legal rules since both common law and customary law tenures have been retained but in the eyes of some commentators the stage has been set for increasing legal integration in the future.

The South African land reform programme stems from the Constitution which mandates the Government to "take reasonable legislative and other measures, within its available resources, to foster conditions which enable citizens to gain access to land on an equitable basis" (Constitution Article 25(5)). The programme has three aspects to it; land redistribution; land restitution; and from a legal perspective, most complex and far-reaching, security of tenure. Legislation on all three topics has been enacted but what may be regarded as the centrepiece – the Land Rights Bill – has, regrettably, been scrapped in the light of changes in land policies consequent on the general election in June 1999. It would have been this law which would have made the greatest strides towards integration – attempting a reconciliation between the norms and practices of customary land tenure, the rather austere and rigorous concepts of Roman-Dutch law and the requirements of the Constitution.

There has been a considerable amount of legal writing on the land reform programme, much of it addressing the issue of the extent to which Roman-Dutch law can accommodate the new approaches. Some of the most thought-provoking writing has come from van der Walt (1997, p. 160) who highlights some of the legal aspects of the programme as follows:

> A number of new rights (or 'rights') completely unknown to Roman-Dutch law have been introduced to improve access to and strengthen the security of 'Black' land rights.
>
> Many reforms are aimed at providing statutory security or backup for traditionally insecure or weak rights and others are characterised by strong policy-orientated efforts to change the current distribution of land rights. Both these categories amount to efforts to change the relative position of 'Black' land rights *vis-à-vis* 'white' Roman-Dutch land rights.
>
> The constitutional arrangements around land reform especially in the 1996 Constitution demonstrate a clear intention to break down the paradigmatic primacy and inviolability of existing (mostly 'white') land rights and create a new, constitutional, balance between the protection of existing rights and the promotion of land reform.

> Some land reform measures demonstrate a tendency to privilege traditional, Roman-Dutch property structures (where full ownership is regarded as the strongest and most secure right); others demonstrate a tendency to opt for a greater fragmentation of land rights (where a wider range of differentiated rights is promoted and, where necessary, bolstered by statutory security of tenure).

There seems to be general agreement amongst commentators that Roman-Dutch law will be able to accommodate the new approach to land tenure but only, according to van der Walt (1995, p. 205), if it adopts an alternative approach to property which fits in with the values espoused in the Constitution:

> However, such an alternative approach to property would require a very decisive move away from the civil-law tradition, both with regard to its methodology and its substance. What seems to many to be the strongest point of the civil-law tradition, its conceptualist methodology, poses perhaps the greatest threat to the new legal order. The new legal order cannot afford to use 'tradition as a substitute for value choices' while covertly relying on the seedy and seamy underside of the seemingly respectable pre-1994 civil-law tradition. Property lawyers will have to 'search for social conditions, including cultural understandings of law, legality and rights, under which collective determinations of aspects of social life are consistent with personal freedom'.

This challenging statement could well be taken as a general text for lawyers concerned with land tenure reform in Africa for too many of whom, at least in Anglophone Africa, a little bit of tinkering with old English land law, bringing in a bit of new English land law, represents the height of ambition (Kludze, 1974).

Some general conclusions

On the basis of the foregoing analysis some tentative conclusions may be drawn which may be of use to policy-makers and lawyers thinking about land reform via law.

First and foremost, and perhaps obviously, no country starts with a clean slate when it comes to land law reform. This point is not just about the existing legislative texts. It refers to the contending philosophies which lie behind the texts and the existing vested interests which support the texts. The principal thrust of this paper is that one cannot avoid the past; the baggage of negative attitudes to customary land tenure bolstered by statutes passed in colonial times, but still applied, remains an impediment to the kind of land reform which Botswana, South Africa, Uganda and Tanzania have embarked upon and hopefully, other countries will be embarking upon.

What the past also tells us is that land laws in African countries, as in all other countries, have been first and foremost, the products of politics not of "objective" considerations of what is best for economic or social or sustainable development. Being products of politics, they have been enacted by and are directed to bolstering and benefiting the ruling group or class in each country. It might seem obvious that a simpler land law or a land law that integrates the people's law with state law would be a positive good to be aimed for but it might not be seen that way by the political and administrative elites; a complicated law and a law which denies rights in the land to the majority of people, leaving them at the mercy of administrative discretion, provides opportunities for accumulation of land and rent-seeking behaviour by those elites that they may not wish to give up. Independence was three or more decades ago for most countries in Africa; why has there not been a greater effort to develop more relevant people-friendly land laws all over the continent?

The attitudes of the legal profession cannot be ignored. They often have a vested interest in the status quo. Recent scholarship has shown how the English legal profession slowed up and had a powerful role in shaping the final form and substance of the English property law reforms of 1925 and it would be unwise to assume that the legal professions in countries in Africa will put the national interest before their own professional concerns. For many of them in Anglophone Africa, and I would suspect in Francophone Africa as well, law reform which departs from the metropolitan model is instinctively regarded with suspicion.[8] The formal superiority of the received law is allied to a concern to perpetuate the law they practise and know best.

Allied to the conservatism of the legal profession and indeed an aspect of it is the question of language. There are two aspects to the language of the law; the technical legal language which lawyers write and speak in; and the European language – Afrikaans, English, French, Portuguese – in which even now most laws are drafted and most of the higher courts conduct their proceedings. The technical "foreign" languages of the received land law represent a barrier to most landowners' ability to make use of that law in acquiring or protecting rights in the land and so weigh the balance against the majority. More important has been the constant problem of the "translation" or transliteration of the concepts and ideas of customary land tenure into received law. In the past the "solution" has too often been to ignore or, in effect, suppress interests which could not be accommodated within the confines of received law; this has tended to affect the interests of women adversely. With a greater awareness in many other parts of the world both of the importance of the language of the law and of the need – in some cases the constitutional need – to accommodate indigenous rights within statutory systems, there is less excuse now than there may have been formerly to ignore interests that fit uneasily into the strait-jacket of received systems.

This leads on however to an important point. There should be a much greater willingness on the part of land law reformers to look beyond the metropolitan models. The common law world, for instance, has a wealth of experience and models to draw on, many of them of infinitely greater relevance to land reform in Africa than the products of the English Law Commission, valuable though these are. One matter can however be learned from the English experience, and now too the South African experience: land law reform is best not done piecemeal. Allied with tenure reform should be reform of the law relating to transactions; a new tenure reform law aimed at simplifying obtaining title and directed to small-holders will be frustrated if the law on dealing with land remains rooted in, *e.g.* old English land law or in the case of Uganda, old Victorian land law as well.

This need for reform would be for several reasons: first, there would be a mismatch between a law on tenure that attempted to accommodate the integrationist perspective and a law on transactions that did not; it might be difficult for some persons with "new" statutory rights to deal with them. Second, the old law is couched in language even more difficult to understand than much modern land law. Third, there is a greater willingness to make use of standard forms in modern land law – the best example of this is the Malaysian National Land Code – so greatly simplifying and reducing the costs of transactions. Fourth, just as tenure change must be geared to the needs of the country, so should any law on dealings with land; there may be a need for some restrictions on dealings or some special procedures that have to be observed before a dealing can be valid which are relevant to the special circumstances of a particular country. Such provisions exist in England, rooted in the particular historical circumstances of the land law of England but there is no need for such provisions to be replicated elsewhere as is too often the case where English law is followed uncritically.

The received wisdom now is that the way of integration or assimilation between the received and the indigenous law is the way to go. The other ways have been tried and found wanting. It is always tempting to think that the present generation have found *the answer* to problems that have proved so intractable in the past but in this case, it is difficult not to believe that an approach that seeks to marry up the law recognised as legitimate by the populace at large – customary law derived from local concerns and needs – with state law – a law that can and should take account of the wider national and international interests – is indeed the most appropriate way forward for those involved with land tenure reform. While such an approach does not dictate any particular solution, being concerned with the method of analysing and developing possible solutions, two possible approaches to solutions may be noted.

The first approach is the enactment by the Government of a national land law which attempts to integrate local laws and the most appropriate of imported laws into one unified law. This must be preceded by a thorough study of the existing land tenure situation and part and parcel of any such an approach must be the duty given to dispute-settlement bodies to advance the development of a common land law through their decisions which should blend the local with the national. This may be seen a basically top-down approach but one informed by information and views from the grass-roots (Sachs and Welch, 1990). The second approach is to leave it all to the grass-roots and replicating the evolution of the common law, accept that it will be many generations before a national integrated land law emerges from a multiplicity of local decisions and local law making. Whatever the theoretical advantages of adopting such a pure bottom-up approach, the practicalities of governance in the modern world suggests that the former approach is the more realistic one to adopt.

A further point must be made about law reform goes a little beyond the strict confines of a chapter about the diaspora of law but does tie in with other conclusions. This is that alongside any programme of law reform, perhaps almost as a pre-condition of law reform, must be a plan for implementation of the new law including the costing of implementation and some facing up and planned response to opposition to implementation. This was not done in Uganda so that it was only after the enactment of the Land Act, 1998 that the relevant Ministry began to realise the implications of what had to be done: the huge financial costs; the revolution in styles of land management and the relative balance of power between the Ministry and local authorities; the training needs of new land management authorities; the organisation of the new judicial system of over 1000 Land Tribunals; the need for a plethora of rules, regulations and forms; the need in short for a major programme of capacity building. It is not to be wondered that things moved very slowly and even with, or perhaps because of, external assistance from the British Government, with a great deal of tension within the relevant Ministry as officials tried to come to grips with new roles – more guidance and facilitation than command and control – and the need to operate in partnership with local governments and institutions of civil society.

So too in South Africa, although a good deal of preparatory work took place in 1999 in respect of the modalities for the implementation of the Land Rights Bill, there must remain a doubt as to whether the politics of implementation – the loss of political control over land which will likely face many traditional rulers as a result of enactment of the Bill – might not yet derail the whole process.

Will the wheel then come full circle? The diaspora of land law from Europe to Africa was to facilitate the grabbing of land from Africans for, and the governance of Africans by the colonial power, its officials and settlers. The idea that the law relating to land was also part of the law relating to governance and existed for the benefit of the ruling class was embedded in the culture of colonialism. But it was also, in many existing African societies, part of their culture too so that at independence there was an easy transference of the colonial approach to land law to the new independent governments. Pressures to liberalise the law, to remove the central organs of the state from the management of land, to allow a market in land to develop thus pose fundamental governance and power challenges to central governments. Both liberal market reformers and what may be called peoples' rightists – those espousing reforms aimed at conferring rights to own land on the people – may then be disappointed as, whatever the form of the new laws, the lure of the old approach will be too powerful for governments totally to reject. Let Calvino who inspired the title to this chapter have the last word (1997, p. 158):

> ... no matter how far you go from the city, will you only pass from one limbo to another, never managing to leave it?

*First published in Toulmin C. and Quan, J. (2000) *Evolving Land Rights, Policy and Tenure in Africa*, London. The book was the outcome of a conference on the same issues which took place in March, 1999.

The title is based on the well-known sentence from Italo Calvino's book *Invisible Cities* (London, 1997) whose theme is that all cities are basically the same: "Only the name of the airport changes" (p. 128). My thanks to Professor William Twining for drawing my attention to this sentence.

Notes

[1] The word "European" is in inverted commas to denote that it is referring to the law of different European countries. Increasingly, in legal discourse, European law is taken to mean the law of the European Union.

[2] A good deal of work has been done on this topic in France and in Francophone African countries but my command of French is not so good that I have been able to go very deeply into the French literature on this. There is some English writing on the subject of the clash between civil land law and customary tenure, not all of it based on African examples, and this will be drawn on in this paper.

[3] There are different legal systems and bodies of common law for England and Wales, Scotland and Northern Ireland. A certain uniformity is applied by the final appellate court of the House of Lords but the systems remain distinct. It was the common law of England and Wales that formed the basis of the reception clause; not Scottish law or the law of Northern Ireland (or Irish law as a whole as it was at the time of all reception clauses except Tanzania Mainland – Tanganyika as was).

[4] The "reception clause" arrangements for these two countries were not exactly the same as for Anglophone countries although the effect was the same. It is the case that Portuguese law in the case of Mozambique and French law in the case of Francophone Cameroon was and remains the basic non-customary law of those countries.

[5] [1926] AC 518. Miller was a major landowner in Swaziland. His name still graces the main street in the capital, Mbabane.
The other leading cases were *In re Southern Rhodesia* [1919] AC 215 and *Amodu Tijani v. Southern Nigeria (Secretary)* [1921] AC 399.

[6] Constitution of Uganda 1995, Article 237. See too the Land Act, 1998 which fleshes out the general principles enshrined in the Constitution.

[7] Interestingly, one of the areas where both Uganda and Zambia have tackled old English land law is trusts. Uganda introduced a variant of the English Trustee Act, 1925 via the Trusts Ordinance in 1954, the relevance of which to the majority of the population was absolutely nil, while Zambia via the Trusts Restrictions Act of 1970 repealed the old English law of trusts, settlements and future interests,

replacing it with a more restrictive regime. See on the Zambian law, Moses Kaunda (1986–92).

[8] In Uganda, for instance, in connection with the Land Act, 1998, there were not wanting lawyers who were unhappy at the notion that freehold tenure in Uganda could be different to freehold tenure in England. In Namibia, the legal profession were very unhappy at attempts to develop a new intermediate urban tenure to facilitate the urban poor gaining access to land and made plain that they would not recommend it to the banks as a safe form of security for lending. See too Moses Kaunda (1986) who recommends the re-introduction of trusts and settlements into Zambian land law and Kludze (1974).

5 The best laid schemes o' mice an' men: the diaspora of town and country planning law in Africa and Asia*

Introduction

It is a happy coincidence that 50 years of law at SOAS is being celebrated in 1997 – the same year as the 50th anniversary of the passage of the Town and Country Planning Act, 1947, a law which may rightly be seen as being one of the foundation stones of post-war British society and government. 50 years on, the basic structure of planning, development control and enforcement carried out by local authorities, with supervision by and appeals to the central government created by that Act remains in place, despite many changes of both substance and procedures in the details of the planning system, a remarkable tribute to those involved in the construction of that law. Equally too, despite constant criticism of the system, most stridently in the 1980s, there has never been any serious move to dismantle it, to sweep away the structure and start again with something completely different.

The same 50-year period in which law at SOAS and town and country planning in the United Kingdom has flourished, has witnessed a diaspora of English town and country planning laws and practices throughout the developing countries of the Commonwealth. Scarcely a country in Anglophone Africa and Asia has not had, does not in some cases still have, a town and country planning law which is modelled on English law and which has been promulgated or enacted since 1947. Is not this then a further remarkable tribute to the creators of the 1947 Act; just as M. Jourdain spoke prose without realising it, so they created legislation apt to plan the whole world or at least the English-speaking parts of it, without realising it. Furthermore, in many cases, a law enacted in the 1950s and 1960s, remains largely untouched and unaltered, a veritable law of the Medes and Persians. At the same time, the law and the system which it provides for are subject to ever increasing criticism designed to make the case for sweeping the whole system away and replacing it with an entirely different one.

This chapter will explore and reflect on this phenomenon; the apparent success of town and country planning law in the United Kingdom; its apparent failure in Africa and Asia. What is the driving philosophy behind the law here; what were its mainsprings in Africa and Asia? (And indeed in the Caribbean too for it would be misleading to leave out that important part of the story.) How does the law and the planning system it provides for differ in the developing countries of the Commonwealth from that existing here? Why has there been resistance to changing from the British system? And if there were to be change, what should take the place of the existing system?

This chapter cannot claim to be a detailed and scholarly history of the growth and operation of town planning law and practice in Africa and Asia. Much work remains to be done on that subject even after Home's pioneering overview (Home, 1997). Still less is it a survey of urbanisation in Africa and Asia over the last 50 years. It is a reflection on a particular aspect of law and development; town and country planning law and urban and rural development; it tries to build on work that has been done by many people over the years both in the field and in the library. It offers some thoughts on why in this area, "the best laid schemes o' mice an' men gang aft a-gley?"[1]

The British system of town and country planning

A start may be made by setting out succinctly but hopefully not too simplistically the fundamental philosophy of the British system of town and country planning introduced by the Act of 1947 for it will be useful to keep that philosophy in mind as the growth of town and country planning law in Africa, Asia and the Caribbean is examined. It is easy to forget the revolutionary nature of the 1947 Act. Piecemeal reforms to the Town and Country Planning Act, 1932 had been introduced during World War Two but these had been associated with wartime necessities. The Act of 1947 heralded an entirely different approach to peacetime planning. It introduced a comprehensive and compulsory system of planning; all land had to be planned via development plans; all development required permission unless otherwise exempted from the need to obtain permission by the law and with a very few limited exceptions, no compensation was payable for a refusal of permission to develop land.

Writing in the early 1960s for an American audience, Sir William Hart, former Clerk to the London County Council made the point that the absence of a written constitution in the UK gave the widest scope for legislation which by long tradition had been used to override individual rights of ownership in the use of land, and he gave the usual examples; control of building in London after the Great Fire in 1666; enclosures in the eighteenth century, compulsory acquisition of land for railways and canals in the nineteenth century (Hart, 1964). These were, however, very different in nature to comprehensive planning control; they were for specific purposes; affected limited numbers of people and, on balance, were enacted for the benefit of the landed classes. Indeed, given the veto powers of the House of Lords at that time, it could not have been otherwise. But planning control was designed to affect everyone, especially the landed classes, all the time in respect of anything they wanted to do on the land. However much the nation might have been prepared for change as a result of the three great reports – Barlow (1940), Scott (1942) and Uthwatt (1942) – in the early 1940s, the Act of 1947 represented a watershed in how the British relate to land; public interest was put before private right in respect of the development and use of land and whatever the changes and vicissitudes which have taken place in law and practice since then, that fundamental principle remains at the heart of British planning law and thus, of the British approach to land development.

The origins of colonial town planning

Was this same philosophy behind the development of planning and its legislative backing in what were then the colonies in the post World War Two era? To attempt to answer this question, it is necessary to go back to much earlier in this century; not just before the establishment of the Law Department at SOAS but before even the establishment of SOAS itself. Colonial town planning, that is town planning based on laws introduced by British colonial authorities as opposed to indigenous or traditional or national town planning, did not commence in the colonies after World War Two. In India, town planning laws *eo nomine* were being enacted in the first two decades of this century, within ten years indeed of the enactment of the first British town planning Act of 1909. Even before that, planned urban renewal and redevelopment had taken place in some of the major Indian cities often under the aegis of an Improvement Trust, the statutory powers for which were based on the English Housing for the Working Classes Act, 1890. The first such trust was set up by the City of Bombay Improvement Act, 1898.

This particular institution and its powers has been very influential in the development of town planning in Asia and Africa and has interesting parallels in certain developments in the UK in the 1980s so it deserves a slightly extended treatment. In the words of a publication produced by the Calcutta Improvement Trust, itself established by the Calcutta Improvement Act, 1911 (Das Gupta, 1974, pp. 15–16):

> A feature of urban machinery in Calcutta common to other large cities of India, is that the Improvement authority does not derive its status from the Municipal authority, but is a co-ordinating body in direct relation to [the State] Government. A slight degree of friction generated by this state of affairs in one or two other cities is, however, happily absent from Calcutta ...

According to the then Secretary of the Trust, what this form of words carefully concealed was that the trusts began to be established at precisely the time that the Indian Congress Party began to win power in the major cities of India and the aim behind these trusts was therefore to take away from elected local governments important powers over urban development and vest them instead in the colonial provincial government which could ensure the presence of "safe" persons on the trust.[2] Certainly, the first Board of Trustees of the Calcutta Improvement Trust appointed in 1912 included 7 Europeans amongst its 11 members and one of the 4 Indian members was a KCIE, unlikely therefore to have been a stalwart of the Indian Congress Party.[3] This model of unelected urban authority spread very rapidly throughout Britain's Asian colonies; Rangoon in Burma, Colombo in Ceylon, Singapore and from Asia it crossed over into Africa with the creation of the Lagos Executive Development Board in 1928.

It is easy to recognise the British parallel; the creation of, first, the London Docklands Development Corporation in 1980 taking planning and urban development powers away from six Labour controlled London local authorities and vesting them in a Conservative appointed Urban Development Corporation, and then upwards of a dozen other Urban Development Corporations in areas where Labour local authorities were resistant to Conservative urban development prescriptions. Truly, a case of the Empire striking back![4]

More to the point from the perspective of this chapter, this Indian precedent highlighted two matters; first, town planning was not, in the eyes of the colonial power, safe in the hands of elected local authorities. Second, to quote Evenson (1989, p. 114):

> According to [Patrick] Geddes [the famous British town planner who spent some time in India in the first quarter of the twentieth century] British planning in India seemed to be drawn from outmoded sanitary byelaws 'with their enormous product of mean streets in our industrial towns ...' The delicate urban fabric of Indian quarters was often subject to brutal renovation in the name of sanitation and improved circulation, 'a matter of doing puja to the straight lines of the drawing board and set squares'.

In short, planning law and practice was seen as a matter for "non-political" experts introducing "objective" standards of health and safety in order to "improve" local urban areas which local people either could not or would not manage properly.

Town planning laws and practices came to Africa before 1947 and here too the historical legacy must be referred to so as to understand evolution over the last 50 years and in particular since the 1960s. The driving force here was segregation. Some examples may be given. Writing of Nigeria, Adeniyi (1981, p. 34) states:

> The first systematic attempt at physical planning in Nigeria was provided by the Township Ordinance of 1917. Its main purpose was to 'establish the broad principle of Municipal responsibility, graduated according to the importance of the community and the measure of its ability to accept and discharge satisfactorily independent or quasi-independent powers' (Lugard) ...
>
> One major feature of the township ordinance was the major emphasis on guidelines for the physical layout of the towns and cities, particularly in the 'European' and Non-European reservations. The impact of these guidelines is still very evident in the physical layout of the GRA,[5] and the grid-iron pattern of the layout of such towns as Kaduna, Jos, Minna, Enugu, Port Harcourt and also the new districts of most of our cities.

The first legislation with town planning in its name was the Lagos Town Planning Ordinance of 1929 which provided the legal backing for the Lagos Executive Development Board which was to carry out the duties of re-planning, improvement and development in Lagos, much the same tasks as had been given to the Improvement Trusts in Indian cities, with much the same tension, Adeniyi referring to the conflicting roles of the

Board and the City Council. Interestingly, Lagos, unlike all other urban centres in Nigeria, had an elected element in its local authority; four elected persons out of a town council of ten persons. Town planning legislation on a national scale arrived with the Nigeria Town and Country Planning Ordinance of 1946, modelled on the English Town and Country Planning Act of 1932, which extended to all Nigeria the aims of the 1929 Lagos Ordinance. The Governor was the central authority for all planning in the country, although in practice he delegated his powers to officials throughout the country.

In East Africa, town planning operated initially through public health laws which provided the formal *raison d'être* for segregation. Thus, Professor Simpson, a major protagonist of urban racial segregation throughout Eastern and Southern Africa in the early years of the twentieth century and the principal begetter of town planning in Kenya and Uganda wrote in a report on Nairobi in 1913 (Werlin, 1974, p. 53) that:

> In the interests of each community and of the healthiness of the locality and country, it is absolutely essential that in every town and trade centre there should be well-defined and separate quarters for Europeans, Asiatics and Africans …

He repeated the same advice to Uganda where in 1915, he became Kampala's first town planner. McMaster (1973) writing on district towns in Uganda notes that Simpson recommended ethnic town zoning with intervening green belts. It was no doubt in order to implement that policy that in Hoima and Masindi, the towns' anti-malarial vote was spent on the upkeep of the golf course.

The importance of the public health dimension to nascent town planning may be judged by the juxtaposition of two events in the early 1920s. In 1922 Lugard's seminal Dual Mandate in Tropical Africa was published in which in the chapter on British Staff and Conditions of Life in the Tropics the following passage occurs (1922, p. 148):

> …[W]here segregation is compatible with work and duty, commercial firms, no less than the Government, incur a moral responsibility not to expose employees to infection which can be avoided.
>
> With this object in view, new townships are divided into European and native reservations, separated by a non-residential area 440 yards in breadth, cleared of high grass and scrub. Europeans are not allowed to sleep in the

native reservation and natives, other than domestic servants and other necessary employees may not reside in the European quarter.

In 1923, the then Government published a White Paper; Indians In Kenya which prohibited separation of the races in towns by means of legislative enactments. Werlin, writing of Nairobi, comments that the same effect was achieved by means of restrictive covenants (Werlin, p. 53) and McMaster writing of district towns in Uganda states that the White Paper made little difference because Crown land leases and building standards regulations could operate effectively to the same end (McMaster, 1973, p. 24). In each case then, officials used their powers under existing laws to circumvent the policies announced in the UK.

Thus, the formal absence of town and country planning legislation in East Africa did not inhibit, may indeed have facilitated, segregated urban development by allowing it to be justified on public health grounds and smuggled in via a variety of legal devices. In Nigeria on the other hand, town planning legislation provided the legal basis for separate development but again with a public health justification. In each case, it is worth noting, further spurious justifications was wont to be put forward: it was in the interests of the native or the Indian as well and it was not really a segregation of races but a segregation of "social standards" to quote Lugard who also opined that "they" *i.e.* the natives who "love to drum and dance at night which deprives the European of sleep...have no desire to abolish segregation" (Lugard, p. 150). How easy was it then to deal with the problems of "the neighbours from hell"; just build a golf course between them and you.

The notion of social segregation was addressed centrally in those terms in the Nairobi Master Plan for a Colonial Capital, prepared by a team of three planners from South Africa between 1945 and 1946 who exhibited some rather muddled thinking in trying desperately not to call a spade a spade (Thornton White *et al.*, 1948, pp. 23, 24):

> ... [F]or the European [in Nairobi] the problem of class differentiation [inter se that is] is of minor importance.
> The present trend of non-European society is quite different. Class differentiation is taking place and already engages much interest ...
> [Then follows the policy]
> *Thus the Master Plan must allow for a fair degree of economic class differentiation among the non-European population.*
> [Then comes the subtlety]

> For like reasons, it is not difficult to see why there is a drawing away of the main upper income group, *viz.*, of the Europeans from other groups.
> Ethnic 'nucleation' is common in all towns with a mixed population irrespective (sic) what Government policy or the law do and say .... Sometimes feelings mount to explosion point and there are racial and communal riots.

It may be thought a little odd that there might be racial riots when its really all a case of social class.

The idea that racist town planning was not racist in intent died hard. I can recall being assured in the pleasant surroundings of the Salisbury Club in Harare in 1981 by the chairman of the Administrative Court with which the Town Planning Court of Zimbabwe had recently been amalgamated that what looked like the racial segregation in Harare was in reality only a concern to protect property values; objections to re-zoning land from single family residences set in spacious plots to flat development were concerned with the possibility of lower-income people moving into a high income area; the race and colour of the lower-income people was immaterial.

The diaspora of post-1947 British town and country planning law

The 1947 Act heralded a new approach to town and country planning in the UK. The approach of the 1932 Act – the planning scheme with compensation payable for certain refusals of planning permission – was completely displaced. It is not too much of an exaggeration to say that there really was a sharp break in the continuity of town planning in the UK and history began anew in 1947. Can the same be said of the diaspora of planning legislation which commenced in the colonies in the 1940s?

The starting point in law for the post-war history of colonial planning is the Colonial Development and Welfare Act, 1945, which provided £120 million over a period of ten years for development and welfare in the colonies. Now this was not the first such act, although it is always pointed to as the beginning of a new approach to colonial administration. The first Colonial Development and Welfare Act was in 1940 where it replaced the Colonial Development Acts which provided money solely for agricultural and industrial development. The 1940 Act provided the first impetus towards spending on social improvements which included slum clearance and the extensive replanning of urban areas but the sums of money provided for those purposes were minuscule. The importance of the 1945 Act was that it provided significant sums of money and indirectly stimulated and encouraged planning in the colonies (Arnold, 1962). Colonies were required to draw up co-ordinated development plans for capital works and bids for CDW money and exchequer loans. These capital works included a good deal of social expenditure. Indeed, Lord Hailey estimated that by 1951, 43% of the expenditure included in the Development Plans for colonial territories was allocated to social expenditure of a capital nature (Hailey, 1957, p. 1325). This tended to be urban expenditure; hospitals, roads, housing and schools. Such co-ordinated development plans for urban expenditure clearly implied the need for some kind of urban development plan.

It was not surprising then that the Colonial Office turned to consider the question of town planning. A Colonial Housing and Town Planning Advisory Panel was set up and advised both the Colonial Office and different colonies on housing and town planning matters. The Colonial Office developed a model town and country planning law which drew on both the 1932 and the 1947 Acts. An important input into this law however was the Town and Country Planning Ordinance of 1938 from Trinidad and Tobago (Home, pp.182–83). We find then starting in the late 1940s, the promulgation of town and country planning ordinances in African and Caribbean countries, nearly all of them having the same general shape and content.

Each territory to be sure varied the basic law to suit its own particular circumstances – Tanganyika's Ordinance, promulgated in 1956 was not the same as Nyasaland's, promulgated in 1948, or Uganda's promulgated in 1951, being much more detailed in every matter, which was perhaps a reflection of what had been learned from the operation of those earlier laws – but more likely was a reflection of the very dominant personality of the chief town planner of Tanganyika. Countries in the Caribbean followed the Trinidadian model fairly closely but, as befitted islands, had rather different arrangements in respect of the development plan which was an island development plan.

In India too there were moves to revise town planning laws. Chandrasekhara (1969, pp. 278–83) noted that while town planning Acts existed in many provinces prior to independence, they only permitted zoning schemes that were partial and not comprehensive either in scope of extent. However:

> In the post-independence period there has been a concerted effort on the part of the state governments to enact comprehensive planning legislation which

> would enable zoning to be applied more systematically and effectively to achieve the objects of the comprehensive plan ... Zoning is positive and constructive rather than negative ... it helps the individual user appropriately to develop his property most profitably for himself as well as for the community and at the same time promote the interests of the community by protecting the quality of the environment and by enhancing the taxable base of the community.

At this point, I propose to put forward a hypothesis based in part on published documents from the Colonial Office. We must bear in mind that in the 1940s and 1950s, there was a genuine belief in the efficacy of planning and public action to overcome urban problems. The concern of the Colonial Office was to tackle bad housing conditions in the colonies just as successive governments were tackling bad housing conditions in the UK. The annual report on the Colonial Territories for 1956–57 (1958, pp. 24–25) is a good summary of these concerns:

> Most of the territories are at stages of development where men and money cannot be spared to make a concerted attack on bad housing conditions and where the role of Government is to ensure that existing accommodation and such limited resources as can be applied to new building are used to the best advantage. This calls for well-considered long-term building policies, adequate legal, financial and administrative arrangements and close co-operation between the many agencies concerned with various aspects of housing and town planning. Conditions vary considerably from territory to territory but there are two problems which arise in acute form wherever there is rapid urban growth. The first is the problem of clearing and replanning the congested and often out-of-date central areas of large towns and rehousing population ... The second is the re-development of fringe areas, where squatters' shacks and other sub-standard dwellings are continually growing up ... .

The report then went on to highlight the work of the Singapore Improvement Trust, established in the mid-1930s, that had been energetically tackling those two problems and that of the Lagos Executive Development Board where it was noted that town planning as well as housing was the responsibility of the Board.

My argument is that officials in the Colonial Office acted and gave advice on the basis that town and country planning was an essential part of a positive programme of public sector led urban development which would have as its overall objective the betterment of the lives of the inhabitants of the cities within the colonies. This was, after all, what town and country planning was thought to be about in the UK where until the mid to late 1950s, most urban development was, similarly, public sector led, and the development control aspect of town and country planning – the control of private development – was of less importance. It followed too that a legal framework for town and country planning should be based on that which was generally thought to be the most advanced and successful in the developed world, namely the UK system. The leading town planning lawyer of that era, Desmond Heap, was certainly of that opinion and reacted rather vigorously to suggestions that town planning laws of the colonies should deviate from the British model. Town planning then was seen in positive terms; a definite public good.

In thinking and acting in this way, colonial officials were not out of kilter with international thinking and action about urban development and the role of planning therein. Consider this striking panegyric to planning by Marc Nerfin, a Regional Adviser to UNECA (1965, pp. 559–63). After stressing the role of housing in bringing about the modernisation of society, he goes on to say:

> Physical planning is an important tool in the geographical creation of the modern nation; it involves the integration of the 'traditional' areas with the 'enclaves' linked to overseas economies ... [In] the more important settlements, the big towns and the capital cities, new town planning will mean social integration and the optimum technical use of land ... [T]he other fundamental aspect of the new town planning [is that] it will deliberately break away from the segregation, both racial and social, which up to now has characterised most African towns.
>
> ... [W]ith few exceptions, bourgeois town planning was essentially, even in the best cases, carried out *a posteriori*, in order to correct the most pernicious of the territorial effects of the free market economy. Africa generally speaking has refused to be bound by the constraints of a *laisser-faire* system; a new dialogue seems possible in future between economic planners, social planners and physical planners, so that 'modern town planning may be definitely regarded as an important factor in the building of a democratic community'.
>
> In the immediate future, town planning will have priority over housing projects ... Evidence shows that no one dreams of disputing the role of government with respect to town and country planning ...

It is perhaps unlikely that any British civil servant would write in that vein but Franklin, the adviser to ODA on planning in the late 1960s and early 1970s before going on the UN Centre for Planning Housing and Building – the predecessor of UNCHS (Habitat) – certainly thought in that way when he advanced the opinion in 1972 that developing countries needed 14,000 planners then and would need 63,000 by the year 2000.

By the early 1960s as countries in Africa, the Caribbean and South East Asia became independent, an English-style planning law had become a part of many countries' modernisation package. Older approaches to town planning were assumed to have been left behind as they had been in the UK itself. The new independent governments and the elected urban local authorities could now address the problems of the majority of the urban population armed with the requisite planning tools. We know however with the advantage of hindsight that that has proved to be a chimera; why?

Why the export model of British planning law failed

Over the last two decades, there has been no shortage of criticism of the kind of urban planning system inherited by countries at independence or introduced since independence but still based on the metropolitan model. I want to try and isolate those criticisms of planning which can, plausibly, be related to the law and the institutions of town planning which, even as independent governments took up the reins of power were beginning to be voiced. One of the earliest criticisms was made by Abrams (1964, p. 62) who commented on:

> The tendency in a number of countries ... to copy the complex [building] codes of England, Germany or the United States as well as their zoning and planning laws, though they are irrelevant and though the talent to enforce, construe and adapt them may be completely lacking.

At that time, I think the first half of the criticism was a little misplaced at least as regards countries in the Commonwealth for they had not so much copied English laws as a matter of choice as had them imported or imposed as a part of the colonial experience.

Nevertheless, however the laws came into existence, they have contributed to the evolution and operation of planning systems which are the antithesis of what Nerfin and Colonial Office planners hoped and anticipated would emerge: negative rather than positive; socially divisive rather than integrational and egalitarian; authoritarian rather than democratic.

The British planning system has always had its negative as well as its positive side. If development plans are designed to channel, locate and stipulate development, development control is designed to do just that; control development. That can often be or seem to be a rather negative exercise although in practice it has always been the case that well over 80% of all applications are always approved and enforcement – stopping development and demolishing what has been put up has always been very much the exception. But this is in a society where close on 100% of all development is carried out in a legal milieu; that is, it is carried out on land by or on behalf of persons with rights to the land; or on buildings that have been lawfully erected in the first place and by people who do, generally, observe the laws relating to development because on balance they consider that it is in their own interests to do so.

Planners who trained in the UK or attended the old RTPI Summer Schools for planners from developing countries would have learned about development control and enforcement and how both were essential parts of the total planning system as provided for by the law, the same kind of law they had back home. Indeed the law they had almost everywhere seemed to elevate development control to a superior position to development plans. Thus, in the Tanzanian Town and Country Planning Ordinance, virtually unchanged since its promulgation 46 years ago, where the Minister is of the opinion that a general planning scheme should be made for an area, he declares that area to be a planning area and causes a scheme to be made. However:

> Notwithstanding any other law to the contrary, no person shall develop any land within a planning area without planning consent or otherwise than in accordance with planning consent and any conditions specified therein (s.35 T&CPO Cap 378).

Equivalent provisions were to be found in the Nyasaland Ordinance of 1948 and the Trinidad and Tobago Act of 1960 to take just two other laws almost at random. Since there was and is no provision which limits the life of a planning area if no scheme is made or which compels the Minister to reconsider whether a planning area should continue in being, the message to planners is plain: control of development is more important than development, or the planning of same. Indeed, the preamble to many acts and ordinances referred to legislation "to make provision for *orderly* and progressive development" (italics added).

Now, apply this message to the cities of developing countries in the Commonwealth. We are all broadly familiar with the nature of these cities: a relatively small modern-looking Central Business District and administrative centre; some high-income residential areas in what are the geographically better parts of the city; some industry, often a source of pollution and, down wind of it, vast areas of low-income housing, much of it unauthorised urban settlements, located on land which does not belong to the occupier, self-built, unplanned, overcrowded and with a total lack of adequate or indeed in many cases, any infrastructure.

To planners brought up in the British system, these areas of unauthorised settlements are anathema; they are contrary to everything that they have been taught that planning is all about and furthermore to everything that planning was before independence; slum-clearance, relocation, re-development. That they are also illegal adds insult to injury. Naturally therefore, the planners are concerned to apply the law, or if that is not immediately possible, then they are equally determined to hold the line, that is to set their face against "regularisation", a modish word for condoning illegality. In this they are usually supported by politicians who are offended both by the sight of slums and by being told by foreign consultants that they should "accept" them; and in some cases are also only too aware of the value such land would have if it were to be cleared of squatters. So development control which, in the UK, has always been seen as the tool for assisting lawful development to take place at the right time and in the right place, in many developing countries is seen as the weapon to attack and demolish development which has occurred in the wrong place, using the wrong materials and is unlawful.

An excellent example may be given from Trinidad and Tobago, in many respects one of the most efficient and committed planning departments I have ever had the privilege of working with. The senior officials there constantly stressed the word "orderly" in the preamble to their legislation; that's what they were there to ensure and that involved enforcement against illegal development. They were not prepared to countenance or support an innovative and indigenous way of providing low-income housing – the Sou Sou Land movement – since that did not follow, indeed deliberately ignored planning law and the planning system which the organisers of Sou Sou Land regarded as unconstitutional since it deprived people of their right to land and to use it as they saw fit (Mohammed, 1997). They were concerned when I proposed leaving the word "orderly" out of new legislation I was drafting to replace the 1960 English orientated Act that had been prepared for them by Desmond Heap, the doyen of English planning lawyers. Similar views about orderliness and legality have often been voiced to me by senior planners in Tanzania and Lesotho.

Looking back with the advantage of hindsight on the British planning system, the optimism of its early years now seems almost naïve. It was meant to be but never was a socially inclusive system; it operated in different ways for different classes of the community. Similarly with the legal system that provided the legal framework for that planning system (McAuslan, 1980). One of the most comprehensive surveys of the British planning system – The Containment of Urban England – sums up the aims of the planning system in that title and make some further points, highly relevant for the arguments being put forward here (Hall *et al.*, 1973, pp. 68–71):

> British planning'[s] ... methods stem from a characteristic model of political organisation, which Meyerson and Banfield have called *unitary*. In it, decision-takers have an organismic view of the public interest; all other interests are subordinated to that of the social 'organism' ... A unitary concept of politics ... is natural to upper- and upper-middle class people ... Such an approach tends to an extremely lofty yet imprecise definition of the public good ... and are characteristically presented in terms of the absolute virtue of a concrete set of policy measures ...
>
> There are important implications here for the study of the British planning system. From the start we have seen throughout the study, British planning has been based on a narrow physical concept and on the implicit belief in environmental determinism. There has been little explicit attempt to relate the physically-defined policy objectives – such as urban containment or the protection of rural land – to fundamental objectives related to the value systems of people ... it seems clear for instance, that the objective of urban containment has in practice proved inconsistent in some important ways with the objective of providing cheap owner-occupied housing.

We can cast our minds back to the early colonial approach to town planning – racial segregation – allied to a belief, explicit in Africa but implicit elsewhere I believe, that towns were not the "right" place for Africans or other essentially rural people to be. If we ally those beliefs to the principal post-World War Two British one of urban containment, we have a planning system in developing countries that is distinctly anti-urban or rather distinctly anti-indigenous urban. Consider through a lens informed by such an approach the statements quoted earlier from the Colonial Office report of 1956–57: "the rehousing of population on the outskirts of towns or in new towns"; "the redevelopment of fringe areas where squatters' shacks and other sub-standard dwellings are continually growing up." The values of the upper and upper-middle class in Britain were reproduced, as might be expected in the colonial planning legislation created in the 1950s and 1960s and inherited at independence and so made the implementation of such policies that much easier.

I would go further. Behind any arguments about the needs of public health providing the justification for segregation in colonial cities lay a deeper concern; the fear of the urban mob and the urban riot. This has always been present amongst the upper classes in England and this fear was translated into town planning in the colonies, particularly India after the Indian Mutiny, the most vivid demonstration of what can happen if the mob is not contained. The most important colonial development in Indian cities was the military cantonment, the substantial military base placed, usually, between the "native" city and the colonial city or near to the native city so as to be on hand to quell riots. King (1973, pp. 210–13) describes the situation in Delhi after the mutiny:

> The cantonment, established in the city in 1803 but removed three miles away in 1828 was now brought back into the city. As re-established in 1859, it occupied an area enclosed on three sides by the city wall ... South of the Fort, property was confiscated and cleared ... Effectively the cantonment occupied one third of the spatial area of the city ... Occupants of dwellings demolished for the Military Zone either crowded into the indigenous sector of the city ... or joined the rapidly growing extra-mural 'squatter settlements' ... The most important component defining the structure of the city was the wall ... The reason for its retention was that of 'military security' ... As a physical barrier around the indigenous culture area of Delhi, most of the wall remained intact until the formal ending of colonial rule.

Cantonments were replaced by green belts and golf courses in most African cities and towns but the intention was the same. Now this fear of the mob, of the urban poor, has remained a *leit motif* of urban governance in the developing world. The almost universal dislike of the informal sector, the sporadic sweeping away of informal commercial structures (King, 1996; Tripp, 1997); the removal of hawkers, their designation as vagrants, the harassment of informal transport systems (aided in Nairobi, by the too easy giving in to the anti-competitive demands of Stagecoach to ban matatus from the city centre); in some cases, the banning of public transport from the upper income parts of cities; the assumption that unauthorised urban settlements are full of thieves, prostitutes and illegal activities; the over zealous use of force by the police when confronted by large numbers of the urban poor – for instance, the use of lathes on the poor struggling to view the coffin of Mother Theresa in Calcutta and the shooting of urban demonstrators in Nairobi in 1997 and Jakarta in 1998 – all testify to this.

Amongst the tools available to urban governors to contain the mob is the planning system and its battery of sanctions and powers to keep the urban poor at a distance and, as it were, off balance by denying them any lawful abode in the city. This is why there continues to be resistance to attempts to develop and introduce inclusive planning systems and planning laws which emphasise public involvement and regularisation. It's not just that this would be to accept the continuation of the "slum"; it involves a totally new approach to planning; one that sees the people as partners and not as threat. It involves in a word, democratic planning.

Before turning to this issue of democratic planning, I want to turn and briefly consider another aspect of the planning system and the way it has perceived people as threat as this too bears on the notion of democratic planning. This is countryside planning and the creation of National Parks. In the UK, National Parks were first statutorily provided for by the National Parks and Access to the Countryside Act, 1949 though the movement for national parks goes back to the late nineteenth century. Two points may be made. First, from the beginning, National Parks in the UK as the second half of the title of the Act indicates were part of a movement to facilitate the access of ordinary people to the countryside and had to overcome opposition of large landowners, particularly in Scotland, who resisted this opening up of land to the people. Second, National Parks were to be managed by a combination of centrally appointed and locally elected people. People lived in the parks and there was never any suggestion that they should cease to do so or that their interests would be ignored.

Contrast that with National Parks, particularly in Africa. Here, the influence of South Africa has been important. The Kruger Park was established in South Africa in 1898, the first such National Park in Africa. National Parks in African countries have involved the removal of people from the parks and the complete displacement of local interests and local involvement in management. Colonialist conservationist legislation in Africa proceeded on the basis that the recovery and development of human and livestock population from its historically low base which was existing at the outset of colonialism was unnatural, threatening and ecologically unsound. In the words of the conclusions of an International Union for the Conservation of Nature (IUCN) workshop in 1985, reported by Bell (1986, pp. 86–89):

> There is no room for complacency on the overall conservation situation. The fundamental problem is recognised as the rapid human population increase.

Bell goes on as follows:

> There can ... be no doubt as to the reality of the conflict with local interests. Most conservation agencies are paramilitary armed and uniformed organisations ... Under rural wildlife legislation in many African countries, normal rural existence is nearly impossible without breaking the law ... In many African countries, armed confrontations between 'poachers', that is those acting contrary to wildlife legislation, and enforcement staff are commonplace and deaths and injuries on both sides are regular occurrences. The international community has in the past come to apply a double standard with regard to conservation and development, applying more rigorous constraints to development to the Third World and Africa in particular than to the developed countries.

It is only in the last decade that policies and laws have begun to change in many countries and local communities are now beginning to be involved in both the planning and management of wildlife reserves and in their exploitation, deriving income therefrom. Bell refers to this as conservation with human face and points out that it differs from the orthodox approach of strong central control based on the assumption of the immanence of a man-induced ecological collapse. Here too then, the fear of the mob, albeit the mob is that of herders and pastoralists is a colonial holdover and operates to inhibit democratic planning.

So we come back to the issue of democracy and planning. Nerfin, it will be recalled, saw the new planning as being an important factor in the building of a democratic community. The authors of the chapter from The Containment of Urban England on the other hand saw the unitary approach to planning – the approach transmitted from the UK to the developing Commonwealth – as being undemocratic as it has no room for constant adjustment to the pressures and desires of different groups through a sensitive political machine. The point being made there is important; planning is about the allocation and use of scarce resources and political factors are bound to play a part in such decisions. That book was reviewing the first 20-odd years of planning in the UK and by the time it was published in 1973, significant changes had taken place in the legal framework and legal culture of British planning. Three may be mentioned; inspectors' reports into planning inquiries were now published and beginning to be regularly challenged in the courts; the Town and Country Planning Act of 1968 had introduced the structure plan system with a much greater emphasis on the policy aspects of the development plan; and plan-making procedures now had written into them a much greater element of public participation. There was then a much more open acceptance that planning and politics were inextricably linked. This new approach to planning had in any event built on a basis which linked planning and politics at the formal level; it has always been elected local authorities and an elected Minister which made the decisions on both plans and planning applications.

Now, the planning systems set up by law all over the Commonwealth do not, generally, reproduce this part of the British planning system. Several strands of thinking went into what was created. First, in keeping with the apolitical approach to planning prevalent in the UK in the early years of the modern post-World War Two system, politics were not thought to be relevant in the decision-making process. Second, in any event in some of the colonies, politics was not thought to be helpful – period. The unitary approach to planning was paralleled by what might be called the unitary approach to the colonial mission – that it was an unalloyed public good and anyone disputing that clearly had evil intent. Third, there was the older colonial experience; the Improvement Trusts of India and South-East Asia, and the Lagos Executive Development Board, appointed bodies carrying out planning functions. Thus, there was a tendency to locate decisions in appointed rather than elected bodies; Boards; or committees with both appointed and elected persons – the latter in a minority. So planning never got off even to a formally democratic start in most developing Commonwealth countries.

While planning in the UK has become more participative, more open, more political in the last 30 years – all features bolstered and a large extent mandated by the law, it has become less so in many developing countries in the Commonwealth. Colonial traditions have been continued in several ways. First, in very many countries, elected local governments in the large cities have been replaced by central government appointed Commissions or in the case of some of the Indian cities, a Commissioner. No geographical area of the Commonwealth has been immune from this disease – Acquired Immunity from Democracy Syndrome. The stated reasons given for this are corruption, inefficiency, misuse of council funds; the unstated reason is sometimes the fact that the opposition party is controlling the city – shades of the Conservative Government and the GLC in 1985. Whatever the reason, the formal democratic element disappears. Second, in many countries again, especially in India, Pakistan and Nigeria, Boards and Authorities have been established or re-established to which planning and land development functions have been transferred from local governments and the membership of these bodies are in the gift of central or state governments.

Third, and this is a factor which is very prevalent in countries in Africa, master plans made by consultancy firms from abroad working to the orders of the Ministry's chief planner are not conducive to the development of a democratic input into plan-making. In my experience, they are not conducive either to complying with any planning law. In short, the planning systems in Commonwealth developing countries provide a good example of the "democratic deficit" and the absence of good government; the weakness of the institutions of civil society; the overbearing nature of the bureaucracy and the casual approach of that bureaucracy to observing the law. Even where, as in Malaysia and Zimbabwe, the post 1968 British planning system of structure and local plans has been introduced into the country via a new planning law, the public participation elements of that law have been left out.

The current British system of town and country planning introduced in a mood of optimism by the Town and Country Planning Act, 1947 and leading the way more or less consistently ever since towards a more open and participative style of governance in the UK bolstered, when introduced into the colonies after that date, a system of planning which must be seen as very much a part of the colonial system of governance and has never really recovered from that inauspicious start. It was then and has remained the antithesis of open and participative governance. Whatever the thinking of the colonial officials who were responsible for the diaspora of British town and country planning law, the law has been used in country after country to keep the urban masses at bay; to deny them lawful homes and livelihoods; to reinforce the powers of officials; and to weaken the institutions of civil society.

It may seem paradoxical after such an indictment to go on to suggest that this outcome is not wholly the fault of the planners and that they were and are as much victims as perpetrators of this state of affairs. Why is this? Crawford Young (1994, pp. 283–87) puts the matter thus:

> ... [T]he colonial state during its phase of construction in most cases created entirely novel institutions of domination and rule. Although we commonly

> describe the independent polities as 'new states', in reality they were successors to the colonial regime, inheriting its structures, its quotidian routines and practices, and its more hidden normative theories of governance. Thus everyday reason of state, as it imposed its logic on the new rulers, incorporated subliminal codes of operation bearing the imprint of their colonial predecessors ...
>
> The state as theologian of development, appeared to speak a new language. But more closely examined, if not deconstructed, one might detect a subtext of continuity ... [D]evelopment was a managerial art; the role of the administrator was 'encadrement' of the populace, to secure compliance with the edicts through which development policy was transformed into administrative law ... In short, what Mbembe terms a principe autoritaire informed the inner ethos of the postcolonial state ...

Is not this just as true for many South-East Asian states? And even in India, does not the IAS have a somewhat similar attitude to its work? And where the state does not, as in *e.g.*, Caribbean states, the planners certainly see their role as "encadrement of the populace".[6]

Conclusion

The principal criticism which must therefore be made of the diaspora of British planning law throughout Africa and Asia is that it reinforced the authoritarianism and paternalism of the colonial and postcolonial state. Planning always has this possibility – Hayek pointed that out over 50 years ago – and it needs therefore, and has always had in the UK, a strong culture of democracy and scepticism to be bearable. It may be that as country after country within Commonwealth Africa and Asia makes a determined effort to address the democratic deficit and measure up to the principles of good governance, town and country planning will begin to play the same positive role which it has done in the UK in advancing more open and participative governance.

One can already point to heartening examples of what can be done; South Africa's pathbreaking Facilitation of Development Act, 1996 and its Green Paper on Development and Planning (DPC, 1999) which owes nothing to British planning law; Namibia and Zimbabwe's legislation to introduce partnerships in wildlife management and Tanzania's acceptance in its National Land Policy and enactment in the Land Act, 1999 of the need to provide titles and security to unauthorised urban settlements are

African examples and many encouraging albeit small-scale examples of participative planning in India and the growth, against heavy odds, of environmental NGOs in Malaysia are Asian examples. It is to be hoped that in the next 50 years it will be these examples that will be built upon to develop legal frameworks of town and country planning more likely to support each state's democratic philosophy and practice than the imported model has proved able to.

---

*A revised version of a lecture given on 27 November 1997 as part of the Golden Jubilee Lectures of the Law Department of the School of Oriental and African Studies and first published in Edge, I. (2000) *Comparative Law in Global Perspective*, Ardsley, NY.

Notes

1 Robert Burns, *To a Mouse*.
2 Personal communication from Mr Das Gupta, November 1983.
3 "There was no public body in Calcutta so intensely unpopular and so cordially disliked. Called by the Calcutta residents 'a scheme to gratify the white population of Calcutta', it was kept under tight official control." Home, *op. cit.* p. 172.
4 One might perhaps take the parallel a little further: many of the urban authorities which lost planning and development powers to UDCs had substantial ethnic minorities which were beginning, in the 1980s, to make the break-through to elected local government.
5 Government Residential Area; formerly, the European Residential Area. Renamed throughout Nigeria in 1938.
6 At the first International Conference on Planning Law in Africa (ICPLA) in Maseru, Lesotho in December 1991, planners from Zimbabwe were at pains to stress that people had to adapt their ways of living to the plan and planning law and not vice versa.

6 Bringing the law back in: urban law in Africa and the Habitat Agenda*

Introduction

Habitat II – the City Summit – was designed to chart the way forward for urban management into the twenty-first century. In the three years since the Summit was held, there has been a very muted response to the Habitat Agenda and in particular to the Global Plan of Action (GPA) which sets out in considerable detail the strategies for action to meet the goals and commitments agreed to in the Agenda.[1] The contrast with the reception of the Rio Declaration and Agenda 21, the output of the Earth Summit in 1992 is very marked and suggests either or both that the City Summit was a "summit too far" or that cities as a topic for global action is thought to be neither practicable nor very urgent. The first follow up meeting to Habitat II was the Global Forum of Parliamentarians for Habitat in January, 1998 when they took the topic of legal action to implement the GPA as their theme. The aim of the meeting was to sensitise Parliamentarians from around the world to the Habitat Agenda and to the responsibilities of governments to take national action to comply with its precepts.

This chapter considers the response from African countries to this challenge. Rather than give a very general overview of the subject which would run the risk of not doing much more than paraphrasing the Agenda, I intend to move from the global through the continental to specific countries and then a city within a country – specifically the city of Dar es Salaam in Tanzania. Hopefully, some general lessons may emerge from this case study.

The theme of this chapter is the evaluation of existing national legal frameworks for urban management and development in the light of The Habitat Agenda and the promotion of new or amended legal frameworks to reflect and advance that Agenda. There are therefore four matters which need to be addressed; first, what are the fundamental principles which inform The Habitat Agenda and which would be expected to inform urban law reform in any country; second, what is the connection between The Habitat Agenda and law reform; what stress is laid on law reform by the Agenda and why; third, what are the underlying themes or assumptions of existing urban law in, specifically, states in Africa; and fourth, to the extent that those existing themes do not conform to or reflect the principles of The Habitat Agenda, what is being done or should be done to bring about a convergence between these internationally agreed principles and national law. This is a vast canvas to try and cover; I intend therefore to concentrate on the areas of law that I am best qualified to write about which also is the area on which The Habitat Agenda lays great stress: urban land management; specifically, land tenure and land use planning and institutions of urban management.

The Habitat Agenda

First then, The Habitat Agenda. At the risk of oversimplification of an extremely complex, densely packed and significant document, I would suggest that its fundamental principle which informs all the detail and helps make sense of it is that of enablement. In order however to make sense of enablement, to understand how it has been used in the Agenda, it needs to be broken down into three parts – market enablement; political enablement and community enablement. In making this distinction, I follow the framework developed by *The Challenge of Sustainable Cities* (1997), a publication which was the product of a conference held as part of the world-wide preparations for Habitat II.

Market enablement involves the withdrawal of the state from the provision of many goods and services; *i.e.*, in the urban sector, housing and utility services, the provision of which should be privatised. It involves deregulation, particularly of the market for land and of the use of land since attempts to regulate and control land supply and use via state bureaucracies stifle initiatives, limits competition, increases costs and contributes to corruption. Governments should be confined to facilitating and promoting the formal and informal business sectors and markets and monitoring their performance; legal, institutional and financial arrangements should be put in place to achieve this. Governments should contract with the private sector via competitive tendering for the provision of goods and services, rather than supply them themselves.

Political enablement involves the transformation of the structure and functions of central and local government, the relations between them and their relations with the market and the community. It is achieved through decentralisation at both political and administrative levels, democratisation, managerial and institutional reforms, the use of NGOs for governance functions, particularly in the delivery of services and the adoption of enablement strategies towards the market for urban goods and services as already outlined. But there is more to it. The reasons for political enablement are similar to market enablement; centralised governments are inefficient, inequitable, prone to rent-seeking behaviour, proliferate overlapping agencies and lack accountability. Equally however local governments are also inefficient, unaccountable, and lack financial resources and discipline so political enablement is also directed to rolling back the local state. Powers are to be decentralised but they would also be restructured to emphasise the enablement approach.

Community enablement in the words of *The Challenge of Sustainable Cities* (p. 151):

> can be defined as a strategy adopted by central and local government to coordinate and facilitate the efforts of community- and neighbourhood-based organisations to initiate, plan and implement their own projects according to the principles of self-determination, self-organization and self-management …
>
> This position contrasts sharply with previous attitudes and policies towards community participation …

These had seen communities especially those of the urban poor as the objects of planning which had proceeded on a top-down basis and which too often selected communities and neighbourhoods to be benefited on subjective, political or "technical" criteria. There had also been considerable suspicion of community organisations working in poor areas or having as their objective the enablement of the poor; these were, and in many countries still are, regarded as subversive.

The similarities between the Agenda and this model are plain. Chapter III of the Agenda is Commitments. Commitment C of the Agenda is headed Enablement and Participation and stresses the central role of enablement in the future management of human settlements. References to enablement however recur constantly in this chapter; Commitment A: "Adequate shelter for all" commits governments to recognise that they have an obligation to "enable people to obtain shelter and to protect and improve dwellings and neighbourhoods". Commitment B: "Sustainable human settlements" commits governments to "creating an enabling international and domestic environment for economic development, social development and environmental protection ..." Commitment E: "Financing shelter and human settlements" commits governments to "strengthening regulatory and legal frameworks to *enable* markets to work, overcome market failure and facilitate independent initiative and creativity ..." (my italics).

Chapter IV of the Agenda is the Global Plan of Action (GPA) which sets out the strategies for implementation of The Agenda. This emphasises the importance of establishing and ensuring the effective operation of a land market and all the actions set out in paragraphs 76 and 77 under the head: **Ensuring Access to Land** and in paragraph 114 under the head: **Sustainable Land Use** proceed on the basis that the objectives of policy reform should be to promote an efficient land market. So, there is the injunction in paragraph 77 to:

> review restrictive, exclusionary and costly legal and regulatory processes, planning systems, standards and development regulations

followed by paragraph 79 which urges that:

> to facilitate access to land and security of tenure for all socio-economic groups, Governments at the appropriate level, including local authorities should:
> adopt an enabling legal and regulatory framework ... so as to stimulate partnerships with the private business and community sectors ...

Political and community enablement comes through even more clearly in Section D of the GPA dealing with Capacity-building and institutional development. Paragraph 178 asserts:

> An enabling strategy, capacity-building and institutional development should aim at empowering all interested parties, particularly local authorities, the private sector, the cooperative sector, trade unions, non-governmental organizations, and community-based organizations to enable them to play an effective role in shelter and human-settlements planning and management.

Paragraph 180, setting out actions to be taken, recommends that:

> Governments, at the appropriate levels should:
> review and revise as appropriate legislation to increase local autonomy and participation in decision-making ... and encourage the participation of the

inhabitants in decision-making regarding their cities, neighbourhoods or dwellings.

Paragraph 182, setting out actions to be taken to encourage and support participation, civic engagement and the *fulfilment of governmental responsibilities* (my italics) urges Governments and local authorities to put into effect at appropriate levels:

> institutional and legal frameworks that facilitate and enable the broad-based participation of all people and their community organizations in decision-making and in the implementation and monitoring of human settlement strategies, policies and programmes.

These frameworks would be aimed at, *inter alia,*

> (b) facilitating the legal recognition of organized communities ...;
> fostering an understanding of contractual and other relationships with the private and other non-governmental sectors ...;
> providing access to effective judicial and administrative channels for affected individuals and groups so that they can challenge or seek redress from decisions that are socially or environmentally harmful.

Other aspects of this section of the GPA are in similar vein.[2]

The role of the law

What is very striking about the GPA is the stress laid on the central role of law in its implementation, particularly at the national level. An explanation of the reasons for this and the evolution of thinking on this matter is necessary. Between the mid-1960s and the early 1990s, a legal dimension to development in general and to human settlement development in particular was not thought to be important. The World Bank did not rate law as a significant development discipline and did not therefore see law as an aspect of governance which needed attention paid to it.

Although I was employed as a consultant on legal aspects of urban planning by Habitat almost from its very beginning – my first mission as a UN consultant was to Tanzania in 1977 to work with the Capital Development Authority there on the legal framework of its planning and urban development – I and others employed as legal consultants were so as a response by Habitat and its predecessor, the UN Centre for Housing, Building and Planning to government requests. Law was not a discipline which found a place in Habitat. Even when in the research phase of the Urban Management Programme, a joint Habitat/World Bank/UNDP initiative, law featured in the programme's land management component, it had no immediate impact on policy. Keynote urban policy documents produced by the World Bank and UNDP in the early 1990s made no reference to the role of law in the implementation of recommended policies. Indeed, if anything there was a certain antipathy to law; law was seen as synonymous with regulation, control and too much government and the early approaches to what has now become the philosophy and strategy of enablement was hostile to any "interference" as it was seen then, to the market.

The breakthrough came about from two directions which impacted on two aspects of enablement; market and governance. The market breakthrough came from the collapse of the command economies in Central and Eastern Europe and in the CIS; the governance breakthrough came from the internal and external pressures on governments in Africa to democratise themselves. In the first case, it quickly became apparent that the whole legal edifice of the command economy erected by Communist regimes had to be replaced by ... a legal edifice of a market economy. Policy guidelines were not enough; they had to be backed up by what market economists and World Bank personnel had hitherto taken for granted – law; so law reform has featured very strongly in all programmes of external aid in what are referred to as the Transitional Countries, including law reform on such matters as land law, housing law and urban planning law and the creation of financial institutions to service urban development.

In the second case, the drive towards democratisation in Africa often took the form of new constitutions, the introduction of Bills of Rights into existing constitutions, reform of electoral laws to facilitate multi-party political activity and elections and the introduction of new or more effective means of redress of grievances against unlawful government action. To this must be added the impact of structural adjustment to African economies; whereas at first, the thrust of external pressure to reform economies was to remove constraints on the operation of the market, *i.e.*, remove, *inter alia*, legal constraints, by a transference of experience from the Transitional Countries, it soon became apparent that structural adjustment would entail legal reforms as well. Furthermore, this would not just be narrow legal reforms to improve the operation of the market; it would be wholesale legal reforms to, *e.g.*, the judicial and legal system; local government and tax administration systems.

Just as market reform has a substantial legal reform component, so governance reform has developed a very broad law input, but one which has, as aid agencies have become more involved in law reform in the course of the 1990s, become somewhat detached from its internal political drive. Governance law reform under these external pressures has taken on the hue of market-led law reform; governance law reform has been all about down-sizing government, getting rid of certain governmental functions – not just those of producing or supplying goods and services but also the vital one of regulation – and carefully not directing attention to the political implications of what is being required to be done.

These two strands of law reform – market and governance – have come together in the GPA. That alone would make the GPA noteworthy as giving an international imprimatur to law reform as a major tool of domestic policy implementation. There is however a greater significance to the GPA. A careful reading of the GPA shows that it has connected up the internal political agenda of governance law reform to the external market agenda; it refers to human rights, to a gender perspective to policy, to more open government, to access to justice, to the right to challenge government actions in the courts, to participation and democracy. These are now government commitments in relation to shelter and human settlements management and, enshrined in The Habitat Agenda, they have taken on the status of "soft" international law. The importance of this is that international agencies like Habitat and international programmes, like the UMP, now have a clear duty to assist governments to realise these commitments and governments have a clear international duty to take such actions, including legislative reforms to comply with their commitments. This has immense implications for Habitat (and other international agencies), for national governments and for civil society. These implications have not yet been fully understood at the national level in most African governments.

A further point must be made on the GPA: market-led law reform and governance-led law reform do not always point in the same direction. A governance-led programme focusing on citizens' rights in relation to access to urban land or involvement in urban governance may well give prominence to the need to regulate the market for land to ensure that principles of equity are taken into account or to construct new institutions of accountability to ensure that contracting-out services to the private sector and privatisation of services does not unduly distance the citizen from those who now control her access to services and resources; in each case, this would be a public institutional "interference" with the efficient operation of the market. Market-led reform would tend to eschew institutional accountability, relying instead on the forces of the market to ensure that the consumers were adequately served. This tension can be covered up in a document of broad principles such as the GPA; it is not so easy to disguise it when turning principles into practice.

Behind the principle of enablement then, the GPA poses this challenge to governments: how are they to reconstruct the processes and institutions of shelter and human settlements so as to establish and maintain not just a market for goods, services and resources but an equitable, efficient and appropriately regulated market; not just urban government but a democratically responsive, efficient and accountable urban government; not just putting up with the institutions of civil society but bringing them into a genuine and equal partnership with governments.

If that is the challenge, how fare governments in Africa in meeting the challenge? What is the base-line from which they start; what evidence is there that law reform is beginning to address the challenge in the two areas of concern in this paper – land tenure and urban planning – and that the reconstruction of both along the lines outlined above is beginning.

African cities: the existing socio-legal position

First, we must consider the base-line. Here I can do no better than quote from a major and sobering assessment of the present African urban problematique written by Samba Mukoko of the UN Centre for Regional Development (UNCRD) in 1996:

> The central assumption of this paper is that equity is the layer through which sustainable development can be rendered into practice at the lower level of spatial organisation. At the urban level, equity refers to the use of urban land and the allocation of public resources among spatial and social units. The paper deals with social integration … in sub-Saharan African cities where the spatial and social cleavages created by colonial settlement are yet to be repaired. Cities in sub-Saharan African countries have in common a dualistic nature, a heritage of residential segregation that was the rule during colonial years …

Discriminatory practices in the provision of basic public infrastructure in the earlier stages of urban settlement; outer location of African populations and physical closure of 'modern areas' and population density differentials between the two segments of the cities are the typical traits of urban agglomerations south of the Sahara. These traits have maintained the noticeable distinction within a city of a segment for which a stable framework for property value creation exists and another segment without such a framework …

Urban policies in Africa are still tainted by the old premise that on this continent urbanization itself is an aberration, that city-bound migrants should not have been allowed to move into cities … and therefore the advances of urbanization should be opposed …

Colonial town planning regulations and practices have persisted in most sub-Saharan African cities. The amendments enacted here and there did not change the essence of the regulations because the basic problem (the dualistic aspect of the cities) was left untouched …

One of the most difficult problems in a dualistic city is local governance … It is believed … that urban economies and societies in Africa cannot be strengthened unless the two segments of African cities are physically and socially unified through changes in physical planning, economic systems and social perceptions under the command of a metropolitan authority before allowing for the gradual establishment of autonomous municipalities … [N]ew local governance practices more likely to guarantee sustainable urban development … should be based on allocation policies initiated and controlled by central governments. On the one hand efforts are to be made to foster equitable allocation policies; on the other hand, it is equally important to devote efforts to free the poorer sections whose rights are 'kidnapped' by biased local councils …

Three fundamental points are made by Mukoko which are of relevance here; first, cities in Africa do not by and large have a framework of land law in place which treats all citizens equally; the land laws which exist provide security of tenure and an operative land market for the urban elites while denying secure tenure to or recognition of a land market for, and discriminating against the urban poor. Second, urban planning laws remain for the most part stuck in the colonial mould perpetuating the dual city and denying the urban majority proper living conditions. Third, local governments are ineffective and biased against the poor; central governments cannot just enact laws decentralising all authority to such local governments.

To these three points, I would add an important fourth one about the nature of much of the public law in African cities and indeed at the level of central government also. It was in colonial times a very authoritarian system of law and this too has not changed. This is particularly the case with respect to planning law. Whatever may have been or be the philosophical basis to planning law in *e.g.*, England and France, in African colonies it was developed as an essential part of the colonial system of government – Mukoko makes that point from a planning perspective – and it has never recovered from that inauspicious start. It was then and remains the antithesis of open and participative governance.

The basic position was that much colonial planning law was inspired by a fear of the masses; the military cantonment in cities in the Indian sub-continent set between the colonial city and the indigenous city; the "green belts" created in African cities between the settlers' and officials' city and the African urban areas were there not solely for public health reasons – the official reason – but to distance the colonial and European presence from the people. Similarly the development of legal regimes which denied the indigenous population any legal tenure in the city; this made it easier to remove them as and when the colonial authorities saw fit with a minimum of expense and fuss. These legal regimes still exist; why? Mukoko in putting forward his proposals to bring about an integration of the African city – densification of the "modern" high-income areas of the cities – states that this may be opposed by "politicians motivated by their desire to keep popular masses at bay". The continuation of the colonial approach to planning laws is not therefore the product of inertia; it is for the most part deliberate. Other African scholars besides Mukoko have noted and commented on this.

The base-line of law for implementing the GPA in African countries is then distinctly unpromising. But I must follow that point up by stating that a start has been made in several countries to develop a new approach both to land management and urban governance through the process of policy and law reform. If I concentrate on land matters in Anglophone African countries, this is not because I wish to suggest that only in those countries are such steps being taken; it is because I am more familiar with those countries having worked on these matters in several of them.

Land tenure reform

Let us take the matter of land tenure first. Tanzania, Uganda and South Africa are leading the way in the development of new laws which are geared to meeting the underlying messages of the GPA. In the first case,

Tanzania has created, via a Land Act, 1999 and a Village Land Act, 1999 a legal framework for the operation of an equitable and efficient land market with proper regulatory procedures in place to ensure that those entering the market for the first time are not taken advantage of and with a high degree of decentralisation to small communities to manage their own land. In the second case Uganda has via provisions in its Constitution of 1996 and fleshed out in the Land Act, 1998 conferred ownership rights on the majority of urban and rural dwellers who previously were tenants at will of the state or of large-scale landlords, both of whom were empowered to and often did arbitrarily remove such tenants from the land which they occupied and used. In the third case, South Africa, a major programme of law reform commenced in 1994 to right the massive injustices of the past which involved making restitution of land to those unjustly deprived of it, redistributing land to those refused it and conferring secure tenure rights on those occupying land for long periods with no security.

The new Tanzanian and South African land laws are so significant in the context of the GPA that they are worth looking at it in some detail.

Tanzania

The primary source and authority for the shape and content of the Tanzanian legislation is the National Land Policy, adopted by Parliament in June 1995. The philosophy behind the NLP may be stated in the following six propositions:

- the overriding role of land as a major national resource which must be used and managed in the national interest;
- the primary importance of providing for security of tenure and title to all citizens;
- the need for transparency and accountability in the exercise of public power over land; in terminology well known to lawyers, for openness, fairness and impartiality in the public administration of land;
- the need to create the conditions for the operation of an efficient and equitable land market;
- the need to bring about a greater involvement of the citizenry, both directly and through their representatives, in the management of land;

- the importance of providing an appropriate Tanzanian legal framework for, and mechanisms for dispute settlement and the redress of grievances in relation to, land management.

These six basic principles of the NLP have been translated into a land law of which the following are the principal features:

The role of the national government

The Commissioner of Lands, the senior central government official responsible for land in Tanzania is placed in a central role in land administration. Given this central role by the Commissioner, it is important that the holder of the office and all officials acting in the name and with the authority of the Commissioner can be called to account for the way they exercise their powers. So reasons must be given for decisions, some decisions must be formally approved by courts before they may take effect and other decisions may be appealed, or referred to or challenged in courts, or to specialist bodies. These provisions meet the commitments of the GPA already quoted to provide access for individuals to challenge government decisions which adversely affect them.

The role of civil society in the implementation of the law

The new land law provides a legal framework for the operation of a market in land. Land markets function as part of the private sector of the economy and the principal actors which make the market work are themselves part of the private sector; lawyers; estate agents; surveyors; lenders of funds etc. The new law will hopefully assist the land market to operate more effectively and equitably but it is likely to have some teething problems. It will be essential that the private sector is involved in a formal way in reviewing the operation of the Act and in developing the forms and regulations that are to be the basic building blocks of the functioning of the Act. It is after all the private sector which is going to be in the front line of developing an efficient and legal land market.

It is for this reason that a National Land Advisory Council has been established by the Act with representatives of civil society well represented on it. There is a need to ensure that the voice of outside experts and actors in the market are heard to ensure that any amendments or additions to the law take account of the needs, realities and concerns of the market. There is a further reason why an advisory committee will be a positive aid to more effective decision-making. Such a committee can act as a buffer between the Minister and potentially untoward pressures from the private sector. A feature of a market economy is the rapid growth of special interest groups pressing governments to bend the law or administrative practices in their favour. So such a council can both represent and filter the views of the private sector to the Minister.

Village land and the national interest

The fundamental principle that all land is public land and as such vested in the President as trustee for and on behalf of the citizens of Tanzania is maintained as the bedrock of the land law. The whole of the Land Act and the Village Land Act and the continued administration of land is based on that principle. Within this framework, village land, the land used by the majority of people in Tanzania is given greater protection than it has had hitherto. In a very real sense, the success of any new land law will turn on whether villagers are satisfied that their concerns about not losing their land have been met.

The new law addresses this challenge of greater protection for village land It provides for an elaborate mechanism for the transfer of village land to general public land. This mechanism has been set up to ensure, on the one hand, that very careful consideration will always be given to any proposal to take large areas of land from the villages, *i.e.*, from use by villagers, but on the other, that in the final analysis village land may be taken for national and public purposes. The law recognises that the Government, like governments all over the world, must have the right to acquire land, if necessary compulsorily, from the citizen but government must follow fair procedures in the exercise of this power and must pay fair compensation. This, incidentally, is a matter which has, surprisingly, been left out of the GPA.

Women's rights to land

Right at the outset of the Land Act is a provision which sets out one of the fundamental principles of land policy, the rights of women to equality of opportunity to obtain access to land and thereafter to hold land and deal with it to the same extent as men is affirmed and specific reference is made to Art. 24 of the Constitution which, subject to the relevant laws of the land, of which this Act will be one, grants every person the right to own or hold any property lawfully acquired. Thereafter, in several places in the Act specific provisions are written in to reinforce the general principle which gives legislative effect to the NLP. No land law in Anglophone Africa goes further in providing legal support for a woman's right to acquire, hold and manage land, so meeting to the full the commitments of the GPA on this matter.

Now it is important to stress one point about the provisions that have been written into the law. They are concerned with equality of opportunity. They are not designed to give women preferential treatment in relation to access to land or to loans for land purchase and development purposes. What they are designed to do is to prevent women being given less favourable treatment than men. That this happens in relation to access to land, whether via the market or via administrative means, and to loans is well attested to in Tanzania. This law can only begin the process towards equality by setting out the appropriate legal framework; it will require a determined effort on the part of officials within the administrative system and women outwith the system to make the legal framework a reality in practice. At least, women will now have the law on their side.

The operation and regulation of the land market

In a land market as opposed to total government-controlled land allocation and transfer systems, the nature and style of regulation changes, but the fact of regulation does not. In place of discretionary regulation operated in secret by public officials, there is substituted legal regulation operated more openly by, for the most part, lawyers and private sector professionals, policed by the courts.

The NLP recognised that the market should be allowed to operate free of restrictions but that some controls would be needed. Clearly, there is some ambivalence here and the law had to come up with a way of reconciling what appears on the surface to be conflicting positions.

On the other hand, there is a good deal of evidence from all over the world and from both the present and the past that the introduction of a land market can lead to those inexperienced in market transactions being taken advantage of by those well versed in them. So it is perfectly reasonable to provide a mechanism and a process to review any disposition which may have been tainted by fraud or undue influence. These are grounds well recognised by the law as providing a reason to reopen a transaction. The

Commissioner is given power to ask a court to reopen a transaction; a not unreasonable addition to the law given the likely disparity in such a transaction in resources and market sophistication between a peasant or poor urban seller and a property developer or high income well educated buyer.

The land law of Tanzania always provided for mechanisms to revoke rights of occupancy – the basic land-holding mechanism in Tanzania – if conditions were not met. These had always been essentially administrative mechanisms. The Land Act expands these mechanisms in two ways; first, to provide for a wider range of remedies for breach of conditions; it is, after all, not every breach which merits revocation. Secondly, as befits a law which is designed to meet the need for greater security of tenure and greater transparency and fairness in administration, a person holding land under a right of occupancy or a lease or a mortgage may ask the courts to review the imposition of a remedy by the Commissioner, a landlord or a lender.

Village land administration

At the heart of the new law are the provisions on village land. So important are these that they were hived off from an earlier draft Bill and put into a separate Village Land Act. These provisions give effect to the principle outlined in the NLP that village lands will be administered by the village community. In most cases the Act gives decision-making to the village council and leaves the village assembly, a meeting of all adult villagers, with a back-stopping job; confirming or otherwise some council decisions or initiating others. Village councils are elected and like most other countries with systems of elected local authorities, they are entrusted with the powers to manage resources on behalf of their electors.

Recognising however, that there is always a danger that some councillors might abuse their powers of land management, the Act provides several mechanisms for giving advice to councils; for villagers to call in outside supervision and assessment of the way councils have exercised their powers; and ultimately for taking over the management of village land if there is no other way to clear up a mess.

The law providing for the management of village land is detailed and complex. How can village level officials be expected to comply with such a law? But what is the alternative? Villagers are deserving of no less a proper legal framework for the management of their land than those who do not live in villages. Openness, fairness and impartiality must apply to them as it does to everybody here; they too must have the same opportunity to have recourse to a court to review actions taken against them as holders of granted rights of occupancy do. If they are to have the same freedom to enter and undertake transactions in the land market, subject to appropriate regulations, as others are, then the law must provide for this.

Customary law will still apply to land occupied by villagers and for the foreseeable future most villagers will continue to rely on that law. It would however, be flying in the face of the NLP if a separate and allegedly "simpler" legal regime applied to village land for such a regime would almost certainly dispense with legal safeguards over administrative power and opportunities to challenge administrative decisions in the courts.

Validating informal tenure and transactions

The NLP makes plain that the urban poor who through no fault of their own are living in informal settlements without any proper legal tenure are to have their land holdings recorded and recognised. The Act accordingly provides for a participatory process of regularisation of tenure in informal settlements in line with the commitments in the GPA; this is one of the first examples in Anglophone Africa of provisions in the law to provide for such an approach to regularisation. In addition, the Act makes provisions for creating specific residential licences to be granted or deemed to have been granted to informal settlers, pending the grant of, *e.g.* a right of occupancy. A fuller legal framework needs to be developed on this matter which can only be brought about by reforms to the Town and Country Planning Ordinance and the Land Acquisition Act.

There is however another huge problem of informal settlements; this is the problem of the middle class informal settlements, brought about over the last 15 to 20 years by the operation of the informal land market in Tanzania. As a result of this market, very large numbers of people have bought and paid for land and built substantial houses or otherwise developed the land yet because they did not get consent to the transaction and have not registered their title or their documents of title, technically they have no title to their plot. One cannot pretend that this has not happened; the only feasible solution to the situation is to create a mechanism for people to validate their land holdings and this is provided for by the Act.

The law aim to create a clear Tanzanian statutory framework for the operation of a market for land. Provisions dealing with sales, leases, mortgages, easements and co-ownership geared to the specific needs of Tanzania – this applies particularly to the small mortgage and to the powers of the courts to police the operation of the market in the interests of those entering it for the first time – replace rules of English law going back, in some cases, to mediaeval times.

But the law does not stop there. First, it provides for a dedicated system of dispute-settlement bodies to deal with land disputes and generally police the new land law. Providing a fair, speedy, expert and efficient system of dispute-settlement will greatly assist the acceptance of the new law by people generally and is vital to the operation of a land market and to transparent land management by officials.

It is also the key to the second aspect to the development of a Tanzanian land law; the creative blending together by the courts of the customary land laws of Tanzania and the new statute law, aided in this by using relevant and appropriate developments and precedents from the common law world of which Tanzania is a part.

I believe that this law points the way forward for many other states in Africa for both the NLP which preceded it and the laws themselves apply the principles of the GPA; not just the market-led principles but the politics-led principles as well. Participation and involvement of the people both directly and through their elected representatives is one key to the law; the other is that while a market is to be accepted as the driving force of land management, it is to be carefully monitored and regulated to ensure that it serves and does not oppress the people. In this respect it must be said that the Tanzanian laws go further than the Ugandan Land Act which stops well short of trying to create a Ugandan land law.

South Africa

Space does not permit such a full overview of the South African land law reform programme (Budlender *et al.*, 1997) but some quotations from the Government's White Paper: South African Land Policy (1997, pp. ix, xi, xii) will show how the policies and laws giving effect to them do chime with the principles of the GPA:

The purpose of the Land Redistribution Programme is to provide the poor with land for residential and productive purposes in order to improve their livelihoods ... Land redistribution is intended to assist the urban and rural poor ... Redistribution projects will give priority to the marginalised and women in need ... this will require the removal of legal restrictions on women's access to land ...

The purpose of the Land Restitution Programme is to restore land and provide other remedies to people dispossessed by racially discriminatory legislation and practice. This will be done in such a way as to provide support for the process of reconciliation and development, and with due regard to the over-arching consideration of fairness and justice for individuals, communities and the country as a whole ... [special provisions are set out to deal with the 'multiple complications of the anticipated urban restitution claims'].

Both the above two programmes have now been legislated for.

Tenure reform is a particularly complex process ... The principles guiding policy development are as follows:
tenure reform must move towards rights and away from permits;
tenure reform must build a unitary non-racial system of land rights for all South Africans;
all tenure systems must be consistent with the Constitution's commitment to basic human rights and equality;
a rights based approach and adjudicatory principles have to be adopted which recognise and accommodate *de facto* vested rights (*i.e.* those which exist on the ground) ...

van der Walt (1997, pp. 160, 161) states as follows:

In promoting these policy objectives, the land reforms that were introduced display a number of interesting characteristics:

A number of new rights (or 'rights') completely unknown to Roman-Dutch law have been introduced to improve access to and strengthen the security of 'Black' land rights.

Many reforms are aimed at providing statutory security or backup for traditionally insecure or weak rights and others are characterised by strong policy-orientated efforts to change the current distribution of land rights. Both these categories amount to efforts to change the relative position of 'Black' land rights *vis-à-vis* 'white' Roman-Dutch land rights.

The constitutional arrangements around land reform especially in the 1996 Constitution demonstrate a clear intention to break down the paradigmatic primacy and inviolability of existing (mostly 'white') land rights and create a new, constitutional, balance between the protection of existing rights and the promotion of land reform.

Some land reform measures demonstrate a tendency to privilege traditional, Roman-Dutch property structures (where full ownership is regarded as the strongest and most secure right); others demonstrate a tendency to opt for a greater fragmentation of land rights (where a wider range of differentiated rights is promoted and, where necessary, bolstered by statutory security of tenure).

It is particularly in respect of tenure reform that general lessons may be learned for, as noted by many commentators the vast majority of urban residents in African cities do not have any security of tenure, being on the land either by permission only of the authorities or "illegally". Their *de facto* vested rights need to be recognised and protected as much as do those in South Africa.

Urban planning law

We may turn now to urban planning law. Unlike land tenure laws, Habitat has always recognised that the reform of urban planning laws was a part of its remit and has, at the request of governments, fielded missions to review and revise national planning, housing and other urban laws. Despite that, no research has been conducted on legal aspects of human settlements and no policy papers have been written on the subject within Habitat. This lack of any coherent proactive stance as regards legal issues on the part of Habitat – in contrast, for instance, to UNEP whose Environmental Law and Institutions Programme Activity Centre (ELI/PAC) has made it its business to urge nations to review and reform their environmental laws; to prepare legal guidelines and policy papers and to conduct training sessions on the subject – has contributed to the failure of governments to review their laws and in the case of most states in Africa, to repatriate them; that is, devise laws more suitable to their own circumstances and needs and in particular address the issue of urban planning to combat urban poverty.

There has, then, been no considered, expert and impartial external pressure for reform to counter the internal vested interests arguing for the status quo. The extent of the failure can be measured by the statistic that in Anglophone Africa since the era of independence or transformation in the 1960s, I would argue that only Malawi in 1988, South Africa in 1995, Kenya in 1999 and some states in Nigeria have completely replaced their old colonial or racist planning laws with laws specifically geared to their needs. As Mukoko has noted, reforms in other countries leave the existing fundamentals untouched. Only Malawi's reforms were the product of a Habitat project. Certainly up to the early 1990s, the position was the same in Francophone Africa as was noted in the UMP policy paper Reforming Urban Land Policies and Institutions in Developing Countries (1992). A good recent critique of the continuation of this pattern of urban planning law in Francophone Africa is provided by Njoh (1995, p. 355) who concludes:

> The examination reveals that a very large gap exists between what authorities desire in terms of minimum building standards and what people can reasonably afford. Authorities are generally bent on adopting the sophisticated standards of developed nations. Central to this paper is the argument that such an unconscious adoption of standards is counter-productive to any serious effort to deal with the problem of quantitative and qualitative deficits in housing in penurious developing countries. Therefore if officials in Cameroon and other developing countries are serious in their attempts to deal with the housing problems, they must discard their preconceived middle-class images and pseudo-sophisticated building and environmental design standards.[3]

My comment on that is to reiterate Mukoko's point: there is no "unconscious adoption" of standards from developed countries; it is quite deliberate and designed to "keep the urban poor in their place".

Within states in East, Central and Southern Africa, there is now something of a movement to review and reform urban planning laws, stimulated by the International Conference on Planning Laws in Africa (ICPLA), a biennial meeting of planners and lawyers from those states – other could join in but hitherto have not – supported by SIDA which started in 1991 and has over its period of existence generated considerable interest and even in some respects competition in the reform of planning law. A majority of states within that grouping of around 12 states are or claim to be in the process of reviewing their planning laws with a view to a complete rewriting of them. This is very encouraging and Habitat could contribute to this initiative by emphasising the duty to give effect, in any new laws, to the principles enshrined in the GPA to which the governments concerned are committed. An equivalent initiative was sponsored by the UMP with assistance from the French and German governments for states in Africa in the run up to Habitat II in connection with a review of the laws and practices on tenure regularisation in urban informal settlements.

One country which has made a resolute attempt to develop a different kind of planning law is South Africa with its Development Facilitation Act, 1996 – the title sets the tone for the content. The law is deserving of some comment. The first few lines in the preamble to the Act set out its overall objective:

> To introduce extraordinary measures to facilitate and speed up the implementation of reconstruction and development programmes and projects in relation to land; and in so doing to lay down general principles governing land development throughout the Republic …

The Act is designed to overcome the bottlenecks in obtaining permission to develop and the discriminatory practices of local authorities which operated to the disadvantage of the black community in South Africa. It establishes development tribunals for every province in South Africa, consisting of officers and lay people, meeting in public and these are the bodies that developers can use instead of the existing provincial and local authorities to obtain development permissions.

Provinces and local governments are required to set land development objectives (LDOs), the content of which is set out in the Act through a participatory procedure. These LDOs in effect take precedence over existing plans – master plans, structure plans etc. – which might already exist. They are as the name implies directed to setting out how the land is to be developed adopting national standards and principles to overcome the inherited practices of the past. Development tribunals are enjoined not to approve a land development application if it is inconsistent with an LDO. The tribunals are given very wide powers to impose conditions on any application, including the manner in which members of communities which are to be upgraded are consulted, and the manner in which any person in beneficial occupation of land is to be accommodated in any upgrading.

Two specific innovative aspects to the Act may be looked at in a little more detail. The first is the setting out at the commencement of the Act of the General Principles of Land Development which are to apply throughout the country; to the actions of the State and a local government body; and to serve as guides to the administration of any physical plan, transport plan, structure plan, zoning scheme or other similar plan or scheme and as guidelines by reference to which any competent authority shall exercise a discretion or take a decision on any matter concerned with land development. These General Principles set out an inspiring vision of the desired urban future of South Africa and enshrine a new approach to planning law.[4] They are very much in line with the principles enshrined in the GPA and so have an application beyond South Africa.

The second innovation concerns the upgrading of informal settlements. Two specific Land Development Objectives are:

> (i) the integration of areas of low-income communities into the relevant area as a whole; [relevant area being the area of the local authority to which the LDOs apply]
> (v) the overall density of settlements, with due regard to the interests of beneficial occupiers ... (s.28(1)(b))

This enjoins local authorities to treat low-income settlements occupied by persons with no valid title to the land they are occupying as full members of the local community and as such entitled to proper planning and the provision of adequate infrastructure. Even more interesting however, is section 63 of the Act:

> (1) Whenever land development takes the form of the upgrading of an existing settlement, informal or unregistered tenure arrangements existing among occupants of the settlement may, subject to any conditions [in other sections] be converted into ownership in the manner prescribed.

Subsection (2) sets out the matters which may be provided for by regulations and these make plain that the whole process is to be a participatory one with members of the communities concerned playing an active role in the process of upgrading and upgrading leads to formal layout plans followed by registration of those plans and the new titles in the Deeds Registry. Thus integration of informal settlements is not just a pious sentiment but is provided for in the DFA.

Finally, reference may be made to a new land right created to meet the new requirements of development: "initial ownership" characterised by van der Walt (1997, p. 154) as

> a radical departure in the law of property ... it provides the initial owner with the right to occupy and use the land as if the right were common-law ownership, to encumber the initial ownership by means of mortgage or personal servitude, to sell the initial ownership and to upgrade the initial ownership to full ownership; but not the right to sell the land itself or encumber it in any other way.

This is a radical departure from the law of property because it departs from (Miller, 1998) "the common law dogma of a unitary concept of ownership" and "is clearly a real right 'available against the whole world'". Interestingly, this innovation partakes of some elements of English land law and also of customary land tenure both of which recognise divided rights of ownership and occupation.

This brief summary cannot do full justice to a law which is clearly inspired by a vision that urgent action must be taken to rectify the grievous land development wrongs of the past and that this vision can be and indeed must be driven by the twin imperatives of advancing human rights and democratic participation on the one hand and developing an effective land market on the other. Furthermore, and this is very much in keeping with governance traditions in South Africa, implementation of this vision is through the legal process – through detailed laws, procedures and formal judicial and quasi-judicial processes and hearings.

Now, a likely reaction by many governments in the rest of Africa to this law may be to say that the circumstances in South Africa were so unique and horrendous that a law which facilitates a legal revolution in land development was long overdue; no similar circumstances apply to them. This is not the case however. This is the whole thrust of Mukoko's argument, an argument which can be fully supported by the historical record and by many other African scholars working in the area of urban planning.

The fundamental point here is that South Africa's planning laws and practices were no different in principle, though they were certainly different in the intensity of their application, to the planning laws of other African states, laws which for the most part are still in operation. These laws were based on the principle of racial segregation, the strict division of urban space into a "'garden town' atmosphere" for Europeans, to quote Mukoko, with full provision of urban infrastructure and, set far apart, space for Africans with little or no infrastructure. Although racial segregation has long gone, the division of urban space remains, sanctioned and enforced by the law. What the DFA heralds in South Africa is the beginning of the inevitably long and slow process to integrate urban space and create more equitable urban development. This approach to urban development is needed elsewhere in Africa and the DFA provides a new paradigm of the necessary legal framework to facilitate it; a paradigm moreover which facilitates compliance with the GPA.

The case of Dar es Salaam

From the general to the specific; I want to consider briefly the situation of Dar es Salaam as showing how difficult it is going to be to ensure that any new GPA friendly land laws enacted by central government or GPA friendly urban management policies espoused by central government are applied at the local level. Dar es Salaam, a city of around 3 million persons was, since 1996, run by a central government appointed Commission; the elected City Council was dismissed for corruption and incompetence in 1996. The initial period of the Commission was to be one year and in early 1997 a joint national and international team of consultants was appointed to advise on the modalities of the conversion of a unitary City Council into a three tier structure of 70 ward councils, 3 Municipal Councils and an upper tier City Council on the basis that this was to take place as soon as possible so that elected and more responsive local government could be restored to the city.

No official communication was made to the team during its work between February and June to suggest that the basis on which it was proceeding was not correct so that the report that emerged (Strategic Plan, 1997) set out mechanisms, including legal changes, which would have allowed elections to new local authorities to take place in early 1998 with the new authorities beginning to exercise their new powers around March 1998. One week after the team submitted its report, the Government announced that the Commission's life was to be extended to 1999 from 1 July and since then it has been extended by a further year to 2000. The reasons given for this were that major changes were underway across the board in local government so that the necessary legal changes in the governance of Dar es Salaam would be accommodated within general reformatory legislation and all local government elections would take place in 2000 on the basis of the new legislation.

The extension of the powers of the Commission in Dar es Salaam gave the green light both to a return to a heavy-handed, insensitive and bullying approach to the exercise of powers against the urban poor by the Commission and to central government planners to revert to the use of the bulldozer as the principal tool of urban planning. Tripp (1997) shows how the early 1980s saw the attempted forcible movement of the allegedly unemployed from Dar es Salaam through draconian legislation modelled on colonial precedents. Those operating in the informal sector were deemed to be unemployed and even those in employment who were walking in the streets during the day could be charged with being "engaged in a frolic of his [sic] own at a time he is supposed to be engaged in activities connected to or relating to the business of his employment"(!). "If we don't disturb loiterers, they will disturb us" thundered the late President Nyerere. Tripp notes that "the campaign was destined to fail when the government resorted to coercion against city dwellers with little regard for the realities faced by the urban poor". From the mid-1980s onwards, government changed tack and began to recognise the informal sector, inviting those working in it to "come out of hiding" to help the nation by undertaking productive activities. As Tripp says, there was an element of absurdity in the notion that 95% of the population of Dar es Salaam should come out of hiding, but the changed approach was welcome.

Some 10 to 12 years on, the Commission seemed intent on putting the clock back. It began to conduct a campaign against the informal sector, evicting traders from areas they had previously been allowed to operate in; destroying large number of stalls used by informal sector traders, even those who had licences to be where they were, and destroying too their goods. Youths were rounded up and ordered back to "their" villages, without regard to whether they originally came from a village in the first place. The Commission was impervious to complaints about its conduct and seemed completely unwilling to contemplate any action except demolition of stalls when faced with allegedly illegal informal sector activity.

At the same time, large scale demolitions of houses, shops and stalls were undertaken by central government planners in pursuit of enforcing the 1979 Master Plan of Dar es Salaam (made by a Canadian firm) and of road widening. In the latter case, the government made clear that it was not proposing to pay any compensation as the road reserve should not have been built on in the first place. As more than one dispossessee has pointed out, government stood by and did nothing to deter those building for well over 15 years; how now can it refuse compensation. There were harrowing tales in the press of people reduced to scavenging on rubbish dumps because they had lost both house and livelihood. As was pointed out by some commentators, the government seemed to be reverting to the behaviour of the First Phase government (a.k.a. President Nyerere's governments) when legal niceties and rights were not allowed to stand in the way of "development" and development meant officials ordering the people about. It may also be noted that there is resolute opposition to any changes to the 46-year-old Town and Country Planning Ordinance, notwithstanding that its philosophy is at variance with that of the NLP and with any recognition of rights for squatters.

It may be argued that it is unfair to single Dar es Salaam out; many other cities in Africa are no different. True; indeed at the same time as the unelected City Commission in Dar es Salaam was harassing the informal sector, the elected City Council in Nairobi was destroying a famous informal sector tourist market in the centre of Nairobi with losses amounting to tens of thousands of shillings for the traders and this was done despite a court order restraining the council from so acting. Tripp recounts similar offensives against the urban poor in Ghana, Nigeria and Zambia.

What makes Dar es Salaam special however is this. In 1992, Habitat and the UNCHS/World Bank/UNDP Urban Management Programme launched the Sustainable Cities Project (SCP) in Dar es Salaam; a new participative approach to city planning with all stakeholders involved in the process of small-scale neighbourhood planning and an end to grandiose master planning, and its inevitable corollary, the bulldozer. An SCP office was established in the City Council with a full-time Habitat official working alongside first, the City Council and then the Commission. Large sums of money have been leveraged by the project and it is held out as a major success. What emerges from the saga recounted above, however, is that despite more than six years of efforts by a specific Habitat project which was in fact used as a model for the Habitat Agenda, attitudes to planning and the urban poor on the part of the political and administrative elites had not changed one iota. The colonial urban management approach recounted by Mukoko and backed up by colonial urban planning and land use laws remains the dominant force in Dar es Salaam.

What this suggests is that the immediate post-1994 South African approach is the correct one; changes in practices, whether at the urban management level or at the level of land management must be preceded by changes in the law and the new law must be followed up by a vigorous programme of public education and implementation so that the people can know and insist on their rights against officialdom. Uganda is also proceeding down this road. It is no coincidence that both South Africa and Uganda have governments which came to power owing little or nothing to existing bureaucracies and are committed to decentralisation while Tanzania has a system of governance steeped in a strong centralised bureaucracy, very unwilling to surrender its powers, privileges and the financial benefits that go with it.[5]

Conclusion

It cannot be denied that in the two areas of the laws relating to land tenure and land use planning, most states in Africa have not yet begun the task of revising their laws to bring them into line with the commitments enshrined in the Habitat Agenda signed up to at the City Summit. Their existing laws on these subjects are still based on the mind-set of the colonial past with the old division between colonialist and *indigène* now replaced by the division of rich and poor; the urban elite and the urban masses; the legal and official city inhabited by the former, the illegal and unauthorised city inhabited by the latter.

It would however be wrong to leave the impression that there is no movement and no examples of change. Some states are now beginning to adopt new national land policies recognising the existence of land markets and the need to provide for them in law or are in the process of developing new land policies and land laws. It must be said however that some of these laws do not measure up to the principles of the GPA. As noted above, ICPLA is having a highly beneficial effect on states which are members of the Conference in reviewing urban planning laws. Models of laws do exist which may be drawn on; in Anglophone Africa; these would be the Land Act of Uganda and the Land Act and Village Land Act in Tanzania for a reformed land tenure system and the Development Facilitation Act in South Africa for a reformed urban planning system.

Two elements are lacking to impel this movement forward at a faster pace and focus it more pertinently on compliance with the GPA. The first is internal political momentum from directions and forces that cannot be ignored; the institutions of civil society have an important role here in pressing their governments publicly and privately to live up to their international commitments. The second element is external; a proactive approach by Habitat and other international and bilateral aid agencies and programmes like the UMP to the task of assisting in the development of the new laws necessary to enable African states to comply with the principles of the GPA, and in their implementation. Habitat is taking the lead here with its recently launched Land Management Programme designed to further the GPA, working closely with governments, local governments and institutions of civil society to develop and publicise the new legal principles and practices which are mandated by the Habitat Agenda. Without such externally generated momentum, there would be a danger that the internal political momentum might be brushed aside. "Bringing the law back in" was proclaimed at the City Summit; the task now is to make it a reality.

---

*First published in (2000) *Direito e Governança; Novas Tendenêcias da Gestão Urbano-Ambiental e a Reforma do Setor Público*. First given as a paper at the Global Conference of Parliamentarians for Habitat, in Cancun, January 1998 with a revised version given as a paper to a conference on New Trends in Urban Governance, in Belo Horizonte, November 1998 of which the publication is the output.

Notes

[1] The Istanbul Declaration and the Habitat Agenda, UNCHS (Habitat) Nairobi, 1997.

[2] The many disadvantages of enablement – particularly the problems of who gains and who loses from privatisation of utilities, the less than perfect record of local authorities in urban governance and the rapid growth of MANGOS – manipulated NGOs – are not addressed in the GPA. See however, *The Challenge of Sustainable Cities*, Chapter 9 for a discussion of these and other issues.

[3] And see too Njoh, A.J. (2000) for a more generalised critique of post-independence land policy and land law reforms in Cameroon.

[4] The Development and Planning Commission established by the DFA has produced a Resource Document and a Manual on The Chapter One Principles of the Development Facilitation Act (Pretoria, 1999), which discuss and explain the principles and show how they can be used in specific cases. Some of the most fundamental principles are set out in Chapter 10 (*infra*).

[5] The paper on which this chapter is based was written in 1998. The Mbeki Government elected in 1999 in South Africa has not shown the same commitment to granting rights in land to either the rural or the urban poor.

PART II: OPERATIONS

7 The role of law in urban planning and land development*

Introduction

Rapid urban growth is occurring in virtually all countries of the developing world. This phenomenon necessitates a rapidly increasing demand for urban land; for housing; for infrastructure; for commercial and industrial development; for communications; and for open space. Few governments have the administrative capacity or the legal framework in place to cope with this demand, and the blockages which accordingly occur in the process of making land available for development have several deleterious consequences. The price of such land as is available for development rises. The urban poor – who are the majority of the inhabitants in the developing world's cities – unable to obtain land by legal means and unable to afford such land as is available through legal means, are forced to resort to unauthorised settlements. These, in turn, are by definition unplanned and likely to be in places which will make existing plans difficult or impossible to implement. Where the land on which such settlements have been developed is publicly owned land, or land zoned for some public purpose in the plan, governments are faced with the difficult choice of foregoing some needed public development or removing, if necessary by force, the unauthorised settlements. Where, in an effort to be fair, governments provide alternative land for residents to move to, it is often too far away from work, from one's community associations and, in some countries, may involve settling on land which by custom and tradition "belongs" to another community. There is therefore resistance to leave. Inevitably, relations between unauthorised settlers and government deteriorate and assume a confrontational mode. This, in turn, affects the government's legitimacy in the eyes of the urban poor.

Problems caused by administrative and legal blockages to land development are not confined to the growth of unauthorised urban settlements. Householders and landowners whose occupation and use of their land is perfectly lawful, also suffer from blockages in the land transfer process; from delays and overbureaucratisation in the process of obtaining finance for land purchase and development. They, too, are driven to resort to action outside the law and correct procedures. This, in turn, puts in question the future validity of title to the land and its development, and inhibits the efficient operation of the land market. Once again, usefulness of government and its processes are in question.

Governments, too, are not immune from the effects of inadequate administrative and legal processes and inefficient institutions. Plans cannot be implemented because institutions and processes do not exist or do not function adequately. Land cannot be obtained because, whether market or compulsory acquisition procedures are used, processes are too slow and liable to constant challenge in the courts. A lack of adequate liaison between institutions often causes further delays and confusion. Faced with these apparently intractable problems, governments are wont to plunge into "reform" of the system, without adequate analysis of the problems and possible solutions; reform thus only makes matters worse.

There is then a strong case for an analysis of the major problem areas and key issues in the whole subject of legal arrangements for the administration of land development, together with a discussion of possible approaches to tackling the issues. From the point of view of the consumers of land and government services in respect to land, the overriding issue goes beyond that of the competence and efficiency of public administration and law: it touches on the question of government legitimacy. If government in whatever guise – central, local, or a parastatal – cannot provide land for use when and where it is needed, cannot sanction the development of land which private landowners wish to develop, cannot provide or operate the mechanisms which by law are a *sine qua non* of lawful land transactions, then what purpose is government serving? The temptation is overwhelming to ignore government, law, and the processes of public administration in respect to land development, but all the evidence indicates that adopting that course of action is not conducive to either efficient or equitable land development in the long run. Efficient land development administration is thus a precondition to efficient and equitable land development; this, in turn, requires appropriate institutional and legal mechanisms to be devised and in place. It is to these matters that this paper now turns. It will first consider in broad terms the issue of the law in urban development.

Law in urban development: an overview

Law has profound implications for urban development. It defines the system of urban government, it establishes the system of urban planning and regulation of land development, and it delimits the powers of the urban planners and managers. But law, contrary to the commonly held view, is not a neutral instrument. In this chapter I shall examine the way in which the law is a reflection of the society and the system of which it is a part, and the ways in which the law, its use and abuse, influence the urban development process. From this, I shall then set out some principles to guide the reform of urban law.

In the mid-1960s, most western legal scholars tended to see law as a neutral body of norms, above the struggle for resources or power, policing the struggle, providing remedies where the struggle erupted into conflict, or where people alleged that they had been injured in the struggle. In the early 1990s, largely as a result of the input of other social sciences into legal scholarship and of the work of those lawyers – both academic and in practice – interested in the role of law in development and social change, we now know better (Ghai *et al.*, 1987). The use of law, of certain legal techniques, the decision to subject certain activities to a regime of legal control while leaving others free of such control, the implementation of law, the legal culture of a society, all are value-laden, part of the social struggles within society. Law is a weapon in the struggle over resources, often a very powerful weapon, so that those who control the making and the implementation of law have or may have a head-start on the control of society's resources. So questions about the role of law in urban development cannot just be answered by reference to specific topics which legislation may deal with – finance for housing, control of the development of land, provision of potable water – since the questions inevitably raise issues about power and resources: who controls the development process? To what ends is the process being used? Who gains and who loses from any particular decision to enact and/or enforce or not enforce any law?

The understanding that we now have of the possible impact of law on society also requires us to "tread carefully" before proposing or implementing any particular legal reform, and to consider a range of general matters before doing so. The world is littered with examples of legal reforms and experiments which proceeded without proper consideration of all their implications or which were naïvely based on the assumption that one sector of the population would benefit – for example, the urban poor – whereas a little thought would have shown that the particular legal regime being introduced would be more likely to benefit a different sector of the population.

Thus, behind any existing urban law, or any proposal for a new urban law lie political and policy issues and not just technical issues. If these fundamental questions are not addressed, however inconvenient it may be to address them, then any proposal for a new legal regime is largely valueless and risks misleading those to whom it is addressed. Furthermore, these fundamental questions must be faced before specific topics are reformed or legislated upon, because until they are, it is difficult to know what is the purpose of any legal input into the development process. These points may seem rather obvious to some people, rather subversive to others. They can be best illustrated by a couple of examples with which I am familiar.

Zimbabwe

In 1981 a UN team went to Zimbabwe to advise on that country's urban and regional planning system, and to suggest what reforms might be necessary in the light of the transition to independence. My brief was to survey and report on the legal framework for urban and regional planning.

In 1976 Zimbabwe, or Rhodesia as it was then, had enacted a Town and Country Planning Act which was modelled on the English reforms introduced in 1968. In England, the purpose of the reforms of 1968 had been to introduce a more flexible policy-orientated approach to planning in anticipation of rapid public-sector led economic growth, an approach which in turn fed into the system of development control, so that that too became more policy orientated and wide-ranging in its consideration of individual planning applications. In Rhodesia, however, the new planning system had been designed to fit into the existing planning and development control system rather than replace it. The existing system was rigid, based on strict zoning policed by a Town Planning Court which could, after a formal hearing, sanction departures from permitted uses in zones. In England then, the law and the system of planning were moving in the direction of greater recognition of the policy and political content of planning; in Zimbabwe the system was being maintained as a legalistic one in which policy appeared to be non-existent and law uppermost, despite changes in the law which superficially might appear to be designed to alter that.

Why was the Zimbabwean system as it was? While using the legal language of English town planning law, and the legal institution of a court, presided over by a judge applying "sound town planning principles" – a phrase used frequently – the Zimbabwean system was in reality a key tool in the creation and maintenance of a system of urban separate development – racial segregation. This was done not by the crude methods then in use in South Africa – for officially Rhodesia had been committed to multi-racial development – but by policies of zoning standards, open spaces between zones and strict control of variations of uses within zones. Residential zones were low density, medium density and high density, which corresponded to European, Coloured and Asian, and African areas, which were separated by open spaces, parks and so on. The language of the judgments of the Town Planning Court never, or rarely, referred to racial issues but concentrated instead on "sound town planning principles" which were in reality taken to mean the maintenance of existing property values. The fundamental principles of the old Rhodesian planning system had been the maintenance of existing property values and this in turn had necessitated rigid zoning and strict judicial control of variations within zones. The importance of judicial control was twofold: first, it helped disguise the policy implications behind the implementation of the system – decisions of a court could more easily be presented as value-neutral than decisions of a minister; and second, it erected a system of precedent which bolstered both the status quo – the maintenance of existing property values – and itself contributed to the mystification of the policy implications.

In discussing possible reforms to make the policy-making aspects more explicit, the then Director of Physical Planning, who had served in Rhodesia for many years, stated that the Court, which has existed since 1945, had always been completely free from any political interference. Exactly: planning had apparently been a kind of technical legal exercise in which policy was almost a dirty word; it was sound town planning principles applied to each case on its merits in a series of "judgements" which "were to become highly respected" which had produced the segregated urban areas which existed in that country; any "political" tampering with such a system would, by implication, lead to it not being highly respected (by whom?) any more. Legal reforms were quickly perceived as policy reforms designed to loosen up the urban structure and, it was assumed, contribute to a slump in urban property values, which the planning system existed to maintain. This was not acceptable to those who operated and benefited from the system.

Nigeria

The case I want to consider in Nigeria concerns the type of planning law which that country has. This was a law originally enacted in 1946, which has survived numerous changes in the constitutional position of the country. The only significant change which had occurred in the law was the grafting on to it in many states of an urban development authority or board, whose members were appointed by the State Government and which was given the planning and development control duties under the law. Over the years, much criticism had been directed at the law; it was elitist, authoritarian, allowed for no public participation, and had not been adapted to the needs of a rapidly urbanising Nigeria (Gihring, 1976; Ola, 1986).

A relatively short spell of working in the Kano Urban Development Board (KUDB) in 1979 showed me fairly clearly why the law had never been revised, despite all these criticisms and, over the years, specific proposals for reform. The reason was that the law accorded perfectly well with the views and attitudes of the ruling elite, both civil and military, which in this respect was not too different from those of colonial power with its low-density Government Residential Areas and its Sabon Garis for "foreigners". There was a very clear appreciation, on the part of the authorities, that planning was about power over land and that this was too important to be handed over to bodies over whom governments might not have complete control.

This analysis received confirmation from the Land Use Act, passed as a military decree in 1978, which endeavoured to bring about a measure of land reform by limiting the amount of land any one person could hold and converting all freehold land into rights of occupancy held by the State (James, 1987; Omotola, 1982). The structure of power in the Act was the same centralised, non-participative structure as existed in the town planning legislation; the State Governor was given control of all urban land, and the power to grant rights of occupancy to such land, the only check on his power being a Land Use and Allocation Committee appointed by the Governor to advise him on any matters connected with his management of urban land in the State. Had there been the political desire either then or after the re-establishment of civilian rule in 1979 to bring about a more open or democratic approach to urban land management, that law would have been the obvious means to accomplish such a transformation; instead it further concentrated power in the ruling elite's hands.

Should the law be involved in urban development?

The case for law

A vital issue which must be considered first is whether there is a case for law to be involved in urban development at all. The arguments against can be put at two levels. The cynical level was put to me by a planning consultant in Dodoma, Tanzania. "Why bother?" he said, "Does it really matter whether the agency [in the instant case the Capital Development Authority] obeys the law or not? Wouldn't everything go on as 'normal' if they didn't bother?" It would be hypocritical to pretend that this sort of attitude is unique; it is widespread among officials and consultants not least because it is grounded in reality. In Dodoma itself, the Capital Development Authority (CDA) in response to recommendations from its master plan consultants had "banned" all development in certain parts of the town from early 1974, pending the completion of the master plan. There was no legal authority for such a ban yet it was enforced and observed by many potential developers of houses who left them half finished, roofless and decaying as a result. No legal challenge was mounted to the ban.

Similarly in Kano, a master plan was published in 1966 and successive urban development authorities had attempted to implement it, yet none of the formal legal steps necessary to publicise the plan, consider objections to it, and approve it, thus giving it a legal status, and legal backing to enforcement action, had been taken. No legal challenge has been mounted to any enforcement action. As it was put to me by the Chairman of the Kano Urban Development Board (KUDB), authority and power rather than law was what counted in Kano. The KUBD had the power and the apparent authority to get its way on development issues *vis-à-vis* the average person and where it had to give way, *e.g.* to the State Government or a local notable on such issues, this was because they had more power on their side and not because they had the law on their side.

The other level of argument is in a sense an alternative development argument. This argument says in general terms that the law impedes the efforts of ordinary people to house themselves, to obtain an income, to get access to potable water, electricity and other urban services and thereby to survive and better themselves in an urban environment. Law turns homesteaders into squatters, self-build houses into "slums" and "nuisances" which must be demolished; petty traders into criminals and job seekers into vagrants. The less the law and lawyers have to do with uncontrolled urban settlement and the informal urban economy, the more chance persons in those sectors have of survival and development.

Again, my own experience gives some support to this analysis. The rapidly growing squatter settlements in Dodoma were not acknowledged in official plans for urban development other than as areas to be cleared for urban development. As it was put in one development plan for a "new" residential area, the existing houses were not of a suitable standard and most of them would have to be demolished to make way for the new model community and the existing people would likewise have to be moved elsewhere as they would not be able to afford to live in the new community (Kikuyu Development Plan, Capital Development Authority, 1977). The existing houses provided shelter for a long-established community of well over 1,000 low-income residents conveniently located for work in Dodoma. In Kano, great concern was generated inside the KUDB over hawkers and their "illegal" booths which were clearly meeting a need. The concern was how to get rid of them, not how to adopt planning strategies and policies so as to accommodate them.

What answers then can be made to these legitimate and powerful criticisms of the role of law in urban development?

A general, albeit western liberal-democratic, answer is that government in accordance with the law is likely to be fairer, more respected, more effective in the long run than government in defiance or in disregard for the law; the tragic example of Uganda may be recalled, where a civilian government careless of legal niceties and constitutional forms was rudely replaced by a military regime careless of human rights, liberties and life, which in turn was replaced by a succession of civilian administrations utterly unable to restore law or respect for law within the country and equally unable therefore to mount any programmes of urban or rural development. A totally new beginning ultimately became necessary.

But less dramatic examples can be given. If the Kano Urban Development Board need not obey the Town and County Planning Law, why should the Kano State Government? The result: government intervention and directives to the Board to ignore the master plan which the KUDB had no way or grounds to resist. Some of the difficulties in implementing the master plan in Dodoma stemmed directly from the CDA's lack of legal backing for its plans and proposals; it was a question of who got to which minister's ear first and which minister had more clout in government and party circles – a rather unsure way to proceed with developing a new capital. The presence of law will not obviate the need for inter- and intra-bureaucratic haggling and argument, but it can provide a reference point for the arguments, and in some situations, may reinforce the power of the urban development agency and thus its authority to get its way.

Within government then, law can provide a measure of certainty and support for particular policies and programmes, and institutions whose job it is to executive them. But what of government *vis-à-vis* the people? An example would be a law that confers powers on government, and rights on the people, such as a law permitting compulsory acquisition of land subject to the payment of compensation. Governments are more likely to know their powers than people their rights, and this will result in an unequal application of the law.

The trouble with this argument is that it assumes an idyllic state of "no law" into which law intrudes unnecessarily. There are no states with no laws, although there are certainly states where very little attention is paid to law, where such laws as there are, are more concerned with conferring powers on government than rights on people or checks on government power. But the solution to this is not to decry a legal input into urban or any other sort of development, but to argue for and propose a law which moves the machinery of government just a few steps away from its existing authoritarian stance. The contrast between the official treatment of squatters in Karachi and in virtually any Indian city, reinforces that point: India is a country which, whatever its imperfections, is ruled by law and in which courts can be, and are effective in halting government action against squatters; the famous case of *Olga Tellis v. Bombay Municipal Council* in 1986 well illustrates that. Pakistan has been for too long ruled by military force and the courts have no effective role in the control of such force (van der Linden, 1982).

Law then can be a handle to be used in the struggle for a more humane or reasonable government, and for more humane and reasonable administration of programmes of urban development. A neat illustration of this was provided by two incidents in Dodoma. A decision was taken to move some "squatters" so that the land could be prepared for development – a road. A decision was taken to pay compensation *ex gratia*. But no procedures were followed in this; no proper efforts were made to ensure that the right people were being compensated or that those who got it understood what it was for. The squatters were not in fact moved until three years after payment of compensation, but there had been no adequate preparation of a site for them to move to. Thus the decision to pay compensation, which was admirable, was vitiated by an absence of any kind of legal or other framework for its implementation. No lawyer had been consulted on procedures and no attempt had been made to adapt what legal procedures existed to the particular circumstances of the case. A repeat performance of this was planned for another area – the Kikuyu Model Community – where homes were to be demolished and squatters moved, as they did not fit in with the plans, without any consideration being given in the plan to relocation, compensation or assistance for those displaced. By drawing attention to the various legal provisions governing these matters – contained in both town and country planning and compulsory purchase legislation – it was possible to get the plan rewritten to incorporate both the necessity to pay compensation and the likely costs thereof.

There is a second and equally important reason for placing some emphasis on a role for law in urban development. I refer to this as the repatriation of decision-making. There is a great deal written about the deleterious effect that international – usually western orientated – consultants, planners and administrators can have on national priorities in respect of urban development (Hai, 1981; King, 1977). I shall draw attention here to one little remarked but important side effect of foreign consultancy. The decision to use foreign planning consultants to produce a master plan for an urban area or region has the inevitable effect of passing decision-making not just on the policies and shape of the plan but on its detailed implementation over to those consultants, ignoring or bypassing the national statutory procedures for plan making, approval and implementation. Sometimes this is blatant as in Dodoma, where in the early years of the capital development programme, the master planners did most of their work in Toronto, their headquarters, and provided both in the plan and in their consultancy contract that no changes could take place in the plan without their being involved. The effect of this was that when some of their more far-fetched ideas were seen to be impractical by planners on the spot, a memorandum suggesting changes would be compiled and sent to Toronto; a pause would ensue until the reply came back defending the sanctity of the plan to the last eight-lane highway. The reply would be addressed to the Director-General of CDA bypassing all normal procedures, and hinting that criticisms of the plan were motivated by malice and ignorance. The reply was accepted, and the plan left untouched – and unimplemented.

In Nigeria the process of a foreign take-over of the planning process was less blatant, but no less serious. In Kano State no fewer than 13 master plans were produced for 13 urban areas by five different nationalities of planning consultants: British, Hungarian, Yugoslavian, Danish and a mixed Indian-Egyptian-Nigerian team from the planning department of Ahmadu Bello University, Zaria. None of the plans made any reference to the existing town and country planning laws of the state. The mixed Polish-Hungarian-Indian team of planners and architects occupying the higher posts in the KUDB knew equally little of the planning laws of the state, as did the mixed Swedish-German UN team of planners, so that administration and implementation of the plans, such as it was, proceeded in a kind of a legal Erewhon.

In Uganda the problem was subtly different. My involvement arose out of the laudable initiative of the UNDP and UNCHS (Habitat) to set in motion machinery, men and money to rebuild the two south-western towns of Mbarara and Masaka, destroyed in the war of liberation from Amin. UN agencies understandably had no wish to get involved in the quagmire of post-Amin Ugandan politics and administration. The solution decided upon was a development agency set up outside the regular administration, reporting direct to the President and bypassing local government, central government, boards, commissions and officials. But this too betrayed a woeful ignorance of the existing laws and administration in Uganda and a somewhat astonishing naivety that it would be possible to isolate such an agency from politics and administration merely by making it a separate corporate body by law. The concern for action rather than talk was laudable but was the approach any different from that adopted in Dodoma?

In each case my approach and my aim was the same: to bring the existing law to the attention of the policy-makers and decision-makers, to explain and stress the importance of complying with it; to highlight its defects and strong points; where necessary, to propose the principles that should inform amendments and reforms, and then finally to draft those reforms in close association with the officials of the agency I was advising.

However deficient the planning laws – and in broad outline and many details the planning Ordinances and Acts of Tanzania, Nigeria (inherited by Kano State) and Uganda are exactly the same and derive from the standard Colonial Office package of the 1950s (Stevens, 1955) – they all provided for certain basic procedures to be followed in respect of plan approval: publication of draft plan; a period for the receipt of objections and comments; a consideration of the same; submission to the relevant Minister of the draft plan, proposed amendments in light of comments, and comments on the comments; approval with or without amendments by the Minister; publication of approval and coming into force of the plan. Nothing in the procedures was very complicated or very time consuming: compared to the procedures most British or North American planners have to go through to get plans approved in the UK, USA and Canada, they were amazingly straightforward.

A failure to follow the law, a belief that it was not necessary to follow the law did not arise from a desire on the part of consultants for more participation and discussion than the law required – such participation could have taken place but did not – but from a desire to keep control of the plan making and implementation process and a belief that the local law was beneath bothering about. The attitude was well summed up by a member of the Canadian planning consultant's team in Dodoma who said to me: "In Toronto, we are told that it's planning by the bulldozer in Dodoma and all we have to worry about is getting the approval of the Director General of CDA." The planning team knew nothing and were told nothing of the planning laws.

In both Dodoma and Kano State, the realisation on the part of officials in the agencies I was advising that there were planning laws in existence which had to be, but were not being, followed, transformed, albeit temporarily, their attitude towards laws and procedures. Whereas they had viewed my mission as being designed to give them increased power to implement their plans, they suddenly found that technically they had no power at all, and indeed were highly vulnerable to legal, or, more likely, political attacks from their opponents for their failure to observe existing laws.

In the Uganda case, government officials were wary of UN proposals because these involved bypassing normal administrative procedures which the officials were trying to re-establish, and because they appeared to strengthen the powers of the President which ran counter to the then, prevailing political concern. UN officials tended to see Ugandan officials as tied to British ways of doing things, procrastinating and failing to understand the urgency of action. But no one in the UN team had actually investigated the law and administration governing planning, building, land use and land tenure, local government and sewerage, that would have to be addressed before any agency could be established. I wrote a memorandum summarising the relevant laws; stating that any new agency would have to fit into an existing legal framework; drawing attention to the essential attributes such an agency would have to have; and setting out possible heads of legislation that could be drafted to implement the proposals. This memorandum was effective. The UN officials understood for the first time the complexity and interlocking nature of Uganda's land use, land tenure and local government system, the political reasons for it and thus the need to respect it; the Uganda officials were able to point to, rely on, propose amendments to, a document about their system which was concrete proof that a system did exist and had to be respected and amended rather than ignored and bypassed. Knowledge and appreciation of the law was the key to realistic negotiations and a Ugandan solution to a Ugandan problem, albeit with UN assistance. The Reconstruction and Development Corporation, set up in 1981 had both a reasonable degree of independence from but was also answerable to the executive.

Too much law is as bad as too little

The second matter for consideration is rather the reverse of the first. There may be a tendency to become too enthusiastic about the possibilities of a legal solution to an urban problem. Virtually everywhere that I have been asked to advise or draft new laws, an existing state of affairs has been presented as requiring a legal input of some sort. In Tanzania, it was the general powers of the CDA to plan and develop Dodoma; they were considered to be deficient in some way. In Uganda, the impetus for a legal input into the urban development process came from the UN itself. In the Maldives and Turks and Caicos Islands the need was presented for a new, more effective legal regime to control urban development, hitherto largely uncontrolled. In Malawi, the argument was that a new system of physical development planning working down from a national physical development plan required a brand new system of planning law. In Trinidad and Tobago the effectiveness of the system of development control was seen as, in part, being caused by an absence of sufficient legal sanctions.

All these arguments had some justification, but in many cases they told only half the story. Sometimes existing laws were not being utilised satisfactorily, either through ignorance of what the law was or because the political process prevented the laws being used, so that a new law would not necessarily "solve" the problems unless the underlying political problems were tackled. In Tanzania, there was, and to some extent still is, a fairly casual attitude towards legal procedures and legal backing for the exercise of power. Thus, new laws for one agency could not displace a general administrative culture which placed a low value on law, nor overcome political and administrative scepticism about the value of the whole enterprise of moving the capital from Dar es Salaam to Dodoma.

If Tanzania provided an example of existing laws being under-used, Madras and Zambia provide examples of the opposite – the sheer amount of law and bureaucracy overwhelming the development and land management process so that resort is made to an outside lawyer in a desperate search for a way through the morass.

Madras In Madras there was in the mid-1980s a plethora of laws dealing with the urban land development process, and a multitude of statutory bodies. Apart from a town and country planning law, there was urban land ceiling legislation, slums clearance legislation, housing legislation, special legislation dealing with the housing of Harijans (untouchables), the siting of nuclear power installations, rent control, land acquisition and several land taxation laws. Apart from a Madras Metropolitan Development Authority (MMDA), there was a slum clearance board, a housing corporation, a water and sewerage corporation, upwards of 50 local authorities within the area of jurisdiction of MMDA, housing finance bodies and officials charged with special duties under land ceiling and taxation legislation. The laws themselves were long and prolix; they assumed an understanding of legal procedures quite beyond most people, both those to whom they are directed and those who have to implement them. The development plans required by the planning laws were similarly detailed and rigidly legalistic, or would be if they were all produced, but the process was so time consuming that it is doubtful whether they ever will be. The courts are actively involved in the urban development process, or rather considerable efforts are made to involve them actively in the process but they too are rather slow at reaching decisions. The picture was one of planners and administrators in the MMDA, the body charged with planning and overseeing development within the Madras metropolitan area, feeling themselves weighed down and unable to achieve anything by the mass of law and, as they saw it, hostile judicial decisions confronting them.

The situation in Madras could be paralleled in many Indian cities and is a classic example of an excess of law and legal regulation. So concerned have the authorities been to regulate the urban development process and close every loophole against illegal development, corruption, exploitation of scarce urban resources, wrongful exercise of discretion, that the principal aim of the MMDA – to get orderly and equitable development underway in

Madras and its environs – has been lost sight of. The result was that the laws were not being observed or enforced; illegal and unauthorised development was widespread – and not just by squatters; plans were not being followed; the panchayats on the outskirts of the MMDA had had no input into the plan, could not understand it, and felt no obligation to apply it; and needed development and acquisition of land was being held up by lawsuits. Furthermore, the total *corpus* of law was not consistent; land taxation laws and administration pointed in favour of the development of land that legal plans decreed should not be developed. This was because no increase in the rate of land taxation was allowed to local authorities, thus putting them into a position where the only way they could increase their revenues was by permitting land to be developed, irrespective of what the plan said.

Zambia Zambia has a dual system of land law and land administration – statutory and customary. Title transfer under the statutory system involves a multiplicity of steps and agencies. Presidential permission is needed for any transfer. This power is delegated to the Commissioner of Lands, but the transfer is registered; the Registrar of Titles has to check the transaction to satisfy himself that the price is a fair one. This involves the Chief Valuation Officer and his staff. Title to the land depends on the records confirming that the land being transferred has a correct title and all taxes have been paid. To check on taxes may involve another official. If the land being transferred is not registered, or a subdivision is involved, the Chief Surveyor and his staff will need to be involved. If land in rural areas is to be brought within the statutory system, the local chief will need to be consulted and his approval attained. If the land is commercial farmland a special committee will need to consider the competence of the intending transferee. These different government departments are in different ministries, housed under different offices. It is not unknown for a transaction – *e.g.*, a two-year lease on a flat – to be ended before official permission is forthcoming. The plethora of permissions needed contributes to a thriving black market in land, with under-the-counter payments and a refusal by tenants to pay rent because transactions, not having received official permission, are technically illegal. Numerous reports on the problem of consent to transactions and the need for an updated and simplified legal framework have been written over the last 20 years. No action was taken until the mid-1990s, because to do so would mean confronting two difficult political issues: the role of chiefs in land administration and the role of the market in land transactions. Even when the land law was amended, the issues were not fully tackled.

In these circumstances, the aim must be to reduce the legal content of the development process. Too much law which leads to a paralysis of will is as bad as too little which allows power to be abused. An important matter to realise in such a situation is that there is already a selectivity of enforcement of law; low-level officials in the front line of law and plan enforcement decide for themselves, without much reference to those higher up in the bureaucracy, what laws to enforce and what to ignore. Reduce the legal content of the development process – freeing much development from the need to apply for development permission; expanding the scope of permitted development within different zones; formally delegating power to make decisions away from the centre – will in reality be doing little more than bringing the law into line with practice.

The problem of linkages

A related issue is that of linkages: the interconnectedness between different facets of the urban development and management process and the futility of trying to alter one piece of the jigsaw, while leaving the rest untouched. Two good examples arose in Jamaica and Trinidad and Tobago.

Jamaica There was considered to be a problem of lack of investment in agricultural development in Jamaica; attention focused on the difficulty small landholders had in obtaining a registered title to their land and thus having the necessary security to obtain loans for agricultural development. It was thought that some new or additional legal input or technological input such as computerised land records, into the land registry process would "solve the problem" by speeding up the issue of title. At the same time, a major UN input into the planning and development of Kingston was in process, and one component of this was the design of a "one-stop shop" planning application process – that is, a system whereby all the necessary permissions and approvals needed before development could commence would be obtained at the same time at one office, presumably quicker than the current system. There was no relationship between the agricultural and urban concerns.

My involvement was on the agricultural side but a brief survey of the rural land tenure and development process made clear that an input on the lines of a quick legal or technological fix would solve nothing. The issuing of a document of registered title could not be separated from the process of land surveying or the granting of permission by parish councils – the units of local government in Jamaica – to subdivide land. Sub-division permission in turn involved the Town Planning Department and its role in co-ordinating comments from ten different agencies of government on any such proposal. The methods and modalities of land surveying were in turn determined by the requirements of the Registered Title Act as to what needed to be proved before the registered title could be issued, and the practice of the Commissioner of Lands in allocating plots for smallholder agricultural development. It was clear too from my survey that first, delay in issuing registered title and its effect on the market for land affected urban land no less than rural land and second, an unofficial market in land operated in many rural areas, with land being bought, sold and pledged but never registered because of costs and delays associated with that process. As a result, the Registry of Titles, housed in a splendid Dickensian office full of huge folios and files, stretching back to 1889, the year of enactment of the Registered Title Act, was in practice an inaccurate record of landholdings on the ground.

In these circumstances, it was clear that here was a case for a fundamental rethink of the total system of land management and development in Jamaica, and that furthermore there were officials who were aware of a deep-rooted malaise within the system so that there would be some receptivity to such a proposal. It was also clear that in practice one could not separate rural from urban land management; the same institutions – Town Planning Department, Survey Department, Registry of Titles – were involved in both sectors; the same laws applied to both sectors and the same problems afflicted both sectors. It followed that any reform, even if originating in one sector, would affect the other and would be more likely to be effective if it applied to both sectors.

Trinidad and Tobago Trinidad and Tobago has a planning and land development control system based on a law modelled on English Planning Law as it was in 1947. The administration of the system is in practice centralised, although the law provides for the delegation of certain powers to local authorities. Pressure over the years built up for a more decentralised flexible system, and the coherence and efficiency of the present system began to break down under the pressure. An informal appeal system had been instituted which followed different planning policies to the central Division of Town and Country Planning; this had the result of stimulating appeals, delaying the hearing of those appeals, and making it difficult for the division to know what policies it should be applying. Local authorities pressed for power to be delegated to them, which the relevant law did not provide to be delegated, and this created tension between the local authorities which considered the Division to be negative and procrastinating; the Division on the other hand considered the local authorities lacked the professional and technical expertise to undertake planning and development control work, even if it could be delegated to them.

One official government policy spoke of decentralisation, but practised only deconcentration. Another official policy was to curb the power of the Division of Town and Country Planning by the creation of a central National Physical Planning Commission; in various guises this appeared to have co-extension powers with the minister, to direct the Division to undertake certain tasks or, alternatively, to be little more than an additional source of advice to the minister. What was clear was that different parts of the Government had very different agendas for town and country planning and until these agendas could be reconciled, the process of planning was not likely to be very effective or indeed well regarded.

The importance of surveying the existing legal scene

A thorough survey of an existing system is essential before proposing reforms. It might seem an obvious point but in the haste to introduce a reform or correct what is thought to be a deficiency in a law or its implementation, such a survey is often foregone and the "reform" fails to achieve its aim. Until such a survey is done, it is not possible to know whether the problem is too much law, too little law, out-of-date-law, ignorance of law, law at variance with practice, customs and beliefs, a reasonable law unreasonably administered, law needing wholesale reform, or law needing minor adjustments. Equally, a survey will help uncover the politics of law, the hidden agenda of the legal input.

A survey of the total system, its strengths and weaknesses, the areas where a case can be made for change, and if so what kind of change and by what kinds of mechanisms, may be the first opportunity officials have had to see how the total system is working in practice; this can have an immensely valuable educational benefit.

In addition, if there is to be reform or reorganisation, it has to be sold to the officials who will be implementing it. In practice, this means that officials will be expected to learn and apply new laws, new routines, new practices. They have to be convinced that this is a necessary and worthwhile exercise. The process of putting together a survey is part of this process of educating officials to accept change. Many of them will have had an input into the survey, will have had an opportunity to express their views about the present system, and how it needs to be changed. They will or should have an opportunity to go through the survey and so increase their awareness of the system of which they are a part. Producing a survey then can both create a climate of anticipation for and acceptance of change and contribute to a more aware and informed bureaucracy.

One must, however, recognise the dangers. The longer the delay in producing positive proposals for a new or a revised legal input into the urban development process, the more the possibility that impatient politicians or others will go ahead with some "reform" that will achieve nothing in the long run to cure the underlying problem. Again, a survey of the present system and its defects will give those who at present gain or who see that in the future they may gain from the maintenance of the present system an opportunity to argue for the maintenance of the status quo – as happened in the case of Zimbabwe discussed earlier. Finally, although one aim of the survey may be public education, governments are often reluctant to disclose a critical survey to a wide audience, even within the bureaucracy itself, so change, if and when it comes, still finds many people unprepared and therefore instinctively antipathetic to it.

The question of local relevance

Obtaining a thorough overview of a national system of urban development and its legal dimension will serve to guard against the too ready application of foreign models and "standard" planning law packages.

In Tanzania, officials in CDA were bombarded with advice from their Canadian planning consultants to introduce North American zoning regulations and from their UN adviser from Canberra, Australian principles of land management derived from the experience of the National Capital Commission in Canberra. In Kano State, the Nigerian staff of the KUDB found themselves caught in a veritable cross-fire of conflicting advice from their foreign colleagues; from Indian planners to introduce the kind of detailed zoning regulations which apply in India; and from Eastern European planners to adopt a formal plan-as-law similar to that found in Poland for example. In addition, each master plan made for different urban areas of the State, by consultants of different nationalities, was predicated on the likely existence of a planning system not too dissimilar from the one the consultants knew best, *i.e.* their own.

Calcutta provided an example of the *reductio ad absurdum* of foreign models. The West Bengal Town and Country Planning Act is loosely based on the current English system and includes in its provisions on development control the time-honoured legal phrase that, in considering whether to grant planning permission, the planning authority – in this case the Calcutta Metropolitan Development Authority (CMDA) – should take account of the development plan and "any other material considerations". I found within CMDA a widespread belief that since the same legal phrase about what to take into account in considering planning applications appeared in both West Bengal and English legislation, the English interpretation of, and practice on the basis of, that phrase would be likely to be relevant in Calcutta. As it was put to me by one very senior administrator: "in India, we have followed your planning laws mistake by mistake." However, since the urban scene is very different between West Bengal and England, how development control should be operated in Calcutta must turn on Calcutta's needs, CMDA's capacity and the wider urban socio-political context of West Bengal, rather than on what happened or was presumed to happen in England.

Trinidad and Tobago provides an example of the awful fate than can befall a country that does over-rely on English precedent. The Town and Country Planning Act in Trinidad and Tobago was enacted in 1960, and is based very closely on the English law of 1947, together with some of the amendments of the 1950s.

Part VI of the Act deals with compensation. As a result of the decision of the Privy Council in *Lopinot Limestone Ltd v. AG of Trinidad and Tobago* in 1988, this part of the law has now assumed considerable importance. The Act provides that if it is shown that, as a result of a planning decision involving a refusal of permission, the value of the interest of any person in the land to which the planning decision relates is less than it would have been if the permission had been granted, then the Minister is required to pay compensation to that person, or an amount equal to the difference between the two values.

The relevant section of the Act was copied almost word for word from section 20 of the English Town and Country Planning Act, 1954, which was an integral part of an extremely complex reform of the law relating to compensation and betterment as it had been enacted in the English Town and Country Planning Act, 1947. The full details of that reform are not relevant to the issue here; the essential point however is; and that is that compensation was not based on differences in the market value of land, depending on whether planning permission was granted or refused, but on whether a claimant has a "claim holding" under Part VI of the Act of 1947 against the sum of £300 million provided under that Act for the loss of the development value of the land "nationalised" by that Act. Thus, whatever the theoretical justification for providing or not providing compensation in respect of some planning decisions in England, the compensation so provided is an ever-decreasing amount with an ever-decreasing value, given the incidence of inflation. In Trinidad and Tobago, on the other hand, the transfer of the same provisions and the tying of them to market value has resulted, from the same processes of inflation, in ever-increasing amounts of compensation becoming payable in the event of a claim being successfully prosecuted. While the Government of Trinidad and Tobago was highly unlikely to have appreciated this point at the time it decided to accept the draft of a town and country planning bill prepared for it by an eminent English planning lawyer, it is equally highly unlikely that that planning lawyer did not realise what he was doing.

Three conclusions can be drawn from these examples. First, difficult though it may be, one should attempt to bring to urban legal problems a mind uncluttered by foreign models. Planning and other urban laws – housing, taxation, compulsory acquisition, title, etc. – are country-specific rather than universal and must be geared to the perceived needs, and probable future needs of the country concerned. There may be a good case for as much uniformity of commercial law as possible around the world, though the issue of who gains and who loses from such uniformity tends to be neglected, but there is no case for a similar uniformity of urban laws. This is not to say that there are not likely to be common matters to be dealt with in a town planning or land planning law, but the way they are dealt with will almost certainly need to be different.

Such considerations applied to laws that I drafted for Trinidad and Tobago in 1988 and the British Virgin Islands in 1989. While using the same basic framework for each law, I found that in virtually every clause, it was necessary to alter the Trinidad and Tobago draft to make it applicable to the British Virgin Islands. It was not just that the planning problems were different; the political and constitutional framework was different; the general body of laws was different; and the administrative system and culture was different. Above all, in the British Virgin Islands, there is an immensely strong ideology of private land-ownership. Private ownership of land is the normal pattern of tenure in the British Virgin Islands (BVI). Historical circumstances have led to a very powerful and strongly held notion of what private ownership means: "With land, a person is a free man; without land he is not." There is a very great reluctance to accept that a public agency can control what a person does with his land. At the same time development pressures on a fragile environment require some controls. The challenge posed to the authorities in BVI was to convince fiercely independent landowners that their own best interests would be met by accepting some controls. Any law which was perceived, however misguidedly, as interfering with that ownership would stand little chance of successful implementation, indeed of enactment.

It was necessary therefore to make plain in the body of the draft Bill that ownership was not being interfered with and the words "control" and "enforcement" were conspicuous by their absence. At the same time, there were clear problems arising from overseas developers with large-scale proposals for development bypassing normal channels and obtaining political approval for their schemes before planning and environmental implications had been properly considered. The need here was for mechanisms which ensured proper consideration for schemes whoever took the ultimate decision.

In Trinidad and Tobago on the other hand, while there is a strong ethic of land-ownership, the problem of planning was perceived by the planners as being a lack of order and discipline, especially among the rural population who wished, contrary to the National Physical Development Plan, to subdivide their land, build houses on the subdivision to keep the family together in accordance with traditional beliefs; such subdivisions contributed to ribbon development and increased the cost of the provision of services. Thus, the need was perceived as being for tougher enforcement powers and a way round political and legal blockages on their use. At the same time, at the political level, the problem was perceived as undue rigidity of development control and over-mighty planners, and therefore the need of mechanisms to enable other points of view to have an input into the planning system. The resultant bill provided for more powers for planners but also more inputs into the planning system by local authorities; advisory committees; participation; and formal appeal mechanisms.

Second, it follows from what I have said so far, that I am sceptical of the usefulness of checklists for either laws regulating the urban development process or the contents of such laws. Checklists would either be so general as to be banal, or else be too detailed to be of much use in specific situations. The range of political and administrative factors which have to be considered before a law is drafted or implemented is so great that each country, or each state in a federation needs to work outwards from its own specific situation to solutions which may or may not involve law, rather than work inwards from an imported law or a checklist of topics to be legislated on. There may, however, be a case for a checklist of principles, and I come to that later in the chapter.

Third, however there is one important occasion when legal transplants may be a valid solution. This is in the area of building regulations applicable to large multi-storey and/or "international" buildings – airports, major hotels, office blocks, factories for the manufacture of heavy industrial goods, chemical plants and so on – and pollution control regulations applicable to toxic and hazardous industrial processes and waste. There is a case, on public health and safety grounds, for direct transplants of, say European or North-American building regulations, pollution control regulations and provisions for environmental impact assessment, with any necessary modifications to take account of specified local circumstances such as earthquakes, tropical rain, termites, in situations where there is to be a direct transplant of the type of buildings and industrial processes from the countries where those rules apply.

It is, however, not so much the content of the regulations in these technical areas as the knowledge, skill and competence of the officials enforcing them which will determine their effectiveness. Until those attributes are available, it may be better to proceed by way of requiring bonds from, and imposing strict civil liability with unlimited damages on, international contractors and employers in respect of the safety of the design, construction and operation of their major facilities, such as hotels and factories, rather than have in place a modern up to date code on such matters which cannot be applied because there is no one to apply it. There is also a case for countries which lack qualified personnel making use of UN and other consultants to assist in the monitoring and control of hazardous industrial operations, for example. Such people would be expected to apply the same judgements about the effects of toxic wastes, necessary safety measures to control hazardous activities, and protection of the environment in those countries as in more developed ones. Here too then, the message is that principles may be transplantable, procedures less so.

Bench-marks for urban law reform

If there is any one message in this chapter, it is that a legal input into the urban development process is a matter of politics and policy and not just technicalities. A legal input involves costs for some, benefits for others; that is a political issue. It follows that it is necessary either to discover what principles lie behind any proposed change in the legal framework for urban development or to propose principles which should guide any such change. Without knowledge of the principles behind the legislation, what form the legislation should take is difficult if not impossible to determine. It is also important to ensure that the principles behind any legislation accord with and march alongside the principles behind the urban planning and development process.

Two levels of principles – first order and second order – are discussed here. First order principles are concerned with whether to proceed at all, and second order, with the bases on which to proceed.

First order principles

Three broad principles or options may be considered: Muddling through; incremental change; and fundamental reform.

Muddling through Many studies of bureaucracies, both public and private, have shown that they work by muddling through – a term coined by the political scientist, Charles Lindblom, to describe how bureaucracies actually work – by reacting to events; by trying to accommodate diverse and conflicting pressures; and by juggling inadequate resources and trying to make sense of confused aims. Adopting the option of muddling through would have the merit of facing reality – this is how things work in practice. Once the issues have been pointed out, let the system carry on as before, in the expectation that over a period of time adjustments will be made to meet pressing difficulties. There would be no call for new agencies, new programmes, extra resources to be committed, and thus no possible waste of resources arising from grandiose reform programmes which were never implemented.

A further argument for muddling through is that, what might appear ideal to lawyers and administrators in the capital and other major urban centres, might well turn out to be incomprehensible to the mass of the population, and another burden to which they would be subjected with no discernible benefit. It is preferable to leave things as they are and only alter the law and administration when the mass of the people are ready for it.

Incremental change This option would represent an advance on the muddling through principle. It would involve small-scale programmes, but important administrative and legal changes would be undertaken as and when both internal and external resources became available.

Much of the argument for incremental change is similar to the argument for muddling through; it is what happens in practice. An example from Zambia may be given. The report of the 1967 Land Commission called for radical legal change in Zambia's basic land law and set out a draft bill with commentary. No enactments of any such bill followed, but over the two decades since that report was published there have been a few alterations to the land laws, broadly similar to some of those suggested in the report.

Incremental change will be more cost-effective from the point of view of the use of government resources. Resources will be used as and when necessary, rather than squandered on a grandiose project which never gets implemented. The example of Trinidad and Tobago may be cited here. A major reform of town and country planning legislation was undertaken in 1960. The Act was not brought into effect until 1969. A major land reform law was undertaken between 1978 and 1981. Five important Acts of Parliament were passed in 1981, which between them rewrote the entire land law, including registration of title. Eight years on, the laws had yet to be brought into force, partly because of lack of government facilities and resources, and partly because of lack of enthusiasm from the legal profession. The ultimate result has been to revert to muddling through. Incremental change, on the other hand, could have, as it were, whetted the appetite for more reform, and so led on to major reforms: a major reform which fails sets back the case even for minor incremental change.

Fundamental reform Fundamental reform would consist of a planned programme of major land reform covering questions of tenure conversion, allocation, transfer, regulation, and use, with each part integrated into the others. The whole is a unified and coherent body of law and administration which would form the basis for the operation of an economic, efficient, and equitable land development system.

A strong case can be made for this approach. First, there are powerful precedents in its favour. The major land reform law which was enacted in England in 1925, was the culminating product of a long process of reform designed to create a body of law which would facilitate more efficient operation of a land market. The land tenure law and administrative reforms in Japan in the 1950s are considered to be an important factor in that country's rapid economic development.

Kenya presents another example of major land reform, with the Land Registration Act of 1963, seen as a necessary accompaniment to land reform and change, again being directed to simplifying the law catering to the large numbers of landowners which land tenure reform was designed to create. The fact that almost 40 years on, it is now considered that the land laws need major reform is much more a criticism of failures of administration and any regular programme of revising and updating the law than a criticism of the basic policy of having such a comprehensive law. Malaysia with its National Land Code of 1965 – a revised and modernised land law based on the old colonial law – considered that land law and administrative reform was a necessary precondition for more efficient land development and management and has had a constant programme of updating and revising the Code so ensuring it maintains its relevance to a rapidly developing society and economy. Finally, Colombia's major urban land reform processes in 1989 are yet another example of fundamental reform being seen as inescapable.

In sum, a programme of fundamental reform to which local and external experts and resources are committed over a planned period will be the best possible way of signalling to investors – both private and public, local and overseas, small- and large-scale that governments are serious about the more efficient management of their major land resource.

The principles or options have been deliberately posed in fairly stark form. In practice, governments tend to opt for a combination – either muddling through with some incremental change or fundamental reform on an incremental basis – that constitutes a coherent reform programme, however, recognising that such a programme is going to take considerable time to accomplish. Insofar as reform of administration systems and laws were involved, they should be seen as the beginning, and not as the end of the reform process. Reform would have to be preceded by a thorough review of what the problem areas are, together with proposals for solutions, followed up by training programmes for officials and public education of citizens in the new systems. But the overall importance of drawing attention to these options is just that: to highlight the fact that choices have to be made on what to do, and that both national governments and international agencies have to think about and argue out which option to select.

Second order principles

The concern here is to discuss the kind of principles that should guide any programme in improving and upgrading institutional and legal arrangements for land development administration. Principles will help determine the style, content, and thrust of any reforms, so that discussion and clarification of views about principles are of direct practical reference to improved administration. I would suggest principles as follows: any legal input into the urban development process should aim to encourage, strengthen or introduce a system of planning, regulation and management of that process which is equitable, flexible, environmentally conscious, participative and easily manageable, simple to understand and use, efficient and administratively fair. Counsels of perfection! The principles may briefly be discussed.

Equitable The system should aim to contribute to righting the present imbalance towards the well-off in most urban development processes. It should be made easier to acquire lawful title to land, or lawful occupation of a home, to acquire funds to build a home, to comply with any regulatory provisions governing the development or construction process and to obtain basic services and facilities such as water and power. Instead of the law being used to bolster and maintain a divided urban system between the illegal or extra-legal city of the urban poor, and the legal city of the urban well-off, it should facilitate the absorption of the urban poor into the legal city.

Flexible The system must be such that it can accommodate change and growth, the twin characteristics of most urban development processes. A rigid plan or zoning system is doomed to failure – there are countless examples of this all over the world – and merely leads to frustration, ignoring the rules, corruption, and the waste of scarce skilled personnel trying either to prevent departures from the plan or allowing them. A flexible adaptive planning system, and a development control system which concentrates on essentials, can act as an encouragement to lawful development where a rigid system discourages lawful and encourages unlawful development.

Environmentally conscious It is now much more widely recognised in literature, if not in practice, that development and environmental conservation can and indeed should go hand in hand. To allow or do nothing to prevent urban development in areas needed for water catchments, or where industrial pollution is likely to blight residential areas, or in ecologically fragile areas, will result in development disasters; cities or islands with inadequate clean water, leading to an epidemic of waterborne illnesses; more Bhopals; loss of local livelihoods from fishing, etc. Any law therefore should facilitate the integration of environmental considerations into the development processes and require that a proper balance be drawn between conservation and development. It should be said too, that an environmentally conscious planning and development system is more likely to be an equitable one, for urban environmental disasters tend to be visited on the poor rather than the rich.

Participative and easily manageable By participation I do not mean just the kind of participation which is now an established part of the British planning system – public meetings on plans and pressure group input into the consideration of planning applications. I am concerned with involvement, with a much greater effort to find out the needs and concerns of the urban majority and cater to them and with encouraging that majority to develop either own environment in their own ways, via local self-help schemes. Again, a flexible planning system will be of assistance here as it can more easily respond to needs and concerns fed into it from below. This too is where an easily manageable system comes in. Too many legal requirements of the contents of a plan, or too centralised a system of planning and development control both impede the development of a manageable system. In the words of an Attorney-General of Maldives – "less law, more power" – provide a framework for the management of the urban development process but do not crowd out initiative and flexibility with over many rules, which will in turn need over many officials to administer them.

Simple This follows on from "participative and easily manageable". Any legislation or forms to be used in connection with the urban development process should be kept as simple as possible. Complexity can, in my experience, result as much from administrative requirements as the supposed necessities of legal drafting, so this principle is addressed to all officials involved in the urban development process. Once again, reference to the first principle of equity is relevant here; a regulatory system applicable fairly to all must be one that can be understood and used by all.

Efficient The notion of an efficient system embraces several impacts: the costs of the system must not be allowed to grow too large; the costs of control of development must be related to some reasonably identifiable benefit to be gained from control; control for example, of hazardous industrial processes, may increase the cost of the processes concerned but the gains in diminution of danger to life and of protection of the natural environment justify those costs being imposed on the industrialists. It is likely to be more economically efficient and certainly more equitable that the costs are borne by the polluter than the polluted since the polluter is in a better position to abate the pollution. Control of a range of minor works of construction on the other hand may have no identifiable benefit over and above providing work for the controller; it should not therefore continue. Equally, this principle would direct attention to finding the most economically effective way of achieving a particular end; there is no magic in any one particular system of regulation or management and there should be a willingness to devise a system appropriate to the government and society concerned.

Administratively fair This is an important procedural value which unless explicitly addressed may become submerged in the concern for efficiency and ease of management. It is a particular lawyer-like concern to create a system which ensures, as far as possible, that proper consideration is given before action is taken which is likely to have adverse consequences on people; that where hearings are provided for, they are conducted in accordance with recognised principles of administrative justice; that where compensation is due, it is paid promptly and in full; that there are proper internal checks on the planners and administrators to ensure that they carry out their duties properly; and that adequate external investigations are made of allegations that they have not. One does not have to subscribe to all the details of Indian administrative law in practice to make the point that, as a matter of principle, a system which allows as much challenge to administrative action as that does, is preferable to one that allows none. Again to come back to the first principle, it is much more likely to be the poor who will lose out in an authoritarian administrative system than the wealthy or well connected.

Applying the principles

It must be clear that while these are the basic principles which should determine any legal input into the urban development process, the content of any law will naturally differ from society to society, depending on the circumstances of that society and what its fundamental political philosophy or basic urban policies are. A government whose policies are to encourage self-help and improvement amongst the urban poor via squatter upgrading programmes will focus on different specific areas of law and planning than one whose policies are to be based on large-scale public housing programmes; and a government with little land at its disposal, for example a small island state, will naturally be more concerned with control of land than a government whose principal concern is with the allocation of land which is not in short supply but is badly distributed. But in each case, the precise content of any law and the way it is put together should have regard to the basic principles. An important point must however be discussed here. Inevitably, attempts to meet all the principles will run up against the problem that in practice there may be conflicts between them; equity may not always be reconcilable with efficiency; fair administration may not always be reconcilable with simplicity. Two examples drawn from practice illustrate the problem.

How can one draft a statute creating new institutions and duties of participation, imposing new checks on administrative action, providing new opportunities for informal developments of all kinds and not finish up with a longer more complex law than the old colonial legislation which is being replaced and which basically gave planners and administrators *carte blanche* to “get on with things” with a minimum of checks on their activities?

My experience in drafting a new planning law for Kano State may be used to illustrate this dilemma. It was designed to replace a 1962 Town Planning Law, itself just a repeat for the old Northern State of Nigeria of a 1946 law applicable to all Nigeria, and a 1972 Kano Urban Development Board Edict, the combined lengths of which were 114 sections and 3 schedules. My proposed draft was 96 sections and 2 schedules, but many of the sections were long and the total number of words used in the replacement legislation was not that different from that in the existing legislation. Length and complexity came about from two causes; first, increasing the types of plans that could be made, thus increasing the flexibility of the planning system and stating what the purpose of the plans were – a necessary provision as each planning consultant or planning officer had his own idea as to what he hoped to achieve by preparing a plan and these ideas rarely dovetailed.

Second, a great many words were used to set up and provide the outline procedures for consultation and publicity in connection with the making and approval of plans. These procedures were unquestionably open to criticism from a "bottom up" perspective as being too heavily weighted toward "official" participation about officially made plans, but equally unquestionably they went far further than any planning legislation in Nigeria in the direction of open participative plan-making. All the time I was drafting, I was conscious that every additional provision I put in to sharpen up participation and reduce the possibility of the provisions being ignored made the legislation longer and more complex and so paradoxically perhaps increased the likelihood of administrators, planners and consultants being tempted to ignore it. The draft bill was not ultimately enacted so I cannot tell whether in practice I erred on the side of complexity in this matter; I think I did but I also think that fewer legal provisions would inevitably have meant placing more reliance on the goodwill of officials, and relying on bureaucratic goodwill might not have been too sensible.

One schedule in the draft legislation was long and complex. This dealt with permitted development – that is, development permitted by the law and which did not need specific planning permission. Once again the aim was straightforward, its implementation complex and possibly devious. The aim was to free as much small-scale development and economic activity from the requirements of planning permission as possible, without at the same time negating the principle of development control. The draft Bill therefore contained the principle of development control where there was in existence a development plan (that alone freed most of the state from development control on unimpeachable grounds); the schedule contained the exceptions to development control in those areas where there was a plan and therefore development control.

It is not however very easy to draft provisions exempting small-scale development from control in such a way that the informal sector is left alone but developments which might cause a nuisance or pollution are caught, or exempting residential developments of a traditional kind or a certain size but catching other residential development. The only way to do it is to spell out in some detail what is permitted and what is not. In this way developers and, more importantly, officials know what they may and may not do or control. But spelling out details adds to the length and complexity of the law. The alternative – to give a wide measure of discretion to officials – ran the risk of providing a spurious legal backing to harassment of informal urban development and economic activity.

Thus demands for more participation, for more decentralisation of power, for more protection for informal economic activity and for more controls over official power – demands in short for a more complex administrative structure – led to a more complex legislative structure which in turn gave rise to the possibility of inefficiencies.

My second example came from Trinidad and Tobago, where in my Report on the existing Town and Country Planning Act I had set out the five principles which should inform any new legislation: efficiency, equality, environmentalism, education and public participation, and employment generation. These principles had been accepted as appropriate. The legislation which was to be replaced was 40 sections long; my draft was 90 sections long and some of the sections were themselves of considerable length. Why was this? First, the terseness of the 1960 Act had not been conducive to its efficient administration. Efficiency there was in practice but this was in spite of rather than because of the Act. In some places, the Act was terse to the point where it was not clear what powers were available to officials.

Second, the Act had assumed that flesh could be put on its bones by regulations and orders, but with two exceptions – a General Development Order dealing principally with development control and some regulations dealing with advertisements – no regulations had been made during the life of the Act. So powers which were probably available under the Act were not used because there was no legal framework set out for their use.

This led on to a third point: there were, no doubt, some political reasons why regulations had not been made to flesh out the Act; there was little pressure for a comprehensive system of planning and a good deal of pressure for allowing people to develop land as they wished. But a factor in the lack of regulations was that the Act provided no guidance, no outline of the subject matter on which regulations might be made. Without some legislative indication of what a particular exercise of power might look like, it became impossible to draw up regulations.

I took the view that any replacement legislation had to take note of the fact that regulations might not be made for some time to come if at all, but that their drafting would be easier if there were a fairly detailed framework already set out in primary legislation, *i.e.* the draft Bill. Equally, it should be possible to implement the new legislation, to exercise powers and perform duties under the legislation without being dependent on regulations. Just as important, those outside the bureaucracy should be able to get a fuller picture of what the system of town and country planning as established by law was about; they would be better placed to do that if matters were more closely and fully spelt out in the Act, the document most non-lawyers instinctively recognise and go to when they want find out what "the law" is on a particular topic. Thus efficiency, equity and public education would all be served by a more lengthy piece of legislation even though simplicity and some economy had been sacrificed.

A holistic approach

Any legal input should be made only in the full knowledge of both the existing system and the likely implications of that legal input. This does not mean that any reform however small can be contemplated only after a full survey of the existing system. But it does suggest that any reform or introduction of new legal or administrative arrangements is likely to have ripple effects and these should be taken account of in the manner, style and content of any reforms. It also means that, on occasions, one might have to pause and refrain from a tinkering reform if there is *prima facie* evidence that there are more deep-seated problems which need to be tackled. The case of the Jamaican land tenure and registration system discussed earlier is an excellent example of that: spending money, time and energy on shoring up the existing system of title registration while refusing to acknowledge that the whole administrative and legal system of land management was failing to provide an adequate service would be counter-productive to the long-term aim of creating a viable efficient and simple system of land management for that country.

A holistic approach is easy to argue for but difficult to comply with, especially if one is being pressured to come up with some reform instantly to solve what someone with political influence but maybe not much understanding of the urban development process sees as a problem. How can one, as a matter of practical politics, say in such circumstances: "wait six months, a year, two years, until we have done a thorough survey and can come forward with a considered proposal"? In such circumstances, a tactic of damage limitation may be the best approach; better a hasty "reform" undertaken by those who understand the system than one undertaken by those who know nothing and might therefore make matters worse not better.

But there is a possible solution to this dilemma. Urban land management and the urban development processes are, for virtually all countries, major concerns of government. Political stability, economic development, social change, health, all are greatly influenced by the way cities are developed and administered. At the root of such development and administration is land, its allocation, development and use. Land-use planning is one tool of such a process of management as are law and taxation, but too often the different tools are left in separate compartments of the bureaucracy. They may be brought together only by the, often fortuitous, appearance of a team of outside consultants brought in to try and sort out problems that are thought to have arisen. The alternative to this is for governments to create a standing committee or commission whose function would be *inter alia* to keep under constant review national urban or human settlement policies and their implementation and to produce reports on the same, either on the basis of references to it by governments or of its own assessment of what needs review and monitoring. The commission would have its own staff, could employ consultants both national and foreign, and help to ensure that urban issues were given full and careful consideration before any specific action on such issues took place. Such a commission would be semi-official; it would not be part of government in the sense that government would be committed to accepting all its views but it would be responsive to government in the sense that it would be obliged to consider issues referred to it by government and government would be its prime funder. Some states have such a body, the embryo of such a body, or have developed an equivalent body in respect of environmental protection. It is a proposal which is worth serious consideration as a way of ensuring that the holistic approach recommended here becomes more than a pious aspiration.

Building on existing systems

There is an administrative and legal culture in every society just as there is a prevailing set of beliefs and practices about land, water, homes, taxes and other aspects of an urban existence. These beliefs, practices and culture have to be taken note of in any programme or proposal for a legal input into the urban development process. They have to be worked with rather than against, adapted to new circumstances and demands rather than abolished. It is unlikely that abolition would in practice occur even if it were decreed to occur. Such a counsel of incrementalism, of working with rather than against local beliefs and practices, may be disappointing and sound pusillanimous to those who hope for radical reform in urban development processes. It may also be pointed out that this conclusion might well conflict with some of the principles enunciated earlier; if the administrative culture is not fair, if equity has not been a feature of urban development process, how can one base any reform both on those principles and on the existing administrative culture?

In answer to the first criticism, one has to point out that a radical reform of legal or administrative processes in urban development or any other part of the development process is a consequence of, and not a forerunner of or substitute for, radical political change. Proposing a radical, grass roots, participative land-use planning system in countries where government remains in the hands of military dictators, will achieve nothing. Indeed such a system never would be introduced even if it were recommended for introduction. Only when governments become convinced of the need for radical change, for example, towards greater equity, which can happen with military as well as civilian regimes, will radical administrative, legal and planning reforms become possible.

More problems are posed by possible conflicts between principles and practice. Here too, however, I would suggest that incrementalism is the way forward. If the application of the principle of equity looks likely to conflict with current and apparently long-standing inequitable practices, then one has to try and create a situation where, over a period, principles of equity begin to be taken account of in practice. Similarly with fair administration: to create possibilities for review of decisions; for assistance in complying with administrative procedures; and for forms to be simplified and in a language understood by the urban poor; may over time bring about a fairer administrative process and will provide handles for those who want to assist the urban poor to achieve justice. I recognise that at the end of the day, incrementalism in reform as a way of creating a fairer and more efficiently managed urban development process depends, no less than does radical reform, on a receptive government or ruling elite; absent that and any proposals for reform will fall on deaf ears, or if accepted for public relations reasons, will be largely nullified in practice.

Acceptability and implementability: a balanced law

In one sense this is an elaboration of the principles of simplicity and manageability discussed above. Leaving aside questions of political philosophy, any legal input will be acceptable to government and administration to the extent that it is easy to understand and implement. But this conclusion goes further than that in two directions. First, the law has to be balanced between the regulative and facilitative – between what is sometimes called reactive and proactive. Too often, laws regulating urban development are open to the criticism that they are essentially negative; they prevent development rather than encourage it. It is important for the general societal acceptance of such laws that, while they might control some developments, they facilitate and encourage others.

It is easier to conceptualise and draft controlling devices than facilitating devices, and easier too for bureaucrats to administer negative controls than positive assistance, but the effort to undertake the latter must be made. A few pointers may be given. Not all development needs to be controlled; as much as possible should be free of planning controls though still subject to minimal building regulation in the interests of public health and safety. Simplified systems of regulation, including land registration, may be applied to certain categories of development. Standard plans for low-cost residential development may be made available. Rather than spending money on accommodation out of the financial reach of the urban majority or on large bureaucracies to administer controls, small revolving loan funds could be made available for low cost housing and commercial development, and co-operatives encouraged to manage such funds.

An important suggestion made by the Indian Task Force on urban planning may also be mentioned here: rather than large-scale programmes of compulsory land acquisition which take time and cause great resentment, more effort should be put into land readjustment and land pooling programmes to make more effective use of badly or under-used urban land while not depriving anyone of all their lands. I would suggest too that a more participative legal system – a greater involvement of local authorities, customary authorities where relevant, and people in the areas subject to large-scale redevelopment – is also likely to ensure that the needs of potential developers – large, small, public and private – will be properly considered and taken account of (Salmon, 1987). The question which always needs to be asked is: is this proposal or law or regulatory measure going to impede or assist development; if it is going to impede, will it be impeding development which it is desirable to prevent or not; if it is to assist development, is it development of a kind that should be assisted to take place, and does it need the kind of assistance that is being provided for it?

The second aspect of acceptability concerns public education. The legal regulation of the development process is often presented as a restrictive, negative matter. If a government decision has been taken to have a legal regulatory framework for the development process, then that decision and its implementation needs to be explained to the public or different groups of the public in a manner apt for that particular group. Thus a manual for development outlining legal requirements and administrative practices could be produced for the formal large-scale construction and development industry; this is already the case in Singapore and Jamaica to name but two countries; Cayman Islands has something similar but rather simpler. For the more informal small-scale construction sector, simpler leaflets and guides would be sufficient. In many public or adult educational programmes the positive benefits of regulation should be stressed with emphasis laid on officials' willingness to assist persons to comply with the law. Too often the regulatory system, besides being negative, is utterly unknown to the vast majority of people until some high-handed action is taken – such as demolition of squatter settlements – or some allegedly beneficial programme is announced – such as upgrading of squatter settlements – which will have far-reaching effects on the lives of the recipients of the action. It is hardly surprising in the circumstances that a common reaction to regulation is one of hostility. There always will be a barrier to overcome in terms of the general acceptability of regulation but the barrier is made unnecessarily high by too negative and too secretive an approach to regulation. If it is to be, let it be balanced and open, so that in time it will become more acceptable and more implementable. In the final analysis implementation can be carried out only with the support of both the bureaucracy and the people at large.

Mechanics

This chapter turns now from principles and how they can be and have been introduced into urban law reform to practice. This section addresses the issue of how to set about developing improved systems of urban planning and land development via legal and institutional arrangements. Given the decision to move ahead on reform of some kind, and acceptance of some or all of the second order principles discussed earlier, what is the best way to proceed? A general theme is the challenge involved in devising new institutional and legal arrangements which hold out the promise of improved administration of urban planning and land development, provide continuity and compatibility with existing cultural and social norms, and take account of political realities and limitations. The concern here then is with process: how to proceed in such a way as to maximise the chances of success and minimise those of failure.

The process of preparing a land development plan offers a useful model which may be set out as follows:

SURVEY — ANALYSIS — PLAN — IMPLEMENT — FEEDBACK

Survey

Survey involves a critical analysis of existing processes, administrative systems, laws, and institutions, undertaken via interviews, visits to institutions, investigation of reasons for existing systems, and so forth. The aim is to build up a picture of the existing system.

It is worth stressing the importance of a thorough survey of an existing system before proposing reforms. This might seem an obvious point, but in the haste to introduce a reform or correct what is thought to be a deficiency in a law or its implementation, such a survey is often foregone and the "reform" fails to achieve its aim. Planners would hesitate to draw up a plan before gathering together and assessing information about the area to be planned, architects would hesitate to design a building before familiarising themselves with the site and the area where the building is to be located, and the information required on a major project before most lending agencies will commit funds to it is voluminous. So, too, should be the case of a reform input into the urban development process. Until such a survey is done, it is not possible to know what the problem is.

There is another important reason for a survey. Most officials are too busy working in their particular area to be able to see the system in the round; no one is available to survey the system. They may be uneasily aware that something is wrong; they may have fixed views on what is wrong and how it needs to be remedied, but have little time to formulate a case for considered change. A survey of the total system, its strengths and weaknesses, the areas where a case can be made for change - and, if so, what kind of change and by what kind of mechanisms - may provide the first opportunity for officials to see how the total system is working in practice and how it can have an immensely valuable educational benefit.

This leads on to a third point. If there is to be reform or reorganisation, it has to be sold to the officials who will be implementing it. In practice, this means that officials will be expected to learn and apply new laws, new routines, and new practices. They have to be convinced that this is a necessary and worthwhile exercise. The process of putting together a survey is part of this process of educating officials to accept change. Many of them will have had some input in the survey, and an opportunity to express their views about the present system and how it needs to be changed. They will or should have an opportunity to go through the survey and so increase their awareness of the system of which they are a part. Producing a survey can then both create a climate of anticipation for an acceptance of change and contribute to a more aware and informed bureaucracy.

Analysis

Analysis involves considering what has been turned up by the survey; asking awkward questions; considering the implications of possible alternative scenarios for improved systems; and recognising that any reform or introduction of new legal or administrative systems is likely to have ripple effects that will need to be taken into account in determining the style, manner, and contents of reforms. Analysis will also help uncover the politics of reform, the hidden agenda which will determine whether reform will go ahead or not.

Plan

Plan concerns itself with the programme and timing of the introduction of new administrative procedures and new laws. As noted both above and earlier in this chapter, programmes designed to increase awareness and acceptance of the case for change are a vital part of the process of introducing new systems and procedures. Therefore, it may well be that, while governments are convinced both of the need for change and the acceptability of the particular changes being proposed, there is a case for postponement until the population at large becomes convinced. The case of the British Virgin Islands discussed earlier may be cited here. The government may well perceive the need for increased regulation of land development to match the rapid tempo in land development evident in the islands. But the population at large sees increased regulation, not as protection of the interests of all, but as restrictions to their opportunity to improve their lot. In these circumstances, too hasty an introduction of new systems of land development regulation could prove counterproductive. Another good example of the need to plan carefully comes from Madras; proposals for a reorganised development control system, while eminently rational and apt to increase efficiency, would also have required the redeployment of some 300 MMDA officials. Reform proved difficult to sell. One must therefore ensure that all relevant officials are on board before launching the new arrangements.

Implementation

Implementation is the crucial stage in the process of reform. If the earlier stages have been carefully completed then implementation should get under way without problems. But no amount of planning can cater to the unforeseen; there will be a need to create mechanisms which can react quickly to sort out problems. This leads to a major question: who will be responsible for introducing and continuing to oversee new and improved systems? Discussion hitherto has concentrated on process, but it must also consider institutions.

Feedback

One of the problems of developing improved urban planning and land development systems via institutional and legal means is that the officials who are learning to handle the new systems are also those who are meant to notice the problems, take action to counter them, stand back and observe the total operation of the new system, and then feed into the process suggestions for improvements and changes. This is impractical: what is needed is an agency or a unit whose principal, if not sole function, is to monitor the implementation of new and improved systems, act as a kind of umpire or arbitrator to sort out inevitable conflicts and tensions; conduct seminars and in-house progress reviews; and prepare periodic progress reports on the operation of the new system. Such an agency should be seen as an ally in the process of reform and improvements; it is not there to pick holes and find faults, but to work with administrators on the ground, help with the process of integrating new approaches with old beliefs and practices, and keep an eye on the overall goal: a more efficient, effective, and equitable system of land development administration. Hence, the role of such an agency in feedback: it will be in the best position to know what has gone well and what has not; what needs further thought and improvement; and which parts of the bureaucracy need reassurance and which need revamping.

Action

The final section of this chapter sets out to provide a brief check-list of what needs to be done in the two key areas of land use planning and land tenure, both of which would feature in any programme of urban land law reform.

Land-use and building costs must be reduced

There is no suggestion here that all land-use or building regulations should be abandoned, though it must be recognised that in many cities, most buildings, especially houses, infringe some or all of the regulations. But if there are to be regulations, and if there is to be a determined effort to apply the regulations to everyone, then regulations have to be devised which are meaningful, easy to comply with, and affordable to the majority of the urban population. The following action could be taken to reduce costs:

- Reduce plot sizes to affordable levels but permitting such arrangements on one plot, where local customs sanction both a main house and subsidiary quarters for renting.
- Free up a large amount of small-scale, commercial, light industrial, and personal services development and use of land from the need to seek permission.
- Provide an accelerated track for obtaining permission for certain categories of development.
- Develop a one-stop shop administrative system for obtaining all necessary permission to develop land.
- Revise building regulations by sanctioning the use of local and temporary materials and technologies; adopting a deemed-to-satisfy approach; encoraging an advisory system through the development of better guidelines and building plans rather than inspectorial ones enforcing standards through regulations and demolitions; devise incentives for complying with regulations in addition to sanctions

for non-compliance and consult local builders, contractors, and professionals to review and amend regulations on a regular basis.

- Decentralise the administration of land use and building controls.
- Produce esay to follow manuals, cartoons, videos, and other forms of communication media so that people can develop an understanding on what they should do and why it is necessary to comply with regulations.
- Develop a standard cost-benefit analysis for any proposals for additional regulations.

Revise and adapt urban land tenure systems and transaction processes

Evidence from many countries demonstrates that security of tenure is an essential precondition, both for private investment in housing and for developing a sense of belonging among a city's inhabitants. Equally, evidence indicates that despite the legal and administrative obstacles, land markets are a common phenomenon in most cities, albeit in some countries these are clandestine or illegal. Thus, this set of actions aims to bring law and administration in line with fact and reality.

- In countries where customary law constitutes the basis of much of the land tenure system, develop a form of secure and pledgeable title to urban land which recognises and safeguards the continuing ultimate title of the traditional landholder, whether it be an individual or a community.
- Provide a mechanism for the conversion by the state of *de facto* title to the land which has been obtained by households in many squatter settlements into *de jure* title. The components of such a mechanism could be: Simple and basic land surveys in squatter settlements; use of local knowledge via adjudication committees to determine boundaries and settle disputes; local title registries to record details of adjudicated titles; simple forms to facilitate land transactions; financial incentives to make use of this "junior" title registration system; and rules on prescription.
- Review and, if necessary, revise or, where relevant, develop a code of land law which covers in one or more basic clearly drafted documents the substantive and procedural law on land title acquisition; registration of title or documents concerning land title; land leasing; mortgages and other forms of security provision for

loans against the land title; strata titles (condominiums); and both public and private encumbrances.

- Develop legal, administrative, and financial structures for alternative means of guaranteeing title, particularly system of title insurance.
- Give consideration to and, if feasible, create systems of specialised dispute settlement mechanisms – tribunals, specialist courts, arbitration, and conciliations – for handling land disputes and arriving at final decisions.
- Review all legislation imposing public controls on tenure and transactions – ceiling legislation, price control, rent control – with a view to assessing whether they are achieving their aims, either at all or with economic efficiency and effectiveness, and whether the aims, achieved or not, are apt to increase the supply of affordable land, and make such necessary amendments and alterations.
- Review and, if necessary, reorganise the administrative structure of the offices dealing with land so as to create an integrated and decentralisable one-stop shop for the service consumers, and enable the private sector to become involved in the delivery of the service.
- Establish a joint public/private sector body to continuously review the operation of the legal and administrative framework for urban land management.

Conclusions

This paper is deliberately long on issues, principles, and ideals, and short on prescriptions. The aim is to stimulate discussion, not solve problems. In this area of institutional and legal arrangements for improved urban planning and land development, the overwhelming issue is how to overcome the inertia and conservatism of officials who feel safe continuing to do what they have always done, and threatened when asked or required to do something different. What they have always done is administer a system of land development controls which by and large does not work and creates resentment of and disregard for the law and those who administer it on the part of the majority of urban residents. Thus, even those parts of the regulatory system which could perform a useful function, or which are needed, stand little chance of being implemented.

I am only too conscious that some of the ideas set out here or perhaps all of them may seem naïve and divorced from reality. Reality, it will be urged, is too often corrupt, incompetent, understaffed bureaucracies responding to venal politicians or authoritarian military, who are more intent on preserving a status quo which allows them to grow wealthy at the expense of the majority of the population than set on creating an equitable, open and fair process of urban development. Any argument which stresses the need to take account of existing governmental structures and philosophy and bases proposals for change on incrementalism will merely finish up reinforcing the status quo and giving "reform" a bad name.

I believe that such a picture of reality is a caricature. It would be idle to deny the presence of venality, incompetence, authoritarianism or worse in many parts of the Third World; it would be equally idle to deny that such regimes are often propped up by western support, and are often opposed by many of their own people. Equally, one can point to regimes which are struggling and have over a long period struggled to bring about a more just society, despite internal and external opposition.

It seems to me to be a perfectly proper position to adopt, in putting forward a broad range of ideas on the nature of a possible legal input in the urban development process, that one should try and lend strength and support to those elements within all societies which are likely to be receptive to ideas about equity, openness, fairness and efficiency. Such elements are more likely to be receptive if invited to build reforms on the basis of the better aspects of existing institutions than on throwing them away and starting again. I accept that these ideas are not likely to appeal to the venal, the incompetent or the authoritarian, and may be dismissed by the cynical and conservative administrator or consultant, but my experience is that in every bureaucracy and in every government there are persons of vision, energy, and ideals who will reach out for new ideas and approaches that might help bring about a more responsive and efficient machinery of government and the better delivery of programmes to all sectors of society. It is to these persons that the ideas in this chapter, none of them particularly revolutionary, are addressed.

A final point must be made: at the end of the day, the regulation of the urban development process is going to reflect and support a government's wider economic and social policies and strategies, and any legal input into that regulation and development process will likewise be designed to advance or at least not impede, those wider policies. An awareness of this basic and inescapable fact of politics should assist any discussion of or proposal for any legal input; it will prevent too great a reliance being placed on law alone as a mechanism to bring about fundamental change in the urban development process. It will direct attention to the need to take full account of the political and societal context of that process and any possible changes to it, and of the fact that law is only one of the mechanisms which are available for use in the management and regulation of the process of urban development. Anyone involved in proposing reform of, or a more or less effective legal input into, the urban development process is then steering between Scylla and Charybdis – between the need to take account of existing political and societal realities and the desirability of proposing principled changes or reforms which would have as their objective bringing about changes in the existing political and societal realities. It is to aid that difficult navigational exercise that this chapter has been directed.

---

*This chapter is an amalgam of two papers. The first is The role of law in urban planning, first published in Devas, Nick and Rakodi, Carole (1993), *Managing Fast Growing Cities; New Approaches to Urban Planning and Management in the Developing World*, Longmans. The book was the outcome of a workshop held in September 1989 as a contribution to the celebration of the 75th anniversary of the Royal Town Planning Institute. Many of the people involved in the workshop later played very active roles in the UNCHS(Habitat)/World Bank/UNDP Urban Management Programme.

The second is Institutional and Legal Arrangements for the Improved Administration of Land Development, first published in 1992, *Regional Development Dialogue*, Vol. 13 No. 2 UNCRD, Nagoya and written originally as a contribution to the land management component of the Urban Management Programme.

8 Planning law in the Commonwealth Caribbean: the challenge of reform*

The Commonwealth Caribbean consists of 17 states and territories. I cannot claim to be an expert on the planning laws of such a multitude of countries so I cannot really compare these laws one with another and arrive at a conclusion as to what is the best national law or, rather like picking a Rest of the World XI, what would be the ideal Caribbean law derived from picking sections from different national laws. In any event I am doubtful whether a conference of planners as opposed to lawyers is the right venue for a detailed analysis of different laws. What is perhaps more in keeping with the theme of the Conference is a discussion of the English background to many of the laws, its appropriateness and possible alternatives.

The basic law of the Commonwealth Caribbean is the common law of England supplemented and in some cases replaced by local statutes. Even the local statutes are for the most part drafted in the English style of drafting, follow English conventions, are often based on equivalent English statutes, and when the subject of litigation in the courts, English judicial precedents are often followed. Appeals still lie to the Judicial Committee of the Privy Council which reinforces the "Englishness" of Caribbean law. So much is common knowledge. During the colonial era, it was natural and in some respects a matter of colonial constitutional law and practice that law reform or law innovation, *i.e.* the introduction of new laws on topics on which there was none previously should follow or be closely related to equivalent law in England – not the United Kingdom, but England. One rarely finds much Scots Law in the Commonwealth. So for this general reason we would expect to find that planning law enacted during the colonial era would follow an English model and indeed where the colonial era still persists, as in the Turks and Caicos Islands, this quasi-constitutional pressure to have English planning law introduced also still persists.

But there were additional reasons why the particular models introduced were as they were, which are important to be aware of; first, the Colonial Office from 1945 onwards, took on board a measure of concern for social welfare issues in the colonies in health, education, housing and above all local government which paralleled the new stance of governments in the United Kingdom. As part of this new focus on social welfare issues, town and country planning was thought to be necessary both in the metropolitan country and in the colonies. There was too some pressure from some colonies themselves for town planning laws – Nigeria in particular faced with returning ex-servicemen who were not about to return to the countryside and resume subsistence farming – to enable officials the better to control the rapidly developing urban areas, so the Colonial Office itself produced something very close to a model law on town and country planning – a law which grew to be an amalgam of the English 1932 and 1947 Acts with minor local variation to suit local circumstances. First introduced into Nigeria in 1946, this law was over the next ten or so years introduced as well into most of the English dependencies in East and Central Africa.

This is one important input into the legislation in Jamaica and Trinidad and Tobago. Looking at both these pieces of legislation, it is clear that while there was a higher proportion of pure English planning law in each, reference had also been made to the Colonial Office model especially in respect of provisions relating to the content of plans – itself drawn from the 1932 Act, which had formed the basis of Trinidad and Tobago's first planning legislation in 1938. Indeed, it would have been odd if Desmond Heap who drafted the Trinidad and Tobago Act and I think had an input into the Jamaican legislation had not consulted the Colonial Office model since he was almost certainly consulted by the Colonial Office about planning legislation.

Two further factors were also of great importance in determining the type of town and country planning law introduced initially into the Caribbean. First, English planning legislation was perceived as being "successful", *i.e.* it had created a planning system which worked efficiently and fairly and was helping to create a "better" society. Secondly, and arguably more importantly, the law and the system it established was considered to be ideologically neutral – that is the law was a set of technical value-free statements, 'do's and 'don't's to officials who exercised their technical value-free powers in the public interest, a vague kind of "motherhood" notion to which only the most ill-willed or ignorant could possibly take offence. The "proof" that this was so was that the very extensive system of town and country planning introduced into the United Kingdom in 1947 with all party backing – apart that is from the compensation and betterment provisions which were a party political gloss on the law – that it was this system, shorn of most of the controversial compensation and betterment provisions, which formed the basis of the export models to the Caribbean.

Given this belief about the English law – that it was successful and that it was just a technical value free set of precepts, it is not surprising that it formed the basis of Heap's proposal for Trinidad and Tobago or that it was also used as the basis for the law in Jamaica and Barbados. After all what these countries were being offered was what the salesman represented and clearly believed to be the best model on the market; if not a Rolls' Royce, then at least a Morris Oxford or an Austin Cambridge – those halcyon days when English cars had English names and were made of English components – good solid models capable with careful use of lasting almost for ever. To have argued to Sir Desmond Heap 25 years ago that Trinidad and Tobago or Jamaica or anywhere else in the Caribbean needed its own special planning law for its own special circumstances would have been rather like arguing with God that he should revise the bye-laws of the Garden of Eden because Adam and Eve had had some difficulty in complying with them.

The extent to which the English model was followed; the limited concessions made to local circumstances in respect of the Trinidad and Tobago Act passed in 1960 but put together in 1959–60 may briefly be noted. The whole country was clearly regarded as the county, in respect of which, in the English law, a development plan had to be made and revised once every five years. The Minister was the Minister as in the United Kingdom and as there, so in Trinidad and Tobago, there was no appeal from the Minister's decision on a planning application. The vital difference, that in the United Kingdom, the Minister was in most cases the appellate authority himself and in any event, his decision was preceded by a public local inquiry where the issues relative to the appeal could be debated was ignored. Indeed the argument used by the then Prime Minister of Trinidad and Tobago in introducing the Town and Country Planning Bill into the legislature in June 1960 and defending the no appeal provision were very similar to arguments used in the English House of Commons that same year in defending the Minister's right to depart from the report and recommendations of "his" inspectorate in any planning appeal – the Minister was responsible to Parliament for the administration of the law and one could not have a situation where he was responsible but could not take the decision.

On compensation for refusal of planning permission, the *reductio ad absurdum* of the importation of English law was reached. The relevant and crucial sections of the Trinidad and Tobago Act were copied word for word from an English Act – the 1954 Town and Country Planning Act – in total disregard of the fact that the English provisions were part and parcel of the reform of the complex compensation and betterment provisions of the 1947 English Act and could only be understood or indeed effectively implemented in that special context. In particular, the amount of compensation that could be claimed was geared to a fixed and ever diminishing sum of money; market value had nothing to do with compensation under the English Law.

Twenty-five years on, we know better. The simplistic world of Desmond Heap and his colleagues in the planning and legal professions and in the Colonial Office has gone, never to return. In fact it had begun to disintegrate in the United Kingdom in the mid to late 1960s even before the law drafted by Heap was in force in Trinidad and Tobago. It was, some might say, destroyed from within; the Planning Advisory Group's Report of 1965 with its recommendations for the introduction of structure and local plans, for the embracing within the scope of planning of a much wider range of issues than was assumed to be covered by development plans made under the 1947 or 1932 Acts, and the Skeffington Report of 1969 on Public Participation were two key official documents which did much to undermine the technical neutral world of planning assumed to exist in the United Kingdom and exported to the colonies in the 1940s, 1950s and early 1960s.

Heap himself reacted strongly to those developments and in a series of articles, lectures, speeches and memoranda from then on displayed unremitting hostility to public participation, planning gain and renewed attempts to deal with the compensation and betterment problem; to, in short, the frank and open acceptance of the position that planning was not, had in fact never been, a technical exercise concerned with drawing lines on maps, filling in forms and granting or refusing planning permission in accordance with the neutral and professional advice of officers, but was a highly political activity concerned with the allocation of scarce resources in society in respect of which society both directly via public participation and indirectly via its elected representatives wanted an increasingly active say in decision-making.

This more political approach to planning and its legal framework has not really penetrated town and country planning in the Caribbean countries.

The laws still reflect the old neutralist ideology, and the proposals to change the laws for the most part still accept this same basic legal framework but are concerned to try and make it work better by the addition of various legal technical devices again mostly derived from England. This is certainly the case in Trinidad and Tobago and in Jamaica too, despite a major plan-making exercise over the last six or so years in respect of Kingston and the Parishes of St. Andrew and St. Catherine resulting in the production of integrated Urban Development plans for those areas, the law of planning has remained unchanged since 1957. This is despite the fact that the most explicit criticism was made of it in 1971 to the effect that a strong case could be made for tearing it up and starting again with a simpler model more relevant for Jamaican needs – remarks which, its author says, drew in turn indignant and misplaced criticism from Heap.

Even where new laws have been recommended and introduced, the underlying philosophy has been that planning is a technical exercise concerned with the orderly development of land – what a splendidly technocratic word "orderly" is as if the development of town and cities, the way people live and move and have their being can ever be made to be "orderly" – for which the law provides the power to undertake this exercise but neither the law nor the resultant exercise of power is in any way concerned with social, economic or political implication of public controls on the allocation of the scarce resource of land. Reference may be made particularly to the major UNDP-sponsored planning legislation project in the Eastern Caribbean in the mid-1970s which used Roger Suddards, an English solicitor specialising in planning and property development law in England as its legal expert. His proposals, followed in several islands, certainly made much more effort to tailor laws to the needs of such jurisdictions – they were essentially fairly short pieces of legislation, explained clearly and fully – but the overall impression of his reports is that planning law is a technical matter concerned principally with crossing the 't's and dotting the 'i's of procedure correctly.

The Suddards exercise may be seen however as a bridge between the Colonial Office/Desmond Heap approach and the approach which is argued for here. While Suddards adopted a technocratic approach to planning law reform he did, as befitted a UNDP consultant, make an effort to tailor the laws he drafted to local needs. English law provided a backcloth of ideas to be drawn on, not the basic building blocks as with Heap in respect of Trinidad and Tobago. This was definitely a step in the right direction of relating the law to the social realities of the country in which it applied.

More significant pressure for this approach to planning law reform is coming from the street level bureaucrats, the planning officials who are actually making plans and engaging in the day to day business of development control and enforcement. Their experiences have shown and are showing up the deficiencies of the existing English models especially the attempt in those models to isolate planning from politics. In part this is because, paradoxically, new and equally imported models of the concept of planning, which are being used in the process of plan-making, embrace much wider notions of what planning is all about – not just lines on maps or land use zoning – ideas which still seem to have a considerable hold on the legal profession in the Caribbean – but land use issues such as transport, issues crossing the boundaries of land use and social policy, such as housing and social infrastructure and the newer approaches to land use embraced in the ideas behind environmental and ecological factors.

Plans are now about policies and principles to guide actions and decisions, all of which make much more explicit the allocative and value-laden functions of planning and result in plans about strategies and proposals or for integrated urban development but not many lines on maps. This newer state-of-the-art approach to planning sits very uneasily alongside a law which assumes a much narrower land use plan and has in fact in Trinidad and Tobago given rise to queries as to whether the National Physical Development Plan is indeed a plan as required under the Town and Country Planning Act. The same query could be made about IUDPs in Jamaica.

It is experiences too, in connection with development control which is bringing home to planners the increasing divorce between the model of planning assumed by the law and the model of planning on the ground. Contacts and negotiations with would-be developers and their representatives, the facts of unauthorised development and the types of authorised development occurring; the reluctance of politicians to take enforcement action; the pressure to have an appellate system and the growth of resort to the courts to test the legality – even the constitutionality – of the exercise of powers by the planners all drive home to planners that, however much the law might try and disguise the fact, what they are engaged in is the highly political activity of allocating what in a small island economy is the most scarce and precious of all resources – land. And if planners within the system are becoming aware of the politics of planning, how much more so are applicants or non-applicants outside the system.

Now I do not see this trend as something we should either bemoan or try to suppress. In a society where there is growing pressure on the land – from a growing population, from a growing demand for new uses to be developed, from a growing realisation that scarce resources have to be husbanded and used with care, it is the very essence of an open democratic political process that there should be public debate on and political factors taken into account in the planning and allocation of land. Indeed planners have contributed to this process by the kind of plans they are now producing. Policy orientated plans are bound to produce policy orientated development control, and public debate on plans, will be mirrored by public debate on development control. What then is the relationship between this evolution of planning and planning law?

If, as is being suggested here, there is a need for much more explicit recognition and perforce acceptance of the policy and allocative function of planning, then this must be translated into the law. This in turn means that the town and country planning legislation in every Caribbean state ought to be examined and assessed not for its compatibility with current English law, but for its aptness in providing an appropriate framework for grappling with the existing and likely future planning and development problems of land in each specific state. Furthermore, there should be a recognition that just as plans need to be kept under continuous review and revised where necessary, so too do laws especially planning laws which should not be viewed as a part of the *corpus juris* of the Medes and Persians. Lest anyone think that these ideas are dangerously radical let me assure you that they have the most impeccable legal credentials – English – for we in England make our planning laws fit our local circumstances and change them frequently when political or other factors require it.

If that is one fundamental requirement of planning law in the Commonwealth Caribbean, another is that the law should seek to harness rather than repel the political dimensions to planning. It's there, it's not going to go away and a refusal to take account of it will result in an increasing divorce between the official planning system provided for by the law and the real world of planning operated by politicians and this in turn will increasingly affect the legitimacy of the whole planning system. The law should explicitly allow policy orientated plans and policy documents about land use to be produced; it should encourage, possible even require, opportunities for public debate on plans, policies and major developments;

it should facilitate the harnessing of local community involvement in plan-making, environmental protection and development and it should seek to make explicitly the factors that the planners, on behalf of society, have to have regard to in exercising their powers.

A third requirement is that the most thorough and country specific consideration has to be given to what planning is trying to or can realistically do; too often, the legal tail is wagging the planning dog so that English imports like the Use Classes Order, permitted development etc., become part of the planners' tools of control without much consideration of whether, in practical reality, what they contain bears much or any relationship to what can or needs to be controlled. It may be that a lot less control or different techniques of control could with advantage be pioneered. Only a thorough emancipation from English law will allow Caribbean originality to develop.

Mention may be made too of the role of the legal educator here. Most of the legal policy makers in the Caribbean obtained their legal education in the United Kingdom – at the Inns of Court. Quite understandably, their framework of reference when it comes to legal authorities is English; their knowledge about development and innovation in law is to a large extent confined to England and for many of them, their work has not permitted them to keep abreast even of recent English developments. In these circumstances, in a relatively new field such as planning law it is for the law schools and the legal academics to take the lead in research and writing about the subject and exploring alternative models and their strengths and weaknesses. It cannot be left to practitioners and it should not be left to visiting firemen such as myself.

Increasing emphasis is being laid in international financial and aid agencies on the need for better land management and by better is meant a system of comprehensive land management that combines equity with efficiency and is comprehensive in its coverage. This is as much applicable to rural as to urban land management and indeed the production of Integrated Urban Development Plans which attempt to put the precepts of better land management into practice at the urban level are the urban counterpart of the Integrated Rural or Agricultural Development Plans which have been around in the rural sector for a decade or more. A system of town and country planning has a vital part to play in land management – indeed, it is the foundation, the *sine qua non* of land management and law is in turn the foundation of any system of town and country planning. This then is the challenge facing the lawyers, the planners and the politicians of the Commonwealth Caribbean: to design, enact and then use a law which enables an equable efficient and open system of land management to be pursued in their respective countries.

---

*Presented as a paper at the Second Convocation of the Caribbean Conference for Town and Country Planning, April 1986 and published in a record of the Proceedings of the Convocation.

9 A legal framework for planning and development control: alternative methods for the Madras Metropolitan Area*

Introduction

During the early 1980s, a major programme of innovative planning and development control proposals was pioneered in the Madras Metropolitan Area (MMA), sponsored and guided by the Madras Metropolitan Development Authority (MMDA). These embraced the making of a structure plan for the MMA entitled "Guidelines for Growth" – a joint operation between the MMDA and Alan Turner Associates, a British firm of planning consultants – and a thorough survey and report on the whole field of the management of urban growth, including the vexed question of the extent and effectiveness of the present system of development control, by the same consultants.

This latter report in turn, and perhaps inevitably, raised the question of whether the existing legal framework for planning and development control within the MMA was the most appropriate one for a new era when a more policy oriented approach to land use planning was being introduced (for the MMDA had accepted the policies and approach outlined in Guidelines for Growth) and a more integrated holistic approach to development control reflected in the title of the new study – the Management of Urban Growth in the Madras Metropolitan Area – was being recommended to the MMDA. This chapter considers this question – first summarising briefly the then existing legal framework and its defects and then discussing possible alternative models for the legal regulation of urban growth in Madras.

It should be made clear at the outset that attention will be focused on town and country planning legislation. As in all other states in India, the state of Tamil Nadu has a great array of legislation and public authorities dealing with different aspects of land development, in particular housing and slum clearance,[1] which cannot be, and in the consultants' report, were not ignored, but within the confines of one relatively short paper it is considered better to concentrate on the major and central piece of legislation dealing with land management and urban growth.

Town and country planning law

The present town and country planning legislation applying to the MMA at the time of the preparation of the Structure Plan and the Report on the Management of Urban Growth was the Tamil Nadu Town and Country Planning Act 1971 as amended in 1974 to provide for the creation and powers of the Madras Metropolitan Development Authority, the principal planning authority in the MMA (Rajagopal, 1981). The Act provided for the making of master and detailed development plans, and under the Act, so as to provide for the enforcement of those detailed development plans in the MMA, Development Control Rules for the MMA have been promulgated, providing for a detailed zoning system with equally detailed rules as to the type and style of permitted development within each zone. A good deal of the implementation of these rules was left with the local authorities within the MMA with about 20% of all applications each year being referred to the MMDA for its decision.

As is the case in many other large cities, a great deal of unauthorised development takes place within the MMA, especially within the city of Madras itself; not just the continued development of squatter settlements and the informal economy, but significant developments and changes of uses within the formal economy and construction sector. This type of unauthorised development is by landowners and developers who either do not bother to obtain planning and building permission, or ignore a refusal of permission and subsequent attempts to enforce a refusal – a favoured method being the obtaining of an interim order from the High Court to suspend temporarily an order for the demolition of an unauthorised structure – or obtain permission but then proceed to develop otherwise than in accordance with that permission.

Furthermore, the various public land development agencies operating within the MMA do not pay very much, if any, attention to the master and detailed development plans made by the MMDA and its predecessors, an approach which is made easier by the Act's failure to ensure that priority is given to the plans in the provisions or the resolution of conflicts between such plans and the development proposals of public agencies. The overall picture is, to put it as graphically as possible, on the one hand, an enormous legal edifice of control – the Act and the rules between them are over 200 pages long – operated by officials, many of whom are neither trained nor experienced in planning control, and on the other hand, a large fast growing metropolitan area, with all the manifold problems associated with such a phenomenon, in which the town planning legislation and its administration is at worst completely ignored and at best, seen as a minor irritant to be got round by legal or if need be, illegal means. The divorce between the law in the books and the law on the ground could not be more glaring.

What, in brief, were the main causes of this disjunction between law and practice. It is suggested that they were as follows. First, there was clearly a widespread reluctance, to put it no higher, to accept the need for any sort of public management and control of urban growth. If such a need were accepted in the abstract, it was not accepted in practical or personal terms; individuals believed that controls should take place on land and in respect of developments other than their own. The planning authorities failed to convince the populace of the need for control and management. Secondly the failure of the authorities was a compound of two factors; over rigid and detailed planning and development control and lack of adequate provision for public discussion and debate on plans and policies. Rigid master and detailed development plans as called for by the Act, tend to be out of date long before they are completed; fail to accommodate to a constantly changing urban scene; are too intent on codifying what exists, rather than endeavouring to formulate policies and programmes to guide the future, insofar as that is possible; and are so complex that they are extremely difficult to understand and follow, particularly by untrained local authority officials.

Similar criticism may be made of the Development Control Rules. Their sheer bulk makes them largely incomprehensible and so act as a deterrent to compliance with the law. Changes in zoning needed the approval of the state government; this took time and once again acted as a disincentive to comply with the laws. Furthermore the rules did not reflect the latest thinking on zoning and permitted development which is to reduce the number of zones; broaden out the permitted uses within each zone, and reduce controls as far as possible to what is, and is likely to be seen as, absolutely crucial and fundamental to the welfare, safety and health of the community, and the preservation of the environment (Chandrasekhara, 1980).

Turning to provisions for public debate and discussion on plans, the Act did require that an opportunity be given for comments to be made on a proposed plan and for those comments to be considered before the plan is finally approved. The relevant sections, however, were so open-ended that the style, content and amount of public discussion and consideration of comments was left entirely to the MMDA to determine and there was little encouragement to debate. Public acceptance of the need for planning cannot bring this about but it could be a powerful tool in helping to create the right environment for dialogue and debate on plans and in this respect the Act was sadly deficient. It was even more so in respect of the control of development for there were no provisions which encouraged, let alone required, any public advertisement, discussion or consideration of the views of interested parties on any planning application, so that from the point of view of the ordinary members of the public from whatever income group they are drawn, it matters not whether developments are legal or illegal; they have no say either way. This too is a disincentive to support the law.

Thirdly, brief mention may be made of the role of the courts. It is going too far to argue that the courts are "against" the planners and planning. The courts no doubt share the general scepticism about the rather secretive process which only seems to surface to public viewing when it attempts to stop something happening – it would be odd if they did not reflect and to some extent, whether wittingly or otherwise, help propagate such scepticism – but without going into great detail, a careful reading of cases on enforcement of planning and building controls is that the courts' responses to attempts to control development depends on how those attempts are conducted.

Two cases are instructive here both taken from the area of building controls. The first case is *Ram Awatar v. Calcutta Corporation* (1982),[2] the Calcutta High Court decision in the unauthorised 14-storey building case recently confirmed by the Supreme Court. In that case it was clear that the Corporation had served all the relevant notices correctly; had made repeated attempts, supported by the police, to stop the unauthorised building and arrest the people engaged in the construction work; that all the tenants who moved into the building (the whole of which was an unauthorised structure) did so after a demolition order had been served and knowing fully well that the whole building had been erected in flagrant violation of the law. The courts in other words, supported the correct, vigorous and repeated efforts of the administration to uphold the law.

Contrast with this *Gupta v. Special Officer, Madras Municipal Corporation* (1980).[3] In this case officers of the Madras Corporation had, as found by the High Court of Madras, managed to delay granting a building permission for seven years and in doing so, were motivated by bias and personal animosity towards the petitioner because they disapproved of the granting to him by the Special Officer of a lease of the land on which he wished to build. Again the court found that the officers of the Corporation were acting under powers of the Madras City Municipal Corporation Act which set out specific grounds on which a building permit could be refused yet were purporting to deny a permit on town planning grounds contained in the Town and Country Planning Act. This was something they could not do. The decision of the Corporation was quashed.

The decisions of the courts then are not necessarily obstructive. Even in the area of compensation for compulsory acquisition which has given rise to much constitutional anguish over the years (Meriallat, 1970; Agrawal, 1993), the courts are not noticeably and obviously out of step with the Constitution as amended from time to time as opposed to politicians' and administrators' wishes. Nor have they set about emasculating the Urban Land (Ceiling and Regulation) Act, 1976, an Act designed to limit speculation and hoarding in urban land "with a view to bringing about an equitable distribution of land in urban agglomerations to subserve the common good" (preamble) although the marked lack of enthusiasm with which the Act is being implemented in some states may account for this.

It is not the decisions but the use of the courts, which raises more issues from the perspective of this chapter. Given the inordinate delay in the legal system, a challenge to an administrative decision can delay action for up to three years, sometimes longer. Several challenges on different aspects of a housing agency's operation may effectively bring the total operation of the agency to a halt. Equally, a request, usually granted, for a temporary stay of execution of, *e.g.*, an order to desist erecting a building alleged to be in contravention of the planning or building regulations allows a developer to continue to erect the building; it is much more difficult to justify pulling down a completed building than preventing the erection of it in the first place though as Ram Awatar's case shows the courts are not rigid on the matter.

Given all these deficiencies of the present system, it must seriously be asked whether there is not too ambitious a legal framework for development control and whether a reorganised system with less control being devoted to relatively minor and unimportant matters and more effort being put into controlling and preventing that which is of crucial importance, might not serve both MMDA and MMA better than the present system. Insofar as any new system would reduce the amount of development control, partly in response to the amount of unauthorised development, a counter argument to this must be faced up to. This is the argument by analogy with the law of robbery; one does not alter the law of robbery to the advantage of the robbers because one has difficulty in preventing robbery. The analogy is not a true one: robbery is generally and instinctively known by virtually everyone to be wrong; social practices and beliefs are harnessed by the law to control robbery. As has been pointed out, the same thing cannot be said for unauthorised development and its control; indeed in some respects, amongst the economically weaker section of the population (EWS), unauthorised development is a precondition to official acceptance and assistance. The analogy with the law of robbery is useful in one respect however: it suggests that control of development might have more chance of public and official support if it concentrated on matters clearly seen by everyone to be necessary of control.

Such an approach would in fact be more in keeping with the approach to planning adopted by the structure plan, which focuses on strategic policies and recommends making the best use of existing resources which maximise their cost-effectiveness. It does not propose policies which would necessitate the detailed control of all land use but rather proposes policies which direct attention to key land use issues. Development control should follow this approach rather than, as at present, be at cross-purposes to it.

Reforms to the system of town and country planning

Two possible new approaches to develop control may be suggested, the first of which moves right away from the traditional zoning approach hitherto followed in the MMA, the second of which is based on the proposals of Chandrasekhara cited earlier. The first approach involves moving from a zoning system to a type-of-development based system. Rather than the whole of MMA being divided up into different use zones with uses therein graded as normal, MMA would be seen as one planning entity with two different types or "islands" of special control located at different places within the one entity. Outside the islands, there would be very little development control, the presumption being that any proposed development was permissible and could only be prevented on certain clearly stated grounds.

The "islands" would be of two kinds – developments of special significance and areas of special importance. In the first case, applications to develop would be made to and decided by MMDA. The types of development to be covered would be set out in the rules together with a provision that the minister could add other developments to the list. The criteria to be taken into account in assessing and deciding on the applications would be set out in the rules.

Areas of special importance could either be protected by special legislation, *e.g.*, a Wetlands Protection Act to protect aquifers, tanks, etc., or by a special area plan or both, and within a special area, any proposal for development, other than relatively minor extensions to buildings or changes of use, would again need permission from MMDA. Areas of special importance could include both areas subject to a great deal of development pressures and undeveloped areas that needed to be kept entirely or largely free of development.

The second possibility is to reduce the number of zones at present provided for in the Development Control Rules from ten to five and reverse the presumption of much of what could be developed in the zones. In the words of Chandrasekhara (pp. 58–59):

> With flexibility as the aim the proposed Model Land Use Zoning Regulations ... indicate only 5 zones, *i.e.*, predominantly industrial, open space and parks, and predominantly agricultural. Also, instead of specifying: *(i)* use permitted; *(ii)* use permitted after appeal, and *(iii)* uses prohibited, what is now attempted is to specify only *(i)* uses prohibited and *(ii)* uses to be allowed after appeal in the 5 zones. Thus uses not specified are considered to be compatible with each other ... The proposal ... attempts to eliminate the strait-jacket approach as in segregated land-use planning procedures and practices largely prevailing hitherto.

These proposals concentrate on a looser, more flexible form of zoning and as such are a major step forward. They could in fact be combined with elements of the proposal for areas of special protection and control, in such a way as to ensure that major decisions on development control were taken by MMDA while leaving less important decisions to the local authorities within MMA assisted, if need be, by planners from MMDA. In this way three important elements of a more effective planning system are brought together: first, greater flexibility and responsiveness to change; second maximum local decision-making and involvement with the system: third, the efforts of the premier planning authority would be concentrated on matters of major metropolitan-wide significance.

The issue of public discussion of plans and development proposals may now be considered and along with that, the method of dealing with appeals from refusals of planning permission and other land use decisions, *i.e.* compensation for compulsory purchase may also be discussed. Here too an alternative to the present system may be suggested. This would be to replace the existing and rather complex appellate systems provided for in the Act including the possibility of public hearings on plans with a Planning Tribunal, sitting if necessary in divisions, to which all decisions on planning matters could be appealed. The Tribunal would be staffed by full-time and part-time lawyers, planners and valuers, presided over by a lawyer of the calibre and status of a High Court judge and would be required specifically to take account of plans, planning policies and other relevant matters when hearing appeals. In addition to the parties to the appeal having a chance to put their case forward, provision could also be made for the Director of Town and Country Planning to be allowed, as *amicus curiae*, to address the Tribunal and even, if it were thought appropriate, objectors to the proposal or decision being appealed. When considering objections to and representation about development plans, the Tribunal would allow all those making objections and representations to be heard, and would make a reasoned set of recommendations to the Minister or other relevant authority having the final decision on a plan; in all other cases the tribunal would give a decision.

This kind of forum of which examples are to be found in Australia, Canada, Zimbabwe and within the UK, in Northern Ireland, can be and is, used to build up a jurisprudence of planning policy on a case by case basis. It provides an answer to the problems already identified of reconciling: (a) the need for some flexibility in the system of development control (b) a reluctance to admit too much administrative discretion into the system, and (c) the desirability of more open and public debate about, and acceptance of development control. In a society which pays great regard to the judicial process and in which judicial decisions play a major role in the planning process, a prestigious Planning Tribunal developing planning policies on a case by case basis would seem an ideal institution to create, through which understanding of and respect for the system of planning could be built up.

Conclusion

A more flexible system of zoning, a relaxed approach to development control, a Planning Tribunal as the principal forum for public discussion and decision-making on plans, planning applications and appeals would together with the Structure Plan represent a significant change of style and approach to planning and development control in the Madras Metropolitan Area. They would also require fundamental changes to the Town and Country Planning Act which was enacted barely a decade ago, and to the powers and duties of the MMDA also barely ten years old. But this should not be a cause for concern. Laws, least of all planning laws, are not to be regarded as immutable and when the case for change has been made out, nothing is to be gained by putting off the legislative implementation of change. At the same time, legislation is the beginning not the end of change, it provides the opportunity to implement a new approach which can only be seized if those concerned are convinced of the need for, and committed to the changes. The signs in Madras are good in this respect and one can look forward with confidence to the future evolution of planning and development control in the Madras Metropolitan Area.

---

*First published in 1983, Vol. XV (4) *Nagarlok*, pp. 79–87, the Urban Affairs Quarterly of the Centre for Urban Studies of the Indian Institute of Public Administration (IIPA). The paper is based on work carried out as part of the team of consultants working with the Madras Metropolitan Development Authority. Madras has now been renamed Chennai but the title of this chapter has been left unchanged and reflects the names of places and agencies in use when the work on which the chapter is based was done.

Notes

1 *e.g.*, the Tamil Nadu Slum Clearance Board established by the Tamil Nadu Slum Areas (Clearance and Improvement) Act, 1971 and the Tamil Nadu State Housing Board established by an Act of the same name in 1961.

2 AIR 1982, Cal, 315.

3 1980 (2) MLJ 39.

10 Land tenure, the urban poor and the law in Bangladesh: implementing the Habitat Agenda*

Key aspects of the Habitat Agenda relating to land tenure

The Istanbul Declaration on Human Settlements and the Habitat Agenda provide the international policy and legal context for this overview of the policies, laws and practices relating to urban land tenure in Bangladesh. The Government of the Peoples' Republic of Bangladesh was represented at the City Summit in June 1996 which adopted and approved these two documents. In the eyes of international lawyers, these documents are examples of "soft" international law which give rise to what might be called quasi-legal obligations which cannot be enforced by any international law enforcement agency. Nevertheless, by agreeing to these documents, all governments represented at that Summit put themselves under an obligation – part legal, part moral – to begin the process of reviewing their policies, laws and practices to bring them into line with the principles enshrined in the Declaration and the Agenda. At the outset of this chapter therefore, it is essential to set out the principal provisions of both the Declaration and the Agenda relating to land so that the international legal bench-marks against which the existing provisions may be assessed and any proposals for change may be judged are there for all to see.

It is readily acknowledged that these bench-marks cannot be the only criteria against which existing and possible future policies and laws on urban land tenure in Bangladesh must be measured. It may be suggested however that significant departures from the principles agreed to in Istanbul will need to have a clear and reasoned justification since these principles have behind them the aim of advancing the welfare of the people by making "cities ... places where human beings lead fulfilling lives in dignity, good health, safety, happiness and hope". Any significant departure from these principles then would need to show that the same ultimate goal would be achieved, notwithstanding those departures.

A start may be made from the Istanbul Declaration. Two principles relating to land are set out:

> 8. We reaffirm our commitment to the full and progressive realisation of the right to adequate housing as provided for in international instruments. To that end, we shall seek the active participation of our public, private and non-governmental partners at all levels to *ensure legal security of tenure, protection from discrimination and equal access to affordable adequate housing for all persons and their families.*
> 9. We shall work to expand the supply of affordable housing by *enabling markets to perform efficiently and in a socially and environmentally responsible manner, enhancing access to land and credit and assisting those who are unable to participate in housing markets* [italics added].

The Habitat Agenda is in three parts; Goals and Principles, Commitments, and the Global Plan of Action (GPA). Under Commitments, Governments commit themselves to:

> Providing legal security of tenure and equal access to land to all people, including women and those living in poverty ...
> Ensuring transparent, comprehensive and accessible systems in transferring land rights and legal security of tenure.
> Protecting all people from and providing legal protection and redress for forced evictions that are contrary to law, taking human rights into consideration and when evictions are unavoidable, ensuring, as appropriate, that alternative suitable solutions are provided.

Turning to the GPA, the Commitments are fleshed out in a series of specific actions based on the strategy of "enablement, transparency and participation" which will in turn assist Governments to establish, *inter alia*, legislative frameworks to enable the achievement of adequate shelter for all. A range of actions are proposed for ensuring access to land and security of tenure which are stated to be "strategic prerequisites for the provision of adequate shelter for all and for the development of sustainable human settlements ..." While recognising the existence of different systems of land tenure and national laws, Governments are enjoined to:

> strive to remove all possible obstacles that may hamper equitable access to land and ensure that equal rights of women and men related to land and property are

protected under the law. The failure to adopt, at all levels, appropriate rural and urban land policies and land management practices remains a primary cause of inequity and poverty (para. 75).

Thirty-two specific actions are then proposed in respect of land. Amongst the most pertinent to the subject-matter of this report, the following may be highlighted:

recognise and legitimise the diversity of land delivery mechanisms;

consider the adoption of innovative instruments for the efficient and sustainable assembly and delivery of land, including, where appropriate, land readjustment and consolidation;

develop appropriate cadastral systems and streamline land registration procedures in order to facilitate the regularisation of informal settlements, where appropriate, and simplify land transactions;

develop land codes and legal frameworks that define the nature of land and real property and the rights that are formally recognised;

support the development of land markets by means of effective legal frameworks, and develop flexible and varied mechanisms aimed at mobilising lands with diverse juridical status;

review restrictive, exclusionary and costly legal and regulatory processes, planning systems, standards and development regulations;

adopt an enabling legal and regulatory framework based on an enhanced knowledge, understanding and acceptance of existing practices and land delivery mechanisms so as to stimulate partnerships with the private business and community sectors, specifying recognised types of land tenure and prescribing procedures for the regularisation of tenure, where needed;

provide institutional support, accountability and transparency of land management, and accurate information on land ownership, land transactions and current and planned land use;

explore innovative arrangements to enhance security of tenure, other than full legalisation which may be too costly and time-consuming in certain situations, including access to credit, as appropriate, in the absence of a conventional title to land.

Four other actions from the heading "Popular participation and civic engagement" may be noted as these have a very direct bearing on the development and implementation of land management in accordance with the principles and actions set out above:

facilitate the legal recognition of organised communities and their consolidation;

provide access to effective judicial and administrative channels for affected individuals and groups so that they can challenge or seek redress from decisions and actions that are socially and environmentally harmful or violate human rights...;

broaden the procedural right of individuals and civil society organisations to take legal action on behalf of affected communities or groups that do not have the resources or skills to take action themselves;

facilitate access to decision-making and planning structures and legal services by people living in poverty and other low-income groups through the provision of such facilities as legal aid and free legal advice centres.

If one were to sum up the principal message of these provisions, it is that while a strategy of enablement is to be the preferred mechanism for providing access to land and ensuring security of tenure, the role of governments does not stop at enabling land markets to operate efficiently and transparently, important though these matters are. Governments must also direct their attention to considerations of equity in the operation of land markets – land markets must be enabled to work for the benefit of all and all must be enabled to participate on an equal and fair footing in the land market – and to this end, government at all levels and civil society must be involved in working with the disadvantaged and the poor, removing obstacles to their obtaining land, developing innovative mechanisms, instruments and institutions to assist such persons to obtain access to land and security of tenure via the market, and governments must desist from actions which penalise such persons and lessen their opportunities to obtain and hold on to land.

An important mechanism to bring about the changes necessary to comply with these principles is the law: reforms in the law to develop an appropriate legal framework to facilitate access to land and security of tenure for all people is a *leitmotif* which runs through that part of the GPA dealing with ensuring access to land and helps explain the provisions on access to justice and legal advice in the section of the GPA on popular participation and civic engagement; new laws directed to assisting the poor and disadvantaged however good they may look on paper will change nothing unless active steps are taken to ensure that the laws are implemented and one of the best ways to facilitate that is to assist the beneficiaries of the laws to access and use them to their advantage.

With the background of the Habitat Agenda on the land issue on relation to shelter and human settlements set out and explained, this paper can now turn to a consideration of the urban situation in Bangladesh.

The urban problematique in Bangladesh, with special reference to urban land

Urbanisation in Bangladesh

Over the last decade, a great deal has been written both in official publications and in academic commentaries on the urban situation in Bangladesh and the principal issues on urban land arising therefrom. This section will draw on those writings rather than trying to develop an original analysis.

"Over the last four decades, a substantial urban population increase has taken place in Bangladesh, both in absolute terms and as a percentage of the total population. In 1961, the urban population was 2.6 million people, or only 4.8% of the total population." According to the figures contained in the Bangladesh National Report to Habitat II from which the foregoing quotation comes, the urban population of Bangladesh in 1993 was 23 million which represented just over 20% of the total population. Projections in that report suggested that by 2000, the urban population could be 37 million, representing just over 26% of the total population. Other projections suggest that the urban population is more likely to be around 30 million by 2000. The bulk of the urban population is contained in four cities – Dhaka, Chittagong, Khulna and Rajshani which between them contain about 50% of the urban population. There are however over 200 urban centres with populations from 10,000 to just below 1 million.

According to the Bangladesh Urban and Shelter Sector Review (BUSSR) prepared by UNCHS (Habitat) in 1993, there are both push and pull factors behind this rapid urbanisation. Push factors include increasing rural landlessness and pauperisation of the rural population; the agricultural sector cannot absorb the increasing numbers of the labour force. Natural hazards and disasters too act as push factors.

Pull factors are the assumed or real opportunities for employment in urban areas together with better opportunities for education, health care and other economic and social developments. These may often not materialise but to those from rural areas aspiring to better themselves, the chance is worth taking. It is too the case that the country's efforts to develop industries and in particular the location of industries in the major cities act as a magnet to rural migrants. Despite several government programmes to slow down or even reverse rural-urban migration, the long-term trend is likely to continue.

Accompanying rapid urbanisation has been increasing urban poverty. BUSSR states as follows (pp. 17, 21):

> In recent years, poor landless peasants escaping rural poverty by moving to the cities have brought a new dimension to the poverty sphere. Of the 23 million urban population, more than 50% are poor, while about 30% are considered as hard-core poor or those who are on the border-line of starvation. These are the families whose monthly household income is less than Tk2600, considered adequate to meet at least the daily calorie intake requirement and pay for some other basic needs. Literacy rates among the urban poor are very low (20–30%), less than 30% of the houses have a piped water supply and less than 20% have access to proper sanitation facilities, and there has been an overall decline in caloric intake (from 2310 in 1965, down to 2094 in 1975/76 and down again to 1943 in 1985/86).
>
> Poverty is now widespread in towns and cities in Bangladesh. The incidence of urban poverty resulting from the rapid urban growth is indicated by the proportion of squatters and slum dwellers. In many of the slums, overall conditions are worse than those in rural areas.
>
> Low-income patterns in urban Bangladesh ensure that access to shelter and land is limited to the relatively small percentage who can afford to pay the price. In Dhaka, an estimated 70% of the urban households are low-income, with 28% middle income and 2% high-income. The small proportion of high-income households has access to 15% of the residential land while the vast majority of low-income households has access to just 20%. Similar distributions are understood to apply in the three other metropolitan cities.

These points on urban land may now be elaborated.

Urban land

According to Chowdhury (1992) the availability of urban land for housing and other purposes was then in a critical situation in Bangladesh with the very high price for land in urban areas testimony to that fact. Since no particular policy or practical initiatives have been taken since that date to ameliorate the situation, and the price for urban land remains extremely high (Hoek-Smit, 2000), it may be taken that the situation remains at a crisis point. The crisis is caused by the mismatch between demand and supply of urban land. Demand comes from the continued in-migration of population from rural areas with the consequent need for somewhere to live, from foreign remittances and from urban uses such as offices, factories and roads.

The lack of supply comes from a variety of factors. First, as will be discussed in more detail in the next section, there are legal and administrative barriers to the easy conversion of rural land to non-agricultural purposes via the land market. Where such conversion has taken place, there are further legal and administrative hurdles to overcome before the land may be developed for urban purposes. This is not to say that such conversion and development does not take place. According to Islam and Khan (1992) the participants of fringe land development have tended to be either individual households or public sector agencies. The former are the rural land owners who, without obtaining any of the necessary permissions, sub-divide and sell the land to individuals who thereafter build their houses in an incremental fashion. The same authors report that private housing developers are now beginning to buy land in fringe areas, sub-divide it with permission and provide housing thereafter.

According to Faizullah (1997, pp. 58–59), there are three sets of operators in the urban land market: the buyers, the sellers and the intermediaries:

> Buyers and sellers mostly operate through mutual contact on person to person basis ... However over the years, with increase in demand for land, intermediaries have come up and today they play an important role in urban land market. The first of these intermediaries are ... *dalals* or brokers who perform the role of middlemen ... The second group ... are the developers who are engaged in real estate business in an organised manner ...
>
> Comparable to the developers or real estate agencies there exist housing cooperatives registered with the Cooperative Department of the government ...
>
> The *modus operandi* of the real estate agencies and cooperative housing societies are similar in some respects. Both procure land through direct purchase and develop it on a site and service formula ...
>
> Of late a new class of operators have entered the urban land market, particularly in Dhaka. These are small real estate agencies who look for individual parties owning small parcels of land in high value areas and enter into a joint venture agreement with the owner on a formula to deliver some cash and a number of constructed flats to the land owner [sic] ...
>
> Apart from the above categories of private operators, a new class of underground operators have of late become active in many urban areas ... They

are land grabbers who illegally and at times forcibly occupy vacant government land or even private land. Once occupied, they would either set up slums or sell out the land in a clandestine manner, taking advantage of numerous loopholes in law.

Second, Chowdhury (1992) considers that speculators in the urban land market hold significant amounts of land especially in fringe areas and this too creates pressure on the supply of such land. These speculators would be some of the above private sector intermediaries.

Third, public sector agencies use the powers provided by the Acquisition and Requisition of Immovable Property Ordinance, 1982 to acquire land for public purposes. While the public purposes include the construction of public buildings, land has been allocated for residential purposes and these purposes have on occasions been executed by the private sector. In Dhaka in particular, there has been significant conversion of rural to urban land via public acquisition with some of the converted land being officially used for the resettlement of low-income dwellers from unauthorised settlements within the city, and other areas, originally acquired to be retained as agricultural land, converted unofficially into lower middle class residential areas. Faizullah (1997) considers that "government agencies like RAJUK, CDA, KDA, RAD and HSD" are the most important operators in the urban land market. According to Chowdhury (1992, p. 117) however, "Public sector intervention has gone against the enlargement of the supply of urban land. Areas acquired by government agencies and later distributed for private housing have become low density areas."

Chowdhury (1992) cites a fourth reason for the dearth of supply of urban land. He states that a large amount of vacant land within cities is not released for use. "In Dhaka city, two-thirds of the land within the urban area are vacant or underutilised. In Chittagong, roughly two-thirds of the land in the urbanised area is held by three government agencies. Significant portions of this land area is vacant or in low intensity use" (p. 117). He considers that underutilised vacant land is of significant amount in other urban areas also. The BUSSR opines that "with adequate flood-protection and the development of a fully-functioning land market, there is sufficient underutilised land in Dhaka to cater for double the existing population" (p. 25) and that the non-use of this land for addressing the urban shelter shortage is caused by a failure of institutional capacity within government, a problem which it regards as being extensive and not confined to this one matter. It may indeed be classified as a fifth reason for the dearth of supply of urban land. Set against these views however, the position of Government is that there is a scarcity of land for development in the urban areas, other than on the outskirts of towns, and with building costs being very high, it is not possible to allocate much land for low-income housing within urban areas.

The effect of the mismatch between supply and demand is inevitable: the distribution of land ownership in urban areas is unequal and skewed. Most of the detailed research into this matter has focused on Dhaka with virtually all studies making use of work carried out by Islam and published in 1992. In that study, he showed that 57% of the population of the city owned no land while 4% owned as much as 28% of the city's land. In terms of access to land – via ownership, renting or squatting – he showed that 2% of the city's population – the upper-income group – used about 15% of the land; another 28% who form the middle-income group occupied about 65% of the land and the remaining 70% who constituted the urban poor had access (mostly non-owned) to only about 20% of the residential land. Their access was either via a tenancy or as illegal occupiers.

Even if the situation in Dhaka was and remains particularly bad, it is not to be supposed that the situation in the other principal urban areas differs in substance though it may differ in degree. The urban poor everywhere lack access to land and where they do actually occupy land, the amounts per household are extremely small, and there is no security of tenure. Where they are legally in occupation as tenants, private landlords will dispossess them if greater income earning opportunities present themselves in relation to land occupied by such tenants, such laws as there are on the protection of tenants on non-agricultural land being generally ignored. Where they are occupying private land as squatters, either illegally or with the tacit acquiescence of the landowner they are liable to be dispossessed for the same reason but in addition they are liable to be subjected to the depredations of "muscle men" (Paul-Majumder *et al.*, 1996) demanding "ground rent", *i.e.*, protection money. Where they are illegally occupying government land, they are liable to be evicted at any time and often with minimal or no warning and suffer too from the attentions of the muscle men. In both private and government land squatter settlements, there is for some, the additional insecurity factor of being tenants of a squatter landlord. It is this lack of access to urban land and lack of security on land once accessed by the urban poor that this report focuses on.

Management of urban land

It is necessary now to set out and comment on the governmental institutions with responsibilities for the management of urban land. They may be divided into two: local governments and central government agencies. On local governments, Faizullah (1997, pp. 47, 48) comments:

> According to the Local Government Division of the Government of Bangladesh, there are 115 urban local governments (ULGs) operating in the country (as of 1994) ... The scope and involvement of the ULGs in urban land related matters is rather limited. The limited functions vested in them in respect of master plan is also not performed for lack of manpower, expertise and resources. In the corporation cities, the task of preparing the master plan is carried out by the respective development agencies. In the pourashavas, this is done by the Urban Development Directorate (UDD). In these circumstances the ULGs do not have any vital operational responsibility or control in respect of urban land. Hence they tend to be ineffective.

It is then central government Ministries and agencies which exercise the functions of urban land management. First and foremost is the Ministry of Lands. It exercises management functions over all land in the country and no distinction is made between urban and rural land. Its responsibilities include the collection of Land Development Taxation (LDT); land use planning; land reforms and their implementation; and the undertaking of various development programmes relating to land. Faizullah comments that "the Ministry exercises rigid control over all agencies under it. As a result many matters which otherwise fall within the competence of the field agencies end up in the Ministry for decision".

The Ministry has three attached departments, namely the Land Appeal Board, the Land Reforms Board and the Directorate of Land Records and Surveys. Land management functions are carried out at field level through the Commissioner at the division level, the Deputy Commissioner at the district level, the Thana Nirbahi Officer the Assistant Commissioner (Land) at the thana level and the Tehsildar at the Union level. The Land Reform Board was set up to supervise the functioning of the field offices and the implementation of land management and reform efforts. The Land Appeal Board was established to deal with the large volume of appeals against the decisions of the Divisional Commissioners/Additional Commissioners on land matters. In addition to dealing with appeals, the Board also provides advice and recommendations to the Government on laws, orders and rules applicable to land as and when asked to do so.

Periodic surveys to update records of land ownership and use are undertaken by the Directorate of Land Record and Survey within the Ministry. Although urban areas change faster then rural areas, no special provision is made to survey urban areas more frequently than rural areas. Thus knowledge within the Ministry about urban land is rarely up to date.

The same point may be made about the Collector (Deputy Commissioner), the official of central government set up in the districts to carry out most of the functions of land management. These include maintaining the record-of-rights, separation and mutation, collection of land tax, lease and settlement of government lands, resolution of certain classes of land disputes and land demarcation.

> No separate or exclusive mechanism exists for the urban areas, although the work load of urban units in virtually all respects, is much greater and more complex. As a result, each town or city come under the jurisdiction of one or more thana land offices under each of which there would be several tahsil offices. Although in the big cities like Dhaka some thana land offices and tahsil offices have exclusive jurisdiction, the jurisdiction of others would extend over urban as well as rural areas ... The tahsil office being the lower tier of land management hierarchy ... most actions end up at the tahsil office (Faizullah, 1992, p. 50).

Siddiqui (1997, pp. 386 *et seq.*) is very critical of the field level management operations of the Ministry of Lands. The following summarises his overall position:

> Most of the Union Land Officers are still working without proper accommodation, furniture, equipment, necessary forms and registers, stationery etc. Records are maintained haphazardly, making retrieval difficult and time-consuming. The style of work is old, with no typewriters, and calculators. A development programme is underway to improve the situation but progress has been very slow. Computers have been provided to Divisional Commissioners and the Thana Land Officers will hopefully have computers.
>
> Due to lack of trained and motivated manpower in the Union and Thana Land Offices delay occurs in the discharge of their functions. These offices are also noted for inefficiency and corruption. As the land records are not updated, there is scope for creating confusion, which leads to corrupt practices. Most of the people are illiterate; they are not aware of the land laws and policies, so there is harassment by unscrupulous land management officials ....

Comments made by participants at the Seminar on Secure Tenure in November 1999 (Nazrul Islam, 2000), tended to support these strictures.

The record-of-rights is a system of land records kept for revenue purposes and is therefore fundamental to land management. It has been in existence for over 100 years and is now governed by the East Bengal State Acquisition and Tenancy Act 1951 and the rules made thereunder. It consists of written records and large-scale maps. The maps give the natural features, boundaries and numbered plots while the written record gives details of the owners, numbers of their holdings, class of land and rent to be paid. The procedures which have to be followed in preparing or revising the record-of-rights are complex and time-consuming and need not be rehearsed here.

General revisions are meant to take place every 20th year but irrespective of that, record-of-rights are meant to be maintained and updated at the sub-district level as reports about transfers, subdivisions, amalgamations, should come in on a regular basis from tahsilders. When they do, the parties to the changes should be notified of that fact and asked to come to the sub-district office to confirm the change after which the record-of-right is altered. According to HIFAB International and MARC (1992) parties never turn up so the records are rarely altered. Similarly, notices of transfers registered under the Registration Act should be sent from the land registration offices to the sub-district office but the same report notes that the duplicate records which are sent are illegible and in any event do not record the position on the ground because of illegal land use changes and fraud in relation to the land records.

Central government is intimately involved in the acquisition of urban land. As noted above, land is acquired by the government under the Acquisition and Requisition of Immovable Property Ordinance, 1982, a successor Act to the old Land Acquisition Act of 1894. District Land Allocation Committees (DLAC) and a Central Land Allocation Committee (CLAC) were set up in 1976 to operate the process of compulsory acquisition in order to "arrest what at the time was considered as a practice of too lavish a use of land and 'to ensure the most rigid measures of economy in the use of land for purposes other than agriculture'." (HIFAB International and MARC, 1992). DLACs consider allocations, *i.e.* applications to acquire, up to five acres and the CLAC consider allocations over five acres. Where more land is acquired than is needed, while it may temporarily be allowed to remain in the occupation of the erstwhile owners, government agencies do not release the excess land and return it to those former owners, a practice sanctioned by the courts in a decision in 1998, and a cause of much of the vacant and underutilised government land within urban areas noted above.

Government agencies involved in land development may briefly be noted. The Housing and Settlements Directorate (HSD) and the Public Works Department (PWD), both of the Ministry of Works and Housing are significant developers. The HSD has executed housing projects for low and middle income families and has also developed housing for squatters. Faizullah (1992) argues that the activities of HSD has the effect of increasing land prices and the general prestige of the neighbourhood with the knock on effect that not only are the original owners pushed out through land acquisition but people generally in the neighbourhood are pushed out as land speculators and higher income people buy up the land. He does not fully explain how this comes about – it seems unlikely where HSD develops housing for squatters – but it may be that it is the servicing of the land acquired by HSD which has the effects noted.

Faizullah (1992, p. 53) also notes that the Local Government Engineering Department (LGED) "is an emerging one [agency] in respect of urban land" but in the same paragraph, he states that "the projects of the agency do not involve land question". This apparent conflict may be reconcilable on the basis that the LGED neither acquires or directly develops land although its engineering activities involve the use of land. In any event, LGED and through it, the Ministry of Local Government is well aware of the urban land access and tenure problems of the urban poor. Finally, "In the four metropolitan cities of the country, the role of respective specialised development agencies like RAJUK (the Development Authority for Dhaka), CDA, KDA and RDA is quite prominent. These agencies mainly go for site and service based development of residential enclaves for higher income group."

In relation to Dhaka, RAJUK argues that there are very considerable obstacles to its providing *in situ* rehabilitation for squatters; land grabbing by "big shots"; squatting on land already allocated to other uses and constant legal challenges to their attempted exercise of powers were three such problems mentioned at the November 1999 Seminar. It is for this reason that RAJUK favours and has undertaken several large-scale programmes of relocating squatters to areas on the outskirts of Dhaka. There was however, very strong criticism of RAJUK's policies and practices at the Seminar; it was accused of evicting the urban poor and giving over their land to the elites and of not following its own Master Plan in relation to land development. The World Bank's report on urban issues in Bangladesh (1999, p. 25) too is also critical of RAJUK and other urban development agencies for adopting policies and programmes which have "excluded lower income households and the urban poor from effective access and participation in the formal urban land and housing markets".

Overall then, the conclusion that may be drawn from a survey of the central government agencies involved in both managing and developing urban land is that no special arrangements exist for the management of urban land, notwithstanding that such land poses rather different challenges and has rather different needs to the management of rural land and that very little urban land acquisition and development by central government agencies within urban areas is directed to the needs of the urban poor. What needs to be addressed now is whether this is a result of or in spite of government policy.

Policies on urban land

Many commentators have pointed out that there is no national land policy or national land use policy let alone any specific policy on urban land and that these should be developed. Thus, Faizullah (1997) argues that "The issue of urban land needs to be given specific focus by the public management and development agencies. For this purpose urban land management should be separated from the rural land management" (p. 66). Haque (1992), a former Secretary, Ministry of Lands, called for the formulation of an urban land policy and an urban land management policy, a call endorsed by the conclusions of a seminar on urban land management (Islam and Chowdhury, 1992) at which the proposal was made.

In the absence of specific policy documents on land and urban land, the most relevant policy document is the National Housing Policy (NHP) adopted in December 1993. This document is in the process of being revised but at the time of the writing of this chapter in mid 1999, it had not yet been issued for public comment. In the absence of any revised policy document therefore, the published one may be considered. This contains some important statements about land, the most relevant from the perspective of this survey being:

OBJECTIVES

Make available suitably located land at affordable price for various target groups, especially the low and middle-income group …

PROPOSED STRATEGY

Encroachments on public land and formation of unauthorised constructions will be discouraged …

HOUSING POLICY: Essential Elements

Land

Increase the supply of serviced land for housing for various income groups, particularly the poorest …
Increase access of the poorer sections and vulnerable groups to affordable serviced land with secure land tenure in areas located near, or connected by cheap transport to their work places.
… [L]and will be acquired within the framework of land use plan, if there is any. Government would have the option to use acquired land for any purpose including housing …
Encourage the involvement of the private sector in land development …
Abolish the discretionary quota system for allotment of plots developed by the public sector. Special provisions will however be made for the handicapped, the destitute and the very poor through fixation of a special but reasonable quota for them.
Develop a modern Land Information System and an effective system of registration and transfer of land and immovable properties for better management of land.

Legal and Regulatory Framework

… measures for removing the legal constraints would cover the following:

Making revision of land use plans, planning and building regulations and infrastructure standards by the Government and local authorities to … enable efficient use of land …;
Review and amendment of laws and regulations relating to town planning, particularly the norms and standards for *in-situ* upgradation of low-income settlements and housing;
Making suitable laws for ownership of plots … and for easy registration and transfer of property that conform to non-exploitative practices. Adequate steps

will be taken to protect the interests of consumers against dishonest and fraudulent practices of private developers and to increase the supply of developed land specially for low and middle income groups ...
Removal of constraints to the flow of finance into housing and services, especially larger lending to the poor and in the informal sector household through flexible procedures and collateral requirements as well as repayment schedules and simplification of procedure for registration of documents and execution of mortgages.

Slums and Squatter Settlements

Keeping in view the policies of planned growth of urbanisation, income support and poverty alleviation, and together with steps to arrest the growth of new slums in urban areas, the Government would take steps to:
Encourage *in-situ* upgradation, slum renovation and progressive housing development with conferment of occupancy rights, wherever feasible, and to undertake the relocation of the squatter settlements from the sites that need to be cleared in public interest.

Policies on urban land for housing directed to the urban poor then focus on:

- making land available to the urban poor either by acquisition by Government or through the market and where the latter is to be used, improving, cleaning up and speeding up the process of land transfer and title security via registration;
- revising planning, development control and building control laws to help reduce the cost of housing; and
- a mix of on the one hand, upgrading slums and squatter settlements including the conferment of occupancy rights, and, on the other, the relocation of such settlements.

A second policy document that must be noted is the Bangladesh National Report to Habitat II (BNR) prepared in 1996. This document does not make any specific policy statements about urban land tenure as such but in the section of the Report dealing with the identification of projects over a five year period, a subproject within the Project: Improvement of Access to Land, Finance and Housing is suggested (p. 55):

Improving efficiency of urban land markets through legal/procedural reforms and rationalising urban control mechanisms. This approach is related to efficient transaction under market price but checking illegal possession of land through land titling with computerisation. Intermediaries, *i.e.*, the 'dalals' should be licensed to check malpractices in land transfers in the private sector.

This subproject is aimed to meet the goal of the National Programme to "... simplify procedures for the transfer of land, encourage the involvement of the private sector in land development and increase access to serviced land and secure land tenure and renting for the poor and disadvantaged". There is, perhaps rather surprisingly, no specific project or subproject directed to issues of urban land currently occupied by slums and squatter settlements.

Some comments are in order on these policies.

From information derived from interviews, it appears that no specific actions have yet been taken to implement the NHP in relation to improving access to land and security of tenure for the urban poor. Action has been taken however in the provision of housing for the urban poor away from their present locations. Government is adopting a New Towns policy in relation to urban development with plots being made available to low income groups and is also providing loans and land to slum-dwellers who are prepared to return to their original rural areas.

The heavy emphasis placed on improving the operation of the formal land market and in particular on moving to a system of title registration may be misplaced. This is for the following reasons:

(i) there is no evidence that the urban poor operate or are likely for the foreseeable future to be able to operate in the formal land market, either as individuals or via a collective entity such as a cooperative;

(ii) the development of a system of title registration is a very, very long term programme and will be, initially, very, very costly. It is not the case in Bangladesh as it was in *e.g.*, Thailand, where a long-term donor funded programme of title registration has operated over the last decade or more to upgrade an existing system of title registration, but of starting from scratch, in a situation moreover where commentators claim that approximately 80% of the cases pending in the courts concern land disputes and there is widespread fraud in the operation of the present system of deeds registration.[1] It is no exaggeration to suggest that even if title registration focused only on urban areas, it would be well into the twenty-first century before the urban poor gained any appreciable advantage from the system, assuming for the sake of the argument that there would be clear benefits for the urban poor.[2] To give just one example, Kenya introduced its current system of title registration in 1956; the whole country has yet to be covered and there are no discernible benefits accruing to the urban poor.

A clear message from the NHP is that while relocation and resettlement of squatters and slum dwellers is to be an important strand of housing policy, the Government is also committed to upgrading existing settlements and the conferment of occupancy rights on existing occupiers. This represents a major policy shift from currently operated policies and practices which interviewees have stressed do not encompass any form of security of tenure on existing sites for squatters.

There is a clear recognition that existing planning and building control standards need to be revised "downwards" in effect to facilitate the provision of legal housing for the urban poor. This will have an indirect effect on security of tenure by removing or at least lessening one reason for the demolition of such housing, *viz.*, that it does not comply with such laws. This too is a major and welcome policy innovation.

The NHP and the BNR both recognise the need for new laws on urban land matters. However, these laws are to focus more on urban planning and improving the operation of the land market and do not touch on the development of any specific legal framework for urban land management or for upgradation or regularisation of slums and squatter settlements, as some commentators have called for. There is a case for the development of such laws to enable the policies of the NHP to be implemented and the Government to meet its commitments under the Habitat Agenda.

The land law of Bangladesh with reference to urban land

General

The basic land law in Bangladesh does not distinguish between urban and rural land. Many statutory provisions do however and since some of the rural land law impinges on urban land, it will be necessary to summarise and comment on these laws as well as consider in a little more detail specifically urban land laws.

Land law in Bangladesh is based on the common law system of freehold and leasehold title. Both may be either private or Government. The method of obtaining one or the other differs. In the case of Government freehold or leasehold, there are various official procedures which have to be complied with before Government land can be transferred to a private citizen or entity – corporation, cooperative, partnership etc – and these may take some considerable time to complete. In the case of private freehold or leasehold, the legal framework for accessing land, protecting title and setting out the rights and obligations of the parties to any particular transactions is contained in the Transfer of Property Act 1882 and the Registration Act 1908. These two and other relevant laws may briefly be discussed.

The Transfer of Property Act covers both movable and immovable property. The latter is land. The Act sets out the procedures which must be followed in order to transfer property between two living persons and transfers of property include sale, mortgage, lease and gift. In the case of a sale of immovable property, a contract for sale is a contract that a sale of that property shall take place on terms agreed between the parties while the actual transfer of such property of the value of Tk 100 and upwards, can be made only by a registered instrument, that is an instrument registered under the Registration Act.

Leases

A lease likewise, if from year to year or for any term exceeding one year or reserving a yearly rent, can be made only by a registered instrument, but other leases may, if so notified by the Government, be made by unregistered instrument or by oral agreement without delivery of possession (s.107). More important from the point of view of this report is section 108 which deals with the rights and liabilities of the parties to the lease. Those relevant to urban leases may briefly be mentioned. On the lessor's side, the lessor is bound to disclose to the lessee any material defect in the property of which the former is aware and the latter could not be aware; the lessor is bound to put the lessee into possession of the property and shall be deemed to have contracted that provided the lessee pays the rent and performs the terms of the lease, the lessee may hold the property without interruption during the lease.

On the lessee's side, the following are relevant. If the lessor neglects to make, within a reasonable time after notice, repairs which he is bound to make to the property, the lessee may make the repairs and deduct the expense of the repairs with interest from the rent. If the lessor fails to make any payment which he is obliged to make and which is recoverable against the lessee or the property, the lessee may make such payment and deduct it with interest from the rent. The lessee is bound the pay the rent due under the lease. The lessee is bound to keep, and, on termination of the lease, to restore the property in as good a condition as it was in at the time when he was put into possession, subject only to changes caused by reasonable wear and tear or irresistible force and shall allow the lessor or his agents to enter the property to inspect it and shall make good any defect which it is his duty. The lessee may use the property as a person of ordinary prudence would use it as if it were his own but may not, without the lessor's permission erect, any permanent structure on the property.

An important law dealing with tenancy is The Non-Agricultural Tenancy Act, 1949. This Act provides in greater detail than is the case in the Act of 1882 with the rights and obligations of landlord and tenants with respect to, *inter alia*, urban tenancies. A tenant may use non-agricultural land in any manner not inconsistent with any of the purposes for which such land may be held and which does not materially impair the value of the land. The Act specifically permits tenants to erect pucca structures on the land or where there is, essentially, an informal lease for between one and twelve years, any structure other than a pucca structure. There are restrictions on the landlord's ejecting the tenant during the term or after the tenant has exercised his right of renewal. Ejectment may only take place as a result of a decree of a competent civil court. All non-agricultural tenancies may only be transferred by means of a registered instrument in the prescribed form with the sale price or value of the tenancy stated therein. A landlord may not prevent a tenant from making an improvement to the land during the currency of a lease and improvements include laying out of roads, open spaces, providing facilities for taking water and for drainage. Overall then, the aim of the Act is to provide a framework of law to go some way towards ensuring fairness of dealings between landlord and tenants.

Mortgages

Turning now to mortgages, the Act specifies six different types of mortgages; **simple** – the mortgaged property is pledged as security for a loan and can be sold by the mortgagee if the mortgagor does not repay the loan; **conditional sale** – the mortgaged property is sold to the mortgagee on condition that the sale becomes absolute if the mortgage money is not repaid but becomes void and the property is re-transferred if the money is repaid; **usufructuary** – the mortgagor delivers possession to the mortgagee and authorises him to retain possession and receive the rents and profits of the property until the loan is repaid; **English**[3] – where the mortgagor binds himself to re-pay the mortgage-money by a certain date and transfers the property absolutely to the mortgagee but with a proviso that the mortgagee will re-transfer it to the mortgagor if the money is repaid; **by deposit of title deeds** – available only in towns specified by the Government and created by depositing the title deeds to a property with a creditor with the intention to create a security; and **anomalous** – a mortgage which is none of the above. These too, apart from the mortgage by deposit of title deeds, must be made by registered instrument.

The rights and liabilities of the parties to a mortgage reflect the English law as it was in the late nineteenth century. The mortgagor – the borrower – may redeem the mortgaged property on repayment of the loan – that is, obtain back the mortgaged property free of any continuing or collateral obligations to the mortgagee – the lender – and all documents of title relating to the mortgaged property or in the case of a usufructuary mortgage, may recover possession of the mortgaged property. The mortgagee has, in the absence of any contract to the contrary, a right to obtain from the court a decree that the mortgagor shall be absolutely debarred from his right to redeem the mortgage – a decree of foreclosure – or a decree that the property be sold. A mortgagee may also appoint a receiver to receive the income from the property and is also entitled to go into possession of the mortgaged property in certain circumstances. Various other ancillary rights and liabilities are provided for in the law. In relation to land coming within the East Bengal State Acquisition and Tenancy Act, 1950 – to all intents and purposes, agricultural lands – there are certain restrictions imposed on mortgages of such land and special protections for the mortgagors of such land but there are no specific restrictions on mortgages of urban land. This is very much in keeping with the general position which has already been noted; that there is no special urban land law.

Registration

The Registration Act, 1908 provides for the registration of deeds relating to land and other documents. As noted in connection with the TPA, all transfers of land must be made by a registered deed and as a general rule a document has to be presented for registration within four months of the date of its execution. The Act is however silent on the status of a transfer if the relevant document is not presented within the required time and the parties cannot bring themselves within one of the exceptions to the four-month rule. The details of the system of registration provided for by the Act need not be rehearsed here but one or two fundamentals must be noted. The Act provides for a register of deeds and as such, Simpson (1978, p. 19) points out:

> ... so long as the registers remain in essence registers of deeds, not of title, the title will have to be deduced from scrutiny of the relevant deeds instead of resting on the register. What is recorded is merely evidence of title. The evidence may be complete and conclusive but it needs interpretation; an opinion or judgement must be expressed on the strength of it. Investigation is still required and the deeds register, no matter how well kept, is merely an adjunct of this investigation.

The implication of this quote is that it is essential to ensure that documents which are registered are an accurate record of the transaction of which they are the most important evidence. Unfortunately this is not the case with the system provided for under the Act. While the Act and the Rules made under the Act provide for a coherent and organised system of registration, one crucial provision has the effect of rendering the whole system of very limited utility. This is section 52 and the Rule 42 made under the Act. The section provides that:

> ... every document admitted to registration shall without unnecessary delay be copied in the book appropriated thereof according to the order of its admission.

Rule 42 provides that where the relevant official in the Registry is satisfied that what is presented to him is a deed that is registrable in the register, he shall register it without regard to its possible effects. He is not, in other words, to concern himself with whether the deed accurately records what the parties want to achieve; whether third party rights are infringed by the transaction; whether the transaction is fraudulent; or whether the deed is false, a nonsense, wrong or a complete forgery or even whether registration is against public policy or would involve a breach of the peace. His is merely the mechanical function of ensuring that documents presented for registration are copied (by hand) into the relevant folders and the index updated accordingly.

Thus, even if the local registry offices were models of efficiency and records were easily accessible – and it has to be said on the basis of admittedly limited field work, that this is not the case owing both to lack of resources available to the system and the practice of transferring records from the local offices to District Offices and later Headquarters in Dhaka – the records might bear no relationship to what the parties thought they were agreeing to so that the system encourages litigation rather than reduces it as registration is designed to do.

A critique of the land law

Both the Transfer of Property Act, 1882 and the Registration Act, 1908 are venerable pieces of legislation which in some respects have served Bangladesh well. The Non-Agricultural Tenancy Act is 50 years old so it too has had a long life. These laws are, however, very much land law for the minority; that is, the ability to use the laws depends on access to lawyers, to some basic knowledge about one's rights under the law and on being what may be referred to as a legal part of society; that is landlord and tenant laws apply to the legal relationship of landlord and tenant and not the a-legal relationship between squatters and landowners or between squatter landlords and squatter tenants. As pointed out at the Seminar at which this chapter as first discussed, the process of dealing with land through these laws is complex, time-consuming and extremely expensive; indeed, one participant claimed that the costs of land transfer in Bangladesh were the highest in the world.

These laws have really no meaning or relevance to the urban majority – the urban poor. What is noteworthy however is that while they are so old, there does not appear to have been any recent attempt to develop new laws more apt to grapple with the problems of the urban poor; even the Premises Rent Control Ordinance of 1963 assumes the formal relationship of landlord and tenant; that all parties are literate, and that tenants will have access to courts or the Controller to ensure the application of the law. The Controller for instance is not given any proactive role: he or she may only act on the application of a tenant or a landlord. A participant at the Seminar put it thus: "there is no city where landlords and landowners are so lucky: there is no regulation of them."

Even with respect to that part of the housing and urban land market which is within the purview of the land law, commentators in Bangladesh have drawn attention to deficiencies in the law. Huque (1992, p. 48) notes that:

Due to inadequacies in land registration, both land tenure and transfers are insecure in Bangladesh. Insecurities in the tenure system adversely affect the willingness of occupants or property holders to invest their efforts and savings in land development …

The mortgage market is the single most important source to finance urban development programmes like housing.[4] The mortgage market is closely related to security of tenure. When the tenure systems are insecure or inadequately registered, access to an important source to finance urban development projects dries up.

Also noteworthy is that no substantive changes have been made to the basic mortgage law for over 100 years. Some changes were introduced by an amending Act in 1929 but they did not alter the substantive law. The existing law is complex and provides few safeguards for the mortgagor. The finance of house purchase or building through the mortgage market is very much a minority activity confined to the upper income groups in society and to that extent it could be argued that no changes in the law are needed; such groups are well able to look after themselves either through formal legal processes or through informal arrangements. That may be the case but any serious attempt to developing a more appropriate legal framework for the access by the urban poor to land for housing will need to address mortgage law so as to provide a more level playing field for the parties. What might be done will be considered later in this chapter.

No account of the existing law would be complete without at least a brief mention of the situation as regards land disputes. Land disputes concerning ownership of a parcel of land or any person's share in a particular parcel go through an administrative/quasi-judicial process. The complaint starts with an Assistant Commissioner (Lands) and winds its way up to the Land Appeal Board from where a party may submit a writ petition to the High Court. Other disputes, *e.g.*, arising out of the TPA or the Registration Act or landlord and tenant disputes go through the regular judicial system. Even in cases which commence in the administrative system, if the AC (Land) thinks it is beyond his jurisdiction, he refers the matter to the civil courts. Siddiqui (1997, pp. 357–59) puts the situation thus:

Land dispute cases instituted in the civil courts take a long time to resolve. Sometimes it takes 15–20 years to get a final judgement … The number of cases pending for judgement in the District Judge's Court was 275,140 in 1995. The number of cases for which appeals [from the Munsiff (Assistant Judge)]

> have been submitted to the District Judge's Court was 330,246...[A]ccording to one estimate, 60–80% of cases in civil and criminal courts are related to land in one way or another ... These long-pending cases have a negative effect on land use as owners do not feel secure and hence do not go for long-term investments in such land. If the civil courts are slow and sometimes corrupt, it does nor mean that the adjudicating process under the Land Ministry is any better ... However on balance the adjudicating process with the Ministry of Lands is cheaper and more approachable, and hence it is still preferred by the common man.[5] The rich and powerful prefer the civil court because they can afford it ... Local government bodies at the lowest level have some adjudicating powers but they are not generally involved in land disputes in a formal sense. But they have a strong informal role in resolving land disputes ... Some NGOs and peasant organisations have a positive role in the settlement of land disputes through providing legal aid and legal education to the poor people ... [but] ... local level arbitration has to be addressed in a much more innovative manner.

These comments are clearly directed to land disputes in rural areas. Participants at the Seminar however made similar criticisms of the judicial system in relation to urban land disputes although it must be noted that there are lawyers who have used the judicial process successfully on behalf of the urban poor. What is of interest to note however is the existence of an alternative quasi-judicial system for the settlement of rural land disputes; perhaps something similar needs to be developed for urban land disputes. Interestingly, the World Bank in its draft report on urban issues in Bangladesh recommends the introduction of specialised land tribunals/courts for the speedy settlement of land disputes (World Bank, 1999, p. 30).

The most fundamental criticism which may be made of the existing land law is not of the existing laws but of the missing laws; namely laws which address the tenure problems of the urban poor. This is to some extent but only to some extent a failure of policy. The NHP was approved and published in December 1993; it makes repeated references to improving the access of the urban poor to land by simplifying the law relating to registration and transfer procedures; it refers too to developing occupancy rights for the poor in urban areas and to upgradation of slums and squatter settlements. In respect of all these proposed policy initiatives, some kind of legal framework is a necessary, although by itself it is not a sufficient, condition for implementation. It may be that the ambivalence about granting the urban poor any *in situ* rights on land in the urban areas is preventing the development of any law to enable the policies enunciated in the NHP to be implemented but this chapter proceeds on the basis that the

NHP is the existing policy document on land and housing for the urban poor and that appropriate laws can be and should be prepared to enable such policies to be furthered.

Urban planning laws

In urban areas, land use is regulated through the Pourashava Ordinance, 1977 and the Town Improvement Act, 1953 (TIA). Both laws provide that Master Plans must be drawn up for the urban areas to which the laws apply. Siddiqui (1997, pp. 378–79) summarises the position with respect to the Town Improvement Act:

> The Town Improvement Act (section 73) provides that the concerned authority will prepare a Master Plan for the area within its jurisdiction indicating the manner in which the land will be used and the stages by which development will be carried out ... The concerned authority is responsible for the implementation of the Master Plan. The Master Plan may be amended or altered with the permission of the government. However in practice, there have been numerous instances of deviation from land use as laid down in the Master Plan owing to collusion between officials and vested interest groups. In addition, complications have been created by land disputes, contradictory decisions and delays in court procedures.

While a defence of master planning under the TIA was mounted at the Seminar and the point was made that some plans have been developed with the support of UN agencies, there is general agreement amongst commentators that urban planning laws are ineffective in Bangladesh. The following quotations indicate the scope of the problem. Huque (1992, p. 47) states:

> In Bangladesh, formal governmental rules to regulate land use exist in the four metropolitan cities. The Pourasava Ordinance also empowers the local authorities to set and enforce such rules. However, these rule-settings have proved to be highly ineffective. Among probable reasons that may be advanced to explain why, are the following:
>
> lack of consistent policy and undefined priorities
> lack of manpower and managerial skills
> rapidity of urban growth
> rigidity in planning and implementation procedures
> lack of reliable information and knowledge.

Chowdhury (1992, p. 95) focuses particularly on sub-division control:

> In our country, the existing inheritance law allows unfettered freedom for fragmentation of rural as well as urban land. With the passage of time, land parcels are becoming smaller and smaller, rendering some plots as totally 'unplannable' … In the relevant Registration and Land Records Acts there is nothing prohibiting fragmentation. The present Planning Acts and the Building Construction Acts do not appear to provide powers to prevent land sub-divisions ….
>
> … If we do not amend our existing laws to regulate sub-division of land [it] will continue unabated making … efficient planning impossible in urban areas.

Hussain (1995, p. 66) too argues for an enabling law which will provide for the framing of master plans for big cities and urban areas and for special area plans and controls; subdivision controls and zoning controls, notwithstanding their comparatively easy circumvention. Local and urban authorities

> should be given powers to regulate and control land use within their respective jurisdictions and frame rules and bye-laws for creation of control mechanisms to enforce them effectively.

Thus all commentators call for more effective planning systems with the emphasis on comprehensive legislation providing for considerably more powers of intervention into the land market with particular emphasis on the areas of low-income housing. These views were accepted by the participants at the Policy Seminar on Urban Land Management in 1992 where the first two quoted views were advanced where there was general agreement that the planning departments of the major city development authorities such as RAJUK, CDA, KDA and RDA needed strengthening; an Urban and Regional Planning Act should be formulated backed by adequate zoning plans and laws, sub-division regulations and building codes. At the Seminar too, the view was expressed that more effective planning laws were needed.

With great respect to such knowledgeable commentators, it must be doubted whether more regulations over land use will assist the urban poor to access or use land for affordable housing or other uses. One need not necessarily go as far as Home (1997, p. 220) who argues that the problems of "the teeming cities of the so-called developing countries … have their roots deep in the colonial situation and colonial approaches survive in the policies of government and development agencies ... [with] ... a reluctance to allow local land-use planning and regulation to be controlled by democratically elected local authorities" but he is certainly right to note that physical planning has become discredited "following the manifest failure of planners and their associated bureaucracies to order urban growth or improve conditions for most urban dwellers". Rather than seek to increase control and regulation on the assumption that what was missing in the past was a sufficiency of control and regulation, policies and laws on urban land use management should be directed to harnessing the energies of the urban poor and facilitating their acquisition and use of land as the Habitat Agenda makes clear. No less than on land tenure then, reform of urban planning law in Bangladesh needs to be refocused to enable the NHP to be implemented.[6]

The arguments that are being put forward here are that insofar as the law has a role to play in improving the opportunities for the urban poor to gain access to land and to secure tenure, the direction lies both in developing specific laws geared to meeting the needs of the poor rather than continuing to promote the use of laws which have demonstrably failed to meet those needs; in changing the emphasis of laws from regulation to facilitation; and in being prepared to consider fundamental reforms to the basic land laws of the country as a contribution to improving the operation of the land market which in turn might encourage financial institutions and property developers to move into the lower end of the housing market. The arguments were put succinctly if somewhat dramatically by one participant at the Seminar: "better access to land for the urban poor can only be achieved by drastic legal changes."

Before turning to consider possible reforms in more detail, some examples of land law reforms in other and comparable countries directed to the same end of improving access to land and security of tenure for the urban poor is in order. This will show both that what is being proposed here is very much in line with current practices around the world and provide possible models that may be drawn on if and when the Government decides to institute land law reform along the lines of that suggested in the NHP.

A comparative survey

Laws dealing with tenure issues

The Government is at present contemplating major reform in the area of registration of land titles by moving from the present system of deeds registration to one of title registration. Whatever the merits of such a move, it will do little to assist the urban poor unless, as in Thailand, a determined effort is made from the start to develop a system which is simple, easy to operate without the aid of lawyers, transparent and widely decentralised so as to bring it within easy reach of the majority of the population. It should be noted that that the reforms to land titling in Thailand over the last two decades have first, built on systems of land titling which go back to 1901 when land titling based on the Torrens system was introduced into Thailand and second, have been part and parcel of wider reforms directed to urban development – in housing finance and the development of systems of land sharing sanctioned by law (to be considered below).

Some countries have developed systems of title registration specifically geared to the needs of the urban poor as part of a process of the regularisation of informal settlements. A good example of this comes from Peru. There by a law enacted in 1988, a system of registration of titles in informal settlements was introduced which relies on proof of title as determined in the informal sector rather than through formal documentation; uses the community and private lawyers to verify boundaries rather than state officials and decentralises registration rather than locating the process in a centralised system as is the case with the formal slow and expensive system. In less than a decade more titles had been registered through this system than the old formal centralised system had managed in 50 years. The urban poor had obtained effective security for a fraction of the cost that using the formal system would have entailed. It means that Peru has two systems of title registration which purists may see as a disadvantage but registration is a means to an end – the end being better security of tenure. If this is achieved through having two (or even more) systems catering for all classes of the population rather than having just one system catering for a small minority of the population with the urban majority left with insecure tenure with all the social and economic disadvantages that this implies, then multiple systems would seem to be a positive advantage.

The Peruvian example is also noteworthy for the fact that the evidence shows that the new semi-formal title is an acceptable security for the granting of mortgages. Zambia too in the 1970s developed a simple system of registration of title in informal settlements operated by local authorities – based on the complicated centralised system which had never catered for more than a very small minority of the population – as part of a programme of upgradation of the settlements and this title too was accepted as adequate security for housing loans even though it only provided for a renewable 30 year right of occupancy. South Africa too is developing, via a Registry Facilitation Act, a simplified system of registration as part of its programme of land tenure reform. Namibia is going one step further down this route: it has legislated for a new form of urban tenure – what might be called quasi or interim freehold which only needs a simplified form of survey and registration and is a first step towards full freehold for those living in informal settlements in urban areas. In Malaysia too, a "qualified title" is a title which may be issued in the absence of a full survey of the land and with less formalities than a full title; it gives just as good security but at less cost and more speedily as a full title and is credited with greatly facilitating the operation of the land market in that country.

Certain states in India have also gone down the route of regularising squatter settlements on the basis of providing security of tenure and better facilities for the settlements. A good example is the state of Madhya Pradesh which, through its "Patta Act" of 1984, grants leasehold titles or "pattas" to squatters and through the Madhya Pradesh Slum Area Act of 1976 provides for upgradation of slums where titles have been granted.

A further step down the route of cooperating with the informal sector comes from the activities of the Hyderabad Development Authority (HAD) in Pakistan. The Authority has in effect gone into partnership with private informal land developers (*dalal*); it allows them to occupy land and subdivide it, sell some land for commercial use and use the capital gained to cross-subsidise plots for low-income families. Professional land-grabbers (*thallawalas*) are used to locate and move people to the site. They too are given some plots on the site. The HAD then lobbies for the development to receive utility services. Here, public power backed by law is allied to private profit to produce more land for the urban poor.

Another approach to regularisation and secure tenure is via land pooling or readjustment and land sharing. Land sharing has been pioneered in Thailand, first on the basis of practice but now backed by law. Squatters and the landowner on whose land they are squatting agree that in return for the landowner allowing the squatters to remain on the land, the squatters will move to a part only of the land, thus freeing up some of the land for commercial or other development. The local authority for its part will increase the plot ratio of the development so that the landowner will be able to build to a higher density on that part of the land which has been freed for development than he would have been able to build if he had had the whole plot to build on. In this way the low-income squatters get to stay close to their sources of employment and obtain a secure title to their plot and the landowner/developer gets to build the development he was planning for the site.

Land readjustment for urban development was pioneered in Japan but has since spread to South Korea, Indonesia, India and other countries in Asia. It too is based on community involvement in urban development. A community in an informal settlement agrees to pool or consolidate their land holdings which are then readjusted to facilitate the redevelopment and upgradation of the site. Each occupier of land agrees that a proportion of their holding goes into a common pool which is then available for community purposes – clinics, schools, a better road, open space. Although each person or family might get back less land than they started out with, the holding is likely to be more valuable because it is part of a planned and upgraded development. The key here is that the community has to agree to the scheme; it cannot go ahead without widespread support. Thus in Indonesia, not less than 85% of landowners covering not less than 85% of the total land area have to agree to a scheme before it can go ahead. As with land sharing, so here: occupiers who may have had insecure tenure in an unplanned informal development finish up with a plot with secure tenure in a better planned and serviced development.

A final and slightly different example of legal development on tenure matters comes from Malaysia. Malaysia has a National Land Code and a comprehensive land law which also provides for a system of title registration though the two do not necessarily go together. The Code dates from 1965 though its colonial antecedents go back to 1891. The Code provides a modern comprehensive and comprehensible code of law covering sale of land, leases, mortgages, easements, public regulation of land use via conditions which may be inserted in titles and certain public rights in land such as wayleaves. What is most impressive and perhaps the main lesson to be learned from the Code is the attitude adopted by the Malaysian authorities to its amendment. So often, laws are enacted and then never revised or updated to keep abreast of changing social and economic factors. In Malaysia by contrast, hardly a year goes by without some amendment, maybe small, maybe large and significant like the provision of strata titles, being enacted and incorporated into the Code. In this way the law is a living law, able to accommodate and keep abreast of rapid urban development based on a thriving land market.

On the settlement of land disputes, the World Bank report on urban issues in Bangladesh has suggested that a specialised system of land courts should be set up to deal with land disputes. There does seem to be a trend in that direction. South Africa (to be considered below), Tanzania and Uganda all of whom have recently introduced innovative reforming land laws provide for specialised land courts and tribunals and mediators to deal with land disputes. The State of New South Wales too has had for several years now a specialised land tribunal which handles planning and environmental matters. England too has had a Land Tribunal for 50 years handling specialised land disputes in both public and private land law and has recently re-introduced specialised land tribunals to handle disputes between landlords and tenants. It is worth stressing too that there has been a specialised judicial process for the handling of rural land disputes in Bangladesh of several years now so the precedent is there to be followed.

It is not only tenure laws which provide examples of innovative approaches to grappling with the land needs of the urban poor. It will be noted that many of these innovations are based on a community approach to tenure. There are similar examples of a community approach to financing urban development, particularly mortgages. As Hoek-Smit (2000) shows very clearly, the formal mortgage market is very small in Bangladesh and does not reach below the upper income groups. However, she gives several examples of micro-finance institutions which are beginning to move into housing loans and these developments need to be backed by an appropriate legal framework. Community mortgages where the loan is given to a community organisation which is responsible for repaying the loan and for determining who within the community may receive part of the loan and on what terms have been developed in the Philippines, in Thailand and in Venezuela. The evidence seems to suggest that while informal community credit systems can operate on a very small scale, any replication on a large scale requires the support of the public authorities which in turn will involve the development of innovative laws on the subject.

Urban planning laws

Some of the examples discussed so far have involved a mix of private land law – tenure, titling, mortgages – and public land law – the powers of public authorities to become involved in decisions on land use. Urban planning laws are pre-eminent examples of public land law and ones which have already been commented on in general terms when considering Bangladesh's laws. It has to be said that there is not the same innovative approach to urban planning laws and systems as there is to tenure reform and upgradation.

In too many countries in Asia, particularly countries within the Commonwealth, the model, either explicit or implicit, for planning legislation is still the British system. This is usually inappropriate for the circumstances of towns and cities in Asia. The British system lays great stress on development plans – structure and local plans or unitary development plans (a combination of structure and local plans) is the current vogue – which are then supported by a system of development control which is geared to developers obtaining permits for development. This works quite well since the overwhelming amount of development is in the formal sector with regular builders and property developers undertaking the work. The comparatively few unauthorised developments can be easily detected and dealt with.

In most cities in the developing world however, the bulk of development is in the informal sector and undertaken by persons ignorant of planning or building control laws. The attempt to apply systems of British development control results in two deleterious tendencies; first, a good deal of corruption relating to the grant of planning permissions and to the ignoring of illegal development; and second, most development is technically illegal and being illegal, is not be provided with utility services. Many commentators have pointed out the need for innovative planning laws but little has been achieved.

One country which has made a resolute attempt to develop a different kind of planning law is South Africa with its Development Facilitation Act, 1996[7] – the title sets the tone for the content. The first few lines in the preamble to the Act set out its overall objective:

> To introduce extraordinary measures to facilitate and speed up the implementation of reconstruction and development programmes and projects in relation to land; and in so doing to lay down general principles governing land development throughout the Republic …

The Act is designed to overcome the bottlenecks in obtaining permission to develop and the discriminatory practices of local authorities which operated to the disadvantage of the black community in South Africa. It establishes development tribunals for every province in South Africa, consisting of officers and lay people, meeting in public and these are the bodies that developers can use instead of the existing provincial and local authorities to obtain development permissions. Provinces and local governments are required to set land development objectives (LDOs), the content of which is set out in the Act through a participatory procedure. These LDOs in effect take precedence over existing plans – master plans, structure plans etc – which might already exist. They are, as the name implies, directed to setting out how the land is to be developed adopting national standards and principles to overcome the inherited practices of the past. Development tribunals are enjoined not to approve a land development application if it is inconsistent with an LDO. The tribunals are given very wide powers to impose conditions on any application, including the manner in which members of communities which are to be upgraded are consulted, and the manner in which any person in beneficial occupation of land is to be accommodated in any upgrading.

Two specific innovative aspects to the Act may be looked at in a little more detail. The first is the setting out at the commencement of the Act of the General Principles of Land Development which are to apply throughout the country; to the actions of the State and a local government body; and to serve as guides to the administration of any physical plan, transport plan, structure plan, zoning scheme or other similar plan or scheme and as guidelines by reference to which any competent authority shall exercise a discretion or take a decision on any matter concerned with land development. These General Principles set out an inspiring vision of the desired urban future of South Africa and enshrine a new approach to planning law.[8] They provide, *inter alia,* that:

(a) Policy, administrative practice and law should … facilitate the development of formal and informal, existing and new settlements …;
Policy, administrative practice and law should promote efficient and integrated land development in that they …
promote the availability of residential and employment opportunities in close proximity to or integrated with each other;
promote a diverse combination of land uses, also at the level of individual erven [plots of land] and subdivisions of land …

Members of communities affected by land development should actively participate in the process of land development ...;

(f) Policy, administrative practice and laws should encourage and optimise the contributions of all sectors of the economy (government and non-government) to land development ...;

Laws, procedures and administrative practice relating to land development should –

(i) be clear and generally available to those likely to be affected thereby ...;

(iii) be calculated to promote trust and acceptance on the part of those likely to be affected thereby;

(iv) give further content to the fundamental rights set out in the Constitution ...

(i) Policy, administrative practice and laws should promote speedy land development ...;

(k) Land development should result in security of tenure, provide for the widest possible range of tenure alternatives, including individual and communal tenure, and in cases where land development takes the form of upgrading an existing settlement, not deprive beneficial occupiers[9] of homes or land or, where it is necessary for land or homes occupied by them to be utilised for other purposes, their interests in such land or homes should be reasonably accommodated in some other manner ...;

(m) Policy, administrative practice and laws relating to land development should stimulate the effective functioning of a land development market based on open competition between suppliers of goods and services ...

These principles are very much in line with the principles enshrined in the GPA and so have an application beyond South Africa.

The second innovation concerns the upgradation of informal settlements. Two specific LDOs are:

(i) the integration of areas of low-income communities into the relevant area as a whole ...; [relevant area being the area of the local authority to which the LDOs apply]

(v) the overall density of settlements, with due regard to the interests of beneficial occupiers ...

This enjoins local authorities to treat low-income settlements occupied by persons with no valid title to the land they are occupying as full members of the local community and as such entitled to proper planning and the provision of adequate infrastructure. Even more interesting however, is section 63 of the Act:

(1) Whenever land development takes the form of the upgrading of an existing settlement, informal or unregistered tenure arrangements existing among occupants of the settlement may, subject to any conditions [in other sections] be converted into ownership in the manner prescribed.

Subsection (2) sets out the matters which may be provided for by regulations and these make plain that the whole process is to be a participatory one with members of the communities concerned playing an active role in the process of upgrading and upgrading leads to formal layout plans followed by registration of those plans and the new titles in the Deeds Registry. (Like Bangladesh, South Africa operates on a deeds registry system not a title registry system). Thus integration of informal settlements is not just a pious sentiment but is provided for in the DFA.

This brief summary cannot do full justice to a law which is clearly inspired by a vision that urgent action must be taken to rectify the grievous land development wrongs of the past and that this vision can be and indeed must be driven by the twin imperatives of advancing human rights and democratic participation on the one hand and developing an effective land market on the other. Furthermore, and this is very much in keeping with governance traditions in South Africa, implementation of this vision is through the legal process – through detailed laws, procedures and formal judicial and quasi-judicial processes and hearings.

Now, a likely reaction to this law may be to say that the circumstances in South Africa were so unique and horrendous that a law which facilitates a legal revolution in land development was long overdue; no similar circumstances apply in Bangladesh. It is certainly the case that no racial segregation exists or has ever existed in Bangladesh. But what does undoubtedly exist is the unequal application of planning and land laws to the urban poor and the disinclination to accept that informal settlements and their occupants are an integral part of towns and cities and must be involved in the planning and development of their own future. What the DFA heralds in South Africa is the beginning of the inevitably long and slow process to integrate urban space and create more equitable urban development. This approach to urban development is needed in Bangladesh and is mandated by the Habitat Agenda. The DFA provides a new paradigm of the necessary legal framework to facilitate it; a paradigm moreover which facilitates compliance with the GPA.

Arguments for and against an urban land law for Bangladesh

The East Bengal State Acquisition and Tenancy Act, 1951 provided the legal basis and framework for a fundamental reform, almost a revolution in fact, of the land laws applying to the rural areas of what is now Bangladesh. It did not solve all the problems of the agrarian structure of the state but at least it pointed the state in the right direction of providing a more equitable system of land tenure relations in the countryside.

In 1951 Bangladesh was overwhelmingly rural; less than 4% of the population was urban. Now the urban population is fast approaching 25% or over 35 million people. The time has come to consider seriously the question of whether an equally far-reaching urban land law needs to be constructed to provide Bangladesh with a fairer system of urban land tenure relations and more effective participative land use regulation which will in turn provide the basis for a more equitable urban development. The arguments for and against such a reform may be summarised here.

The arguments *for* are as follows:

First, there is the situation on the ground. The evidence set out in this chapter based both on a literature review of respected and knowledgeable Bangladeshi scholars and commentators and on interviews with a range of public servants and commentators is that there is an urban crisis in Bangladesh. More and more people are coming to the towns and cities; more and more overcrowding exists in informal "illegal" low-income areas and while policies are announced to deal with the problem, these are not followed up with effective action. Unlike many other states both within and outwith the region, there are no laws in place to provide, at the least, the basic framework and the powers to make a start on re-ordering land tenure relations in the urban areas. Thus, even if a decision were to be taken right away to tackle the urban problems of Bangladesh, action would be inhibited through lack of appropriate laws.

Second, there are arguments based on equity. It is not just law which is needed. It is a particular kind of law. The East Bengal State Acquisition and Tenancy Act was concerned to give tenants secure rights to their land and lift the burdens of landlordism from off their shoulders. It addressed the needs of the majority. An urban land law must do the same. The many millions of urban dwellers who are trying to make a living and so are contributing to the economy of the state should be facilitated to do so by being accorded security of tenure through a process of upgradation of both living conditions and tenure in the areas which they are at present occupying. Present policies which are geared to compulsory large-scale removal of the urban poor from the sites they are occupying in or adjacent to town and city centres to outlying areas where they will be separated from their means of livelihood must accordingly be replaced. Equally, urban planning laws should facilitate and legalise the land use patterns of using land for both living and livelihoods which is how the urban poor use land.

Third, equity and efficiency arguments also apply to the issue of the settlement of land disputes. The present system is demonstrably failing all sections of the population and placing a premium on delay and obstruction. The poor suffer the most from such a system as even the modicum of justice available in the formal judicial system is well beyond their financial means.

Fourth, there is the argument based on compliance with international obligations. Present policies and laws cannot be reconciled with the obligations accepted by signing up to the Habitat Agenda in June 1996; they do not and are unlikely to work as the poor slowly come back into town where they can find work. New laws based on participation, access to land, security of tenure and access to justice to enforce rights are the minimum necessary to meet the standards set out in the GPA. It may also be pointed out that some of the laws and particularly the practices on removing the urban poor from their current places of abode cannot be reconciled with the rapidly evolving human rights approach to these matters (UNCHS, 1999; COHRE and ACHR, 2001).

Fifth, there are more general arguments based on economic efficiency. An appropriate law can play a major role in releasing the potential of the urban poor and so increasing urban investment. The urban poor will not, quite rationally, invest in their homes or in their areas when they know that they have no security. So the lack of security acts as a self-fulfilling criticism: the case against leaving the poor where they are is that the areas are run down, unhealthy, overcrowded, lacking amenities with the poor unwilling to help themselves. But why should the poor "help themselves" when they are denied the security of tenure which would make such help economically worth-while and while they are aware that the lack of long-term security is one reason why public investment in their areas is not forthcoming.

The arguments *against* any law which provides for *in situ* upgradation and greater tenure security for the urban poor are as follows:

First, for the most part the urban poor are squatting on public land which is earmarked either for necessary public sector development or for commercial development so that to facilitate the continued use of the land by the urban poor is economically inefficient. It will be cheaper to relocate them to inexpensive land on the outskirts of towns and cities and provide an efficient system of public transport to ferry them to their places of work within the cities. Since the poor are squatting, there is no need for a special law to deal with their removal; administrative practice will ensure that fair procedures are followed in applying the law. Insofar as squatting takes place on private land; if the landowner wishes to reach an agreement with groups of squatters on their continued occupation of the land or part of it, that is a matter for the parties and the law of contract; no new law is necessary.

Second, to enact a law to legalise illegal behaviour will send a signal to actual and potential squatters that the way to obtain security of tenure is to act in an illegal manner. Such a policy will also encourage urban drift. It is not the function of the state to encourage or facilitate citizens to break the law. Orderly development following the regular town planning laws is the correct way forward with the state's role being to release land or arrange for the release of land in appropriate areas for low-income housing.

Third, an adequate land law already exists for the operation of a market in land and to the extent that current thinking stresses that market forces are to be preferred to state intervention, private developers making use of the existing laws can be left to provide for the needs of all levels of urban society. It is true that there are imperfections in the operation of the existing laws but piecemeal reform tackling actual problems as experienced by practitioners is to be preferred to wholesale reform and the introduction of laws based on foreign models which are not suited to the circumstances of Bangladesh.

Fourth, new laws are not wanted. The existing laws are not enforced; why over-burden the system with new laws which are likely to be resisted by everyone, even by the urban poor themselves. The present laws allow the poor to be exploited by the rich. That is no doubt regrettable but it should be remembered that the laws also allow poor people to exploit each other. The poor welcome that opportunity and would resist losing it.

It must be said that while these arguments may appear quite strong on paper, they have all been shown time and time again to be falsified by the facts of the situation. The last argument was put at the Seminar; it seems a counsel of despair and is, in equal measure, cynical and hypocritical.

Behind the arguments about laws and their reform lie policy issues which will need to be resolved before any new laws can be put together.

The arguments *for* urban land law reform are based on a policy of *in situ* regularisation of informal settlements and this in turn is based both on international experience – wholesale demolition and relocation just don't work – and international obligations – the Habitat Agenda (which is itself based on the same international experience). The arguments *against* urban land law reform are based on long-standing and consistent national policies which have always emphasised the sanctity of private and public property and the need therefore to relocate squatters.

It may be suggested that there is something of a false dichotomy in these contrasting positions. The experience of South Africa is relevant here. Planners and land tenure reformers there recognise that rights to land are relative not absolute; that two or more groups of people may have valid rights to the same land but derived from different legal and factual roots; that people who have put down roots in the land cannot just be dispossessed and told or left to move on. A process is needed to "unpack" the conflicting rights; to determine who gets what rights in what land and when; and to make additional land available where both factual and "legal" overcrowding, *i.e.*, the multiple overlapping of rights in the same land, make it impossible for all parties to co-exist on the same land.[10]

Is this not the case in urban areas in Bangladesh? Rights to land gained through inheritance or the market co-exist with or overlap with rights to land gained through actual occupation and use. The South African concept of the "beneficial occupier" is suggestive here. The Thai approach to this is also relevant: land sharing, which, *au fond*, recognises that same basic principle of overlapping rights to land and the need to accommodate them. The South African and Thai experience point to another important lesson: the market cannot be the sole guide as to what is right; the regulation and guidance of rights to own and occupy no less than to use land is not merely permissible but essential if social peace and justice is to prevail in urban areas. But regulation must be directed to facilitating land development, not stifling it. Finally adopting the notion of overlapping rights will guide policy makers towards another essential fundament of a new policy approach: all citizens, whatever their economic or social status are deserving of equality of treatment in respect of their occupation and use of urban land.

The conclusion then is that the sharp contrast between relocation and regularisation is misplaced as it is based on an approach to rights to land which does not accord either with reality on the ground or current developments in legal thinking and practice. The way forward is to blend reality and law in the development of a new urban land law for Bangladesh, the outlines of which this chapter now addresses.

Recommendations for a new urban land law for Bangladesh

It is recommended that the Government of Bangladesh put in hand –

(i) the development of one or more laws which will provide the framework for –
   (a) the implementation of policies directed towards securing tenure rights for the urban poor via *in situ* regularisation and developments on "new" land; and
   (b) an urban planning law which emphasises development and community participation in setting developmental objectives;

(ii) a detailed review of the Transfer of Property Act, 1882 with a view to adapting it to the needs of a rapidly urbanising society with particular reference to Chapters III and IV (sales of immovable property and mortgages);

(iii) law to provide for a dedicated system of land dispute settlement bodies which would include both formal and alternative dispute settlement mechanisms (ADR), the latter of which could draw on traditional systems known to and used by the poor. Any such law should also provide for schemes for legal aid and assistance to enable the poor to access their rights.

These recommendations may now be further elaborated.

A law dealing with regularisation will need to provide for:

- the establishment and empowerment of a central government body which will have overall charge of programmes of regularisation;
- the requirement for the establishment of participatory mechanisms and bodies to enable communities to participate in planning and managing their own programmes of regularisation;
- the content of any plan for the regularisation of an informal settlement;
- mechanisms to settle boundaries and adjudicate disputes over rights within informal settlements as a precondition to upgradation;
- simplified systems of title and/or deed registration operated by communities to provide proof of secure rights to land;

- mechanisms and procedures for land sharing and land readjustment;
- joint ventures between the public and the private sectors;
- provisions dealing with land acquisition in connection with regularisation and claims to and quantum of compensation. If necessary, this could be achieved by amending the Acquisition and Requisition of Immovable Property Ordinance, 1982;
- procedures in connection with relocation;
- the broad content of conditions which may be imposed on any title to land;
- financing regularisation;
- appeals and dispute settlement generally.

A new law dealing with development planning will need to provide for:

- general principles of land development;
- types of plans and plan-making;
- participation and openness;
- the facilitation and regulation of development including the exemption of much actual development on the ground from controls;
- who decides;
- special areas and zones where special types and programmes of development may take place;
- appeals and dispute settlement.

A detailed review of Chapters III and IV of the Transfer of Property Act will need to pay particular attention to mortgage law. Are the current types of mortgages suitable for potential low-income mortgagors; if not what kind of legal framework needs to be developed to facilitate such mortgages? Is there a case for the creation of a special regime regulating mortgages for residential premises? Is the current law apt for the development of community mortgages; if not, what kind of legal framework should be created to assist this kind of mortgage development? Are protections for mortgagors in arrears satisfactory both in law and in practice? There will need to be associated with such a review, a review of the relevant law on micro-finance institutions and their lending powers and functions.

Conclusion

This chapter has reviewed the present state of urban land law in Bangladesh with particular reference to its applicability to the urban poor's need for better access to land and for secure tenure on the land they are occupying. The law was reviewed against the background of, on the one hand, the Habitat Agenda – the international legal commitments entered into by participating countries at the City Summit in Istanbul in June 1996 – and on the other, the urban problematique in Bangladesh – a rapidly expanding urban population which is becoming progressively poorer and which is finding it more and more difficult to obtain either land or secure tenure on land on which to live and earn a living with governmental agencies that seem either unable or unwilling to tackle these problems with anything like the urgency that is needed or with appropriate policies.

It is therefore no surprise that the laws applicable to urban land management are deficient in many respects. First and foremost, there is no specific urban land law which addresses the needs of the urban equivalent of the rural poor whose needs were addressed in the East Bengal State Acquisition and Tenancy Act, 1951. Thus there is no law concerned with upgradation or regularisation of informal settlements, or with providing a simplified system of titling or providing any special loan finance system for the poor. The basic land laws that do exist have served the country well since they were enacted but there is an urgent need to review them and adapt them to meet very different needs in the twenty-first century – an increasingly urban century.

Equally, there is a need to rethink the planning system and law that applies to the country's towns and cities: to move away from a command-and-control top down approach to a more facilitative participative approach where people are encouraged to plan for themselves and manage and develop their own communities. Above all, there is a need for policy and law on land management to recognise that the majority of the urban population are entitled to equality of treatment in the towns and cities where they live.

The arguments being put forward here are bolstered by a comparative survey of relevant laws from around the world. What emerges from the survey is that there are many countries with urban problems similar to those of Bangladesh which have developed innovative policies and laws designed to assist their urban poor; these laws work and they could be adapted for use in Bangladesh. Furthermore, many of these laws accord with the precepts and principles enshrined in the Habitat Agenda which is a further good reason for the Government of Bangladesh to consider adapting them for use in addressing its own urban problems.

Properly analysed, the situation on much land in the towns and cities of Bangladesh is that there are overlapping rights in the land, the beneficiaries of different sets of rights being able to point to different sources of legitimacy for those rights. The way forward then is to make a reality of the National Housing Policy and set about developing land laws which provide the legal framework for the unpacking of those rights and in appropriate cases for the progressive realisation via programmes of regularisation, of secure tenure for the urban poor. Sometimes – perhaps a majority of times – secure tenure will be provided where the poor are actually occupying land through such techniques as land sharing or land readjustment. At other times, secure tenure will be provided elsewhere through programmes of co-operative and participative planning and development of new settlements. At the same time, a major review of the basic land law of Bangladesh should be undertaken with a view to ensuring that its original purpose – to provide a simple, clear and comprehensive land law – is once more realised, though this time for an urban Bangladesh. These are challenging propositions but there is no reason to suppose that the genius of the people of Bangladesh cannot rise to the challenge and make the country an outstanding example of the implementation of the Habitat Agenda and compliance with the human right to land and housing.

---

*First published in Islam, N. (ed) (2000), *Urban Land Tenure and Housing Finance in Bangladesh*, Dhaka. The book is the output of a seminar on secure tenure for the urban poor in Bangladesh and the chapter is based on a report prepared for UNCHS (Habitat) in connection with a project to examine the problems of secure tenure for the urban poor in Bangladesh.

Notes

[1] It might be argued that it will be possible to build on the record of rights system and convert that into a title registration system. But this system itself is out of date, inefficient and corrupt. Also "Most of the litigations of both civil and criminal nature arise from land disputes. These disputes occur mostly due to lack of good and up-to-date land records" (Siddiqui, 1997, p. 344).

[2] A rousing statement of the case for title registration is to be found in Chapter 3 of the FAP – 15: *Land Acquisition and Resettlement Study* (1992), pp. 43–55 which glosses over the difficulties. See in particular paragraph 3.5.2 – Benefits of Title Registration. There is no equivalent paragraph on disadvantages.

[3] That was indeed the way a mortgage was created in England in 1882; now the standard form of mortgage in England is what is called in the Act a simple mortgage.

[4] As Hoek-Smit (2000) shows this is not in fact the case but the general point made in this quotation is still valid.

[5] However, "the Land Appeal Board is ... a dumping ground for officers who have fallen from grace so the morale there is rather low" (Siddiqui, 1997, p. 358).

[6] See too the World Bank, *op. cit.*, footnote 3: "Urban planning in a manner that facilitates land development and urban growth is a lost art in Bangladesh ... The present planning system is highly centralized and lacks public participation and transparency. The plans themselves are highly inflexible and do not reflect economic and financial realities" (p. 28).

[7] The Act was repealed and replaced by legislation enacted by provinces in 2001. It was not thought in practice to have been a great success but I have decided to leave the text as I wrote it in 1999 as I think the Act contains very useful lessons not only for Bangladesh but for other countries in the Commonwealth still too prone to transplant English planning laws into their urban legal soil.

[8] The Development and Planning Commission established by the DFA has produced a Resource Document and a Manual on The Chapter One Principles of the Development Facilitation Act (Pretoria, 1999) which discuss and explain the principles and show how they can be used in specific cases.

[9] "'*beneficial occupier*' means in relation to the occupation of land in a land development area where land development takes the form of upgrading an existing settlement, any person who has been in peaceful and undisturbed occupation of such land for a continuous period of not less than five years" (s. 1 DFA).

[10] This is what the Land Rights Bill designed to meet the constitutional requirements contained in Article 28 of the South African Constitution was directed to. The Bill was dropped after the June 1999 election of President Mbeki in South Africa.

11 Making law work: restructuring land relations in Africa*

The relevance of land reform

Issues related to land reform in Africa are particularly relevant at this time, for a number of reasons. In the first place, the twin emphases of donors, led by the World Bank, on "good governance" and the market economy as the keys to social and economic regeneration in Africa are increasingly seen as necessitating a greater reliance on legal forms and a legal culture similar to those operating in Western, market-orientated economies; conscious moves to adapt legal and judicial systems to that end are thus increasingly part of aid programmes.[1] Secondly, land reform, while never off the African reform agenda as advanced by the donor community, is itself increasingly presented as being a candidate for legal – that is, Western-type legal – solutions.

Consider these comments from the seminal World Bank report on Africa in a section headed Redefining Land Rights (1989, p. 104):

> [F]armers must be given incentives to change their ways. One importance incentive is the right to permanently cultivate land and to bequeath or sell it. Secure land rights also help rural credit markets to develop, because land is good collateral ... Traditional land tenure system need to be codified. Titles could also be provided to groups for collective ownership ... . Nationally legislated land rights are likely to conflict with prevailing customary rights. Judicial mechanisms for dealing with disputes between owners claiming traditional versus modern land rights are urgently required.

The less well-known, but much better informed FAO report by Jean-Philippe Platteau (1992, p. 293) also concludes that:

> Formalization of land rights through issuance of titles or other land-register documents is an urgent step to be taken in all areas where competition for land has become so stiff as to impose high *ex ante* and *ex post* transactions costs on

the agents ... Land markets ought to be regulated in such a way that poor and vulnerable groups gain better protection of their rights of access than they have at present in the context of African dualism of land rights.

Thus, whether arguing for an unregulated free market in land, or for a regulated and supervised market in land in Africa, the means to achieve these ends is seen as involving the introduction of new codes of land law.

There are also factors internal to the region which are equally, if not more significant. In December 1991, the inaugural International Conference on Planning Law in Africa took place in Maseru, Lesotho, bringing together planners and lawyers with an interest in planning and land matters from most countries in Eastern and Southern Africa (and a few outsiders, amongst whom was the author) to exchange ideas and experiences on the role of law in land use management. It was agreed that a second conference should be convened two years later at which countries would report back on the extent to which they had complied with the conclusions and resolutions adopted in Lesotho. A second conference was duly held in Windhoek, Namibia in 1993 and since then conferences have been held in the region every other year.

The first conference was a serious attempt to grapple with practical issues of the implementation of the law. What came through very forcibly at the third conference held in Johannesburg, was the peer group pressure to produce results. Delegates from country after country reported either on new land management laws which had been recently introduced or were planned, or on new policies adopted which would in time lead to new laws. There seemed to be a commitment to take planning law and land law reform seriously, sparked not by external pressure from donors, but by the internal pressure not to lag behind one's colleagues in the Conference.

Quite apart from the impetus generated by these Conferences, land reform of one sort of another, through the medium of law, is high on the agenda of many countries in Eastern and Southern Africa:

- Land reform and redistribution form a central thrust of the reconstruction and development policies of the Government of the Republic of South Africa; a large number of new and far-reaching laws have been enacted to translate policy into action.
- Land reform and redistribution have been major issues in Namibia, both before and after independence, although little urgency has been shown in tackling them. However, significant legislative moves on

agricultural land reform were taken in 1995 and new types of urban land tenure have also been developed.

- In 1992, Zimbabwe enacted far-reaching legislation to speed up land redistribution, although considerable circumspection has attended its implementation. A land reform commission and a new land policy proposed far reaching changes to the ownership and management of the land occupied by Africans but these proposals have yet to be acted upon. At the beginning of the new millennium, however, attention turned to the problem of the highly skewed pattern of land distribution. The Government, unnerved by the first effective political opposition to its 20-year-old rule, began, in the run up to elections to the National Assembly, to encourage and facilitate the illegal occupation of mainly white-owned farms followed by the passage of legislation which empowered the Government to expropriate such farms without the payment of compensation (but not exclusively; the farms of some black opponents of the Government were also the targets of illegal occupation and expropriation).
- In Tanzania, a major investigation into the manifold deficiencies of existing policies and practices on land management was undertaken, via a Presidential Commission in the early 1990s; new policies on land were subsequently formulated in the first half of the 1990s, and the new National Land Policy (NLP) was adopted by Parliament in June 1995. Two major new Acts of Parliament were passed in 1999 to give effect to this new policy. It is the process of developing these new laws which is the subject of this chapter.
- Malawi appointed a Presidential Commission to review and make recommendations on land tenure and its reform in 1996 and its report, published in 1999 foreshadows major changes to that country's tenure system. The Government's White Paper on land was published in early 2002.
- Uganda's Constitution of 1995 provided for new systems of land tenure throughout the country based on conferring rights of ownership on the citizen and removing powers of management from central government. The Land Act, 1998 fleshed out these principles, providing for mechanisms for adjudication and registration of customary and other titles, decentralised systems of land management and dedicated systems of dispute settlement.

In all these countries, the pressure to act is, at least in part, the result of contested democratic politics and the perceived need to meet the concerns of rural voters. This is most obvious in South Africa but also applies to Namibia and Tanzania. The commitment to legislate in Namibia was made just before the general election of late 1994, when the government felt the need to respond to a Peoples' conference on land reform which had taken place that year. The enactment of the Agricultural (Commercial Land Reform) Act (ACLRA) took place just after the election. In Tanzania, the establishment of a Presidential Commission and the drive towards finalising a national land policy occurred as the country moved from a one-party to a multi-party political system.

Land reform as land law reform

However, the commitment to developing a legal response to land reform, to seeing land reform as being, in part, land *law* reform, is driven by something else – an aspect of land reform which is not generally noted by external commentators and the aid industry pressing for land reform.

The South African case may be used as an example. In South Africa during the era of apartheid, indeed from 1913 onwards, there was a plethora of legislation on land tenure so far as it affected Africans. The principal characteristic of this legislation was that it deprived Africans of any rights to land and any security of title and put them at the mercy of administrative whim. Law was used to abolish law. Land reform in South Africa, then, must include land *law* reform because it seeks to change the nature of the legal regime and the legal culture that applies to African-held land. It is to replace, at best, licences or permits held at the mercy of administrators or chiefs , with *rights* guaranteed by law.

The same approach to African land tenure was adopted in pre-independence Namibia and also, as is graphically portrayed in the Presidential Commission on Land Matters, by the post-independence land administration bodies in Tanzania. There, the pre-independence colonial approach of denying to Africans any rights in the land formed the basis of Operation Vijiji, the forced and a-legal collectivisation of peasants in the 1970s. When, in the more open political system that began to develop in Tanzania in the late 1980s, peasants started seeking judicial redress for what they argued was the deprivation of their land during the collectivisation, the government rushed legislation through the National Assembly to stop all judicial proceedings on land issues. It then sought to defend the constitutionality of the legislation before the Court of Appeal in *A-G v. Akonaay* in 1994 – 33 years after independence – by solemnly arguing, through the Deputy Attorney-General, that those persons who held their land by customary law, under what are known in Tanzanian land law as "deemed rights of occupancy", did not have a property right in the land and so were not protected by the constitutional provision against deprivation of property without compensation. As the Chief Justice pointed out in his judgement, the effect of this argument was that "most of the inhabitants of Tanzania are no better than squatters in their own country. It is a serious proposition". The court rejected the proposition and with it the legal foundation of Operation Vijiji that land could be taken without payment of compensation. The Government accepted the judgement and enacted legislation amending the impugned Act, which allowed for the possibility of compensation to be claimed for hardships and losses suffered during Operation Vijiji. The legislation to implement the National Land Policy makes it very clear that all citizens in Tanzania, whatever the legal origin of their right of occupancy (the highest form of land-holding right available in Tanzania) have a property right in the land held through a right of occupancy, and are thus protected by the constitution. Thus in Tanzania, land reform is pre-eminently land *law* reform: the substitution of a law to facilitate the *right* of citizens to access and hold land, for a law which had facilitated the state's *administrative control* over the citizens' access to land.

Ambivalence in land law reform

If there are both external and internal pressures operating on policy-makers in Africa to use the law to restructure land relations, these pressures are pulling in opposite directions. The external, donor-driven pressures are aimed at facilitating the operation of a market for land, while some, at least, of the internal pressures pull in the direction of strengthening the security of tenure of those presently on the land. Facilitating a market in land widens the scope of the rights of landowners, while restricting their ability to dispose of land reduces their rights, whatever the merits of so doing; it is thus not always easy to reconcile these two sets of pressures.

This ambivalence about the market and the problems it might pose for social stability and peasants' land rights is evident in both the Report of the Presidential Commission and the Government's National Land Policy (NLP) in Tanzania. The Report proposed that a special status be conferred on "village land", such land could only be held via a right of occupancy by those ordinarily resident in that village, and could only be assigned between villagers; non-villagers could at best only obtain leases in the land. The thrust of these recommendations was accepted. The NLP proposed that market transfers of land will no longer need prior approval, which is currently required, but at the same time, it stated that special provisions will be needed to protect vulnerable groups from the effects of market transfers. How one achieves these contradictory aims will be addressed later.

Left out of the equation so far is a third pressure applying to land restructuring, which is certainly present in Namibia and Tanzania, and is also to some extent present in South Africa. This is the pressure for the status quo: for using the law to bolster existing arrangements rather than to change them. A new law is for public relations, not for public actions. In Namibia, for example, the ACLRA triggered off significant differences of opinion between two, if not three, sets of officials and politicians. First there were those who argued that economic development and a healthy foreign exchange position require that the status quo of very large white-owned cattle ranches be maintained and very minimal changes be made to accommodate land-hungry Africans from the north of the country. Then there were those who argued that the evidence shows that African smallholders are in fact very efficient farmers, that ACLRA should be implemented and land acquired from the cattle ranchers to settle African smallholders on the land. Finally came those who saw the Act as an opportunity to facilitate land-grabbing in communal lands, with those who lost out being compensated by (inferior) land acquired from ranchers under ACLRA. Thus, at one level, attempts to revise ACLRA, to close its loopholes, to develop criteria and administrative arrangements in order to facilitate its implementation are just technical matters for legal and other consultants to deal with. At another level, however, the issue is whether to *use* the Act to start the process of significant societal transformation for which the 30-year war of independence was waged; to *under-use* the Act to maintain existing land relations with some cosmetic changes – the preferred option of some international agencies; or to *misuse* the Act to allow the new elite to join the ranks of large-scale landowners – the preferred option of some at least of the new elite.

In the case of Tanzania, the pressure for the status quo to be maintained came from some officials and politicians who, as the implications of giving legal effect to the philosophy of the NLP started to become apparent (more rights to citizens, less rent-seeking opportunities for officials, more transparency in, and more opportunities to challenge the exercise of powers by officials), began to voice doubts about the new approach. If the old system worked well – as it did from the point of view of officials who could ride roughshod over citizens' land rights – why change it?[2]

The Namibian case highlights one important point; to move from policy formulation to drafting laws is not, as some people assume, to move from a debate on policy to one on legal technicalities; the move changes the content of the debate but it remains, none the less, a policy debate. In some respects indeed, it becomes a sharper and more relevant debate. The broad general policies set out in, for example, the Tanzanian Government's NLP or the Namibian Government's *Land Reform: To Promote Equity and Fairness* (1994), can be readily agreed to by (almost) everyone. Who, after all, could possibly be against equity and fairness? However, when these ideas are turned into precise powers, duties, limitations, restrictions, procedures, when it becomes clearer who is to benefit and who is to lose out, then objections begin to be voiced. These are not, of course, objections on "policy" grounds but on technical legal grounds; a particular clause "wouldn't work"; a certain provision is "unnecessary": another goes "too far", or is "impracticable". Sometimes, as happened in Namibia with the ACLRA, it is argued that if the law is so deficient, it would be better if its implementation were postponed until it was rectified, thus allowing yet more time for the loopholes in the Act to be exploited and the policy of promoting equity and fairness to be further undermined.

It may thus be concluded that every step down the legal path involves policy: the decision to resort to law, the nature of the legal system to be adopted, the style of the law, the sources of the law, the content of the law; all these decisions are policy decisions. This is not a particularly original point: it is worth making, however, since in the context of development and aid, it is often denied, explicitly or implicitly, and law is portrayed as the technical and relatively uncontentious means through which policy can be implemented. This is a feature of a World Bank report on its approach to legal assistance (1995, pp. 5, 9) which states: "The Bank should ensure that its legal assistance projects are in accordance with its policy of non-interference in the politics of its member countries." At the same time, however: "In the light of the close linkage between economic and legal reforms, it is important that any assistance to the borrowing countries' legal reforms should be part of the Bank's country assistance strategies that identify reform priorities in a range of areas." The Bank does not vouchsafe how the latter statement is to be reconciled with the former.

Drafting laws as practising politics

The business of drafting laws, of turning broad policy statements about land, which may well contain deliberate ambiguities and contradictions, into more precise implementable propositions of law, is a policy function, a political matter. This section will explore some of the problems of drafting land laws in a policy framework; in other words, it will look at drafting as politics, and discuss some of the choices that confront the draftsperson, but which rarely get a public airing.

One of the most fundamental questions is the extent to which it is realistic to use a major and inevitably complex piece of legislation, such as a new code of land law, as a vehicle for radical social reform. Is there not a danger that the act of legislating, the detailed, complex, verbal formulae put before legislators, the minutiae of debate on those details, the need for officials and citizens to master the new rules and comply with them, the inevitable slow-moving bureaucracy which clings, lichen-like, to any new reform programme, the politics of reform already noted in, for example, the Namibian case – is there not a danger that all of this will dull the edge of reform or, worse still, subvert reform by creating a situation where only those with the resources to employ lawyers will be able to benefit from reforms? Far better, if one is serious about reform, especially reform to benefit the majority, to get out and do it and let the law catch up later. This was the Tanzanian way with Operation Vijiji, where what little law there was, was largely ignored. Law was, and to some extent still is, perceived in Tanzania as an impediment to change; therefore, where the law has to be used, the style of drafting has tended to be one of conferring great powers on officials, with few safeguards or external controls. This ambivalence about law is present in many cases: two examples will serve here to illustrate the point.

Example 1: Tanzania

There were two particularly important proposals in the Report of the Tanzanian Presidential Commission. First, villagers should be able to obtain individual customary rights of occupancy to land; that is, the process of individualisation of land tenure should be officially recognised and assisted in Tanzania. The rather tricky business of determining boundaries of individual plots, and who may claim what rights to the land about to be individualised, would be dealt with (GoT, 1994, p. 152) "in the manner traditionally accepted in the village in the presence of members of the Village Council". The revolutionary proposal of individual titles to land was accepted and formed the basis of the policy on land rights in the NLP. Second, it was proposed that the basic dispute settlement mechanism for village land should be *Mbaraza ya Wazee ya Ardhi*, councils of village elders. These bodies were to have original jurisdiction in all land matters, including settling disputes over individualisation of tenure; they would determine their own procedures subject to the obligation to follow the principles of natural justice; they would not be bound by any civil or criminal procedure codes or the law of evidence or have lawyers appearing before them. *Mbaraza*, too, were largely accepted by the NLP, although it remained silent on actual practice and procedures.

Both of these far-reaching proposals involve changes in the law, but the clear message of the Presidential Commission was that the new law should be similar to that which it will replace in terms of drafting style, with a few broad strokes of the legal pen giving vast powers to legally unqualified people and relying on their innate common-sense and sense of justice to get things done – just like Operation Vijiji in fact. In the light of the evidence uncovered by the Presidential Commission of the abuse of power and the chaos that accompanied the latter exercise, this approach could be described as naive. This might be unfair; an alternative analysis is that the approach adopted by the commission is a classic example of "path dependency".

North (1990, p. 99) summarises path dependency as follows:

> Once a development path is set on a particular course, the network externalities, the learning process of organisations, and the historically derived subjective modelling of the issues reinforces the course ... We cannot understand today's choices ... without tracing the incremental evolution of institutions.

Applied to land and the use of law to alter land relations in Tanzania, this tells us that while the policy proposals of the Presidential Commission were indeed far-reaching, the approach to the use of law to implement them was driven to some extent by long-standing Tanzanian legal traditions which stretch back to colonial times. The real revolutionaries, therefore, might turn out not to be those who proposed radical policies but those who, through the NLP, proposed a radical legal methodology for implementing policies; namely a detailed and inevitably lengthy new land code in which legal rules and checks and balances replace reliance on administrative and political action based on goodwill and common sense – which, according to the evidence, are in short supply where land relations are concerned.

Example 2: South Africa

The ANC government now in power in South Africa decided early on in its life that a major programme of detailed land law reform was the key to the radical reform of land relations. To quote from the White Paper on South African Land Policy (1997, pp. 1, 73): "The central thrust of land policy in South Africa is the land reform programme. This has three aspects; land restitution, land redistribution and tenure reform." Furthermore: "To overcome the institutional problems and constraints to the implementation of land reform, the following are necessary: ... the rationalisation of legislation ... ."

The White Paper lists six Acts and two Bills as part of the legislative programme to implement land reform, and many of these laws have established or are proposing to establish judicial institutions as key parts of the implementing mechanisms. More significant is the drafting style of these laws. In contrast to Tanzanian statutes, South African statutes are very detailed and tend therefore to be lengthy. The philosophy behind this seems to be that the detail in the law will facilitate radical action rather than hinder it. If powers and the reasons for them are spelt out clearly, then officials will be able to take, and justify, actions. This same drafting philosophy prevails at the moment in Namibia: ACLRA is a long and detailed statute aiming, on the surface, to bring about significant land reform and spelling out the methods and criteria to be used in doing this.

Here too path dependency can be seen at work. One of the most striking characteristics of the imposition and operating of apartheid in South Africa was the use of law – immensely detailed and complex bodies of laws designed to entrench in a fixed and permanent way a specific social and economic system. Law, in a painstakingly detailed form, was the primary tool used to create and implement apartheid; now, through the Constitution and the land reform programme, the same type of law and the same manner of law-making are being used as primary tools to dismantle it.

Land law as administrative law

The South African approach and philosophy to legislative drafting has three main, and interlinked, merits. First, given the evidence presented in the Tanzanian Presidential Commission Report, officials armed with powers and subject to few or no restraints, cannot be relied upon to behave reasonably. Indeed, they cannot always be relied upon to behave reasonably when they are subject to some restraints – the old South Africa is evidence of that – but at least where there are legal rules and procedures which have to be followed, a challenge can be mounted to unreasonable behaviour. Even under apartheid in South Africa, the courts quite frequently, by a close and technical interpretation of a statute, reined back an unreasonable exercise of power, particularly in the areas of land and housing: because the decision was based on the interpretation of a statute, it was hard to allege that the judges were "interfering" in policy – a charge which becomes more plausible where statutes are very broad and "general principles" of administrative law are used to overturn an administrative decision.

The second merit is one of considerable significance for much of the land reform going on in Africa. In much of Africa, the allodial title to land is vested in either the state, the President (Tanzania), the Nation (Lesotho), or even a National Land Commission (Ghana); this means that the citizen has to obtain land from the state or its organs, with state officials managing the land as landlords or trustees, or with the state reserving the power to bring about fundamental alterations in land relations amongst the citizenry, as in South Africa, Namibia, Zimbabwe and Kenya. In cases such as these, land law ceases to be a matter of private law, but becomes part of public law; it is in fact, administrative law.

It could be argued that over the last 40 years, no branch of the law, with the possible exception of environmental law, has developed more quickly or with such universal approbation as to its guiding principles, than administrative law. Many of the newer generation of African constitutions –

Malawi, Namibia, South Africa, Uganda, for example – now explicitly provide for administrative justice as a part of the Bill of Human Rights. Administrative law or administrative justice requires that official power be bounded by legal rules, be exercised in accordance with certain principles of fairness, allows for hearings and appeals, and be subject to review. How else can this be done except through statutory provisions which go beyond merely granting powers to officials, to setting out the manner and form of their exercise and control?

In drafting the new land law for Tanzania, it became clear that much of the draft was actually applied administrative law. Even where the draft dealt with matters of substantive land law, such as remedies for breach of conditions of a right of occupancy, or determining the rent for a right of occupancy, the manner of dealing with breaches or setting the rent involved principles of administrative law, because it was public officials who were to exercise the relevant powers. It was not possible just to indicate that powers were to be exercised "reasonably". The South African model of spelling out in considerable detail how powers were to be exercised, on what basis and taking account of what factors, was followed. In so doing, drafting became involved in policy-making; substantive matters had to be put into the Bill which were not dealt with in the NLP. This implied that a dual test had to be applied to any assessment of the draft Bill: did it create a new substantive land law, appropriate to the conditions of Tanzania; and: did it provide a suitable legal framework for the exercise of powers by officials?

The third reason for supporting an approach of "more" rather than "less" law is, paradoxically perhaps, the existence of the market. Administrative justice apart, a land law which confers broad powers with few controls on officials may be adequate when the main thrust of the law is about administrative power, and where few private rights are involved. This applied to the land relations of the majority of the population of Tanzania up to late 1994. However, once the land law recognises and protects private rights, and facilitates dealings with those private rights in the market place, the law has to be much more specific, detailed and clear. Such aspects as the nature and limits of private rights; how they may be acquired, disposed of, burdened, lost; the whole issue of third-party rights; and, where the state is to remain involved, a more exact demarcation of state power and its limits, including the payment of compensation in certain circumstances – these all have to be spelt out in detail so that all those who have private rights, or intend to try to obtain private rights in land can predict with reasonable certainty the scope and operation of the law applicable to those rights.

It is no accident that the National Land Code of Malaysia, for instance, is composed of 501 sections and 11 schedules, extending to 400 pages. Malaysia has a market economy and the Code sets out the basic land law of Malaysia, dealing both with private rights and their exercise and with the powers of officials in a market economy. The argument is that a detailed and necessarily somewhat complex land law is an inevitable part of moving towards a more market-orientated private rights based land law. Difficult though the transition will be for many people in, for example, Tanzania, Namibia and South Africa, the alternative – a continuation of a relationship to land at the mercy of officials, or worse, the proposals of the Tanzanian Presidential Commission that undefined collectivities of peasants be given large unregulated powers over land – cannot be seriously entertained.

A clear example of the dangers of a continued reliance on administration as opposed to law may be instanced from Lesotho, with respect to the provisions relating to compensation for loss of land brought about by the Lesotho Highlands Water Project, a major dam-building project. After a somewhat shaky start in the late 1980s (McAuslan, 1987), the Project developed some good principles of compensation for loss of land and livelihood, although implementation of these principles left a good deal to be desired. As part of the process of preparation for another phase of the Project, a major participative study was undertaken of the compensation needs and desires of local people who were to be displaced by that next phase. According to the draft report of the study (Hunting-Consult, 1996, p. 52): "The Compensation Policy [of the Lesotho Highlands Development Authority] has no legal status and cannot be cited in a court of law. It serves as a set of guidelines to assist LHDA in the implementation of its compensation programme."

At a workshop in March 1996 to discuss the study, this statement was picked up and queried: what was the point of the study and the workshop if the LHDA could just ignore their findings? The consultants claimed that they were just repeating what they had been told by the Authority's legal officers; they then attempted to reassure other participants, including representatives from the area concerned, by referring to such concepts as "legitimate expectations" and "reasonableness", implying that even if the proposed policies were not part of a statute, the Authority could not ignore them, and that a court would take account of them in any action challenging the Authority's decisions. However, the damage had clearly been done: local people were dismayed by the statement and many of those present at the workshop had their already cynical view of the LHDA reinforced. Lay people, both formally educated and otherwise, are well aware of the difference between having to rely on administrative goodwill and having rights enshrined in the law.

A new land law, then, is by necessity, a mix of public and private law, for a mix of public (administrative) and private (market) reasons. This same point has been made in more general terms by Ajani and Mattei (1995, pp. 131–32) writing about property law reform in Eastern and Central Europe:

> In all modern legal systems, property law involves private law as well as a good deal of public law. Economists tend to disregard this point but it is crucial for lawyers. Lawyers see private and public law as cooperating in defining property rights. Economists usually see private law as creating property rights and public law as destroying them.
>
> Indeed, in the standard neoclassical economic approach, private law is the province of the market while public law is the province of the state ... In more sophisticated economic terms, however, property law is justified as a cure of externalities ... Each legal system will therefore establish, in addition to a private-law cure, a more or less extended public-law cure of externalities reflected by a larger or smaller role of administrative regulation and enforcement.

The crucial issue, as the authors go on to say, is to strike the right balance between public and private law for each problem.

Controlling dispositions: whether and how

One particular problem is that of controls over dispositions: should they be provided for, and if so, how? In much of Africa, whether as a result of internal policy decisions, or of external pressures from above or, less frequently but not to be disregarded, of social pressures from below, land relations are being restructured to take greater account of the market. The ambivalence towards controls on market transactions is clear in the NLP of Tanzania. On the one hand there is one policy statement, so clear that it could almost have been drafted by the World Bank (p. 15): "The consent of the Minister or his appointed officers is not necessary for market transfer to take place." On the other hand, there are numerous other policy statements which, equally clearly, seek to regulate the process of market transfer:

> No disposition will be allowed unless all development conditions have been complied with.
> Regulations will be drafted to protect risk groups such as displaced persons, children and lower income people.
> Special taxes will be imposed to deter land speculation.
> Land ceilings will be fixed by Government ....
> Land hoarding will be discouraged by strict enforcement of development conditions ...

In addition, special rules will continue to apply to foreign investors in land. Whilst all these provisions may be perfectly reasonable, the problem for the legal draftsperson is in reconciling the two approaches; the private law, free market approach of "no consent", and the public law regulatory approach.

In Namibia, before the enactment of ACLRA, this dilemma was resolved by imposing on the Registrar of Deeds – an official whose position was established for the private law purpose of registering deeds relating to land transfers – the public law duties of checking whether certain public law restrictions had been complied with, before approving the registration of a deed. This led to considerable concern on the part of the Registrar that that office was being misused; acting as a watchdog for other departments and regulatory systems would alter the character of the Registrar's office from an agency which vetted private legal documents (with the aim of ensuring their conformity with the private law and advancing essentially private transactions in the market) to a judgemental agency concerned with public law matters. Although the "watchdog" role of the Registrar is retained under the terms of ACLRA, there is now an additional requirement that all transactions by settlers have to be approved by the Minister, with no provision for appeals in case approval is denied. This is not only unconstitutional (infringing the constitutional provision on administrative justice which requires that any administrative decision may be appealed against), but also totally impractical. People will either not wait for a ministerial decision on a transaction, or will ignore a negative decision, leading to a situation in which virtually every transaction will be "illegal".

In Tanzania, the situation in relation to village land is fairly clear: the village councils are empowered to regulate most transactions, since village land may generally only be transferred between villagers. With respect to land transactions under the jurisdiction of central government, the initial solution proposed was to borrow an approach from English town and country planning law – "deemed consent" for certain transactions and classes of transactions provided for by the Act (the list could be expanded or contracted by Ministerial order), together with provisions requiring that consent be obtained for some specific transactions. This did not find favour with a workshop held to review the first draft of the Bill, which considered it too complicated. A majority view of the workshop was that consent requirements should be dispensed with altogether: that, however, would not have met the policy prescriptions which required some controls.

The alternative form of regulation suggested by the central level was to adopt a two-fold approach; pre- and post-transaction control. At the pre-transaction stage, transactions would be graded by their value, the greater the value of the transaction, the greater the control, with an Allocations Committee to advise the Commissioner of Lands on all major transactions. Minor transactions would escape pre-transaction control altogether. The value of minor transactions was set in the draft Bill at such a level that around 90% of all transactions fell into this category, with no need for consent. However, a supervisory role was retained to check on transactions which might be tainted by fraud, undue influence and the like, with the Commissioner of Lands empowered to refer any suspect transaction to the courts for their review.[3]

In Western societies, regulation focuses on the institutions and personnel involved in market transactions rather than on the transactions themselves. In the UK, for instance, estate agents, solicitors, mortgage brokers and building societies are all now regulated via the Financial Services Agency, Ombudsmen, the Office of Fair Trading and local authorities. However, it is unlikely that such a solution would work in most states in Africa, where the concern is to try to ensure that the introduction of a market in land does not lead to landlessness and indebtedness on the one hand, and a small number of large-scale landowners on the other. It is difficult to see any way of avoiding some regulatory mechanism which, in order to ensure consistency, fairness and transparency, will need to include the involvement of a central authority. This will be a departure from market mechanisms as they operate in Western economies, but not as they operate in Asian market economies;

there, regulations on land transactions have long been a feature of land markets without seeming to inhibit their vigorous operation.

Land law reform and customary land law

The most challenging task facing any programme of land law reform in Africa is the issue of the place of customary law in any reformed system. The cause of customary law has waxed and waned over the years. Platteau (1996) quotes several World Bank studies and reports which attribute the difficulties of improving African agriculture to the defects of customary tenure, with the proposed solution being to move towards a "modern", individualised tenure system based on statute law. On the other hand, he also draws attention to alternative views that customary tenure cannot be ignored but must be used as the basis for any reform programme. A recent statement on this from what may be called the "World Bank stable" is a study by Bruce and Migot-Adholla (1994) as part of some World Bank funded research. The study concludes (pp. 261–62) that the implication for policy-makers of the research is:

> [to] redirect attention to more incremental approaches to change in indigenous tenure systems ... We should be moving away from a 'replacement paradigm' in which indigenous tenures are to be replaced by tenure provided by the state towards an 'adaptation paradigm' ... An adaptation paradigm requires a supportive legal and administrative environment for the evolutionary change in indigenous law. Such a supportive environment implies a clear recognition of the legal applicability and enforceability of indigenous land tenure rules.

These conclusions appear to have been fed into a policy change on customary tenure by the World Bank (World Bank, 2001).

The policy of replacement was not solely a donor-driven policy. Kenya's policy was set in place by the colonial power in 1956 but it has not changed since independence 40 years ago. Tanzania has constantly enacted legislation which purports to abolish customary land tenure, most recently in 1992. Namibia's ACLRA is based on the assumption that the land law by which settlers are to be governed is the Roman-Dutch land law, not customary law, and a draft Communal Land Tenure Bill was, at best ambivalent about the role of customary land tenure. Lesotho's Land Act of 1979 was designed to start the process of replacement. These laws have not worked. Even in Kenya, which has the longest and arguably the most consistent customary land tenure replacement policy in Anglophone Africa, the enactment of the Land Disputes Tribunal Act in 1991 was a recognition that customary tenure could not be abolished. The Act established councils of elders to handle land disputes, applying customary law even for those lands where rights had been adjudicated and which are now governed, allegedly, by the Registered Land Act 1962, applying law based on English land law.

Although Tanzania has not opted for the adaptation paradigm, the practical implications of this were not spelt out very clearly in the NLP. Opting for this approach as a policy does not solve the issues of how to provide for it in a statute, or how to grapple with all the important ancillary problems which then arise, such as women's rights to land, the relationship between customary law and statute law, individualisation of tenure and the provision of appropriate dispute settlement arrangements. These issues will be briefly discussed below.

Issues in customary law

Women's rights

Approaches to tenurial reform in Africa have tended to skirt round the issue of women's rights to land. Namibia's ACLRA (enacted in 1995) and its draft Communal Land Bill (of the same year) were both silent on the matter. This was in spite of the existence of legal and policy injunctions: there are specific provisions in Article 23 of the Constitution that permit the Government, when enacting legislation and applying policies that provide for the advancement of persons who have been socially, economically and educationally disadvantaged by past laws and practices "to have regard to the fact that women in Namibia have traditionally suffered special discrimination and that they need to be encouraged and enabled to play a full, equal and effective role in the political, social, economic and cultural life of the nation". Furthermore, the National Conference on Land Reform of 1991 specifically resolved that a programme of affirmative action be instituted to help women gain access to land, and that all customary and statute laws which discriminate against women be abolished or amended.

Developments in Tanzania have been more fluid and illustrate a reluctance to take concrete actions. When the NLP was brought to the National Assembly in 1995, women MPs objected to the lack of specifics on women's rights; they were only persuaded to withdraw their objections to the policy by oral concessions to the effect that the Constitution requires that everyone be treated equally, implying that women would be treated equally in terms of land allocations under the NLP. In fact, the Constitution's definition of discrimination does not include any reference to gender discrimination; the Chapter on the Bill of Rights actually starts off by asserting: "all *men* are born free and are all equal." More significantly, the NLP (Policy Statement 4) itself is very ambivalent about women's rights:

> (i) In order to enhance and guarantee women's access to land and security of tenure, women will be entitled to acquire land in their own right not only through purchase but also through allocation. However inheritance of clan or family land will continue to be governed by custom and tradition.
> (ii) Ownership of land between husband and wife shall not be the subject of legislation.

The statements about inheritance will ensure the maintenance of the status quo for most women and were criticised by the Tanzanian Women Lawyers' Association and other women's groups. The problem with (ii) is that it was clearly written from ignorance: there has been legislation dealing with property relations between husband and wife in Tanzania since the onset of British colonial rule, and the latest such legislation (the Marriage Act of 1971) is in fact fairly liberal on the matter. The brief on the drafting of the land law did not encompass either succession or marriage law, so those policy statements were not taken on board. They were evidence, none the less, that there is some considerable way to go before generalised statements about women's rights, which are never far from the lips of politicians in Tanzania, were likely to be translated into practical measures on the ground where it matters (Gopal and Salim, 1998).

The draft Bill provided at various points that those concerned with the management of land should have special regard for the needs of women when considering allocation or dispositions of land; that any dispute-settlement bodies located at village level – the *Mbaraza* – must include women in their composition; and that land adjudication in connection with individual customary rights of occupancy must pay particular attention to the interests of women. The first workshop on the draft agreed to these proposals without much enthusiasm. The second workshop approved them *sub silento*. Thereafter, women's groups waged a vigorous and ultimately quite successful campaign to build on these provisions and were quite satisfied with the provisions that were ultimately enacted in the Land Act, 1999. The provisions set the parameters for action, but this issue was heavily tied up with two others; customary law, and the individualisation of title.

On women's rights (as on other matters) South Africa seems to be ahead of the field. Its White Paper (RSA, 1997, p. 33) is much more explicit and far-reaching, proposing, *inter alia*:

> The removal of all legal restrictions on participation by women in land reform. This includes reform of marriage, inheritance and customary law where they contain obstacles to women receiving rights to land.
>
> Specific mechanisms to provide security of tenure for women, including the possibility of registering assets gained through land reform in the name of the household or its individual members.

This continues the trend noted earlier of a commitment to use legislation to bring about major social change, but here too, success will be measured not in what goes into the statute book, but what happens on the ground.

Legislative reform of customary law

The examples of the Tanzanian and, particularly, the South African reforms throw up the issue of customary law and legislative intrusion into that law. The Report of the Presidential Commission in Tanzania played down the necessity or even desirability of significant statutory reform of customary land law, apart from provisions designed to prevent discrimination against women and to facilitate the granting of individual titles. It considered the reform of that law was best brought about by the slow process of judicial decisions, in the same way that common law and equity evolved in England. Desirable though this may be in principle, it is impracticable both in general terms and for Tanzania in particular. In all countries in Africa, there has been legislative intrusion into customary land law; in Tanzania this has been going on for over 100 years, including several attempts to "abolish" it altogether. The "restoration" of customary land law, which the new Act provides for, means that in the future customary law will derive its legality, if not its legitimacy, from statute law; and the attempt to create a Tanzanian common law, which the Land Act explicitly charges the courts to develop, inevitably means that the law will derive its continued legitimacy from the top – reported judicial decisions of the High Court and the Court of Appeal – and not from the bottom, as the Report hoped would be the case.

Individualisation of title

The process of individualisation of title poses the greatest challenge to the evolution of customary law. The creation of an individual right of occupancy and its allocation to an individual or a group through a statutory process *ipso facto* breaks the link between the land and customary tenure, even if the same people occupy the land. In Tanzania, however, the new law provides that the incidents of tenure on the new holding will be governed by customary law. This is a recognition that whatever legislation is in place, in practice customary law would continue to apply – the Kenyan legislation mentioned above also testifies to that.

However, the Act intrudes further: some basic rules of fair procedure are laid down; a person may not be dispossessed of land, and no penalties for "misuse" or other infringement of customary tenure rules may be applied without notice; an opportunity to contest the matter at a hearing and a right of appeal are provided. More contentiously, the law also provides that *inter vivos* transfers and other transactions designed to prevent women from inheriting or acquiring land, or obtaining credit on the security of land, may be disallowed. The justifications for these legislative intrusions are, first, the constitutional principle of equal treatment; second, the principle of administrative justice; and third, the NLP itself.

Can and should legislative intrusion into customary law be minimised? Should more vigorous efforts be made to adapt it to the needs of the market place? To what extent can and should a conscious effort be made to develop a national customary law or a common law via judicial decisions? These were not matters that were considered in Tanzania's NLP, in Namibia's policy documents or even, surprisingly perhaps, in the South African White Paper.

Adjudication

Given the central importance of land in African economy and society, and given that land disputes can and do escalate into violence and serious civil unrest and disturbances – Kenya and Ghana are two Anglophone examples – to say nothing of the total breakdown of civil society which conflicts over land can trigger (see Andre and Platteau, 1996; Besterman and Cassanelli, 1996), appropriate dispute settlement mechanisms are vital to successful land reform. In the past, far too few resources have been allocated to land dispute settlement procedures and institutions. The successful implementation and general public acceptance of new land laws and new rights, obligations, ways of doing things and official powers will depend to no small extent on whether efficient, effective and equitable dispute settlement mechanisms are put into place and then supplied with sufficient resources to enable them to provide justice to the people.

Adjudication and dispute settlement has been recognised as being of fundamental importance not just with respect to solving land disputes but to general respect for the rule of law. The World Bank and bilateral donors are putting increasing resources into programmes to improve the quality of the judicial and legal systems of countries in Africa. With respect to land, the trend within those countries which have embarked on land reform has been to develop specialist land courts or tribunals. South Africa established a Land Claims Court to deal with land restitution claims; Uganda has established a nation-wide system of land tribunals both at first instance and on appeal by the Land Act, 1998 and Tanzania has after some vacillation on the matter, established specialist land courts by the Land Courts Act, 2001. Owing to some politico-bureaucratic difficulties, the land tribunals in Uganda did not take off immediately and it is still too early to say how the Tanzanian land courts will work. Specialist courts will have the advantage of building up expertise in land issues but they will only be effective if they offer a rapid, economical and efficient service. In this respect, any general reforms to judicial systems in Africa will need to be applied to these specialist dispute settlement bodies as well.

Land law reform: an example

Finally, in this section, we will look at the example of Tanzania, where a two-pronged approach to land law reform is being proposed. The first prong deals with substantive law, the second with institutions of adjudication.

First, those holding customary rights of occupancy who intend to deal in them, and those with whom they may deal, may opt for their transactions to be governed by the statutory system; this is an approach used in Botswana and it avoids the problems which may arise from trying to marry up a modern transaction with customary law. A corollary of this approach is that a modern, reasonably straightforward statutory code of land law specifically tailored for the needs of smallholder peasant farmers is developed as a part of the new law. This part of the new law replaces the existing received land law that was imposed on Tanzania at the time of the English colonial take-over after World War One – the land law as it applied in England on 1 January 1922.

Somewhat surprisingly, the Presidential Commission had recommended retaining sections of this received land law, which was greatly at odds with its comment to the effect that a new basic land law should be drafted in as simple a language as possible without sacrificing accuracy. To propose that the gaps in Tanzanian land law be filled with English land law as it was in 1922 is to suggest that large parts of the basic Tanzanian land law should be drawn from laws stretching back to medieval England, couched in language which is at best complex and at worst quite unintelligible, and which in practice makes it quite impossible for the vast majority of Tanzanians to know what the law actually says.

The critical question then becomes: what law should replace the 1922 English land law? It does not seem practical to move too far away from a land law which is grounded in the common law. First, neither the NLP nor the Presidential Commission suggested that Tanzania develop a totally different basic substantive land law. Second, the residual non-customary and non-Islamic law of Tanzania remains the common law as developed in England and modified by almost 80 years of application in Tanzania. Third, the legal profession and those managing land in the public sector are familiar with English legal concepts and some of the basics of English land law and there is much good sense in the comment, made by a working party surveying the land law of Northern Ireland with a view to updating it, that: "The danger of impairing the efficiency of the legal profession [and it may be added in the context of Tanzania, the public sector land managers] by overloading it with unfamiliar law must be taken seriously" (Sheridan, 1971, p. 3).

This is not to say that Tanzania should slavishly adopt modern English land law; the latter is, quite naturally, geared to the needs of modern English society, which is very different to Tanzanian society. In one respect, however, the thrust of many proposals for land law reform coming from the English Law Commission do offer a better model to Tanzania as it embarks on the road to a land market than some of the models and ideas on offer from, for instance, the World Bank. The overall message of the English models is that a free market in land is not self-regulating; there needs to be a regulatory framework in place to ensure that a market works equitably as well as efficiently. This message is reflected in Tanzania's new land law.

There are other models which Tanzania drew on. There are many countries in the Commonwealth which have land laws based on English land law, but which have modified or amended them to reflect their own circumstances and more modern thinking about the role of land law in society. Three may be briefly mentioned.

First, the Malaysian National Land Code (MNLC), enacted in 1965, provides a comprehensive code of land law for Malaysia, covering both the administration of the land by public officials and substantive land law. It is this Code of Land Law that has been in operation during the last 35 years of spectacular economic growth in Malaysia. The Code makes extensive use of standard forms, contained in Schedule 1 of the Code, thus reducing the costs and complexity of dealings in land. An additional aspect of the Malaysian model which holds lessons for Tanzania is that there is a recognition that the land law of a country is a living law which needs constant review and amendment. A year rarely goes by without some amendment being made to the Code; each year, however, two or three commercial publishers publish a revised and updated edition of the National Land Code in both English and Malay ensuring easy access to the basic land law of the country.

The second example was a major Bill published by the New Zealand Law Commission in the form of a report in 1994. This dealt with many of the matters of substantive land law which needed to be provided for in the Tanzanian basic land law, and in part for the same reasons: to abolish some of the outdated common law rules on land – "ancient English statutes dating back to the thirteenth century" (New Zealand Law Commission, 1994, p. vii) which still survived in New Zealand; and to restate others in a clearer, modern legal form: "One of the most important objectives of the new Act is to set forth rules of property law accessibly and in a manner which, allowing for the subject matter, can be readily understood" (*ibid.*, pp. 1–2). The first clause of the Bill indeed states: "The purpose of this Act is to make the law relating to real and personal property more accessible and better suited to present and future needs by restating and developing that law and codifying it in part." This very succinctly sums up the aims of the Tanzanian law. Since New Zealand is a largely agricultural country, with small landowners and with land to which customary law applies, this was a relevant model for Tanzania to examine.

Finally, several parts of the land law of Kenya also provide useful models for Tanzania. The Registered Land Act of 1963 provides a well-drafted example of a modernised and simplified version of relevant parts of English land law adapted for use in an African setting. The Land Adjudication Act, and the Land (Group Representatives) Act 1968 deal with matters which the NLP considers central to Tanzanian land law. The Land Disputes Tribunals Act of 1991 provides useful pointers to the possible powers and procedures of mediation based on customary legal principles in Tanzania.[4] There were, then, no shortage of relevant models from the common law world on which Tanzania could draw in developing its own substantive land law. It needs to be emphasised, however, that at the end of the day, the decisive issue was whether the new proposals are appropriate for Tanzania, and whether the necessary Tanzanian adaptations have been made to laws drawn from other jurisdictions.

Turning now to the second prong of the approach to customary law, the new law proposed a dedicated system of land courts which, staffed by specialist judges, would be able to develop a new common land law of Tanzania out of the multiplicity of customary laws, received laws and statute law. This was suggested by the Presidential Commission and while the NLP agreed with the principle of specialist dispute-settlement bodies, it preferred to cast them in the form of tribunals. The important issues are that any dispute settlement bodies, by whatever name, should be independent of the Executive, should be staffed by experts in both customary and statutory land law, should be regulated by straightforward procedures and should, with a minimum of expense and delay, deal with land disputes via a range of techniques - alternative dispute resolution, formal hearings, public inquiries, and informal meetings. The new law aimed to provide for all this.[5]

Legal personnel and law reform

The final matter to be dealt with in this chapter concerns people; legal academics and the training of personnel. One of the most striking aspects of the wide-ranging public debate on land reform in South Africa over this decade has been the leading role taken by lawyers, for the most part legal academics, in writing about the need and possible models for land reform laws. The quality of the legal contributions has undoubtedly raised the intellectual and conceptual content of the debate and might contribute to better laws as a consequence.[6] In Tanzania too, the Presidential Commission on Land Matters, which has had such an important influence on the content of the NLP and the Land Bill, was headed by an academic lawyer. Concerned and committed progress on land reform or land law reform is unlikely to be made without them.

However, legal scholarship is only one, albeit very important, role for the legal academic. New land laws providing for major programmes of land reform must also involve the training of those who are to implement the laws and those who are to use them. New land laws may well be ignored by the people at large if they do not perceive any benefits to be had from complying with them. This attitude is much more likely to be adopted if no effort is made to explain the new laws and their benefits; if officials continue to behave under the new law as they did under the old; and if lawyers make no effort to adapt their working practices to meet the needs of ordinary people.

The Mexican land reforms of 1992 provide a compelling example of what can go wrong if new laws are not followed up with adequate training and public awareness campaigns. These reforms were designed to introduce market forces into the *ejido* land tenure system, a village communal system of land tenure in which individuals (*ejidatarios)* had limited rights, and the land could not be sold. This system was very similar to customary tenure and villagisation in Tanzania and gave rise to similar economic and political phenomena – low productivity among the peasants; power concentrated in the hands of local party bosses of the one major party, the PRI, and the local *ejidal* commissioners, who controlled *ejido* land; and the growth of an unofficial land market in *ejido* land, with all the rent-seeking behaviour that encourages. The process of reform was largely worked out in secret by a deregulation secretariat in the President's office, and was enacted in 1992. Grindle (1996) analysed the reforms as part of a wider study of reforms in economy, politics and society in Mexico and Kenya in the 1980s and 1990s; she summarised the post-enactment position as follows (p. 91):

> Whether strong opposition existed or not, implementation of the new legislation would be problematic. Unlike deregulation, implementing new rights in property would require an extensive administrative infrastructure. Under the new laws and regulations, each *ejido* could decide whether or not its members would receive individual property rights. In order to grant individual title to land, the government needed to settle a vast number of outstanding *ejido* land claims. It also needed to clarify the individual status of *ejidatarios* and to assess the value of agricultural land if a market in land was to be introduced. An extensive system of land courts was set up as part of the reforms, but their operation was not clearly understood, even by the reformers. *Ejidatarios* needed to be informed of their new rights and how to implement change.

Much of Grindle's summary reads like a remarkably prescient forecast of the contents of the Tanzanian Land Act and Village Land Act and the likely implementation problems. As the summary makes clear, little of what was needed by way of implementation of the reforms was provided for; opposition duly grew culminating in the peasant uprising in the southern state of Chiapas in January 1994 in which the peasants demanded (amongst other things) the repeal of the revision of the Article 27 in the Constitution which had preceded and made possible the land reform. This is not to suggest that similar failures of implementation in Tanzania, or indeed elsewhere in Africa, will lead to such a dramatic result, but the message is plain: enactment of a law to bring about fundamental changes in land relations must be accompanied by a planned programme of implementation in which training and public education are central both for citizens and for the professions.

Programmes of training and public education in law are a major challenge to the legal profession as whole but particularly to its academic branch. They are also a challenge to the donor community which urges land law reform on countries in Africa. To give just one statistic; according to policies enunciated in the NLP, considerable powers of land management are to be vested in village councils in Tanzania by the new law. There are over 8000 villages in Tanzania: it is doubtful whether even 5% of these have officials with any expertise in land management. Unless a quite extraordinary programme of training in the new law and how to exercise the powers provided under that law is mounted for village officials, aiming to provide no more than one trained official per village, the law will never be effective and may in fact be counter-productive, contributing to widening the gap of comprehension about land and law between the peasants on the one hand, and central officials and educated elite on the other. Such a programme can only be mounted with donor support.

Equally, to ensure that the new specialised land courts and *Mbaraza* are staffed by persons with some knowledge of the land laws of Tanzania will involve considerable resources. While donors might supply funds and some technical training expertise for these training programmes, the intellectual and human resource input must come from inside the country concerned.

Lawyers, and particularly academic lawyers, thus face two major challenges related to land law reform in Africa. First is the challenge of scholarship; to rise above the merely descriptive and analytical approach to writing about land law and adopt a more policy-orientated and innovative approach which offers new models and creative ideas as solutions to practical problems of land management; and, if the opportunity presents itself, to become involved in the challenging business of turning these ideas and models into legislative drafts – a scholarly endeavour, for which creative and not just critical scholarship is needed.

Second is the challenge of education and training. Here too there is a need to set aside the traditional, rather narrow functions of the undergraduate legal educator. Innovative programmes – of mass legal education, of the development of distance learning materials and instruction, of interactive learning via computer programmes, of the use of radio, television and videos – and intensive short courses for all levels of officials and lawyers, will need to be developed and taught. Lawyer-reform will need to accompany law reform.

Conclusion

There is no one right way to tackle the issue of land tenure reform in Africa. The reforms in Tanzania have been the product of a good deal more thought, investigation, preparation and participation than has occurred elsewhere in Africa, with the exception of South Africa, and the Government deserves considerable credit for that. Continued debate can only improve the prospects of success for the reforms, as more people become aware of them.

It is essential that the reforms, once introduced, are carefully monitored, so that adjustments may be made as and when needed. At the end of the day, while land law reform might, just, still be the preserve of the lawyer, the products of that reform – the new laws – are the property of the nation and the nation must be assisted in embracing and working within those new laws. Only in this way can law be made to work to restructure land relations in Africa.

---

*This chapter is based on an article of the same name published in 1998, *Development and Change*, Vol. 29, pp. 525–52 and is a revised version of the Third Alistair Berkley Memorial Lecture, given at the London School of Economics and Political Science on 30 May 1996.

Notes

[1] For example, Tanzania embarked on a major multi-donor supported programme of legal system reform, the Financial and Legal Management Upgrading Project (FILMUP) in 1994. This began with a series of studies of different facets of the legal system which led to a single report by a Legal Task Force to the Government of Tanzania for onwards transmission to donors. See Mark Bomani, Report of the Legal Task Force (1996) 4 *Change*, pp. 83–89. The World Bank funded a programme of law reform in Uganda in the late 1990s and a Kenyan equivalent of the Tanzanian FILMUP also funded by the World Bank commenced in 1998.

[2] Two small illustrations of this attitude. First, a provision was put into the draft Land Bill providing that an official who forcibly entered on to land, or who while on land wilfully did any damage to that land should be liable on conviction to a fine not exceeding Tshs 1 million (Tshs 1200 = £1) or to imprisonment not exceeding two years. A committee advising on the drafting of the Bill (of which a majority were officials) proposed reducing the fine to a maximum of Tshs 1000 "otherwise officials would fear to carry out their duties". Exactly: the whole point was that officials should fear to abuse their powers; but officials thought officials should not be impeded from exercising their powers as they saw fit. Second, a proposal was made to create the office of a Land Ombudsman to deal with complaints against officials and overcome the problem of the Commissioner of Lands having to deal with complaints against his own officials. More horror: there were already too many opportunities for people to complain about officials. The proposal never saw the light of day.

[3] In the event, the worst of all possible worlds was adopted. The "limited consent for special categories of transactions" approach of the NLP was used by the author

in drafting the Land Bill. The text of the relevant clauses was accepted by the Ministry but during the process of turning a consultant's draft into an Act, someone somewhere got cold feet about "letting go" and there were tacked on to the consultant's draft Bill sub-clauses and new clauses providing for full administrative control of dispositions. The resultant provisions of the Land Act, 1999 are contradictory, confusing and likely to give rise to many problems of practice and interpretation. See ss. 36–41.

[4] In late 1999, the Kenyan Government announced a wide ranging inquiry into its land laws and their administration headed by a lawyer who had played a major role in the introduction of English land law via the Registered Land Act in 1962. Very few amendments had been made to the Kenyan Act since its enactment so that some changes are probably needed. The major problem in land in Kenya however is not the law but the flouting and violation of the law by the land-grabbing elite.

[5] Here too the process of turning the consultant's draft into a law has produced some considerable difficulties. The Government preferred to develop new District Land and Housing Tribunals which would merge existing Customary Land Tribunals and Rent Tribunals. Unfortunately, apart from vesting *exclusive* jurisdiction in these new bodies, the relevant Part of the Land Act, 1999 was silent on them. They were not established by the Act; their composition was not set out; nor were their powers and duties; nor the appellate structure. There was then a great hole in the law. The problem was specifically drawn to the attention of the Ministry in April, 2000, but not until the Land Courts Act, 2001 was the gap in the law filled.

[6] Oddly however, the Department of Land Affairs never made any use of the large number of academic land lawyers, even as consultants to comment on drafts of laws, during the period 1994–99 when the bulk of the work on land reform laws was underway.

12 As good as it gets: politics and markets in the making of Uganda's Land Act, 1998 *

Our position has four points and is based on double reform – controlled rent and no power to evict. The points are: recognise ownership of the landlord, accept controlled or nominal rent, a landlord should not evict the tenant as he likes but go through a tribunal and set up a fund so that poor people can also get money to buy land. For me, I am ready to be hanged on these four points.

Yoweri Museveni, President of Uganda, The New Vision, 19 May 1998

Introduction

This chapter charts the evolution of the Land Act of Uganda, which was required by the Constitution of Uganda to be enacted into law on or before 2 July 1998 and the first steps in its implementation. It is in many respects a revolutionary law, overturning a century of land relations in Uganda and laying the groundwork for the evolution of a market in land based on the individual ownership of land, and not surprisingly therefore, it sparked off a vigorous public debate on the matter. This debate pitted the local politics of land in Uganda against the dictates of the market for land and so is of wide interest.

Of equal interest, at least for those concerned not just with the evolution of the market economy in countries in Africa but with the evolution of good governance as well – transparency, accountability, participation, respect for the rule of law – this case study also records the openness and quality of the public debate, the willingness of the Government to listen to alternative views, the interaction between Parliament and Government and the emergence as a consequence of a greatly improved law and a better informed populace.

The third theme is the nature of the law that is the vehicle for the introduction of the revolution, the impact that the draft Bill as published in March 1998 had on the debate and the way different approaches to the business of drafting laws can play an important role in the reform process. The final theme is that of implementation and the importance of planning for that before rather than after the Bill became law.

A brief history of land relations in Uganda in the colonial period

Students of land relations will know that it is difficult to understand the present state of land tenure in any country without an awareness of its history. Even where a revolutionary change occurs, its rationale lies in the past and the chances of success of the change will also be determined in part by the past and the extent to which path-dependent patterns of development can be overcome. Uganda is no exception to these generalisations so this chapter must start by sketching the history of Uganda's land tenure and its legal framework.

The modern history of Uganda starts with the Uganda Agreement of 1900 – an agreement in equal measure about land and about governance. The Uganda Agreement was made between the British Government and the Kingdom of Buganda, one component of the modern state of Uganda. The Agreement defined the judicial and administrative functions of the Kabaka (King) and Lukiiko (Government) of Buganda *vis-à-vis* the British colonial authorities and by Articles 15–17 made provision for a general land settlement. In the words of Henry West (1972, p. 17), the foremost authority on land relations in Buganda:

> This land settlement was fundamental to the whole Agreement and should be viewed only as an integral part of it. Johnston [the British colonial official who was responsible for it from the British side] used it quite patently for political purposes. He seemed to have no realisation of the changes he was making … Briefly, the total area of land in Buganda was assumed to be 19,600 square miles which was to be divided between the Kabaka and other notables on the one hand and the Uganda Administration on the other. Thus the Kabaka, certain members of the royal family, the Regents, county chiefs and certain other leaders were to receive either private or official estates totalling 958 square miles and 'one thousand chiefs and private landowners' were to receive 'the estates of which they are already in possession'. These were computed at an average of 8 square miles per individual making a total of 8,000 square miles … The remaining area, amounting to an estimated 9,000 square miles was to be vested in Her Majesty's Government. It was this land which came to be called Crown Land; its designation being changed to Public Land by the Public Lands Ordinance of 1962.

The land thus granted to the Kabaka and the chiefs was not vacant land; it was occupied by peasants and the relations between the peasant occupiers and the chiefs was up to the time of the Uganda Agreement, governed by a intricate system of law which as tends to be normal in pre-market societies, mingled public (government) and private (access to use and occupancy of land) law. The land granted to the chiefs became known as 'mailo' land, mailo being a reference to the square miles of land so granted and the tenure in which it was granted was English freehold tenure. Prophetically, the Foreign Office in considering the Agreement in June 1900 commented that the "introduction of the law of England in regard to land, which appears from the wording of the Agreement to be the intention of the framers, may create a very complicated system". Johnston however in West's words "saw individual property rights as a fundamental principle of civilisation and social order" and was more concerned to confirm Ganda leaders in their private landholding than guarantee the continuance of traditional relationships between chiefs and their subjects (bakopi).

Thus was one time-bomb embedded in Uganda's political and socio-economic structure; relations between landlord and tenant within Buganda have always been fraught with tension; the landlords reluctant to accept that the restrictions of customary relationships should limit their absolute ownership of their land, as they understand freehold ownership to imply; the tenants totally refusing to accept that they have no rights in land which they regard as being theirs by virtue of customary law. Freehold tenure then was taken to be something very different in Uganda to that which it was in England; in Uganda it was taken to denote absolute ownership – it was freehold ownership; in England, it was and had always been a freehold estate; a fundamental part of the system of divided rights of ownership which characterises English land law and which permits more than one party to have rights in the same plot of land. English freehold could have accommodated both landlords and tenants in Buganda; Mugandan freehold could not.

The 1900 Agreement however planted a further time-bomb; the "Lost Counties". In the run-up the Uganda Agreement 1900 and the British acquisition of Uganda, there was, inevitably, fighting between the British and various states and political groupings in the geographical area of modern Uganda. One such state was Buganda; another was Bunyoro. At the crucial time, Buganda threw in its lot with the British; Bunyoro did not and fought hard against the British. The 1900 Agreement rewarded Buganda by taking a portion of Bunyoro and transferring it to Buganda, subjecting it (and those living in that area) to the new regime of mailo land – Ganda chiefs with freehold ownership of land occupied by Banyoro with a burning sense of grievance over the "Lost Counties".

Finally, the Agreement had another perhaps unforeseen but in retrospect, inevitable effect which was the third time-bomb planted by the colonial power. The Agreement had divided land in Buganda into two categories; freehold (mailo) land and Crown Land. In respect of mailo land, customary land tenure was not recognised as giving any secure rights to the land to those occupying land in accordance with it. *A fortiori* with respect to Crown Land as the Crown Land Ordinance of 1903 made clear. This Ordinance set the pattern for all land in Uganda other than mailo land; persons occupying land under customary tenure were never regarded as owning the land; they were no more than tenants at will of the Crown. The colonial Government could and often did grant both freehold and leasehold titles of land which such persons occupied to persons who applied for such land, with the customary occupiers thereafter being required to move off the land so granted or remaining specifically as tenants at will of the new owner.

For the sake of completeness, the fourth time-bomb must be noted. This is the Registration of Titles Ordinance, 1922, now the Registration of Titles Act, Cap. 205, which governs the registration of land titles in Uganda. Its genesis and effectiveness are well described by West (1972, pp. 166–68). He recounts that the Registration of Titles Ordinance 1908 based on laws from Fiji and the Sudan was a short and simple law but was never regarded as more than a temporary one. The Torrens system of title registration was thought to be appropriate for Uganda so reference was made to Australian experience:

> By 1916 opinion had swung in favour of an ordinance based on the most recent Torrens style legislation, namely the Transfer of Lands Acts of 1915 and 1916 of the State of Victoria ... A draft Bill was sent to the Secretary of State ... [and] ... was eventually approved by the Uganda Executive Council in 1922 ...
>
> It will be remembered that there was at that time no fund of English experience from which to draw. In fact, in England, prior to 1925, registration of title may be said generally to have been a failure ... Of the two lawyers chiefly concerned with the Bill in its final stages, one had some experience in Australia and the other in Ireland; neither of them had any length of experience of conditions in Uganda.. So the result was the transfer of an institution from one context to another with the minimum of criticism and adaptation ...

> Almost since the day of its enactment, the Registration of Titles Ordinance has been criticised by those who have had experience of its operation ... As a piece of legislation it has a sophistication still generally uncalled for in either rural or urban areas of Buganda [or it might be added Uganda generally]. It has 211 sections and 22 schedules; much of its couched in abstruse phraseology; many of its sections still have no application in practice. Its very complexity has weighed against its successful operation in a number of ways ...

West mentions the failure to translate the law into Luganda and the impossibility of doing so; the confusion of which courts had jurisdiction over disputes arising under the Ordinance; the ineptitude shown over the reference system connecting the register and the ground; the neglect of a proper system of survey. "These and other problems could have been avoided if ... greater wisdom and common sense had been exercised in the process of legalistic plagiarism" (1972, p. 172).

If some time has been in setting the scene in Uganda, it is because it seems to me as if some of the lessons that could have been learned from the colonial past in Uganda not just for Uganda but generally in respect of land tenure reform in Africa have been but imperfectly learned by the protagonists of market-orientated tenure reforms in both national and international aid and lending institutions.

As at the beginning, so at the end: as the colonial enterprise was wound down in the early 1960s, the British colonial authorities slipped a couple of poison pills into the morass of land tenure and governance in Uganda in 1962 just before independence. First, as a "solution" to the "Lost Counties"; it was agreed and provided for in the independence Constitution that a referendum would be held in the "Lost Counties" to determine whether they should be returned to Bunyoro or remain as part of Buganda; no mention was made of the ownership of land in the area. The referendum took place in 1964 with the result a foregone conclusion; the "Lost Counties" voted to become part of Bunyoro again and were made so eventually as the District of Kibaale but the festering sore of Baganda landlords and Banyoro tenants remained.

Second, as part of the deal done between the British, the authorities in Buganda and the political parties in Uganda in the run up to independence, it was agreed that Crown Land should be transferred to the state of Uganda and vested in and managed by a Land Commission but that in Buganda, Crown Land should vested in and managed by the Buganda Land Board. For the Baganda, this was the "return" of "their" 9,000 square miles taken by the colonial authorities by the Uganda Agreement in 1900. The Public

Lands Ordinance, passed in March 1962, before independence provided for this. This law also provided for the possibility of the conversion of customary tenure to freehold tenure via a process of adjudication.

Land in Uganda 1962–85

The history of Uganda's independence has been a troubled one and at the heart of the troubles has been the land question. The referendum on the "Lost Counties" in 1964 went against Buganda and soured relations between the coalition government of the Uganda Peoples' Congress and Kabaka Yekka – the Baganda only political party. Two years later the Prime Minister and leader of the UPC, Milton Obote overthrew the Independence Constitution of 1962, abolished the kingdoms in Uganda, sacked Mengo – the capital of Buganda, chased the Kabaka into exile, wound up the Buganda Land Board and vested all public land in Uganda in the Land Commission. The Public Lands Act 1969 gave legislative backing to this new dispensation. It left untouched the position of customary tenure however; land occupied under customary tenure was public land and could still be alienated in freehold or leasehold but only with the consent of those occupying the land under customary tenure and such persons would be entitled to compensation where such a grant was made. No change was made to tenure in Kibaale District nor was the Registration of Titles Act touched.

Obote was in turn overthrown in 1971 by Amin, the army chief whom Obote had used to lead the sacking of Mengo. Amin was persuaded to try his hand at land reform. The Land Reform Decree 1975 attempted to deal with the problems of mailo land by abolishing it and indeed all freehold land. All land became public land, held, at most, on a 99-year lease from the state. At the stroke of a pen, mailo landowners became tenants of the state and all landlord/tenant relationships were governed by the Decree. As before however, customary tenure was untouched although the position of customary land holders was significantly worsened; land which they occupied could be alienated without the need to obtain their consent.

Interestingly too the Registration of Titles Act was tackled; the Mortgage Decree 1974 replaced many of the provisions of that Act dealing with mortgages. This decree was in part inspired by Amin's anti-Asian policies; there was (and is for the decree was still in force at the end of 2001 with no reform in sight) significant discrimination against non-

African mortgagees, but in part the decree represents an attempt to up date the law on mortgages. The decree was not well drafted and more of the provisions of the Registration of Titles Act dealing with mortgages were repealed than were replaced which leaves unfortunate gaps in the law.

There are not wanting those in Uganda who argue that the Land Reform Decree was the best effort yet to grapple with the colonial legacy since it represented a root and branch attempt to get rid of the poisoned chalice of private landlord/tenant relations and sought to impose a uniform system of land administration throughout the country. In practice however it was never fully implemented. Amin was overthrown in 1979; an interregnum of some 18 months gave way to a regime known as Obote II, the product of a rigged election in 1980, which was dominated by internal civil strife and, in turn, after a further brief period of musical presidential chairs in 1985–86, gave way to President Museveni and the National Resistance Movement Government.

The market approach to land reform

This is the present government, legitimised by the new Constitution of 1995, and the elections which took place under it in 1996 and 2001, and it is the actions and decisions of this government that need to be concentrated on for it is this government that set in train the policy processes that led up to the Land Act. There were two forces behind the Act; they may be called the World Bank force and the Constitutional force. The former represents the forces of the market; the latter the political force.

The World Bank began to involve itself in agriculture policy reforms in Uganda in the early 1980s. In 1987, a working group on land tenure reform recommended that the effect of the Land Reform Decree be studied and a sound national land tenure policy be formulated, conducive to agricultural development and consistent with positive steps to rehabilitate and update the Land Registry. The Bank, together with USAID funded this major study of land tenure in Uganda which was carried out by the University of Wisconsin Land Tenure Center (LTC) together with the Makerere Institute of Social Research (MISR).

The study, which reported in 1989, consumed large sums of money but did not probe very deeply into the more intractable problems of land tenure in Buganda. It recommended that the Land Reform Decree be repealed and that policy on land should be to facilitate the development of a market for land based on freehold titles with mailo owners, mailo tenants, leaseholders on public land and customary tenants (those holding public land under customary tenure) able to obtain freehold title to the land they occupied and freely deal with it thereafter. Mailo owners would be compensated for land occupied by tenants which was converted to freehold through a process of leasehold enfranchisement under these proposals. No development conditions should be imposed on freehold titles.

These recommendations were accepted by a workshop which met to consider them and a technical committee was then set up to “reduce” these policies into land legislation. The Committee was also to carry out a “rapid reconnaissance exercise” throughout the country to obtain the views of the people on the proposed policies. That committee produced a draft law which was, in some respects, a repeat of the Public Lands Act 1969 but with some significant differences; mailo land was not reinstated but freehold tenure was; customary tenure remained in its usual state of limbo but the possibility of conversion to freehold via a process of adjudication was provided for. Leasehold titles could be automatically converted to freehold title. A high degree of administrative management of land via the Uganda Land Commission which was retained in a central position was provided for.

Further consultation took place on these proposals. Another committee was established to carry out a nation wide consultation exercise particularly with respect to the implications for customary tenure of proposals to enable conversion of that tenure to freehold. As a result of that exercise, a new Bill was put together by the Technical Committee on Land Tenure Law Reform which reported to the Agricultural Secretariat of the Bank of Uganda in June 1993. This new Bill steered an uneasy course between the Scylla of freehold tenure and the Charybdis of state control to be exercised by the Land Commission and various district level bodies and local authorities. Entitled the Tenure and Control of Land Bill, this too never got beyond being part of a committee report.

Overall however, the consistent thrust of this strand of land policy making was in the direction of a uniform system of land tenure in the country based on freehold tenure, the solution to landlord/tenant relations on mailo land being left to market forces with the Government facilitating leasehold enfranchisement, and customary tenure being phased out as freehold titles replaced occupation under customary law.

The constitutional approach to land reform

It is at this point that the constitutional dimension to land tenure reform must be considered. Starting in 1992, a major exercise in constitution-making got under way in Uganda. A Commission sat for almost two years, touring the country widely to obtain views on the most appropriate form of constitution for Uganda. Its report together with a draft constitution was then subjected to a further detailed scrutiny by a Constituent Assembly elected for the purpose. Land was a major issue both before the Commission and in the Constituent Assembly. After much debate, various important and not wholly consistent provisions were adopted which need to be set out here.

The Preamble to the Constitution consists of 29 National Objectives and Directive Principles of State Policy. Several are concerned with recognising and enhancing the role of women in society – an important factor in later debates on the Land Bill. Directive XI deals with the role of the state in development. Paragraph (iii) states:

> In furtherance of social justice, the State may regulate the acquisition, ownership, use and development of land and other property, in accordance with the Constitution.

Directive XXVII deals with the environment. Paragraph (i) states:

> The State shall promote sustainable development and public awareness of the need to manage land, air, water resources in a balanced manner for the present and future generations.

Article 26 of the Constitution provides that every person has a right to own property either individually or in association with others and further provides limitations on the state's power compulsorily to acquire private property. This may only take place if it "is necessary for public use or in the interest of defence, public safety, public order, public morality or public health" and prompt and prior payment of fair and adequate compensation is provided for.

Chapter 15 of the Constitution, comprising Articles 237–45 deal with land. Article 237 is central to the debate on the new Act:

> (1) Land in Uganda belongs to the citizens of Uganda and shall vest in them in accordance with the land tenure systems provided for in this Constitution ...

Land in Uganda shall be owned in accordance with the following land tenure systems –

customary;
freehold;
mailo; and
leasehold

On the coming into force of this Constitution –

(a) all Uganda citizens owing land under customary tenure may acquire certificates of ownership in a manner to be prescribed by Parliament; and

(b) land under customary tenure may be converted to freehold land ownership by registration.

(5) Any lease which was granted to a Uganda citizen out of public land may be converted into freehold in accordance with a law which shall be made by Parliament …

(8) Upon the coming into force of this Constitution and until Parliament enacts an appropriate law under clause (9) of this article, the lawful or *bona fide* occupants of mailo land, freehold or leasehold land shall enjoy security of tenure on the land.

(9) Within two years after the first sitting of Parliament elected under this Constitution, Parliament shall enact a law –

(a) regulating the relationship between the lawful or *bona fide* occupants of land referred to in clause (8) of this article and the registered owners of that land;

(b) providing for the acquisition of registrable interest in the land by the occupant.

It is clause (9) which drove the enactment of the Land Bill by 2 July 1998, the second anniversary of the first sitting of Parliament elected under the Constitution.

Four matters are of particular note in this Article, all of them representing a different approach to the market dimension. First and arguably most revolutionary, given the history of the matter, is the conferring of rights of ownership on persons occupying land under customary tenure. No longer are they customary tenants on public land, subject to the whims of officials willing to grant that land to whomsoever they see fit or will pay. Given that under the Land Reform Decree, all land in Uganda was previously public land and even under the Public Lands Acts and their predecessor Crown Lands Ordinances, all customarily occupied lands were public lands, the effect of this provision is virtually to eliminate public land as a category of land in Uganda.

Second, as a concession to Buganda, mailo land is restored. In practice, as successive committees recognised, the incidents of mailo tenure are the same as the incidents of freehold tenure but the symbolic significance of mailo land was too great to be ignored. However, given its restoration, it was equally necessary to tackle the problem of landlord/tenant relations on mailo land, the more so since during the guerrilla war in the bush which preceded the coming to power of the NRM Government in 1986, commitments were made to the peasant occupiers of mailo land that their interests would be catered for. It was also necessary to grapple with the continuing sore of land relations in Kibaale District. It was impossible to reach agreement within the Constituent Assembly on these matters – the third matter of the four referred to above – so clauses (8) and (9) were inserted to deal with this problem; a temporary freezing of the status quo with the long term solution thrown into the lap of the new Parliament. Just to compound the difficulties, no definition of lawful or *bona fide* occupant was provided in the Constitution.

Fourth, clause (5) provided for leasehold enfranchisement in respect of leases of public land – not automatically but in accordance with provisions to be made by Parliament. This provision however was consistent with the aim of eliminating public land which is the corner-stone of Article 237. No effort was made to address the issue of any potential conflict of land rights between customary occupants of leasehold land and the leaseholder. That too was left for Parliament to sort out.

To complete the record, the other Articles of Chapter 15 may be summarised. Article 238 provides for the establishment of the Uganda Land Commission; Article 239 provides for its functions – little more than the Government's estate agent and property manager, though as will be seen below, it has been given very important functions by the Land Act. Article 240 establishes District Land Boards for each district and Article 241 sets out their functions – to hold and allocate land not held by any person or authority and to facilitate the registration and transfer of interests in land – providing for them to be independent of the Commission and any other person or authority but required to take account of national and district policies on land. Article 242 empowers the government to make laws regulating land use. Article 243 requires Parliament to establish land tribunals to deal with land disputes, Article 244 requires Parliament to make laws regulating the exploitation of minerals and Article 245 requires Parliament to enact laws to the protect the environment.

The Land Bill, 1998: a drafting critique

The Land Bill published in early March 1998 was designed to take up the matters specifically remitted to Parliament by the Constitution. An earlier version, while never officially published was the subject of a public debate in September 1997 where some critical comments were directed at the paucity of its provisions dealing with the land rights of women and with matters of customary tenure. The Government, in the person of the Prime Minister, welcomed the comments, undertook to take the Bill back and rethink some of the provisions and indicated a willingness to work with the critics. At this point however, it is fair to say that general public debate about and awareness of the contents of the Bill was minimal.

Despite the considerable input via research and official committees over the preceding decade to developing a national land policy for Uganda, no specific document has ever been published setting out in clear non-legal language what the aims of a national land policy are and how a Land Bill will achieve them. Thus, when the Land Bill was published in the Government Gazette, it was, for virtually everyone, the first indication of government thinking about how to implement the provisions of Chapter 15 of the Constitution. As the debate on the Bill developed, this was a major charge levelled against the Government; that it was trying to bounce Parliament and the public into accepting a law which had not been subject to adequate public debate. The Government's response was that the proposals in the Bill had in fact been the subject of considerable public discussion all over the country, both during the debate on the Constitution and while the various committees were developing their policy options on land over the last decade. The conflict of views is a familiar one; the Government had indeed held public consultations but on an agenda usually determined by Government; there had, however, been no open-ended public debate either on land policy or on the specifics in the Bill which as the ensuing debate showed, were highly contentious.

At this point, it is necessary to outline the author's role in the making of the Land Bill and so provide the justification to narrowing down the discussion to legal specifics. He was invited to participate in a workshop on the Bill organised by a Uganda NGO for Parliamentarians in late April – the date was put back by a month to accommodate the visit of President Clinton to Uganda – which was designed to sensitise MPs and launch a public debate on the Bill. He was asked to consider whether the Bill as drafted was workable and provided adequately for accountability. His answer was broadly, that it was not possible to say because the draft Bill was too vague, had too many open-ended provisions that left it unclear who was to do what and with what effect, had provisions that were virtually meaningless or did not appear to comply with the Constitution, and did not provide adequate certainty for the rights being granted to the citizen.

Two specific examples of drafting deficiencies in the March Bill may be given. They both come from the paper the author gave at the workshop. The first comes from the provisions dealing with the conversion of customary tenure to individualised holdings (1998, pp. 5–7).

Conversion of customary tenure to individualised tenure

> Clause 3 of the Bill repeats the constitutional position on the four types of land tenure. Clauses 4 to 8 encapsulate the primary purpose of the Bill. Clause 4 provides for a person holding land under customary tenure on former public land to obtain a certificate of customary tenure. This is an enabling device to allow land held under customary tenure to enter the market. Clause 5 enables a person to bypass a certificate process and covert his/her customary holding of land straight to freehold title in accordance with the provisions of clause 8. Clause 6 provides that a group of persons who hold land communally may also obtain a certificate of customary tenure and proceed to freehold ownership. Land holdership in such circumstances will be by trustees.
>
> There are some problems with these provisions. They assume only individual or group ownership of land under customary tenure. They leave out family or household ownership, something wider than a joint tenancy provided for in the Registration of Titles Act but less than a group (which is, surprisingly, not defined in the Bill). They are very unclear as to what powers and duties the Parish Land Committee has to deal with an application for a certificate of customary ownership. How is it to 'verify' customary rights over the land to which the application relates? Are there to be hearings? Who may appear? What does verification mean and what are the consequences of verification or non-verification? Can it verify a customary right but recommend that it be ignored or set aside with compensation paid so as to facilitate the grant of a certificate? Can a certificate be granted subject to one or more customary rights which are to be vested in other persons? Can more than one certificate be granted in respect of the same piece of land to reflect the position that under customary law, there may be different kinds of ownership rights in the land vested in different persons?
>
> Even more serious, what happens to customary rights, verified or otherwise when land is converted to freehold ownership and the customary rights have no comparable or parallel rights in the common law? This is a particular problem with the rights of women. Some customary systems may recognise a wife's

right to use land for the growing of certain crops. The right might not attach to any particular piece of land. How is this right to be categorised in common law terms so that it can be entered on the register of title. It is not a lease or a joint tenancy because it does not attach to a particular piece of land; it is not a profit *à prendre* for the same reason. The nearest 'modern' equivalent is a usufructuary right recognised in Roman-Dutch law but not in the common law. Without some guidance in the Bill, how is the Committee to know what to do?

What powers does a Committee have in respect of inspecting and marking boundaries? These words do not seem to include adjudicating on boundaries; *i.e.*, deciding between different points of view about where boundaries are which will inevitably occur when individual rights are being determined. Are boundaries to be 'fixed' or 'general'; or to use the terminology of the Registration of Titles Act (to which no reference is made); could a freehold title be issued 'Limited as to Parcels'? Why may a person aggrieved by a decision of the District Board under clause 4 (certificate of customary ownership) or the Parish Land Committee under clause 6 appeal to the Land Tribunal (which Land Tribunal?) but not someone aggrieved by a decision of the Board under clause 8 (freehold ownership)? The lack of appeal here seems to infringe Article 42 of the Constitution (which provides for a right of appeal to a court of law in respect of an administrative decision taken against him or her). Who is a person aggrieved? What are the time-limits for appealing to the Tribunal? These matters need to be provided for in the Bill.

Further issues arise on two institutions created or provided for by these clauses. First, trustees of communally held land. These trustees are to be chosen 'according to the customs of the group'. This assumes that groups know of trustees; that is, that trustees are a recognised body of persons in all customary laws applicable in Uganda. Are they? And if not, how can they be chosen according to the customs of the group? No provision is made for changing trustees in case of dissatisfaction with the performance of one or more. How many trustees must/can there be? The Bill states that only one trustee need be appointed; this would be most undesirable since there would be no check on the behaviour of that one trustee. Is it to be assumed that any matters connected with the performance of trustees are governed by the Trustees Act and determined by the High Court? If so, it is unlikely the system will work very well.

Relations between bona fide *occupants of land and registered owners*

The second example comes from the provisions dealing with relations between lawful or *bona fide* occupants and registered owners of land (1998, pp. 10–11).

Lawful and *bona fide* occupants covered by the Bill are granted security of occupancy which is clearly meant to be different to tenure and all such occupancy, whether *bona fide* or lawful (and there is a difference – the *bona fide* occupant being either a *bona fide* squatter or a person settled on land by the Government while a lawful occupant is a species of tenant) is converted into a statutory tenancy. Apart from provisions about the paying of rent which is contained in clause 10, there is nothing else in the Bill about the rights or duties of a statutory tenant. Does the conversion from occupancy to statutory tenancy entail a switch from customary to common law as the law governing the incidents of the relationship between owner and occupier? The Bill needs to provide for this. One puzzling point on a statutory tenant is this: under the common law, a lease is a tenure of land for a defined period and the Bill so defines it; what is the length of a statutory tenancy? It seems to be potentially perpetual: is this correct? If so, statutory tenancy needs to have its own special definition in the Bill.

Clause 11 deals with some incidents of a statutory tenancy. Statutory tenants may be issued with a certificate of occupancy following the same flawed process as applies to those persons dealt with in clauses 4 to 8. Subclause (4) needs to be revisited since it may be impossible to comply with. The intention seems to be that a certificate of occupancy is issued once rent begins to be paid as a statutory tenant. However, first, it may be impossible for certificates to be processed sufficiently quickly for them to be issued on the first payment of rent ('a certificate shall be issued …'). Second, the way the subclause has been drafted would require a certificate to be issued once a first payment of rent had been made even if that first payment were a payment made in arrears and there were other payments outstanding. The subclause needs to be amended to provide that a certificate will only be issued when payments of rent are up to date.

The logic behind the provisions dealing with dispositions is a little difficult to follow. First, the registered owner must be given the right of first refusal if the occupant wishes to sell the right of occupancy; what happens if the registered owner fails or refuses to react to the notification of the right of first refusal arising? There are no provisions about how the occupant notifies the owner or the time-limit for the owner to respond to any notification. The principle may be sound but without some statutory provisions about how the principle is to be implemented, it will not work.

Second, on a proposed transfer of the right of occupancy, the registered owner must give prior consent (which may not be unreasonably withheld and any such withholding may be appealed against to a Land Tribunal [which one?]). What is to happen if the registered owner cannot be found or fails to give any decision on an application for a consent? What is the time-limit for a consent to be given? What kind of grounds might constitute 'cause'? What are the powers of a Tribunal if cause cannot be shown? The Bill is silent on this so the Tribunal is given far too much open-ended discretionary power. There are plenty of precedents for setting out in an Act the grounds which might constitute good cause for a landlord's refusing the request of a tenant to transfer his/her interest.

Third, with a proposed mortgage or pledge, it is only required that the registered owner be given notice, which notice however has to be delivered to the Committee who forwards it to the Recorder who posts it on a notice board. It seems odd that you give notice to A by sending it to B who sends it on to C. There is clearly a case for any mortgage or pledge to be recorded by the Recorder (as is the law under the Registration of Titles Act) but it is surely not necessary to inform the Recorder that an occupant is proposing to pledge or mortgage his/her interest. This provision needs revisiting.

Fourth, it would appear that leasing the right of occupancy escapes any control by or notice to the registered owner for leasing the right is not transferring the right – transfers and leases are dealt with in separate sub-parts of Part VI of the Registration of Titles Act – and I am not sure that the draftsperson has catered for subdivision and the creation of joint tenancies. It must too be queried whether conferring on a lawful occupant with a certificate of occupancy the right to lodge a caveat in accordance with the Registration of Titles Act to protect his/her right will be very beneficial since this is a complicated process for all parties involving the expense and delay of a High Court action which could sterilise the land for some time.

Approaches to drafting legislation in the light of the Land Bill

There are, very broadly, two styles of drafting, the detailed and specific and the broad and general. The latter concentrates on principles and consciously allows those implementing and interpreting the laws considerable latitude in developing the law. The former is concerned to set out the new law clearly and in some detail so that the citizen, officials and judges know what their rights, liabilities, powers and obligations are, what they have to do and how they have to do it to achieve certain specific ends. In the case of a land law which is to confirm and protect private rights and interests in land; to facilitate the acquisition of certain sorts of private rights by administrative action; to regulate hitherto contentious relations between citizens in connection with land; and to establish and empower new administrative and quasi-judicial bodies (which may well for some time to come be inadequately staffed) to exercise powers and determine disputes in respect of privately owned and occupied land, the author's position is that it is absolutely essential that the new land law is clear, and in sufficient detail and precision so people know where they stand and relatively inexperienced officials have their discretions carefully structured and controlled. This can be done without making the resultant Bill too long or inflexible. This model of legislative drafting has in fact been followed in Uganda in the drafting of the Constitution and in general legislation, to give two recent examples, in the drafting of the National Environment Statute 1995 and the Local Government Act 1997. This approach should be followed with respect to the Land Bill.

The author's overall conclusion was that the Land Bill as it stood needed more work to be done on it if it was to provide the foundation for a new workable and accountable system of land management in Uganda. His argument was that law alone is not a sufficient basis for effective and equitable systems of land management – trained and experienced personnel and adequate resources are equally important – but it is a necessary basis and an inadequate law, particularly one that leaves so many issues unresolved; gives such wide and unstructured discretionary powers to officials and official bodies; and is not meshed in with existing land laws as is the case with the Land Bill, will run a very grave risk of exacerbating the land problems of the country, rather than providing the basis for their solution. It would be a great pity if the philosophy behind the Land Bill – provide the people with secure rights to their land and so release their potential for development, provide a lasting basis for the settlement of long-standing disputes between citizens – failed to be realised because the contents of the Bill made it impossible to be realised.

In his presentation to the workshop, the author was at pains to concentrate on the technicalities of the Bill and eschew comments on the policies being implemented by the Bill. Other comments did focus on these matters, with particular emphasis being directed to women's rights – the organisation running the workshop was the Forum for Women in Democracy (FOWODE) – and the inadequate provisions on those matters in the Bill; customary tenure and the lack of adequate protection for community rights to communally owned and used land; and the position of land in Buganda and the relations between landlord and tenants on mailo land (Alden Wily, 1998).

The Land Bill: approaches to amendments

These matters of substance had also been the subject of debate and proposed amendments to the Bill in the Sessional Committee of Parliament which was at the time of the workshop in the process of examining the Bill. A Sessional Committee has a much more important role in the legislative process in the Parliament of Uganda than, *e.g.*, a Standing Committee of the UK Parliament which considers Bills at their committee stage after the Second Reading debate. The Sessional Committee is formed and meets to consider a Bill after its First (formal) Reading. After that reading, the Bill becomes, as it were, the property of Parliament, and the Sessional Committee will go through it as in a committee stage, rewriting the Bill if it considers that is required. It may also invite submissions from the public on the Bill or receive unsolicited suggestions for changes.

There may be very little contact between the Ministry and the Committee; certainly no Minister or official from the sponsoring Ministry will be in attendance at the Committee – a matter which in the instant case of the Land Bill generated some tension between the Minister and the Committee. The Ministry can submit proposals for amendments to the Committee and ideally, after negotiations, reach a more or less agreed text with the Committee. Once the Committee has finished its work, it will submit its report to the full Parliament, indicating where it has been unable to reach agreement with the Minister. The Bill goes to Parliament for its Second Reading and is likely to pass through all its other stages with little debate or amendments, although the Minister has the opportunity to put his case for his amendments. Thus, it is at least as important to convince the Sessional Committee of the desirability of changes to any Bill as the Ministry and while the Bill is with the Committee, probably more important, for if the Committee is not persuaded, it might dig its heels in over any amendments later suggested by the Ministry.

The upshot of the author's critical comments on the Bill was that he was asked by the Minister to assist in the preparation of amendments to the Bill which would meet the thrust of his criticisms. On being approached by the relevant UK Department of International Development (DFID) official – DFID had funded his workshop visit and was being expected to fund his return visit to draft amendments – the chairman of the Sessional Committee also agreed to this drafting mission and invited the author to assist the Committee in drafting its amendments to the Bill.

Thus, the author found himself in the position of an unofficial liaison person between the Ministry and the Sessional Committee and also inevitably involved not just in technical drafting amendments but in what may be called policy drafting amendments. In any event, even technical drafting amendments have policy implications – filling a "gap" in the draft

Bill on *e.g.*, certificates of customary ownership may facilitate the retention of customary controls over land transactions or make clear that they no longer operate once certificates are obtained – and in the case of the Land Bill there was the added complication that the Ministry's technical committee which had been responsible for the draft Bill was divided on the merits of the author's approach to drafting, outlined above.

While one key official saw the comments as vindicating his stance on many matters in the draft Bill, another equally, if not more, key official – a lawyer – was opposed and his position had won out in the draft. He repeatedly summed up his views by likening the Land Bill to the British Constitution; largely unwritten but everyone involved in it knows how it works and what to do; there was no need for detailed written rules; if there were problems of implementation, they would all be sorted out by the Tribunals being established by the Bill or in other ways. He was also rightly concerned that the Bill did not become so long and detailed that it ceased to be user-friendly. There is no doubt that his was a sincerely held view, and one shared in fact by many administrators and ministers in governments in East Africa who, in the author's experience, do not relish being tied down by rules and have never really regarded written constitutions as imposing serious limitations on their powers. It did however appear as if both the Minister and the chairman of the Sessional Committee – both lawyers as well – had been convinced by the author's arguments and it was on that basis that he proceeded.

The main issues that will be addressed in the rest of this chapter are those which highlight the overall theme of the paper; how the pristine approach of facilitating the operation of a market for land in Uganda by basing land tenure on the private ownership of land governed by "modern" law, *i.e.*, the received English-based common law and doctrines of equity has been or is likely to be diluted by political factors which are concerned to maintain aspects of customary tenure, and greatly reduce the scope of leasehold enfranchisement both in respect of public land and in relation to the traditional private landlord/tenant relationship.

Reform and customary tenure

Amongst those Ugandans, particularly in the North of the country who still occupy and use land under and in accordance with customary tenure, there was considerable concern about the long-term implications of a move towards the individualisation of tenure on the basis of certificates of customary ownership or even more so on the basis of the acquisition of a freehold title. The concern was that there is a functioning system of land tenure which holds a proper balance between the rights of individuals and the needs of the community and if that is disturbed by individualisation and the introduction of an unrestricted market in land, landlessness will rapidly develop and social relations will break down. Less commendable, it was also made clear that "modern" ideas contained in the Bill about women's rights were totally unacceptable to traditional communities which would endeavour to ignore them if they remained in the Bill.

The solution proposed to concerns about customary tenure was threefold. First, new provisions were drafted which distinguished between land occupied and used by individuals and households for their own purposes and land occupied and used for communal purposes – common grazing, gathering of woodfuel and medicinal plants, hunting etc. – with individualisation limited to the former category of land only. Second, new institutions, modelled on the South African Communal Property Associations Act 1995 but considerably simplified, together with a legal framework for the establishment and operation of common land management agreements by Communal Land Associations were substituted for the unwieldy and inappropriate law of trustees to provide a basis for communal land management that could embrace both traditional customary tenure, "modern" customary tenure via certificates of customary ownership and freehold tenure.

Third, the bodies charged with the duty of "verifying" customary tenure as a prelude to recommending and issuing certificates of customary ownership and/or freehold titles were given a clearer set of functions; charged with specific duties to safeguard "third-party" rights when converting traditional to "modern" customary tenure or to freehold tenure and given specific powers to grant certificates of customary ownership or freehold titles subject to conditions which can be used to ensure that community considerations are taken into account both before and when market transactions are undertaken. Market purists will no doubt be horrified at this proposal – one or two very conservative Ugandan lawyers were but mainly because they were reluctant to accept that freehold tenure in Uganda could or should be different to the "fee simple absolute in possession" freehold tenure in England – but conditional freeholds are not unknown in other common law jurisdictions – indeed the Public Lands Act,

1969 provided for them in Uganda – and few countries allow a completely unregulated market in land to exist.

Reform and land relations in Buganda

Customary tenure affects the majority of rural dwellers in Uganda but the issues surrounding it in the Bill did not give rise to contentious public debate. Land in Buganda represents less than 20% of the land mass of Uganda but the provisions in the Bill sparked off most of the debate. The issues centred round landlord/tenant relations on mailo land; land in Kibaale District (which is in Bunyoro but the land issues involve the Baganda) and the land wrongly and illegally taken from Buganda by Obote in 1966 in the aftermath of the coup engineered by Obote which propelled him into the Presidency and which some claim should be returned to Buganda.

The Bill followed the Constitution in using the terms "lawful or *bona fide* occupants" to categorise those persons who were to have their land-holding rights regulated by 2 July 1998. Lawful occupants were defined in the Bill as persons occupying land under certain specific laws, or who entered land with the consent of the owner or who were on former public land as a customary tenant but whose tenancy was not disclosed or compensated for at the time of the grant of a lease. There was little controversy about this category as such and it is designed to embrace all tenants on mailo land and other land whose relationships with their landlords have hitherto been governed by customary law or various local laws passed during colonial times modifying customary law.

Bona fide occupants in the Bill were defined so as to include squatters – persons on land for an undefined period who occupied or utilised it "genuinely believing that no registered owner … was available from whom the occupant could obtain consent …"; those who have been on land unchallenged by the owner for 12 years or more – the length of the limitation period for claiming a possessory title under the Limitation Act – and those settled on land by government. The controversy focused on the first category of people for it was and still is claimed that no one, particularly in Buganda, could possibly settle on land without knowing who the owner is and to give such persons rights to remain on the land or acquire a freehold title to the land is to reward illegality. The counter-argument was that long-standing confusion over titles and boundaries in respect of mailo land – fully discussed in West – social and political problems over the last two decades, and the rapid development of informal settlements in urban areas have all contributed to "illegal" settlement which cannot now be undone. Parliament was not convinced by these arguments; the Sessional Committee proposed that this group of persons be removed from the category of *bona fide* occupants and this was accepted. Special provisions, to be discussed below, were provided for them.

The principal controversy however was on the arrangements proposed in the Bill for regulating relationships between occupants and registered owners. These are summarised and discussed above. The effect of the proposals was that owners of land retained their freehold title but lost virtually all effective rights of ownership in the land; the occupants were to have rights of permanent occupation, subject to paying a nominal rent, able to use the land as they see fit, subject to complying with the law of the land, and able to deal with the land, subject to what appeared in the Bill to be very limited rights of refusal by the landlord. The proposals, by giving security of tenure to the tenants of mailo land and reducing landlords' rights to "bare" ownership – and although the Bill will apply nationally, it is on mailo land that the landlord/tenant problems are most acute – met the political undertakings made to the tenants during the guerrilla struggle of the NRM in the early 1980s but go way beyond the proposals made by the various committees which examined the problem from a market perspective. Their solution was to leave substantive powers with the landlord but subject them to controls in the interest of the tenants, with Government's role being "to create policies which provide incentives to facilitate the negotiation between the two parties to reach an acceptable settlement" (Technical Committee, 1993). The sentiments, which were admirable, seemed to ignore the history of relations between landlords and tenants on mailo land.

Issue was joined in the Sessional Committee and outside on this matter. The President raised the political temperature with his speech to the FOWODE workshop where he declared that no-one in Buganda owned land. His statement was political hyperbole; lawyers would understand it as meaning that where the rights of both landlords and tenants are unclear, no one can, with confidence, invest in the land and use it productively as an owner could.

Opponents of the Bill in Buganda however chose to regard it as "proof" that the Government was intent on grabbing land in Buganda and depriving the Baganda of it. The Bill was denounced as unconstitutional as it was proposing to deprive landlords of their property rights without compensation contrary to Article 26 of the Constitution. The argument was widened: the only way that land in Buganda could be safeguarded was if the 9,000 square miles of public land wrongfully taken away from Buganda by Obote in 1966 was "restored" to Buganda by being revested in the Buganda Land Board which had been established to manage the 350 square miles of land returned to the Kabaka as his land when the Kingdoms within Uganda were restored as cultural institutions under Chapter 16 of the Constitution.

At this point, it was clear that notions about markets in land had been put on one side. The issue was political pure and simple: who was to control land within Buganda? Was it to continue to be the traditional landlord class, individually on mailo land and collectively, via the Lukiiko, on public land or was it to be the peasants – the erstwhile tenants who were being given ownership rights in the land? As the quotation at the head of this chapter shows, President Museveni had made absolutely clear that it was to be the latter while many politicians and leading public figures in Buganda, by claiming that the Bill is designed to facilitate taking land away from the Baganda, have aimed at getting the peasants to throw their lot in with the landlords and support the maintenance of the status quo on mailo land. In language that was almost reminiscent of Smith in Rhodesia in the 1960s talking of relations between African and Europeans, the author was told by very senior Baganda persons that there was no need for changes to the law on mailo land as relations between landlords and tenants were very good and only outsiders wanted to disturb things; the solution was to revert to the independence settlement on land.

A careful reading of the Constitution and the Land Bill showed that many of the arguments of the opponents of the Bill could not be sustained. First, public land; as noted above, public land was former Crown land which was land occupied by persons holding it under customary law. Colonial legal theory, taken over at independence in the Public Lands Act, 1962 and its successor, the Public Lands Act, 1969, did not accept that persons occupying land under customary law could own it; hence the ownership of such land was vested in the Crown and its successor state, the Republic of Uganda via the Land Commission, or between 1962 and 1966 within Buganda, in the Buganda Land Board.

The Constitution of 1995 however has brought about a legal revolution in respect of customary law. For the first time in Uganda's history, customary law is now recognised as a legal foundation for land ownership.

This is absolutely explicit in Article 237(1) and (4)(a) of the Constitution. At a stroke therefore, the ownership of land occupied under customary law which used to vest in the Crown and then the Republic of Uganda as public land has ceased to exist; it has, as it were, been merged with the customary occupation to provide the new customary law ownership of land. Public land as it used to be has ceased to exist and therefore there is no "9000 square miles of public land" within Buganda to vest in any authority.[1] The only public land in the old sense which under the Bill continued to exist was the freehold reversionary interest of leaseholds granted out of former public land which Article 237(5) of the Constitution provides may be converted into freehold together with unowned land (if any such exists which is disputed).

Second, the constitutionality of proposals on landlord/tenant relationships. There are several misconceptions here, compounded by the Bill. It was assumed, and the assumption derived some support from the Bill as it was originally published in March, 1998, that the mailo tenure being legislated for in the Bill was the same as the mailo tenure provided for in the 1900 Agreement. It was not. That mailo tenure was abolished by the Land Reform Decree in 1975. Mailo tenure now derives its legal authority from the Constitution of 1995 – a point reaffirmed by the Land Bill which was redrafted on this matter to bring it into line with the Constitution – and the provisions in the Constitution quite explicitly gave lawful and *bona fide* occupants absolute security of tenure for two years on mailo land with provisions to follow on future relationships including the acquisition by such occupants of registrable interests, *i.e.*, freehold title, in that land.

Far from the Bill then unconstitutionally depriving landlords of their property rights, it actually restored some rights to them. Under the Bill, now the Act, tenants are required to pay a nominal ground rent for their new perpetual lease and may lose their lease if they do not pay that rent. More important, landlords have a right of refusal to consent to transactions by tenants (which right may not however be unreasonably withheld) but there is nothing in the Act to say that the landlords cannot charge for their consent. Thus, if a tenant by occupancy – the term for such tenants in the Act – wished to assign his/her tenancy to a developer for a commercial development, the landlord could quite legally (subject to the provision on reasonableness) propose a joint venture with the tenant and the developer to ensure that s/he obtained some of the capital value of the development; indeed section 37 of the Act which provides for the possibility of landlord and tenant agreeing to share the land as joint tenants or as tenants in common seems to contemplate that eventuality.

In another very important softening of the provisions of the Constitution, the Bill went no further than providing that tenants might negotiate with landlords for the purchase the landlord's interest. No change was made to that provision by Parliament. There is to be no compulsory leasehold enfranchisement although the plain language of Article 237(9)(b) of the Constitution would seem to require that that be provided for. The Government was persuaded that any such provision would infringe Article 26 of the Constitution and that Article 26 took priority over Article 237. The argument for that is shaky and in any event the decision of the European Court of Human Rights in 1986 in *James v. United Kingdom* (the *Duke of Westminster's case*) is powerful persuasive authority that compulsory leasehold enfranchisement comes within the scope of acquiring the citizen's land in the public interest (provided for under Article 237(2)(a)) and is permissible where Parliament considers that it is necessary to right social injustices.[2]

Amendments proposed to the Bill did not seek to depart from the policy of vesting rights in the tenant and leaving the landlord with few residual rights. As with the provisions on customary tenure, they aimed at creating a more workable legal framework and greater certainty for both parties – something which both a market orientated and a politically orientated approach would be likely to agree on. Perhaps over-optimistically, they aimed too to lower the temperature of the contest over the Bill by creating a more level playing field in terms of procedures between landlords and tenants – this was an approach which some members of the Sessional Committee urged.

Thus, rather than the vague provisions criticised earlier in this chapter, clearer procedures were provided for; criteria for refusals of consents were set out; and a new institution was proposed to assist the parties in their negotiations with each other. On squatters, rather than eliminate all provisions on squatters' rights as the Sessional Committee proposed or leave them untouched as the Government would have preferred, section 31 of the Act ultimately provided that where a person has occupied or utilised land unchallenged by the registered owner for less than 12 years and does not therefore qualify as a *bona fide* occupant, it shall be the duty of such a person to take reasonable steps to seek out and identify the registered owner for the purpose of negotiating with him concerning his or her occupation of that land. This rather odd provision was substituted by the

Sessional Committee for one proposed in the amended version of the Bill under which landlords were to have two years to challenge such a non-*bona fide* occupant's right to remain on the land, with various possibilities available to both parties to reach an accommodation. Failure by the landlords to take action would have resulted in this category of occupant being automatically upgraded to the status of perpetual tenant with all attendant rights. Section 31 leaves matters in the air so to speak; if the parties do not reach an agreement, with or without assistance, the Act is silent on what is to happen.

The new institution is the Mediator – persons of good standing in the community who will be made available to the parties to help them resolve differences, negotiate agreements or consents and so avoid the expense and delays of contested actions before the new Land Tribunals. Mediators are expressly referred to by section 31; either party may invite a Mediator to assist them in their negotiation but as befits such an office a Mediator "shall not compel or direct any party to a mediation to arrive at any particular conclusion or decision on any matter the subject of the mediation" (section 90(5), Land Act).

Leasehold enfranchisement

The final matter where politics and markets conflict is enfranchisement of leases of public land. Article 237(5) of the Constitution provides that such leases may be converted to freehold tenure in accordance with a law made by Parliament. The Bill as originally published provided that such conversion should be automatic and in this it reflected and, in respect of urban land, went further than the various committees which looked at land tenure from a market perspective. It was, however, consistent with the thrust of basing the new land law on ownership of land and reducing the role of the state in land administration.

However, it did not prove acceptable to the Sessional Committee which noted that Article 237(5) of the Constitution did not require any automatic conversion of former public land leaseholds to freehold. The Committee's view was that it is unwise to provide for any such automatic conversion because it would give a small number of people undeserved and unjustifiable large capital gains and reduce the availability of future land stocks. The Committee considered that leaseholders on former public land should be entitled to apply to District Land Boards for the freehold reversion to their leases but should have to pay for them. Indeed, at one point the Committee wished to prevent any enfranchisement at all until it was pointed out to the members that the Constitution had provided for it.

The Bill was amended accordingly and the Act therefore provides, by section 29, for leaseholders to apply for enfranchisement of their leaseholds. Where the leasehold is less than 100 hectares, then, provided the lease was "authentic and genuine" – a reference to leases granted under rather dubious circumstances under past regimes – and that the interests of customary tenants were properly taken care of at the time the lease was granted and that all development conditions have been complied with, conversion will follow and does not involve any payment. Where an application for conversion is for an area of over 100 hectares however, the District Land Board must be satisfied that it is in the public interest that it should be converted to freehold and payment of the market value for the conversion must be made. Public interest is undefined. In addition, Boards are empowered to impose conditions on any freeholds that are sold and the rights of sitting occupants are protected. Here then the processes of the market – selling valuable property rights rather than giving them away – are harnessed to a political end – imposing costs on obtaining a freehold which may deter leaseholders from doing so. The result is not "logical"; there is no particular magic about 100 hectares but the section was a compromise between those who didn't want any enfranchisement at all so that "foreigners" *i.e.*, people from outside a particular area, could be prevented from acquiring freeholds in that area and those who saw nothing wrong (or stood to benefit) from Ugandans being able to acquire freeholds anywhere in Uganda.

The passage of the Bill: the case of the "lost amendment"

The work of redrafting was completed by the end of May. MPs had one month to complete their work of examining the Bill and passing it into law to meet the constitutional deadline. The Sessional Committee examined the proposed amendments to the Bill and as discussed above accepted the majority of them, although in some cases, inserted amendments of their own. However, that was not the end of the process of amendments. Women's groups had been very active and very effective in arguing for changes to the Bill so as to enhance women's rights to own land. This was despite the President's, at best, lukewarm advocacy of women's rights to land. Women were concerned that clause 40 which provided for certain restrictions on the transfer of land by family members – spouses had to consent to any such transfer of land on which the parties ordinarily resided and a transfer without such consent would be void but consent could not be unreasonably withheld and appeal against a refusal of consent lay to the Land Tribunal – did not go far enough. They wanted to see introduced into the Bill a provision dealing with land ownership rights between spouses generally.

As June, 1998 drew to a close, the pressure on MPs to pass the Bill so as to comply with the Constitution became intense. The Minister had made it clear he would not propose any amendment to the Constitution to allow for more debate. The President made clear his unshakeable commitment to see the Bill passed. Towards the very end of June, a foremost leader of the women's caucus in Parliament proposed an amendment to the Bill to deal with the question of married women's rights to ownership of land. The gist of it was that land acquired by either spouse before marriage remained the property of that spouse – too often, particularly in customary law, a married woman would in effect forfeit any land she owned – and land acquired after marriage by either party either as the matrimonial home or as the land for the maintenance of the family would automatically be jointly owned by the spouses (the amendment as moved did not specify whether joint ownership would be as joint tenants or as tenants in common, a matter of considerable importance). The amendment was published for debate.

At this point, there is no agreement on the remembrance of what happened. Most women MPs claim the amendment was passed but in the final hectic hours of debate – MPs were kept in the chamber at nights and during the last weekend of June to ensure the passage of the Bill by the end of June – the amendment somehow slipped through the net and when the Bill received presidential assent on 2 July – deadline day – and was thereupon published, the amendment was not in the Act. The Speaker was sympathetic to the women's concern and made plain that if it could be shown that the amendment had indeed been passed he would certify to the First Parliamentary Counsel that a mistake had been made and a corrigendum would be published incorporating the amendment into the Act. The Chairman of the Sessional Committee made plain his support for the amendment and his willingness to ensure that if necessary, time would be found formally to pass what had already been agreed to. The problem was that there seemed to be no firm evidence that the amendment had been moved let alone passed. At the crucial period of the debate, the mover of the amendment was not in the chamber, having left for another engagement and it was not clear whether the amendment had therefore ever been formally moved. Another version of events is that the amendment was not formally moved because the Cabinet had not formally indicated its acceptance of it which was necessary before any such amendment could be moved at that juncture.

The argument continued notwithstanding the coming into force of the Act on 2 July. Perhaps somewhat unwisely, certain donors joined in the argument and adopted uncritically the position of women's groups that the amendment had been passed but had been "lost" deliberately owing to the opposition of male MPs to it. The British Government took a strong position on this and hinted that aid programmes, particularly those directed to assisting in the implementation of the Land Act might be affected if the Government did not ensure that the amendment was passed.[3] Unlike the position in the British House of Commons, however, the Government does not have an automatic majority in the National Assembly in Uganda – a no party Parliament means that in practice, there are no whips; MPs are virtually uncontrollable and for each piece of legislation, a coalition of interests has to be built up to ensure its passage.[4] The Land Act undoubtedly benefited from the constitutional deadline; at the end of the day, MPs gritted their teeth and passed the Bill because of the perceived importance of adhering to the Constitution. Any amendment to the Land Act, particularly one of such far-reaching import as that on the land rights of spouses has no external force behind it and cannot therefore be guaranteed to pass.

It was well into 1999 before the Ministry of Water, Lands and the Environment – the relevant Ministry – began to address the issue of the "lost amendment" and what to put before Parliament (Kawamara, 1999). It was not male opposition to the amendment that caused two Ministry workshops (funded by DFID) held in July and September 1998 to plan a programme of implementation and determine priorities to decide that the three most pressing priorities were; first, dissemination of the Act to the public through publicity, user-friendly literature and sensitisation workshops; second, the making of regulations to provide for the modalities of acquiring certificates of customary ownership by a process of adjudication of interests and boundaries, and certificates of occupancy and their registration by Recorders; and third the appointment of members of District Land Boards and Land Tribunals together with their training.

Conclusions

What lessons can be learned from this saga for land law reform elsewhere in Africa? First and foremost while the law can be reformed, history cannot. The history of land tenure and land relations in Uganda since 1900 clearly played a much more important role in shaping the final outcome of the Land Bill than the decade of market-orientated donor-sponsored committee reports on land tenure. The political compromises negotiated within the Sessional Committee, between the Committee and the Minister and between the Government and its critics, especially within Buganda, diluted the pure milk of the market solution and although the resultant law may look messy, a law of compromises which recognises the continuing strengths of the indigenous land tenure system will have a better chance of successful implementation than a law which seeks to set them aside and replace them with a law based on "legalistic plagiarism".

Second, the vibrant nature of the political debate on the Bill, led from the front by the President and featured in all the national daily newspapers and on the various radio stations played a major part in generating public awareness and interest in the subject. MPs consulted with their constituents so spreading awareness of the Bill amongst those likely to be affected by it but would not normally involve themselves in political debates. In addition, NGOs, especially the Uganda Land Alliance, a consortium of many small NGOs, and the Uganda Women's Network played a significant and constructive role in sensitising people to the Bill, researching on their needs and publishing well thought-out specific suggestions for amendments to the Bill. The Government was constantly open to suggestions for changes and willing to make amendments to the Bill. There were, for instance, considerable changes to the published March 1998 Bill from the unpublished late 1997 version and considerable further changes from the March 1998 Bill to the Land Act.

There appeared, to an outside observer-participant, to be a spirit of co-operation between government, Parliament, the citizenry and the principal donor involved in the process, with external participation welcomed, which led to a better Bill and may be contrasted with the spirit of confrontation which characterised relations between government and Hakiardhi, the Tanzanian NGO equivalent of the Uganda Land Alliance in respect of that country's Land Act, 1999 and Village Land Act, 1999 with the NGO scapegoating the external involvement in the process, blaming it for deficiencies in the internal political process.[5] The result in Tanzania, perhaps predictably, is that the two Land Acts as passed showed remarkably few changes from the work of the external consultant, completed more than two years before thc Bills were finally passed and those that were introduced as a result of external input came from women's groups willing to work with the relevant Ministry. It may be an obvious point to make but it is a lesson that still has to be learned on both sides: co-operation between civil society and government is more likely to achieve both specific results and advance the cause of the democratic polity than is confrontation.

Third, the nature of the content of the Land Bill must be addressed. I make no apology for returning to a theme I have discussed earlier. My judgement (shared it may be said by some persons in Uganda) is that the over-broad and general draft that was published in March 1998 was a significant contributory factor to generating opposition to the Bill. Its lack of clarity, the very wide and unstructured powers given to new public bodies being established in the Bill and the rather poor definitions of key terms used in the Bill reduced support for the Bill because it was too unclear as to what it was aiming to achieve and so allowed opposition to criticise it both for what it appeared to contain and for what it did not contain. Much of the criticism of the Bill could have been avoided if there had been more specifics in the Bill for much criticism was about gaps in the Bill; the lack of safeguards and protections and procedural arrangements for customary tenure, for women's rights, for settling landlord/tenant disputes and for the functions of new boards, committees and tribunals.

It is not the case that a short law is user-friendly and a long one is not; the nature of the subject-matter and the aims of the reforms dictate the shape, content and size of a law. Land tenure reform is always a major and sensitive issue and where as is the case in many states in Africa, and indeed in Eastern Europe, reform is moving from public control of, to private rights in, land, the law needs to spell out clearly both the new rights and their incidents and the limits on the residual powers of public officials. This necessarily leads to a detailed and sometimes complex piece of legislation.

It is a truism that complex legislation will not be understood by the vast majority of any population, let alone one where the majority of the population are not overly proficient in the language of the law – in the case of Uganda, English.

The solution to this or at any rate a partial solution to this, and this is the fourth lesson to be learned, is the need to follow up any new legislation on land with programmes of public education and awareness and the rapid development of legal literature at all levels to explain, analyse, comment on and criticise the new law. Donors increasingly use the academic and NGO community to prepare reports on all manner of issues. Perhaps serious consideration needs to be given to hiring academics from the law schools to write the texts and other literature and undertake the programmes of public education needed to accompany the new land laws now coming on stream in African countries; there are clearly no internal funds available for this and no legal scholar, however dedicated, can be blamed for preferring to earn money either in practice or in writing reports for donors on the deficiencies of existing laws rather than writing a textbook on a new law for a derisory fee from a local publisher – assuming one such can be found. The sums of money involved would be quite small in donor terms; the returns would be substantial.

Fifth, land law reform has to be seen as a continuous process and not as something that is accomplished when the new "Land Act" dealing with tenure reform is enacted. The model here is the National Land Code of Malaysia, first enacted in 1965, but amended almost yearly and reprinted in a new consolidated version every year. As society's needs change, so must the law. Mention has been made earlier in this paper of the Registration of Titles Act, first enacted in 1922 in Uganda and its well-known and oft cited deficiencies. If that law remains untouched as it has been (apart from minor reforms on titling in 1958 and botched mortgage law reform in 1974) then, whatever the merits of the new Land Act, implementation will likely fail and the mechanism for an operative market for land will never provide value for money nor be transparent. There have been more changes in the last 80 years in customary law in Uganda than to the RTA over the same period. The same point may be made about the Acquisition of Land Act 1967, which provides for the compulsory acquisition of land. It cannot stand alongside the Constitution and needs to be rewritten. My impression – an impression confirmed by the papers given at a DFID conference on Land Tenure Reform in Africa held in February 1999 (Toulmin and Quan, 2000) is that apart from South Africa, states in Anglophone Africa moving down the path of land reform have yet to address the subject in the round; public land law – town and country planning, compulsory acquisition, regularisation of informal settlements, housing – all need to be reformed as well as all private land law – transactions as well as tenure, succession, and the regulation of the actors in the market.

The final lesson to be learned is the importance of planning for the implementation of the new law before rather than after its enactment. No thought was given to implementation in Uganda until after the Bill became an Act. Several problem areas immediately came to light. First, it became apparent that over 20,000 people would be needed to staff all the bodies established by the Act to enable full implementation to take place. This was clearly well beyond any likely funding of the Act.

Second, the Ministry had not provided in its budget for any costs of implementation for the financial year 1998–99 yet had to meet certain deadlines for the appointment of District Land Board members by January 1999 as well as prepare land regulations to enable these Boards and other bodies to function. Funds were not made available until early 1999 and even then, in the absence of a well-argued case for substantial funds to be made available for the financial year 1999–2000, the Ministry of Finance was reluctant to provide adequate funding for substantial implementation in that year, yet no contingency plans existed for partial implementation.

Third, the Act provided that as from its commencement, courts, apart from the High Court, would cease to have jurisdiction over land disputes, all land cases henceforth being dealt with by Land Tribunals to be appointed by the Chief Justice on the recommendation of the Judicial Service Commission (JSC). More than two years after the Act came into effect, not a single member of a Land Tribunal had been appointed; the JSC claimed it could not appoint until funds were forthcoming; the Ministry had established a unit to manage the Tribunals – a matter the Ministry had addressed in October but decided that it was not the appropriate Ministry to undertake that task, a decision reversed in April 1999 but not thereafter acted upon – and tribunal procedural rules were made.[6] These had to be made by the Chief Justice but, despite the judiciary being reminded of this in September 1998, no action to develop any rules was taken until early 2000. Meanwhile land disputes continued to fester and the credibility of the Act suffered. Questions began to be asked in Parliament about the non-application of the Act.

Overall then, the fundamental lesson to be learned from Uganda is the central importance of ensuring that land law reform is and is perceived by the actors involved and society at large to be a national exercise with a firm sense of ownership located within the national body politic. This is as important from the point of view of countering internal political opposition – Buganda's opposition, for instance, can be portrayed as sectional and divisive rather than as an alternative national vision – as of countering internal criticism of external involvement in the reform process – where everybody is encouraged to be involved, the external involvement becomes that much less significant. Politics not markets then are and will remain the driving force behind land tenure reform in Africa; governments, both African and donor, international agencies and consultants will forget this at their peril.

---

*First given at a Conference on Land Market Reform in Africa, Eastern Europe and Latin America, Lincoln Institute of Land Policy, Cambridge, Mass. July 1998. The work on which this paper is based was done while acting as a Department of International Development (DFID) UK consultant in Uganda during 1998. Nothing in this paper must be taken as in any way representing the views or policies of DFID or any body or organisation I worked with in Uganda.

Notes

[1] There is a somewhat involved legal argument on this matter which may briefly be rehearsed here. Buganda's public land was illegally taken away from Buganda by Obote in 1966 when he illegally overthrew the 1962 Independence Constitution. Everything that has happened since then is therefore illegal; the only way for Uganda to get back to legality is to go back to the 1962 Constitution and proceed from there. Under that Constitution, Buganda controlled its own land so all that is being asked for now is the restoration of the legal status quo. The argument overlooks the decision in *Uganda v. Commissioner of Prisons ex parte Matovu* [1966] EA 514 which decided that once a coup has taken place the courts have no alternative but to accept the new reality: a new Grundnorm comes into existence and legality is thereafter judged by the courts on the basis not of the old discarded Grundnorm but the new one, *i.e.*, the Constitution of 1966 which confirmed the taking away of Buganda's land. This reasoning, while not very brave, was perhaps realistic, followed decisions made in Pakistan and Cyprus in similar circumstances and received a modified approval in the Judicial Committee of the Privy Council in *Madzimbamuto v. Lardner-Burke* on appeal from the then Rhodesia in 1968.

[2] An issue which remains to be fought over is that Article 26 does not specify "public interest" as a ground for compulsory acquisition while Article 237 does. Does Article 26 being in the Bill of Rights prevail over Article 237 or does the later provision *pro tanto* repeal the earlier to the extent of any inconsistency between the two? In the interests of getting the Bill through, the Government in effect accepted the first proposition.

[3] "An amendment to the Land Act dealing with co-ownership of land by spouses was passed in principle by Parliament but not included in the published Act. Government of Uganda is pursuing a strategy to have the amendment reinstated. DFID will monitor progress on this and in the event that the issue is not resolved

by the end of the first session of Parliament of 1999, DFID will consider whether to withhold further support until such time as the matter is resolved." (UK Government 1998, para. 5.1.4.)

[4] Political parties are not banned in Uganda but may not campaign as such for Parliament. All candidates for Parliament are deemed to be members of the "movement political system" and as such are elected to political office on "individual merit". Thus, while there is a movement caucus in Parliament consisting of backbench MPs, there is no party discipline and MPs cannot be whipped into the Government lobby. This makes for greater democracy in Parliament but creates considerable difficulties for the Executive. Many Ministers have been forced out of office because of critical reports of Parliamentary committees on their handling of their Ministries. It is an ironic commentary on the notion of democracy that the Ugandan system is regarded by donors as not fully democratic because political parties cannot contest seats in Parliament yet, as a result, the Executive has far less control over the Legislature than in most Western European states.

[5] See Shivji (1998), especially the Appendix at pp. 111–18 for a deliberately inaccurate attack on the author's work as the consultant who assisted the Ministry of Lands, Housing and Urban Development in 1996 in preparing a report in the form of a draft Land Bill to implement the National Land Policy approved by Parliament in June 1995.

[6] These reasons were not convincing. Tribunal members could have been appointed and training given with their actual starting date to be set later when funds were made available. The Ministry of Finance is unlikely to provide funds until there are Tribunal members in existence.

13 Men behaving badly: a narrative of land reform*

Introduction

This is the story of a land reform aid project. It was a project to assist in the implementation of an important new piece of legislation, the Land Act, 1998 of Uganda. It was developed with the best of intentions but despite some limited achievements in some areas was, judged by its own terms, largely unsuccessful. The argument to be put forward in this narrative is that its failure was caused by three interrelated factors. First, there were fundamental and irreconcilable internal differences about both the Act and the project within the host Ministry where the project was located which were known about but glossed over in order to get the project started. Second there were internal political differences between offices within the aid agency about the merits of the project and a lack of commitment to the project from the key regional office of the agency compounded the difficulties the project experienced from local differences. Third, the project was miscast; its stated purpose – to lay the foundation for the effective and equitable implementation of the Land Act – could not be realised because the underlying requirements for such a realisation were not addressed by the project.

This story is a case study on the implementation of a new law about space, albeit national space – land law; and how the best of intentions of the Ministers and Parliament can be corrupted and subverted by bureaucrats. Such a case study is thought likely to be of general interest to all those concerned with more than just the text of a new law. Land reform is very much back on the agenda of both governments and aid agencies but as this story will seek to demonstrate, land reform involves much more than land law reform, reform of land relations or the facilitation of a land market. It goes to the heart of governance and a failure to focus on that will likely undermine any good intentions to promote land reform.

The project in question was entitled Securing Sustainable Livelihoods through Land Tenure Reform (generally referred to as the Land Act Implementation Project or LAIP). It was a 15-month exercise funded by the Department for International Development (DFID) of the British

Government designed to assist the Government of Uganda to begin the process of implementing the Land Act, 1998. The author had assisted in the process of drafting the Act in 1998, and was invited to become the Senior Technical Adviser to the project in 1999. He worked with the project for one year from March 1999.

His detailed Terms of Reference fell into four main areas:

- Getting the project up and running, advising and working with project institutions to ensure the production of project outputs;
- Assisting the Ministry of Water, Lands and Environment (MWLE) to prepare its budgets and liasing with donors to generate additional resources for implementing the Land Act;
- Plan, co-ordinate and work with the Medium Term Implementation Study (the Land Act Implementation Study or LAIS) and ensure that its outputs feed into the development of the Ministry's longer term implementation plan which in turn was to be fully integrated into national budgetary and planning processes;
- Advising and assisting the Permanent Secretary and Ministers on project activities and other matters as requested.

This paper is based on his experiences while undertaking these tasks. The story starts out with a summary of the principal provisions of the Act so providing the necessary background to the project and its work. It moves on to summarise the structure, activities and outputs of the project up to the time the author left the project. It then considers the problematics of the project: its institutional environment. It concludes with some reflections on land reform, governance and aid.

The Land Act, 1998

One important piece of background information to the Land Act which must be emphasised is that while much policy-related work had taken place on land tenure issues in the preceding 15 years, the Government had not produced any "White Paper" or even a "Green Paper" on a national land policy. Insofar as there was a national land policy, it had to be pieced together from the Act itself, other laws, and statements by the President and Ministers both in discussing the Act in and outwith Parliament and in discussing such matters as agricultural development, environmental protection and poverty alleviation. The Act itself has been represented at various times as being a positive contribution to all those three matters. The extent to which it is or may be either or both a necessary or sufficient condition for this was one of the issues which the project was to explore. What must first be addressed however, is the content of the Act. Irrespective of what the Government hoped it will achieve, what does the Act say: what bodies with what functions have been created to carry out what purposes in what manner? The Act addresses five principal concerns which may now be outlined.

Customary ownership

The Constitution provides that persons occupying land under customary tenure shall henceforth be owners of the land they are using and occupying. The Act provides that such persons may obtain a certificate of customary ownership as documentary evidence of that ownership. This is to be achieved via a process of adjudication and demarcation of boundaries and rights in the land conducted by Land Committees at the level of the parish (PLC) who will pass up their recommendations on applications for certificates to the District Land Boards (DLB). On the recommendation of a DLB, a Recorder, located at sub-county level, will issue a certificate of customary ownership and open a register where such certificates will be registered in a simplified system of title registration. The Act makes provision for third-party rights in land – rights of persons other than owners to use the land for certain specific purposes – to be recorded at the time of adjudication and certificates of customary ownership will be issued subject to those third party rights being protected. Adjudication of customary rights is entirely voluntary and is based on a process of sporadic adjudication; no specific provision is made for systematic adjudication of areas of land on the basis of a majority decision by persons in the area to proceed down that route.

Persons owning land under customary ownership may undertake the full range of transactions in land – both commercial (sale, lease, mortgage etc.) and family (gifts, devises by will). Where certificates of customary ownership have been issued, they will be the medium of transactions which to be valid will have to be recorded in the register. The Act expressly states that a certificate of customary ownership "shall be recognised by financial institutions ... as a valid certificate for purposes of evidence of title" though no sanction is provided if financial institutions decline to comply with that peremptory and somewhat unrealistic command.

The Act provides for persons wishing to own and manage land under customary or any other tenure on a communal basis to form themselves into a Communal Land Association which will be able to hold land which may be used by persons or families on an exclusive basis and hold and manage land to be set aside for the common use of members of the Association in accordance with rules agreed to by members.

Persons owning land under customary law may, instead of applying for certificate of customary ownership proceed to apply for a freehold title. The same processes of adjudication of rights will have to take place but the demarcation of boundaries and the measurements of the relevant plot will have to comply with the standards set out in the Survey Act and registration of the title will be under the Registration of Titles Act, a much longer and more costly process than obtaining a certificate of customary ownership. Freehold ownership may be granted subject to conditions which will be designed to protect third-party rights.

Tenants' rights

Tenants of private landlords – known in the Act as lawful or *bona fide* occupants of land – are enabled to obtain certificates of occupancy in respect of their occupation of land by a process similar to that available to customary owners wishing to obtain certificates of customary ownership. Certificates of occupancy are issued by Recorders and are registered in the simplified register kept at sub-county level. Tenants by occupancy have in effect perpetual leases for which they are required to pay only a nominal rent (though they may lose their lease if they do not pay the rent and have no reasonable excuse for not so doing). They may bequeath their lease as of right but with respect to commercial transactions – sale, sub-leasing, mortgaging etc. – they must obtain the consent of their landlord which consent may not be unreasonably withheld. In the event of a dispute between landlord and tenant on, *e.g.*, the grant of a certificate of occupancy or a consent to a transaction, appeal lies to a Land Tribunal.

Tenants wishing to sell their leasehold and landlords wishing to sell their freehold reversionary interest must first offer their interest to, in the first case, the landlord, and in the second case, the tenant. Where agreement cannot, even with the aid of the services of the Mediator, be reached on the sale, the parties may sell their respective interests on the open market. As an alternative to sale, the parties may agree between themselves either to subdivide the land in agreed proportions, each becoming the freehold owner of a portion of the land or to become joint owners of the land. In urban areas, the local urban council may require as a condition of granting permission for any development that landlord and tenants agree together on a programme of planned development which must include arrangements for the future ownership and occupation of the development. This provides the legal basis for the parties to agree to land sharing or land readjustment projects.

Tenants are empowered by the Act to acquire their landlord's interest; *i.e.*, the Act permits leasehold enfranchisement but does not give the tenant any right to require the landlord to sell his or her interest to the tenant. This is despite the Constitution's requiring by Article 237(9)(b) that Parliament shall enact a law "providing for the acquisition of registrable interest in land by the occupant" which would seem to imply that the occupant should be given the right to acquire the landlord's interest. This provision was directed particularly at the long-standing tenure problems in Kibaale District. It is this opportunity to acquire the landlord's reversionary interest which was the original driving force behind the creation of the Land Fund.

Tenants holding leases granted out of former public land are also empowered to apply to the DLB in which the freehold reversionary interest is vested for leasehold enfranchisement. Where the application is in respect of less than 100 hectares, it may be granted if certain conditions connected to the lease are met. The enfranchisement is free. Where the application is in respect of more than 100 hectares, then first, in addition to conditions relating to the lease, the application must be in the public interest – undefined in the Act – and second, the applicant must pay the market value for the freehold reversion.

Decentralised land administration

The Act repeats and fleshes out the provisions of the Constitution on District Land Boards. The most important of these is that in the performance of its functions, a DLB shall be independent of the Uganda Land Commission and shall not be subject to the direction or control of any person or authority but shall take into account national and District Council policy on land.

There shall be for each of the 45 Districts a District Land Board of not less than five persons of whom not less than one-third must be women.

Their functions are to hold and allocate land in the district which is not owned by any person or authority; facilitate the registration and transfer of interests in land; take over and exercise the powers of a lessor in respect of leases granted out of former public land; and compile and keep under review compensation rates payable where land is to be compulsorily acquired. Boards may acquire land; alter, improve and demolish buildings; and sell lease or otherwise deal with land held by them. Expenses and fees of the Boards are to be charged to District Administration funds.

In addition to any staff the Boards may have, each District Council is to have a District Land Office which is to consist of a District Physical Planner, a District Land Officer, a District Valuer, a District Surveyor and a District Registrar of Titles and this office is to provide technical services to the DLBs to facilitate them in the performance of their duties.

Below the DLBs are the parishes. For each of the approximately 4517 parishes, there shall be a Land Committee (PLC) and in each of the 64 gazetted urban areas and divisions of a city, a Land Committee (ULC). PLCs and ULCs consist of a chairperson and three other persons of whom at least one must be a woman. PLCs are the first port of call for those wishing to acquire certificates of customary ownership and are responsible for carrying out the processes of adjudication of boundaries and rights. Their recommendations on titling and on the protection of third-party rights are passed on to the DLBs and, if accepted, form the basis for the issuance of a certificate of customary ownership by the Recorder. As such they play an absolutely fundamental role in the implementation of the Act.

Recorders are to be appointed for each of the 917 sub-counties, each gazetted urban area and each division in a city. They are to be responsible for keeping records relating to certificates of customary ownership and certificates of occupancy. The notion of "keeping records" is somewhat ambiguous; it is being assumed that Recorders are to be responsible for registering the certificates of customary ownership and occupancy rather than just holding certificates registered elsewhere as a type of post box.

Land tribunals and the mediator

The Act provides that, as from the commencement of the Act, courts, other than the High Court, shall cease to have jurisdiction over land disputes. Instead, for each District there shall be a District Land Tribunal consisting of a Chairperson who is qualified to be a Magistrate Grade I and two other members. All the members of the Tribunal are to be appointed by the Chief

Justice on the advice of the Judicial Service Commission. For each sub-county, gazetted urban area and division of the city there shall be respectively a sub-county Land Tribunal and an urban Land Tribunal. All these members are to be appointed by the Judicial Service Commission. The Act however is silent on which body will be responsible for administering and funding the running costs of the Tribunals.

The Land Tribunals have jurisdiction over land disputes relating to the grant, lease, repossession, transfer or acquisition of land whether arising under the Act or otherwise and whether between individuals or involving the Land Commission or other authorities with responsibility relating to land. This is a very large jurisdiction for taken literally, it would mean that the Land Tribunals would have jurisdiction over land in forests and national parks if issues concerning the above noted topics arose. Tribunals also have jurisdiction over amounts of compensation payable for land compulsorily acquired. District Land Tribunals hear cases on appeal from Sub-county and urban Tribunals and appeals lie from the DLTs to the High Court. Special rules of procedure are to be made for Land Tribunals by the Chief Justice.

In addition to Land Tribunals, the Act provides two alternative channels for dispute settlement. The first is customary dispute settlement and mediation: traditional authorities may continue to exercise their functions of determining disputes over customary tenure or acting as mediators between the parties to a dispute. Second, a Mediator may be appointed by a Land Tribunal to assist parties to a land dispute to reach an amicable settlement. A Mediator is not required to have any special qualifications; she or he must however be a person of high moral character and proven integrity who must exercise her or his functions in accordance with the principles of natural justice and general principles of mediation and conciliation.

The Uganda Land Commission and the Land Fund

The Act provides for the Uganda Land Commission, a body of five persons all of whom are appointed by the President with the approval of Parliament.[1] The Commission's principal function is to be the Government's estate agent and property manager and to that end it may undertake the full range of transactions and activities in relation to land. One important activity that it will have to perform is to arrange for the surveying and titling of the land used, occupied or set aside for public purposes in Uganda – in effect the residue of public land. In the past, when virtually all land was public land and it was a simple process to order people occupying land under customary tenure to move from the land, there was no need to survey and register land used, occupied or set aside for public purposes. Now however, when most land is privately owned, the lack of clear boundaries to public land is causing grave problems for public development projects.

The Act gives another function to the Commission – that of managing the Land Fund. The Land Fund is established by the Act. It comprises monies appropriated by Parliament, loans obtained by Government, grants from donors and funds from other sources approved by the Minister responsible for lands in consultation with the Minister responsible for finance. The Fund is to be utilised for four purposes; to give loans to tenants to enable them to acquire registrable interests referred to in Article 237(9)(b) of the Constitution; to enable government to purchase or acquire registered land to enable tenants by occupancy to acquire registrable interests pursuant to the Constitution; to resettle persons made homeless by government action, natural disaster or any other cause and to assist other persons to acquire titles. The Fund was to be duly established by 2 July 1999 – one year after the Act came into force.

Women's rights to land

This matter was not amongst the central economic and constitutional imperatives which lay behind the enactment of the Land Act but it emerged during the public consultative process on the Bill and has since assumed considerable importance both within and outside Parliament and played an important part in the development of the project. A brief summary of the saga is therefore necessary.

Women's groups had been very active and very effective in arguing for changes to the Bill so as to enhance women's rights to own land. Women were concerned that clause 40 (now section 40) which provided for certain restrictions on the transfer of land by family members – spouses had to consent to any such transfer of land on which the parties ordinarily resided and a transfer without such consent would be void but consent could not be unreasonably withheld and appeal against a refusal of consent lay to the Land Tribunal – did not go far enough. They wanted to see introduced into the Bill a provision dealing with land ownership rights between spouses generally.

Towards the very end of June 1998, an amendment to the Bill to deal with the question of married women's rights to ownership of land was proposed. The gist of it was that land acquired by either spouse before marriage remained the property of that spouse – too often, particularly in customary law, a married woman would in effect forfeit any land she owned – and land acquired after marriage by either party either as the matrimonial home or as the land for the maintenance of the family would automatically be jointly owned by the spouses (the amendment as moved did not specify whether joint ownership would be as joint tenants or as tenants in common, a matter of considerable importance). The amendment was published for debate.

Owing to factors which are not of direct relevance to this paper, the amendment did not appear in the published version of the Act. It has since become known as the "lost amendment" and argument continues to rage as to what happened in the final stages of the debate on the Bill.[2] In June 1999, the Speaker ruled that the amendment had never been passed by Parliament so that amending legislation would be needed if the matter of spouses' land rights were to be provided for.

One of the conditionalities of the project was that the "lost amendment" should be re-introduced into Parliament before the end of the first session of Parliament in 1999. It was not and DFID quietly dropped the condition. The project itself was active in developing a revised and fuller version of the amendment which was finally agreed to by the MP who had introduced the original amendment (by then a Minister) and various NGOs fighting for the cause at a meeting between the Minister of State (Lands), the Minister in question and the NGOs in January 2000. It was to be introduced as one of the amendments in the Land (Amendment) Bill which the Ministry of Water, Lands and Environment (MWLE) was preparing to bring to Parliament. In February 2000, however, the Cabinet[3] decided that the amendment should not be part of the Land Act but instead be part of the Domestic Relations Bill, a highly contentious piece of legislation being drafted by the Uganda Law Reform Commission. The general assumption was that the lost amendment had been killed off for good.

The structure and functions of the project

The purpose of the project

The principal purpose of this chapter is to offer some comment and analysis on the project. In order for this to be comprehensible however, it is necessary to set out very briefly the management and operational structure of the project and the activities undertaken and accomplished. The overall goal of the project was:

Sustainable development and livelihood security through effective implementation of the Land Act

with the purpose of the project being:

To lay the foundation for the effective and equitable implementation of the Land Act

The project was designed to lead to three outputs:

- basic awareness by the general population of the content of the law and its implications through the production of a range of resource materials, public information campaigns, and support to local governments and NGOs to mount their own such campaigns;
- the essential least-cost institutional framework for effective and equitable implementation of land tenure reform through support for the development of guidelines and regulations governing the operation of land administration and dispute settlement, through training and through the development of a financial and management plan for the Land Fund;
- a realistic and affordable medium/longer term implementation plan developed and fully incorporated into the national planning and budgeting process through the provision of technical advice.

It is important to note that these three outputs, taken almost verbatim from the Project Document (Prodoc) which is the "constitution" of the project are not so much outputs *of the project* but how it is hoped that the world outside the project will change *as a result of the project.* The project could therefore meet all its targets and complete virtually all its activities, objectively verified by stated indicators, but with some of the outputs neither fully nor even partially achieved. For instance, given the non-establishment of Land Tribunals and with no indication by the end of March 2000 of when any Land Tribunals were to be established, let alone start work, there was no possibility that the project could *during the life of the project* make any contribution to cost-effective dispute settlement even if guidelines and regulations had been developed and training materials prepared. Similarly with the Land Fund; given the view of the Land Act Implementation Study (hereafter LAIS) Report on the Land Fund, the project would actually have been acting in a counter-productive way if it had assisted in the development of a financial and management plan to enable the Land Fund to execute its existing statutory functions.

Project management

A fundamental feature of the project was the multi-institutional nature of its management and operation. The basic principle behind this was that implementing the Land Act necessarily involved institutions, agencies and persons over and above officials in the Ministry of Water, Lands and Environment (MWLE) and the project must therefore engage with these other entities. The law indeed is based on this principle: land administration is decentralised by the Act so that local authorities and the Ministry of Local Government assumed important roles, taking over, in effect, roles and functions previously exercised by officials in the MWLE. *A fortiori* with Land Tribunals and the courts.

The project itself with the amount of activity geared to sensitisation, training and the production of information about the Act aimed at laypersons had to use the skills of persons and the experience of institutions other than those of the Ministry and officials in the Ministry who did not have these particular skills. Given this basic principle, it followed that the units of management and of operation of the project were themselves multi-institutional.

The Multi-Institutional Steering Committee (MISC) which determined the policies of the project, as set out in the Prodoc consisted of officials from central Government of which only two were from MWLE, members from local authority associations and members from organisations in civil society with the Project Co-ordinator as Secretary. The Technical Advisory Panel (TAP) which was designed to exercise quality control on the project outputs consisted of four officials from the Directorate of Lands and

Environment (DLE) of the MWLE representing technical land management expertise and four other persons from the public and NGO sectors representing different skills and organisations, with again, the Project Co-ordinator as Secretary.

The Focus Groups were the engines which drove the project; they did or were responsible for the basic work and when they functioned well, outputs were forthcoming and project activities were realised. When they did not work well, the reverse occurred. All the Focus Groups were multi-institutional and in all the Focus Groups, officials from the DLE were in a minority emphasising that while they were the biggest single group in any Focus Group (except the Sensitisation Focus Group), they were part of a team and implementing the Land Act was a team effort.

The final piece of the multi-institutional and multi-disciplinary jigsaw was the Project Secretariat which managed and co-ordinated the project. The Secretariat was designed to embrace within itself the key skills needed to manage the project and provide technical advice to the Focus Groups; a senior Ugandan administrator as Co-ordinator to provide the administrative and managerial expertise and liaise with other relevant Ministries and governmental agencies; a senior technical adviser focusing on legal and policy issues; and a social development adviser to focus on sensitisation and training and doubling up to assist the DFID Project Officer and the Co-ordinator in the management of DFID funds. These latter two officers were paid for by DFID.

Tasks of the project

By the end of its initial 15-month time-span, what had the project accomplished; to what extent were these accomplishments likely to enable the project to meet its purpose; and what were the constraints and difficulties that may have impeded the project's successful forward momentum? These questions may addressed by reference to the three Project outputs outlined above.

Output 1: Basic awareness by population of the Land Act

Considerable efforts of the project were devoted to this output. The Sensitisation Focus Group (SFG), advised and assisted by the social development adviser held regular meetings and were very active in commissioning the preparation of a multiplicity of publications designed to acquaint the population with the contents of the Act and the rights accorded to them by the Act.

By the end of March, 2000, however, only the *Citizens' Guide to the Land Act* in English and Luganda had been published and distributed to the Districts and various other persons. Five other local language versions had yet to be published. A Simplified Version to the Land Act, a section by section explanation of the Act for lay administrators and Land Tribunal members had been dogged by too many inaccuracies in the first two drafts which had to be corrected and its progress was temporarily held up by TAP refusing to consider the first draft on the grounds that the Act might be changed so that it was not appropriate to proceed with the activity. The translations took much longer than expected and these too were plagued by inaccuracies and the inevitable difficulties in translating Anglo-Ugandan legal concepts into languages not as advanced in legal terminology as English. It was almost inevitable that distilling, translating and simplifying a complicated piece of legislation would take time. When even lawyers do not get it right, it is evident that translation is by no means an easy task.

A poster and radio campaign was held up for two months by a ruling by the Project Co-ordinator that the Ugandan Central Tender Board had to sanction any contract for services valued at over Ushs 2 million shillings (£850) and the CTB's subsequent requirement that radio outlets not hitherto utilised by the project be approached to participate in the radio campaign. This matter was only resolved when the First Secretary (Development) of the British High Commission made it plain that British aid funds did not have to go through such a process and that campaign got under way in October, 1999.

Were all these publications and campaigns likely to lead to the achievement of Output 1? It may be argued that they were more likely to than not. However, it may equally be argued that the general population will never become aware of the content of the law and its implications within the time-span of the project. First, while an effective, clear and simple campaign can get messages across in a fairly short span of time, the messages being put across on the Land Act were inevitably complex and it proved very difficult to simplify them; the assumption in the Prodoc that a media campaign would enable simple messages to get across was perhaps over-optimistic.

Second, even professionals and Government officials didn't yet know the full "implications" of the Act. Third, although considerable numbers of the population do have access to radio, developments in the media sector which have resulted in a fragmentation of the radio audience into smaller and smaller units listening to specific radio stations will inevitably mean that significant sections of the population may not hear the messages relayed over only some stations.

The second aspect of the work of the SFG was to plan sensitisation and familiarisation campaigns in the field and contribute to them. One nation-wide sensitisation campaign was undertaken in all Districts and although inevitably it reached only a small number of people, these tended to be opinion formers within the Districts and the feed-back was positive.

In a society which is still in many respects reliant on oral face-to-face rather than written communication – outside the professional and administrative elites in the urban areas – these sensitisation and familiarisation courses and programmes and the subsequent follow up sensitisation meetings they facilitated should have a major impact on increasing the awareness of the general population about the Act. To that extent, it was not unreasonable to hypothesise that by the end of the project, if, first, all the literature being produced by the project had been produced and widely distributed; and, second, a wide range and considerable numbers of familiarisation courses and workshops etc had taken place, it is more likely than not that Output 1 will have been achieved.

Much more problematic however is whether the achievement of Output 1 will contribute to the realisation of the purpose of the project or the overall goal of the project. On the purpose, two matters have to be considered. First, a decline in public expressions of opposition to the Act. Second, uptake by the population of the facilities and services provided by the Act.

The first matter may be addressed. What were these "public expressions of opposition to the Act"? Four may be identified. First, the traditional authorities in Buganda concerned about the "loss" of 9000 square miles of "Buganda's land". On this, it may be noted: there has been no "loss"; insofar as the status of former public land in Buganda has been altered, this was done by the Constitution and not the Act; and the opposition is essentially political with the general public in Buganda being manipulated to oppose the Act by being misled as to its contents. This opposition may well change when the full import of the Act is brought home to those in Buganda who stand to benefit from the Act.

Second, landlords concerned about the loss of their "right" to get rid of their tenants as they saw fit without let or hindrance. It is quite possible that opposition from this group will grow in proportion as knowledge about their rights percolate down to tenants and tenants begin using their rights. Increased opposition from landlords could then, paradoxically, be taken as a measure of success of the second leg of the purpose.

Third, women concerned about the "lost amendment" and men concerned about the possible "finding", *i.e.*, enactment, of the lost amendment. A major and long term programme of sensitisation will be needed to convince men of the justice and workability of provisions about common ownership of matrimonial land. Women will remain dissatisfied if the provisions are not enacted. The project was in a no-win situation: whatever was done or not done on this issue would stimulate opposition to the Act and was outside the control of the project.

A fourth source of opposition to the Act must be mentioned. This is the general population, who, sensitised to the advantages to be gained from using the services and facilities provided by the Act, then become increasingly irate that they cannot actually use the Act because Boards and Committees and Recorders and Land Tribunals and Mediators are either not in place or have not been resourced adequately or have no regulations in place which enables them to function. By the end of March 2000, this was a real possibility. Effective sensitisation then might stimulate rather than lower opposition to the Act.

Now to the second matter. By March, 2000, this was a non-starter. The population had not begun to take up the opportunities provided for under the Act. They could not for reasons which will emerge later in this chapter.

Output 2: Least cost institutional framework for implementation

There were considerable problems with this output arising from factors *dehors* the project. Indeed the Objectively Verifiable Indicators (OVIs) set out in the Prodoc attached to this output are not within the powers of the project to ensure. The OVIs required that 45 DLBs, 45 District Land Tribunals (DLT), sub-county and Urban Land Tribunals in seven districts would be in place and working and consultative partnerships between central and local governments would also be in place and working. These may be considered *seriatim*.

District Land Boards First, by the end of September, 43 out of the 45 District Land Boards were in place and had started meeting. They were not then, nor indeed by March 2000, in a position to issue certificates of customary ownership. First, few Parish Land Committees, the institutions which commence the process of titling were in place; second the Land Regulations had not been enacted; third, very few districts had their full complement of land officials as stipulated in the Act, and fourth, there was no money in local government budgets to fund the Boards. Training of Board members had not yet taken place and the budgetary arrangements for paying for the Boards had yet to be implemented.

District Land Tribunals Second, the state of affairs on Land Tribunals was even more gloomy. No Tribunal members had been appointed by March 2000 and the process for appointment was clearly going to be so long-winded that it was unlikely that any Land Tribunals would be in place before the second anniversary of the passage of the Land Act in July 2000. Amendments to the Land Act had been developed by the senior technical adviser at the request of Ministers as far back as June 1999 to try to overcome the logjam on tribunals but these had yet to be brought to Parliament before it was adjourned in May 2000 for upwards of two months.[4] No Tribunal (Procedure) Rules had been made by the Chief Justice by the end of March 2000 as was his duty under the Act.

Two further matters may be considered which although not specifically referred to in project logframe, are relevant to this output; the Land Regulations and the arrangements for the management of the Land Fund. Each are worth considering in some detail as in their different ways, they demonstrate some of the difficulties the project had in achieving outputs and matching outputs to purpose.

Rules and Regulations On the first matter, the Rules and Regulations Focus Group (R&RFG) together with the Survey Methods and Standards Focus Group (SM&SFG) worked well together at the very outset of the project to examine and revise the draft Land Regulations prepared under a DFID consultancy by a local and an international consultant in December 1998. The TAP considered and accepted the work of the two Focus Groups at a meeting in early April 1999 and the draft was then passed on to the Ministry for Ministry consideration and onwards transmission to Cabinet, the First Parliamentary Counsel (FPC) and Parliament.

Unfortunately, these further steps took over a year to complete. Ministry officials considered that once the project had completed its work, the draft should go straight to the FPC. Agreement was reached between Ministry officials and the FPC on the draft but Ministers were not brought into those discussions. Ministers were then presented with the agreed draft to take to Cabinet. They considered the draft for the first time in May 1999 and proposed changes to a draft that the FPC had apparently indicated should not be further changed before being submitted to Cabinet. Ministry officials did not act on proposed Ministerial changes for six months as work on the regulations got caught up in disputes within the Ministry about the project and the role of officials and Ministers in implementing the Land Act. Once the regulations were taken up again in November 1999, work proceeded very slowly and although the draft regulations were finally approved by the Cabinet in February 2000, they had not been formally put to Parliament before its adjournment in May 2000.[5]

Land Fund The management of the Land Fund had not progressed even that far by the end of March 2000. If the SFG is the success story of the Focus Groups, the Land Fund Focus Group (LFFG) is the reverse. After a year of meetings, the Group had produced nothing. The Group believed and wrote an interim report to the Permanent Secretary on the matter that the cause of their lack of productive labour was the constant blockages that the senior technical adviser had put on their initiatives. The senior technical adviser's position was that the problems were caused by the Group's disinclination to focus on their core activity as set out in the Prodoc – developing the management structures and processes and the regulations to go with them for the operation of the Land Fund – in preference for a much wider role of considering the management and funding of land reform programmes generally, a role for which the Group was not equipped. Consequently the senior technical adviser was unwilling to agree to DFID funding or to recommend to the Ministry spending on this wider activity. In this, he was supported by the first Project Co-ordinator.

Efforts to arrive at some *modus vivendi* between the two positions did not prove successful. The appointment of a consultant to work on the Land Fund – provided for in the Prodoc and strongly supported by the Minister of State (Lands) – did not greatly assist matters since the consultant recommended a very small role for the Land Fund in the future implementation of the Act with a very limited budget, while the Group maintained that the Fund should occupy a central role in implementation and funds must be found for this to be made possible. An offer by the senior technical adviser to fund a workshop to work on the details of management structures and the principles to be put into regulations in the light of the consultant's report received no response from the Group. Thus, project institutions did not work and outputs were not forthcoming. The Steering Committee was not invited to mediate on the impasse; in retrospect, perhaps it should have been. However, the Chairman of the Steering Committee in his capacity as Permanent Secretary was aware of the problem but took no action on it.[6]

What contribution to the purpose of the project did Output 2 make? The answer is: none. The principal reason for this was that the project assumed that the Ministry would work reasonably efficiently and effectively and that there was a commitment within and outwith the Ministry to implement the Land Act. Neither assumption was correct as will be explained in more detail below.

Output 3: Medium and longer term implementation plan developed and fully incorporated into national planning and budgeting process

A Land Act Implementation Study (LAIS) was to be the project vehicle to kick-start this output. A multi-disciplinary national and international team of consultants – reflecting in their composition and disciplines the basic principles of the project – worked hard and harmoniously together for over three months – late May to early September 1999 – to produce a report providing the basic information, analysis and proposals for implementation for the development of the plan envisaged in Output 3.

The LAIS's purpose was to assist the Government of Uganda (GoU) to determine appropriate and affordable implementation priorities by examining the institutional, legal, financial and technical needs for implementation and assessing the social, economic and environmental implications of the Land Act. The Study concluded that as set out in the Act, implementation was beyond the financial capacity of the GoU and even when modified in ways proposed in the Study, would still involve a considerable financial burden for the country in respect of which there were no clear and identifiable social or economic benefits to be gained.

Notwithstanding that conclusion, the Report recognised that the Act introduced major reforms into the system of land holding in the country, had considerable political capital invested in it and that it would be a significant set-back for the development of Uganda if its promise could not be realised. The Report identified a range of "development initiatives" to build capacity to enable the Act to be effectively implemented. These were:

Pilot Operations	Limited pilot exercises to test the operation of the proposed systems prior to full implementation.
Policy Development	Development of national and local land policies to guide the process of tenure reform.
Legal Reform	Requirements to replace out of date and inconsistent legislation to harmonise with the Land Act and other relevant modern legislation.
Technology and Infrastructure	Acquisition of modern surveying equipment, and information technology (hardware, software and systems design) and communications systems. Specialist equipment/furniture. Vehicles.
Human Resources Development	Developing appropriate human resources management and human resources development systems, and the costs of "initial" training for each of the implementation institutions. Also provide for development of more general professional and technical education and training to increase the pool of appropriate skills in the population.
Financial Management	The development of appropriate financing and financial management policies and systems.
Sensitisation	A range of sensitisation, public information and participatory planning activities to raise awareness, selectively encourage titling where appropriate, and mitigate negative effects and abuses.
Monitoring and Evaluation	Quality assurance procedures to monitor quality of service and cost effectiveness, and survey-type activities to monitor and evaluate impact.
Co-ordination	A Steering Committee and Secretariat to oversee implementation.

These nine heads of activities on capacity building followed on from the Study's analysis that "the current infrastructure, expertise and human and technological capacity is far from being able to deliver the Land Act services" and capacity building activities will be needed if there is to be any likelihood of effective, efficient and responsive implementation of the Act. What may be further noticed is that these heads of capacity building are very broad – they do not just focus on training – but offer, in other words, a coherent and integrated vision of what is needed if implementation is to have any chance of success and what, inferentially, might be the subject of donor assistance.

A major three-day workshop bringing together all key stakeholders discussed the draft report in August 1999 and was in broad agreement with the analysis in the report, the suggestions for changes in laws and administrative arrangements to facilitate implementation, its proposals for how to proceed and where donor inputs could be invited. The only major disagreement was on the Land Fund where the members of the group discussing that, dominated by the LFFG members, without addressing the report's findings that the Land Fund as set out in the Act would be financially ruinous, economically disastrous, socially regressive, and unappealing to donors as a consequence, nonetheless considered that the need to tackle historical injustices – in particular buying out landlords in the "Lost Counties" and allocating the land to tenants – required that the Fund be activated to the fullest extent possible as soon as possible.

The LAIS report was one of the if not *the* most important activity of the project: it was to form the basis for future GoU and donor input into the planned implementation of the Land Act. After the report was submitted to the Minister on 6 September, the senior technical adviser wrote a memorandum to the Permanent Secretary to urge rapid action. The Minister of State (Lands) called a meeting to decide how to proceed. Against the advice of the senior technical adviser, it was decided to "recycle" the report back into the project with TAP meeting to review it followed by the MISC doing the same.

What then transpired was exactly as the senior technical adviser feared would happen: the report was more or less buried by the DLE. It was the DLE meeting as TAP[7] in October which produced a thin comment which more or less dismissed the LAIS analysis and all the proposed savings on implementing the Act. The DLE which by September had "captured" the project by getting the first Project Co-ordinator removed and one of their members put in her place then made no move to call a meeting of the MISC for six months. Thus by the end of March 2000, no progress has been made on developing a medium and long term implementation plan on the basis of LAIS. The Ugandan Joint Team Leader of the LAIS Team was right when he said at a workshop in January 2000 that the Report had been sidelined.[8] There was then no possibility that Output 3 would be achieved by the planned end of the project.

The institutional environment of the project

In keeping with the writing of any project document for an aid project, there had to be a risk appraisal of the project; an assessment of the principal risks to the project and what action would be taken to meet those risks. One of the risks as described in the Prodoc was "lack of motivation within the Ministry of Water, Lands and Environment ..." This was later explained as the possible lack of support by members of the MWLE Directorate of Lands to the participatory implementation strategy and the devolution of authority over land administration.

What was not considered was what in fact transpired: the overt and continuing hostility of senior members of the Directorate of Lands to the project itself and the effect this would have on the ability of the project to carry out its activities and achieve its outputs and on the morale of the members of the Secretariat of the project. No purpose would be served by recounting the details of the sustained, unjustified (and unjustifiable) attacks on the project, its personnel, members of the Ministry and DFID itself by members of the DLE. Suffice it to say that the attacks which started as internal Ministry conflicts were given wide publicity by the DLE by being made to the Parliamentary Sessional Committee on Natural Resources, in the press and on radio and television.

Behind the unpleasant personal attacks lay a fundamental structural problem which the risk appraisal did almost put its finger on: the difficulty the DLE had in coming to terms with the new multi-institutional and devolved approach to land management which appears to leave them without a clear and useful role in the Ministry coupled with the threat, as they saw it, of being "agentised". The project was seen as being the primary vehicle for their marginalisation and they reacted accordingly. This part of the paper seeks to explain how this came about.

The opposition of the DLE

Whatever the published aims of the project – assisting land tenure reform as a contribution to poverty alleviation and sustainable development – it was in practice a project about institutional reform and capacity building: building the capacity of decentralised land administration agencies and land dispute settlement bodies through training and the provision of a framework of rules and guides to regulate and structure discretionary power; building the capacity of the citizenry through expanding their knowledge about the new laws and the opportunities provided by the laws to acquire and safeguard their right to land; and building the capacity of the Government of Uganda generally by providing it with the information and tools necessary to develop a coherent, cost-effective and responsive plan to implement the Land Act in the medium and long term. There was, at best, a heroic assumption – perhaps, pious hope would be better – that if capacity were to be built in the way envisaged, poverty alleviation and sustainable development would follow.

Like M Jourdain who spoke prose without realising it, the project then was about capacity building without realising it. But seeing it as capacity building allows one to understand (without in any way condoning) the attitude and activities of the officials in the DLE who consistently opposed the project from its commencement. Why was this? The matter can be put thus: to plagiarise the aphorism which Dean Acheson used about the British Government in 1962, the Act had created a situation where the DLE had lost an empire but had not yet found a role. The project was the outward and visible sign of this and was therefore bound to attract opprobrium from the DLE.

To elaborate: until the coming into effect of the Constitution in October 1995, most land in the country was public land and the central government was the primary manager of that land; district land boards were very much subordinate to the Land Commission and the Ministry responsible for land. Within the Ministry, officials with technical and professional qualifications relating to land – surveyors, valuers, lawyers, physical planners – managed the land. This had gone on for so long that it had become an article of faith, part of the ideology of land management within the DLE, that not only was it right and proper that technically and professionally qualified officials should manage land but that it would be wrong and improper and subversive of good land management if persons without those particular skills and qualifications should engage in the business of land management, either directly or indirectly.

Even after the Constitution was promulgated, nothing much changed. True, the Constitution had made some pretty radical pronouncements about who owned the land and who was to manage it but the basic law of land management remained the same. Then along came the Land Act, 1998 which has turned the world of the DLE upside down. Overnight, literally, officials were stripped of their powers of land management which were vested in District Land Boards. Even worse, the inherent powers of land management which are inseparable from land ownership also disappeared from the public domain and became vested in millions of peasants and urban dwellers: the grand words of the Constitution had been made a reality by the Act.

But perhaps most shattering of all was that the loss of powers was accompanied by loss of control over resources – funds hitherto available to the centre were to be allocated to the districts. What then was to be the future role of the officials and what access would they have to public and donor funds? At the very least, they assumed that they would be in charge of implementing the Act so that they would be in a position to control the pace and nature of the changes mandated by the Act and so the allocation of resources for implementation. In order to achieve this indeed, they had established a Task Force within the Ministry on the morrow of the enactment of the Act to plan for the implementation of the Act.

Even that, however was denied them. The Ministry or in the eyes of the DLE, the higher echelons of the Ministry, without regard to the skills, knowledge or opinions of the DLE, conspired with the British Government to introduce into the Ministry a "project" which involved personnel with no professional or technical knowledge about land from outside the Ministry – administrators, sociologists, journalists, professional educators, officials from other Ministries – making decisions about land management and how capacity to manage land should be developed in the future. At the outset of the project, the Ministry's Task Force was to be abandoned. A major feature of this "project" was to be a study about the long term management of land in Uganda in which non-professionals with limited knowledge about land in Uganda – whether Ugandan or non-Ugandan was beside the point – were to dominate. It was hardly surprising that members of the DLE did not wish to give such a study a spurious air of legitimacy by participating in it while being in a minority or that when they had the chance, they would rubbish it and sideline it.[9]

The professional and technical officials were, in their own eyes then, sidelined *by the project*. In truth, they were sidelined by the Constitution and the Land Act in the sense that they were no longer to be the primary managers of land in Uganda and what is worse, the bodies that assumed their functions are specifically stated by the Act "not [to] be subject to the direction or control of any person or authority ..." so they could not even indirectly manage land by, as it were, operating through District Land Boards. The project's purpose was to facilitate the implementation of the Land Act and that necessarily involved concentrating on the new institutions of land management.

The Land Fund and the budget

The saga of the Land Fund which on the surface appeared to be a rather petty squabble between officials and the senior technical adviser can be better understood in the light of the analysis offered here. Of all the new institutions introduced by the Land Act, the Land Fund was the only one, the administration of which was located at the centre. It thus became absolutely essential for officials to argue that the Fund should be seen as *the* most important institution created by the Act and that those charged with developing its structures and management processes should be facilitated to expand their role and thus the role of the Fund. The senior technical adviser was seen as the agent of those within and outwith the Ministry who were responsible for cutting the DLE down and this fuelled the bitterness of the dispute between the LFFG – composed entirely of officials from the centre – and him.

Further support for this analysis is provided by the sub-plot of the development of the budgets for land activities in the Ministry. The Ministry of Finance allocated £1.2 million; £2 million and £3.2 million for Land Act implementation in the three years 1999–2000, 2000–01, and 2001–02. This was however, coupled with a decision that the Directorate or the bulk of it should be "agentised", that is converted into an executive agency operating at arms length from the Ministry and that no funds should be allocated to the normal land management activities of the DLE from the financial year 1999 – 2000 onwards. This decision had nothing to do with the project and had been taken before the project commenced; it was, however, taken with no consultation with the officials in the DLE and further soured relations between them and the whole process of implementing the Act.

The DLE was thus faced with loss of power over land via the Act and loss of resources for land administration via a Treasury decision. Neither were acceptable to the officials and alongside the fight against the project, they set out to fight the decision over funding. Unfortunately the project was at the centre of this fight too. This was because the Project Co-ordinator, already anathema to the DLE owing to the fact that she was an outsider with no land management expertise brought into the Ministry by the Minister precisely to ensure that the DLE were kept at arms length from the project, was also the Under Secretary in the Ministry responsible for the budget, and, as such, responsible for ensuring that the Treasury's decision on funding for land management was adhered to.

A bitter battle was waged by the DLE against the Co-ordinator and the project with unsubstantiated and unsubstantiatable allegations made over some four months to Ministers within the Ministry and, outside the Ministry, to Parliament, to the Government's anti-corruption agency and to the press about the project and its alleged mis-management. Ultimately the DLE won; Ministers sacked the Co-ordinator in mid August 1999 and allowed the DLE to select one of their number to take over the post. Immediately, the DLE, which up to that point had not been prepared to discuss the 1999–2000 budget with the Under Secretary, agreed to form a task force with officials from other Ministries involved in Land Act implementation to revise the budget. A revised budget allocated considerable sums for expensive 4x4s for officials in the DLE and for other central expenditures.

This revision was but a prelude to the DLE's proposed expenditure plans for the next three years. First, the officials decided to dispense with a multi-ministerial task force despite a specific direction from the Minister that the existing such task force should continue with the work of preparing the budgets for the following years. Second, the proposed budgets allocated over 80% of projected funds to the centre and less than 20% to the decentralised local agencies which were mandated by the Act to implement the Act. The figures for the Land Fund say it all. The budget proposed that Ushs 6.46bn/= (£2.75m) be allocated to the Land Fund over three years while only 2.64bn/= (£1.12m) be made available to the 45 Districts via conditional grants (grants earmarked for specific purposes) from the centre during the same period. The contrast is even more striking when the figures are put in percentage terms of the proposed GoU budgets for the three years:

2000/01: Land Fund: 17%	Conditional Grants: 13%
2001/02: Land Fund: 25%	Conditional Grants: 11%
2002/03: Land Fund: 29%	Conditional Grants: 8%

The officials then were determined to hold on to resources and powers at the expense of any programme to implement the Land Act. To the extent that the project appeared to obstruct that aim, it had to be opposed until they could get control of it and then emasculate it thereafter.

The DLE and the control of the project

The project however was not completely blameless. Since the project was designed to be about poverty alleviation and sustainable development, it had to meet the developmental criteria of both DFID and the GoU on those matters. Indeed, that is, in reality, putting the matter the wrong way round. Poverty alleviation and sustainable development drove the project; if it couldn't be related to those aims, it wouldn't have got off the ground. But concentration on these lofty aims which it was thought could be met by capacity building of the citizens and decentralised land administration bodies, diverted attention from what, arguably, was the most important need for capacity building: capacity building or the re-engineering of the skills and knowledge of the officials at the centre; the DLE. The project, in other words had been designed, perhaps unwittingly, to concentrate on the new institutions of land management *at the expense of the old institutions*. They had been cast adrift by the Act. The Directorate was not to be in control of the project; it seemed that its members were outside the scope of the project; they neither ran it nor seemed to be beneficiaries of it.

Was it any wonder then that the principal aim of the DLE from the commencement of the project was to obtain control of the project and argue that without that control, the project was not "owned" by the GoU; *i.e.*, that a project about the management of land in Uganda could only be legitimate if it were run by and to the direction of the professional land managers employed by the GoU. Perhaps more cynically, one could say that the DLE's perception was that if it gained control of the project, officials would be in a position to re-assert their central role in land management and sideline all these other organisations and persons who had been allowed to usurp that central role. The fallacy of that was obvious: as noted above, it was the Act and not the project that had removed the professional officials from centre stage but it was the design and outputs of the project that fuelled the resentment of central officials by not specifically including them within the scope of capacity building.

If DLE officials showed interest in accessing the GoU budget after winning the battle of the co-ordinatorship, the reverse was the case with the project. There was no doubt that the pace of and interest in implementing the Land Act within the Ministry diminished once the original Project Co-ordinator was replaced in mid August 1999. In part, this was because from mid August to late November there was no full-time Project Co-ordinator[10] (though that in itself was symptomatic of a loss of enthusiasm and momentum within the Ministry) but there were other factors at work here, both structural and personal.

First, the DLE had from mid August, at least in its own eyes, taken over the project which became just a part of the DLE. The very approach the Minster of State (Lands) warned against in a meeting with members of the DLE and the senior technical adviser in November, *viz.* that he did *not* want the project to become part of the DLE and so be swallowed up in Ministry bureaucracy, occurred. Too often, project matters were referred to the Director by the new Project Co-ordinator before any action was taken and this inevitably either slowed things down or stopped them in their tracks altogether.

Second, it is not just that the project became part of the bureaucracy of the DLE. A determined effort was made, entirely in keeping with the mind-set of the DLE, to turn it from a multi-institutional project in which equal partners work together to implement the Land Act, into a sub-programme of the DLE in which the pace, direction and nature of implementation is determined solely by the DLE.

The evidence for this was overwhelming. First there was the refusal to continue the task force work in developing future budgets and the medium and long term plan after the task force completed its first task of rewriting the 1999–2000 budget in November. Second, there was the side-lining of the MISC (the DLE unilaterally changed its name to the *Inter*-Institutional SC which was in itself significant); only one meeting took place between mid August 1999 and the end of March 2000 compared to four meetings between February and mid-August 1999.

Third, there was the heavy emphasis in the DLE's Budget Framework Paper produced in February 2000 that the overwhelming amount of resources for Land Act implementation would remain under its control with the involvement of others, including donors, being very much that of junior partners with no directive or policy-making role. Fourth, there was the sidelining of the LAIS Report with its emphasis on multi-institutionality and the primacy of decentralised land management.

Fifth, there was the Permanent Secretary's decision – part of the concordat which ended the stand off between the higher management of the Ministry and the DLE – that he would delegate most matters of land management and project implementation to the Director of the DLE which meant that since mid November when the Director returned to duty from his 6 months enforced leave,[11] the Permanent Secretary showed only spasmodic interest in Land Act implementation. Implementation had passed into the hands of those who were not committed to implementation.

The upshot of the state of affairs as at the end of March 2000 may be put thus. At the time the senior technical adviser wrote the issues and options paper on possible future DFID input into land reform in Uganda on the morrow of the submission of the LAIS report in late September 1999, it was not clear how the project would develop and how Land Act implementation would proceed in the aftermath of the removal of the then Project Co-ordinator.

By the time he left at the end of March, the position was clear. The DLE had succeeded on all fronts; the project was just a part, and a rather small part at that, of the DLE's activities. Land Act implementation and its resources have been subsumed under the DLE's drive to equip itself with the latest 4x4s, "high-tech" toys – survey equipment, printing presses etc – study tours, international conferences etc and qualifications without regard to whether these will have any positive impact on poverty eradication and sustainable livelihood development, or indeed on implementing the Act. By not providing them with positive benefits, the project had set in train a course of events whereby the officials in the DLE acted on the basis that their survival necessitated the emasculation of the project and the non-implementation of the Act.

The analysis so far has concentrated on the problems that the DLE had with the project and their successful efforts to preserve their own positions at the expense of the project. The Directorate was not alone however in finding its traditional functions had been, to some extent, undermined by the Act. Much the same analysis can be applied to the Judicial Service Commission (JSC) in relation to the Land Tribunals.

Land Tribunals

The JSC and the Chief Justice are mandated by the Act to appoint the members of the Land Tribunals and the Chief Justice is mandated to make procedural rules for the tribunals. Up to the end of June 2000, two years after the Act was passed, no members had been appointed; no Tribunals were operative; and this was imposing an increasing social and economic cost on the country; people were being killed over land disputes because there seemed to be no other way to settle disputes and advice was being given by local authorities to people involved in land disputes to allow the land in dispute to lie fallow and unused pending the settlement of the dispute.

What was not fully appreciated was that the Chief Justice and the JSC whose whole *raison d'être* is to advance the interests and work of the courts and the judicial system had suddenly been required to establish a rival judicial system designed to marginalise the courts in probably the most important area of civil law in the country; namely, land disputes. It is not to be wondered therefore that the only public speeches the chairman of the JSC made about Land Tribunals was to suggest that since there had been unavoidable delay (sic) in getting them off the ground, the Act should be amended to restore the jurisdiction of courts to deal with land disputes, and that when the JSC did finally begin to put together a programme for appointing chairpersons and members in early 2000, it found it needed 4x4s, considerable sums of money for allowances (both of which were, apparently to come from the Land Act implementation budget) and that the process would take many weeks if not months to complete. Here too, perhaps the project should have included within its components, some element of capacity building for the JSC in relation to the roles and functions of tribunals.[12]

The project as institutional reform

It has been noted above that the project was based on a set of assumptions about the purpose of the Land Act – it will assist in poverty alleviation and sustainable development – that are, in the view of the LAIS Report, highly unlikely to be borne out in practice and these assumptions dictated the activities to be pursued by the project. In consequence, too little attention was paid to the actual central thrust of the Land Act in practice: *that it is a major exercise in institutional reform* and such exercises generate a whole host of problems, challenges and opposition which need to be addressed if reform is to have any chance of being successful.

The recently published book *Getting Good Government* (Grindle, 1997) which focuses on capacity building in the public sectors of developing countries suggests that:

> ... good government is advanced – although by no means ensured – when skilled and professional public officials undertake to formulate and implement policies, when bureaucratic units perform their assigned tasks effectively, and when fair and authoritative rules for economic and political interaction are

regularly enforced and observed ... Getting good government means, among other things, efforts to develop human resources, strengthen organizations and reform (or create) institutions in this sector. Table 1–1 (below) indicates that these three dimensions of capacity focus primarily on personnel, management, or structures and imply distinct activities if they are to be developed, strengthened, or reformed.

TABLE 1–1
Dimensions and Focus of Capacity-Building Initiatives

Dimension	**Focus**	**Types of Activities**
Human resource development	Supply of professional and technical personnel	Training, salaries, conditions of work, recruitment
Organizational Strengthening	Management systems to improve performance of specific tasks and functions; microstructures	Incentive systems, utilization of personnel, leadership, organizational culture, communications, managerial structures
Institutional reform	Institutions and systems; macrostructure	Rules of the game for economic and political regimes, policy and legal change, constitutional reform

The study goes on to make the point that ideas about the role of the state have changed over the years but that there is now a general consensus that "effective government performance [has become] central to a changed definition of the role of the state in development and to its ability to create the institutional conditions for market-oriented economies, secure and productive populations and democratic political systems". Building effective state capacity is a continuous process with no easy solutions. In designing projects, there is a need to take account of a wide range of factors, many of them outside the immediate subject-matter of the project, which will affect the likely success of the project.

These points are no doubt well known. They are made here to draw attention to the fact that a project focusing on capacity building is a complex exercise – in its design, in its implementation and in any measurement of success – and one that may need to extend over several years. It goes beyond training – along with sensitisation, the principal focus of human resource capacity building in the project under review here – and embraces organisational structures, management practices and the "rules of the game" – all matters which are central to effective land tenure reform programmes in Uganda. Any such project would have to extend beyond the confines of one Ministry so that although it might focus on one central matter – land tenure reform – it will have to be designed to encompass all the principal actors and stakeholders involved in that activity.

Capacity building and institutional reform are intimately linked. The following quotation brings this out (Grindle, pp. 19–20):

> Few can have witnessed or participated in capacity-building initiatives without being impressed by the extent to which organizations are deeply embedded in their environment and the extent to which this larger context must be considered in addressing their capacity. For this reason capacity development often requires addressing problems of institutional reform.
>
> Institutional reform means altering the rules of the game in which organizations and individuals make decisions and carry out activities ... Thus capacity building through institutional reform would involve initiatives such as the development of legal systems, policy regimes, mechanisms of accountability, regulatory frameworks, and monitoring systems that transmit information about and structure the performance of markets, governments and public officials ...
>
> As indicated, much of the emphasis of capacity-building initiatives traditionally has focused on human resource development and on the organizations (or projects) that carry out specific tasks.

Implementing the Land Act fits into this analysis remarkably aptly. The Land Act has introduced a new (land) legal system – new organisations to administer and decide disputes about land; new policy regimes – the emphasis in the Act is to facilitate the acquisition and protection of titles to land vested in private individuals and entities; new mechanisms of accountability – the somewhat awkward relationship between the District Land Boards, District Councils and the centre illustrate that; new regulatory frameworks – the whole Act is just that in relation to land management. Where it is weak is on new monitoring systems and it is precisely in that area that the project could, if the introduction of the Land Act had been understood in this light, have focused some attention which would in turn have necessarily involved officials at the centre. Similarly, can we not understand the perceptions and actions of officials in the DLE and in the JSC as being, at least in part, driven by their "deeply embedded" environment to which too little attention was paid in the pressure to get on with implementing the Act.

On this analysis, the inescapable conclusion is that the problems of the project went beyond personal relationships and structural issues. The project was based on an incorrect appreciation of the issues that needed to be addressed if implementing the Land Act was to proceed with any likely degree of success: these are, quite simply, *issues of governance; capacity building in the context of institutional reform which needed to embrace all elements of existing organisations and personnel therein which were undergoing change mandated by the Act*.

As it was, the project in practice was a contributory factor in the breakdown of relations between officials in the MWLE and between some officials within the Ministry and DFID; it was a causal factor in some officials in the Ministry behaving in a reprehensible and unprofessional manner; in some cases, it probably delayed rather than promoted implementation; to some extent, it delayed the development of the necessary restructuring of the role and functions of Ministry officials professionally responsible for land management; and it was used as a stick to beat the Ministry with in connection with the slow progress of the implementation of the Act and as a pawn in various intra-Ministry battles over access to resources and compliance with proper procedures.

This is not in any way to decry what the project against the odds, succeeded in accomplishing between its commencement in January 1999, and the end of March 2000. Significant progress was made in the development of excellent materials for sensitisation and training and sensitisation in the field got off to a good start. The Land Regulations – essential for the new organisations established by the Act to exercise their powers – were an early successful product of the project; it was not the project's responsibility that they were not then carried forward. Similarly with efforts made to get the Land Tribunals started. The centre-piece of the project, the LAIS Report, was the product of a very successful multi-disciplinary multi-national team effort that produced a first class report on time which provided the essential policy basis and analytical framework for the GoU to develop its long-term strategy for implementing the Act.

Self-assessment

Writing in *Getting Good Government*, Clive Gray quotes from the UNDP study on *Rethinking Technical Cooperation: Reforms for Capacity Building in Africa* as follows (Grindle, p. 414):

> The expert concentrates on getting the work done rather than on training, is often good at his job but bad as a trainer, upstages the counterpart in influence, and sometimes blocks the counterpart's progress by staying too long. Counterparts are too few and often are not right for the job, are selected too late in the life of the project, are too lightly trained, or quit for better jobs.

This seems a useful peg on which to hang an attempt at self assessment, although it by no means covers all the points that could be made on the relationship between expert and counterpart. It is more sensible at this juncture to use the personal pronoun "I" as I endeavour to sum up my own role in the project.

I concentrated on trying to get the job done, the job being the achievement of project outputs in order to meet the project purpose. When it seemed to me that an output was not being achieved or that there was a blockage in a project activity, I endeavoured to suggest ways to overcome the blockage or speed up the achievement of the output. I either met with counterparts (taking that term to mean officials in the DLE) the Permanent Secretary and/or the Minister of State (Lands) or wrote memoranda to try and get things moving. This, it must admitted, was not always successful, and this was usually because the root cause of the blockage was not susceptible to rational Weberian type administrative solutions which I was apt to suggest.

This leads on to a second point, not sufficiently addressed by the above quotation but discussed in the Grindle book. It is not just training that an expert fails to give but the expert also is usually not him- or herself sufficiently versed in the nuances of African public administration which often relies far more on informal networks to get things done than formal rules and procedures (nor, even if he/she is, can he/she participate in such networks). This was certainly the case with this project. I relied on the formal bureaucratic procedures to get things done; so did the Permanent Secretary, the Minister and the first Co-ordinator; the DLE, on the other hand were much more adept at using informal networks, by-passing regular procedures and channels to ensure that they could get their way. (Their use of MPs, other Ministers and civil servants and the press to attack the project and the Minister is a good example of that.) I had a great many contacts in the higher reaches of the Ugandan political and legal establishment: I did not make use of them. I played it by the book.

I did not engage in any process of formal training. That said, occupying the same office as the Project Co-ordinator and discussing with successive co-ordinators what I was doing; what they were doing; how to overcome problems of the project or in the Ministry is bound to lead to the transference of some ideas and approaches – good and bad – from myself to the co-ordinator (and in the case, certainly, of the first co-ordinator, vice versa).

It is necessary to distinguish between co-ordinators here. I worked with the first co-ordinator for over five months and I think some of my approaches to land matters probably did assist her. The second co-ordinator from the DLE who succeeded her never moved into the office so there was in practice very little day-to-day contact with him during the two or so months he acted as a part-time co-ordinator. It is more difficult to say whether any of my approaches or skills were transferred to his successor, with whom I worked for just over four months. His point of reference was the Director and he continued to work as much with the DLE as in the project.

This is where the point about the counterpart in the quotation at the beginning of this section is relevant. The first co-ordinator was selected for the job of co-ordinator by the Minister and was a good choice; she was a good administrator, if a little rigid; was not part of the hidebound thinking of the DLE; was sufficiently senior to get through to senior people in other Ministries; had worked in many other Ministries and therefore had a knowledge of how the Ugandan bureaucracy worked; and clearly had the respect of other officials in other Ministries. She didn't know much about land issues but was willing to learn. She clearly too wanted the project to make a difference.

The other two co-ordinators could not have been more different. They were selected by the DLE as people who would *not* act independently of the DLE; they were not very senior; as professional officers, they had not worked in other Ministries; they did not know how the bureaucracy works (their struggles to access funds from the 1999–2000 budget was eloquent witness to that);[13] and they did not have the contacts amongst officials in other Ministries which would have enabled them to get things done. They did not want the project to make a difference insofar as "making a difference" meant doing things which the DLE would have preferred not to have done. So in some respects, I would have to say that while the first co-ordinator and I were on the same wave length, that was not the case with her two successors and this made me less effective as an "informal trainer".

I did not "network" with the senior members of the DLE. That was a mistake. It might have prevented the stand off between the Land Fund Focus Group and myself that certainly did not help the progress of the Land

Fund. In my defence I would say that while the first project co-ordinator was in post, such was the animosity felt by the senior members of the DLE for her and the project that any informal relationships with them were more or less out of the question – one member actually refused to speak to her even when they sat on committees together. After her replacement, the relationship between the DLE and the project thawed so that personal relationships finished up perfectly correct without being particularly warm.

I think that there was some resentment at my easy access to the Minister and the Permanent Secretary. But this was also mixed with disagreement with my attitude to Ministers. I adopted what might be called the conventional British civil service attitude to Ministers "deferential, glad to be of use; politic, cautious ..."; they are Ministers and as such entitled to respect and to be listened to. That was not the approach of the DLE. Ministers, for the DLE, are in the way (as, on one notorious occasion, the Director shouted at the Minister at a meeting of TAP) and need not have much attention paid to them. (The second co-ordinator in particular and in my presence expressed very critical remarks about Ministerial involvement in land matters – not about *e.g.*, corruption but about ignorance.[14])

So my easy access to Ministers was quite probably because Ministers quickly felt that I regarded them with respect and treated them as equals in the business of the implementation of the Act and the project. Upstaging my counterparts was in the circumstances, unavoidable. It may be noted however, that after mid August 1999, when the DLE took the project over, the Minister and the Permanent Secretary had fewer meetings with me alone and involved the Project Co-ordinator and the Director far more.

In retrospect, it is not too difficult to see where I could have done things differently. A greater effort at the outset of my work to bring the warring parties together might have helped, although once the DLE's round robin letter of 29 April 1999 attacking the project, its personnel and DFID had been delivered to Ministers, the battle lines were drawn and there was, from then on, all out war against the project until the DLE's victory was achieved in mid-August. I should have had more personal contact with individual members of the DLE. Again however, the opportunity for this to occur with the two most influential members via working together on the LAIS team fell through when both of them, although invited to join the team and initially accepting, later decided not to do so. Towards the end of my contract, my memoranda etc. began to be couched in fairly forthright language; this probably did not help them to be acceptable.

These are micro matters. The macro matter is this: did the organisational environment, administrative culture and mind set of my counterparts in the DLE change as a result of my being a part of the Ministry for one year and working alongside them on land issues? The answer is: *not in any way whatsoever*. Indeed their conviction that they and they alone, as people with the requisite professional and technical qualifications, should manage land and be in sole and exclusive control of the implementation of the Land Act was, if anything, strengthened over that year as they successfully saw off every attempt to interfere with their monopoly, including, in their own eyes, the project.

The role of DFID

An important dimension of the project was the interaction between DFID and the Ministry. The DFID EA Uganda office was always very supportive of both land reform in Uganda and the project and helpful to both the senior technical adviser and the social development adviser. The office was instrumental in getting the project off the ground and enjoyed good relations with both the Minister and the Permanent Secretary. The office tried to encourage the Minister and the Permanent Secretary to move forward on important aspects of the project, particularly budgeting and preparing the medium to long-term plan. It was no fault of the office's that its efforts on that score were no more successful than those of the senior technical adviser's.

It was a different story however with the DFID Nairobi office which had an overseeing role on the project. To put the matter bluntly; that office was insufficiently supportive of the project and the personnel in the project when the project, the Project Co-ordinator and the social development adviser were under scurrilous, unjustifiable and continuous attack by the DLE between April and mid-August. This was despite specific requests for such support.

When, without any prior consultation with or even warning to DFID, the Project Co-ordinator was relieved of her post in public at the workshop on the draft LAIS Report, if there was any adverse reaction by the DFID Nairobi office (who were present at the workshop), it was so low key as to be almost invisible and certainly had no effect on the subsequent situation which left the project effectively without a co-ordinator for over three months. The Outputs to Purposes Review (OPR), conducted by the DFID

Nairobi office, which took place in mid-October 1999, provided the ideal opportunity to draw the attention of the Ministry to its responsibilities; the report, which according to DFID procedures should be sent to the project being reviewed within a week, did not come in for over six weeks and matters which the report indicated the DFID Nairobi office would undertake to try and help the project forward were not taken.

This apparent lack of support for the project did not help the project. It did not go unnoticed. The DLE kept going with their attacks on the project because they were never answered. They found a ready audience amongst MPs. In the world outside the Ministry, the assumption was made that there was no smoke without some fire somewhere. When a Minister told the senior technical adviser in mid-August, after he had had to give in to DLE demands that the co-ordinator be removed, that he found he had no friends, was he just referring only to his Ugandan colleagues?

When DFID EA Uganda became more pro-active in respect of the project in relation to utilising the GoU budget for 1999–2000, there was an immediate if, as it turned out, only, temporary improvement in the willingness of the DLE to work with other stakeholders in the spirit of the project. It was noticeable how, once some external adverse comment was directed at the Ministry on its performance on implementing the Land Act – the last one before the senior technical adviser left being in the donor statement on the Plan for the Modernisation of Agriculture made at the donors' Consultative Group meeting in March 2000 – there was an immediate response in the Ministry to try and move things forward. It was no part of DFID's role to try and run the Ministry but if there had been more overt support for the project from the DFID Nairobi office, when it was needed and asked for, it is difficult not to think that the project and so the Ministry would have made more progress in achieving project outputs and implementing the Land Act.

Why was the DFID Nairobi office so apparently unenthusiastic about the project? Basically for reasons as old as the existence of bureaucracy: a feeling that it, the "rightful" office to develop projects in East Africa had had its nose put out of joint by a pushy young DFID official in Uganda who had gone ahead to develop the project and had as it were "bounced" the Nairobi office into supporting it. Quite apart from the clear evidence of lack of support shown to the project (of which the most glaring was the extremely casual attitude to finalising and then acting on the OPR report) information obtained unofficially by the senior technical adviser throughout his tenure in Uganda was to the same effect; the DFID Nairobi office gave a very low priority to dealing with the project.

Conclusions

The recent World Bank publication *Assessing Aid; What Works, What Doesn't and Why* (1998) has this to say about making aid more effective:

> ... [P]olicy-based aid should be provided to nurture policy reform in credible reformers. Experience has shown that donor financing with strong conditionality but without strong domestic leadership and political support has generally failed to produce lasting change.
>
> ... [P]rojects need to focus on creating and transmitting knowledge and capacity. The key role of development projects should be to support institutional and policy changes that improve public service delivery ... In many cases innovative approaches to service delivery will involve greater participation by local communities and decentralisation of decision-making.

The second of the two quotes is a fair summary of what any future land reform project in Uganda should concentrate on; the first of the two quotes is a fair summary of why any such project is unlikely to be successful if it were to be located in the MWLE as it was constituted and managed during the time I was there.

Without in any way seeking to minimise my responsibility, as senior technical adviser for the comparative failure of the project during my period with the project, my conclusion now is no different to the analysis in the Issues and Options paper of September 1999. The project was doomed from the start. There were deep and probably irreconcilable differences between the DLE's view of how land should be managed and the Land Act implemented, and what the Act (and the Constitution) required and the Minister of State (Lands) in particular wanted to see happen. There were equally deep divisions between how the Permanent Secretary saw the Ministry being run and how the DLE would like their bit of it run. There were too deep divisions between those in the Government pushing for executive agency status for most of the functions of the DLE and the DLE.

The project straddled the fault line of all these divisions from day 1 and very quickly became the principal battleground (perhaps prize would be the better word) over which the contest raged. Output 1 of the project dealing with dissemination of information about the Land Act was on the whole achieved precisely because there was no real contest over it: everyone was agreed on the need for sensitisation and dissemination and no senior persons from the DLE were involved in the Focus Group that was responsible for that output.[15] Outputs 2 and 3 were not achieved precisely because there were contests over them over which the project had no, and could never have any, control. The LAIS Report was, on this analysis, at the very heart of the struggle for the soul of the implementation of the Land Act. Not surprisingly then, the least progress was made in dealing with its proposals.

The overall conclusion which may be drawn from this saga might seem fairly obvious but it clearly needs to be spelt out. Laws relating to land involve issues of governance – the English legal historian Holdsworth long ago made that point – and governance involves the exercise of power and the use of public money by public officials. Any fundamental changes in those laws, particularly changes designed to remove powers from and therefore access to and use of public money by public officials are likely to be opposed by those officials unless they can see some specific benefits flowing to them from the reforms.

Opposition may take many forms but the usual kind and the one which was used in the Ugandan case was bureaucratic sabotage: undermining a project designed to assist in the speedy implementation of the Land Act by attacking it from the outside and then, once that had proved successful and control had been obtained of the project, emasculating it and its outputs from the inside. The whole nature of the project (and this goes for aid projects in general) facilitated this exercise. Implementation of the Act could be and was painted as donor-driven and the supporters of the project as not putting the interests of Ugandans first; opposition was portrayed as patriotic and being concerned with national "ownership" of the process of implementation.

In the particular case which this chapter has dealt with, an additional factor was the comparative political skills and ruthlessness of the two sides of the contest over the Act: the officials in the DLE were more skilled and more ruthless in their opposition to the project and the Act than were the Ministers and the Permanent Secretary in their support of the project and the Act. There was a lack of leadership in the Ministry. From the time that battle was well and truly joined early on in the project, Ministers allowed the DLE to make all the running. Ministerial instructions were constantly ignored by DLE officials with impunity. The Permanent Secretary was always looking for a way to arrive at a compromise with the DLE, an approach regarded and acted on as a sign of weakness by the DLE.

Without the appropriate political environment and support for land law reform and/or an aid project to support such reform in the key parts of the government machinery, reform won't take place – whatever its merits and whoever in general terms is likely to benefit from it (and there are considerable merits in the Land Act which properly implemented would benefit the population at large) – and it is a waste of aid money to fund projects which lack that essential political support. As the Ugandan case showed, it is also a waste of money to fund the wrong project; a land reform programme is first and foremost a governance reform programme. A failure to grasp that fundamental point will render land reform programmes promoted either internally or externally so much wasted effort and resources.[16]

---

*This paper was written for the annual conference of the International Research Group of Law and Urban Space (IRGLUS) in Cairo, July 2000.

Nothing in this paper must be taken as in any way a statement of or to reflect the views of the Department for International Development or any official therein or to represent any official DFID position on the project discussed in this paper or any possible future project supporting land reform in Uganda or elsewhere.

Notes

[1] Sections 47(1); 48(1); (5) and 49(1); (5) and 50 (a) of the Land Act repeat verbatim parts of Articles 238 and 239 of the Constitution which deal with the Uganda Land Commission. Technically therefore the Land Commission was established by the Constitution, with further details being provided for by the Act.

[2] There is no agreement on the remembrance of what happened. Most women MPs claim the amendment was passed but in the final hectic hours of debate – MPs were kept in the chamber at nights and during the last weekend of June to ensure the passage of the Bill by the end of June – the amendment somehow slipped through the net and when the Bill received presidential assent on 2 July – deadline day – and was thereupon published, the amendment was not in the Act. The Speaker (who became Speaker during the course of the Bill's progress through Parliament, having previously been the Minister for Lands and as such started the Bill through Parliament) was sympathetic to the women's concern and made plain that if it could be shown that the amendment had indeed been passed he would certify to the First Parliamentary Counsel that a mistake had been made and a corrigendum would be published incorporating the amendment into the Act. The

Chairman of the Sessional Committee who played a key role in getting the Act through Parliament made plain his support for the amendment and his willingness to ensure that if necessary, time would be found formally to pass what had already been agreed to. The problem was that there seemed to be no firm evidence that the amendment had been moved let alone passed. At the crucial period of the debate, the proposer of the amendment was not in the chamber, having left for another engagement and it was not clear whether the actual amendment had therefore ever been formally moved. Another version of events is that the amendment was not formally moved because the Cabinet had not formally indicated its acceptance of it which was necessary before any such amendment could be moved at that juncture. Another version is that the women's caucus was indeed stitched up by the male MPs who didn't like the amendment and made sure by various underhand means that it did not appear in the published version of the Act. The mover of the original motion, at a meeting attended by the author, in January 2000 admitted that she was responsible for the failure of the amendment to get through Parliament owing to her ignorance of Parliamentary procedures.

[3] The Cabinet meeting in question was chaired by the President himself, a rare event. Usually Cabinet is chaired by the Vice-President, a woman. The President followed up the decision by making speeches advising women that their demands might destabilise society and the economy.

[4] Information made available to the author at the beginning of June 2000 is that the Cabinet has rejected the proposed amendments to the Land Act on Land Tribunals (having agreed to them in principle in February) so that the whole question of the management and financing of the Tribunals is up in the air once again.

[5] Information received in mid June was that the relevant Committee in Parliament has decided that it wants to consider both the Land Regulations and the Land Fund Regulations together. The latter have not yet been drafted so the prospect of the former being in place and facilitating the operation of the Act have receded into the distance.

[6] The Permanent Secretary did not reply to the complaints of the Group set out in its Interim Report submitted to him in August 1999. This upset the Group which re-submitted its report in January 2000 with a request for a response. The Group almost certainly suspected that the senior technical adviser had had a hand in the non-response of the PS but this was not so. The PS was overwhelmed by paperwork and the senior technical adviser's memoranda were often not attended to.

[7] As noted above TAP was 50:50 DLE officials and others. The meeting to consider the LAIS Report was called at short notice; met out of town; included other members of the DLE and few if any non-DLE members. A point to note is that civil service regulations in Uganda allow officials to claim attendance allowances for sitting on committees specially convened to consider some matter even when these committees are committees of civil servants. So it paid the DLE

to sit as TAP out of town rather than sit as the DLE in their offices in the Ministry reviewing the report.

[8] The workshop was laid on for the visiting head of the Sustainable Livelihoods Division of DFID to enable him to learn something about the project. The two DFID advisers to the project put together the programme which provided for the Ugandan Joint Team Leader of the LAIS to make a presentation. The DLE attempted to remove him from the programme.

[9] Two senior officials of the DLE were invited to participate as members of the LAIS team. They initially accepted then changed their minds and pulled out.

[10] The member of the DLE selected by the DLE to be Co-ordinator never formally took office. The first Co-ordinator refused to hand over the post on the grounds that she had been appointed to it by the Head of the Civil Service and could not therefore be removed by the Permanent Secretary of the Ministry. Then the member of the DLE decided that his health would not permit him to take on such a stressful job (it didn't help that he was not given any increase in pay) but he would remain as an acting Co-ordinator Designate for a month or so. After he ceased to be even that, there was a hiatus when no-one was Co-ordinator. Another member of the DLE was finally prevailed upon to take the job but it was not until mid December that the post was formally handed over.

[11] He had been sent on enforced leave in May 1999 on the grounds that he was the leader and orchestrator of the attack on the project via a DLE manifesto sent to Ministers and others on 29 April. Despite direct Ministerial directives to withdraw the letter (which made some fairly serious allegations against DFID as well) members of the DLE refused to withdraw it. The Director paid the price. Ministers tried to get him out of the civil service altogether but his colleagues (some of whom were a good deal more responsible than he for the manifesto) went in to bat for him with other Ministers, Parliament and the Public Service Commission and stopped the move to oust him from the civil service.

[12] The chairman of the JSC was elevated to be Chief Justice in late 2000. In February 2001, the Land Amendment Act was passed which extended, "until the Land Tribunals are established and commence to operate", the jurisdiction of the courts to deal with land disputes.

[13] The inter-Ministerial task force referred to above finished its work on revising the 1999–2000 budget in early November 1999, four months into the financial year. Five months later, by the end of March 2000, less than 25% of that year's budget had been spent and the Ministry's project 2000–01 land budget was cut by 40% on the grounds that as it had failed to spend its 1999–2000 budget, it clearly did not have the capacity to spend a larger budget. The failure to spend the 1999–2000 budget was caused by the refusal of the DLE to address the issues of the budget in the first four months of that financial year followed by their lack of know-how in actually accessing the available funds once they did address the issues. The project had funds available to help the Ministry in putting together its

1999–2000 budget and thereafter accessing funds but the DLE rejected the need for that assistance.

[14] The Minister in question had been, earlier in his career, an agricultural extension officer and so knew a good deal about the land issues of Uganda from practical field work experience.

[15] Interestingly, the DLE's budget strategy paper for the financial years 2000–03 allocated huge sums of money to dissemination, all of which was to be controlled from or spent by the DLE.

[16] I recommended in my end-of-mission report that no more funds should be committed to support land reform in Uganda unless and until there was evidence that attitudes to supporting land reform and administrative practices were changed in the MWLE. DFID allowed the project to continue on a no-cost basis (*i.e.* existing funds could continue to be used for project purposes but no new funds would be committed) but even nine months later at the end of 2000, the funds had still not all been spent as actions had not been taken by the Ministry or other agencies in the GoU which were a precondition for funds to be spent. Early in 2001, DFID decided to give substantial budgetary support to the Ministry, *inter alia*, for land reform and more or less publicly declared the project a success: I was awarded an MBE for my efforts in the 2001 Birthday Honours.

14 Land in the city: the role of law in reforming urban land markets*

Setting the scene

There are few better summaries of the phenomenon of urban growth, which forms the essential background to this paper, than the 1991 UNDP Policy Paper: *Cities, People and Poverty*. To quote from the introductory overview to the paper:

> The relentless growth of cities is inevitable and irreversible. Standing at 2.4 billion in 1990, the world's urban population will rise to 3.2 billion in 2000 and 5.5 billion in 2025. The developing countries' share in these totals – 63% in 1990 – will rise to 71% in 2000 and 80% in 2025. By the end of the 1990s, Mexico City will have almost 25 million people, and Sao Paulo almost 22 million, Calcutta, Shanghai and Bombay will each have more than 15 million residents. And 13 other cities in developing countries will have more than 10 million: Seoul, Cairo, Dacca, Delhi, Lagos, Beijing, Bangkok, Manila, Jakarta, Karachi, Tianjin, Buenos Aires and Rio de Janeiro. In addition to the growth of these megacities, the growth of small and medium-sized cities will also continue.
>
> For decades this growth was seen as inimical to human development. Cities already benefited disproportionately from national development efforts, urban development was more costly than rural development and the growth of cities merely added to unemployment – these were the prevailing views. So, government policy and international assistance gave greater attention to the countryside.
>
> Today the growth of cities is seen increasingly as essential for human development. The GNP per capita numbers are much higher in countries with more of their people in cities. The economies of scale in large cities generate goods and services far in excess of their share of the total population. This higher productivity of urban labour means that wages are higher and employment opportunities greater, especially for women. Cities also give their residents the knowledge and skills to become more productive – a propitious

cycle. Cities promote the modernisation of agriculture, provide markets for farm goods and reduce pressure on the land.

Despite the obvious efficiency advantages of cities, the negative consequences of urbanisation for low-income groups are overwhelming. Simply, many city dwellers in developing countries live in crushing poverty – more than 300 million, or a quarter of all those in urban areas. That number promises to swell. By 2000 more than half the developing countries' poor will be in cities and towns: 90% in Latin America, 45% in Asia and 40% in Africa. Their living conditions are alarming, for their numbers far outstrip the supplies of water, waste removal, transport and clinics. Nor do they and their richer neighbours help the environment – using natural resources and discharging wastes in disturbing quantity, with all the predictable effects.

One central and overwhelming issue stands out from this phenomenon of relentless city growth: the need for land in the city. Land for housing, for infrastructure, for employment, for open space and recreation, and for waste disposal. For many years, this need for land and the problems associated with meeting the need have been either not addressed at all or subsumed under some other head such as shelter needs, or master planning or improving the lot of the poor. There have been no shortage of books and articles on the subject – some of them influential – but at both national and international level there has been a shying away from facing up to the problem of land in the city. What this paper seeks to do is answer several questions: what is the problem of land in the city? Why is there a reluctance to face up to the problem? Where attempts have been made to deal with the problem, what have they been, have they been successes or failures and why? What is the way forward? And, interleaved with all these questions, what has been, is and should be the role of law in dealing with land in the city?

What is the problem?

The word "problem" in this sub-heading is in many respects a misnomer; the word "crisis" would be more accurate: the crisis of inadequate amounts of land being made available for urban development and in particular for urban development by and for the urban poor. Why is this? At the root of the current crisis is that, usually with the best of intentions, governments have adopted policies which *have contributed to land shortages rather than land availability.* The policies have emphasised control and regulation over land use, rather than enabling and facilitating the supply and use of land. They have stressed the maintenance of standards, often standards taken over or accepted uncritically from erstwhile colonial powers, rather than focus on the affordability and appropriateness of standards. The policies have either shied away from, or attempted to impose inappropriate legal regimes on, traditional land tenure practices which have thereby inhibited the release of land with clear titles for urban use. Finally, the policies have placed too much emphasis on the public ownership, management and development of urban land and the attendant bureaucracy has too often impeded the release of land. Some examples of all these defective policies may be given.

Control and regulation of supply and use

There are few better examples of attempts to control the supply and price of urban land than the Urban Land (Ceiling and Regulation) Act 1976 of India. Buch (1984, p. 2) had this to say about the Act and its operation:

> This Act was aimed at socializing all land in excess of a given quantum on payment of a nominal amount thus making available large chunks of strategically located land for use by the common man. Exemptions can be granted from the operation of the Act. The phenomenon of granting exemptions to large property owners, bogus cooperative societies who enter into agreements to purchase land, commercial builders, etc., is universal with the result that the very purpose of the Act has been defeated.

The National Commission on Urbanization has likewise concluded that the Act has failed to achieve any of its objectives. This has not however prevented a very rapid rise in urban land prices all over India and a continuing shortage of affordable land for housing for the Economically Weaker Sections (EWS).

Nigeria may be instanced as another country where similar legislation – the Land Use Act of 1978 – has done nothing to bring more land forward for urban development, but has created yet another layer of bureaucracy and corrupt practices which must be overcome before land can be developed.

Even where the supply of land is not controlled, its use too often is. Inappropriate metropolitan models of town and country planning legislation, some of them dating back 70 or more years, with emphasis on control of development, and the obligation to seek, via official forms, permission to build a house render the self build efforts of would-be upwardly mobile poor people illegal and liable to demolition.

The maintenance of standards

Two aspects of this deficiency are plot size and building regulations. Over-large plot size requirements in Jordan severely handicapped efforts to develop low cost housing until a fortuitous down turn in the economy caused plot owners themselves to see the good sense of sub-dividing their plots in order to increase income and reduce building costs. Many site and service schemes have been beyond the reach of the urban poor because the price of the large plots has been beyond their capacity to pay and the costs of running services to the plots have further raised prices.

Few countries have yet made a concerted effort to revise their building regulations so as to allow for more appropriate standards. In some countries and cities the building regulations are more than 50 years old and are still, in theory, in operation. Two examples may be given: in Nairobi, insistence on old standards in the regulations held up the commencement of a major site and service project. In Madras, refusal to countenance cheap and unconventional materials and practices being used in building in site and service schemes effectively eliminated most of the EWS from the schemes.

Customary tenure

Africa is littered with examples of inappropriate efforts to grapple with customary tenure. In Lesotho, a World Bank inspired land reform programme broke down because of suspicions that, in so far as it applied to urban areas, it was designed to facilitate foreigners acquiring choice urban plots under a law which only they could understand. In Tanzania and Zambia, a refusal to countenance a market in land has led to an unofficial market in land with consequent problems of the recordation and security of title. In Nigeria, the imposition of public controls on an evolving market in land has inhibited the evolution of the market without any positive benefit.

Public ownership and management

A favourite device used here is the urban development authority which is empowered both to purchase land in advance of use and release it in due course for use of the urban poor and develop land itself. The example of the Delhi Development Authority shows that whatever the theoretical merits of the policy, in practice it can have disastrous results. 50,000 acres of land were notified for compulsory acquisition and thus frozen for private development. The DDA, in order to balance its accounts, has allocated nearly 50% of the land it has released to the Higher Income Group (HIG) with, after an initial allocation in its first year of operation, less than 10% going to the Lower Income Group (LIG) and EWS. Land prices have at the same time rocketed. According to Buch (1984, p. 6):

> ... regardless of its efficacy in servicing desired goals, the fact remains that this policy for Delhi, supported by hefty financial aid from government, was sought to be replicated in other states with calamitous results ... Funds or the expertise to assess needs, plan and execute development programmes or to manage the land were not provided.

Urban Development and Capital Development authorities in Pakistan, Nigeria, Tanzania and Brazil likewise have a poor record of providing affordable land for the urban majority, many of whom labour to construct buildings they will never be able to afford to use.

Over and above all these technical and legal deficiencies, however, is another factor which perhaps is the most important one and provides the link between the question being considered here and the next question to be considered.

Why the reluctance to face up to the problem?

The missing factor in the above catalogue of deficiencies is the socio-political. The present systems of the allocation and use of land for development in the city may be, objectively, and judged by criteria of efficiency or equity, inefficient and inequitable but it would be a mistake not to realise that these systems confer benefits on those who operate them and that is why they are as they are. Senior politicians and public servants in cities all over the world manipulate or ignore the law and administration relating to land allocation and development so as to line their own pockets and those of their families, friends and political allies. A process of land allocation based on secretive administrative criteria as opposed to open market criteria lends itself to malversation and those in charge of such systems have not been slow to take advantage of that fact. Lower down the scale of the bureaucracy, where the actual acquisition of land may be more difficult to achieve, there are plenty of opportunities for illicit gain. A file can only be located out of the disorganised heap and thereafter processed if money is paid. An "illegal" structure can be left undisturbed if money is paid. An invasion of land by squatters can succeed if money is paid, and services can be acquired – water, electricity, etc. – if money is paid.

What this adds up to is a system which if not designed then at least is adapted to facilitate the exploitation of the poor. It is the poor who live in "illegal" structures; who squat and who cannot afford lawful connections to services. But the present system goes further in its facilitation of the exploitation of the poor. By being weighed so heavily to those who have the financial or political power – the latter often precedes the former but the two are usually ultimately joined together – the system facilitates the development of the exploitative relationship of landlords and tenants in the cities of the developing world rather than that of owner occupiers. Much research has shown that contrary to the ideal put forward by Turner and others and supposedly facilitated by international aid programmes, what is happening in these cities is the commodification of shelter: shelter as a scarce good sold to the highest bidder without any effective restrictions or controls on the transactions. The urban poor in such circumstances are forced into less and less salubrious accommodation with fewer and fewer rights. The fact that their accommodation does not measure up to legal public health standards triply disadvantages them: first, the inferior accommodation affects their health and welfare; second, at any point in time their landlord can evict them in the interests of "complying with the law"; and third, if their landlord falls foul of the authorities, demolition may follow, again "to comply with the law".

Indeed there is some evidence in some cities to suggest that demolition is in fact used to facilitate the growth of landlordism. The bulldozing of squatter settlements inhabited by owner-occupiers of houses both forces such persons into rented accommodation and frees land for the development of further rented accommodation. Even where the demolition is done with the best of intentions – that is, there is a genuine belief that "slums" are being demolished so that their inhabitants can be rehoused in something better – too often the "something better" is unaffordable to the "slum dwellers" who finish up in worse conditions further from where they can earn a livelihood while the "something better" finishes up in the possession of the better off.

This then is the crux of the matter: present systems of land allocation and use in the cities benefit the urban elite. The urban elite either run or have influence over the government of the cities and indeed the national governments which usually have a significant role in urban land management. This fact is well known to observers of, and international aid donors to, governments who consequently are extremely reluctant to propose programmes involving urban land reform. Where there is an absence of any external or internal stimulus to urban land reform, in too many countries reform doesn't happen or where it happens on paper – *e.g.* Nigeria and India – reform consists of yet more bureaucracy, and loopholes in the law and its administration are quickly discovered and remain unplugged.

This section has deliberately painted a gloomy picture of political and administrative abuse of power preventing any meaningful addressing of the crisis in urban land delivery with the role of the law being either a cover up, a fig leaf for baser activities or a weapon to be used to carry out those baser activities, or, less frequently, the basis for well-meaning but misguided bureaucratic action.

What might be the results of continuing with present policies? The following are suggested as the more major costs:

- Land prices will continue to accelerate and there will be a corresponding decline in the number of people who will be able to afford to obtain land in the official systems.
- There will be an increase in unauthorised urban settlements. People will not cease to come to cities but they will cease to be able to do otherwise than slot into already overcrowded squatter settlements or take part in land invasions.
- The development of ever larger squatter settlements without adequate services and a deteriorating environment, both of which phenomena know no boundaries.

- Large cities will begin to be seen as places to avoid investing in. This will in turn contribute to rises in unemployment and further decline in living standards.
- Large cities, full of unemployed and the poor, too few of whom have a stake in the system through the ownership or secure possession of land or regular employment, will be beyond the capacity of city governments to deal with and may begin to pose problems to the security of the state and the stability of democratic political systems.

What efforts are being made to tackle the crisis?

Hitherto this paper has proceeded on the basis of a problem or a crisis with the implicit assumption that there is a solution to the problem or crisis. This is not the case. There are several crises – maybe going back to one cause, the politics of land – and it follows that there may be several solutions. It will be argued that the solutions too can and should be grounded in a set of common principles but implementation will take different forms. To take just one example out of many, while the commodification of housing is apparent in African and Latin American cities, political, social and legal factors are so different in those cities that solutions which may work in Latin America or some cities there will need very careful scrutiny and adaptation before they are tried out in African cities if indeed they should be tried at all. And vice versa.

This is by way of prelude to this section of the paper. Are there any examples of efforts to address the crisis, that is to develop systems of the management of urban land which go some way towards meeting the needs of the citizenry? And, if so, are there any common themes that seem to lie behind them?

Three case studies may be referred to in some detail – one from each of the three regions of Africa, Asia and Latin America and the Caribbean (LAC). Conclusions will follow.

Botswana

The position in Botswana may best be summarised by two quotations, the first from a Presidential Commission on Land Tenure which reported in

1983 (pp. 2–3), the second from John Bruce, of the Land Tenure Centre at the University of Wisconsin, Madison (1988, pp. 106–07) who has studied and been involved in land tenure reforms in Botswana for most of the 1980s:

> In the final analysis ... it became apparent that the desires of people are not for new and radical forms of land tenure but rather for easy access to land for citizens of Botswana, their ability to utilize it as an instrument of development and at the same time the retention of such developed land as a family asset to be passed on from generation to generation. Tribal land tenure, whatever its drawbacks, possesses many of the characteristics meeting such desires. The Commission has thus become convinced that any existing or suggested land tenure system must meet the twin objectives of giving people rights in land that can be used as an economic asset both saleable and bankable, and at the same time ensuring that land is inheritable and that a landless class is not created. These objectives often contradict each other, but the challenge is to balance them.
>
> Many Batswana stand today with one foot in the traditional sector and the other in the developing cash economy. New needs exist but old needs persist. Government has sought since independence to accommodate both these needs. In the townships, Government has created new forms of tenure, namely the Fixed Period State Grant and the Certificate of Rights. For the rural areas and major villages, the Tribal Land Act (Cap. 32:02) provides a new system of administration for tribal land and new tenure forms such as the common law lease for commercial holdings, to meet the demands of a changing society. It leaves intact, however, the customary rules governing residential, arable and grazing land. The Tribal Grazing Land Policy (TGLP) of 1975 provides for the extension of the common law lease to areas of tribal grazing lands which have been designated commercial to facilitate the development of commercial ranching operations.
>
> The land tenure policy which has been pursued by Government may be described as one of careful change, responding to particular needs with specific tenure innovations. The alternatives would have been a wholesale change in forms of tenure or retention of the status quo. The approach taken by Government has much to commend it. Land is a very special resource, the very base on which the nation stands. The way in which it is administered is a profound expression of national values. Since the economy of Botswana is still largely agricultural, land is the only resource available to most of its citizens from which to earn a livelihood. Land tenure is thus a matter of grave importance and any change required must be made with great care (Presidential Commission).

The Presidential Commission on Land Tenure opted for a long-term leasehold rather than freehold for residential land in the villages. A long-term lease is a readily mortgageable interest; the loan is secured with the unexpired term of the leasehold by the borrower/lessee. Before turning to its detailed recommendations on long-term leasehold, however, it is useful to ask why the freehold option was rejected. To answer this question it is necessary to refer to tenure policy as it had evolved and was confirmed by the Commission. The introduction of freehold in the villages would have implied a fundamental reversal in that tenure policy. It would have placed in question, at least in the long-term, the role of Land Boards created by the Tribal Land Act in 1968, to replace traditional leaders and to maintain the policy of social control of access to land. The Commission's report notes the 'grave concern' it found among those who gave evidence to the Commission over the possibility of a citizen losing his residence (paragraph 2.16), and elsewhere it argues the 'Government cannot afford to introduce expensive social security systems which would become necessary if there were an unemployed and landless class' (paragraph 2.33). A decision for the freehold adoption in this particular case would also have been difficult to reconcile with two other long standing government policies which were affirmed by the Commission: (1) use of less-than-freehold tenures for urban development (*i.e.*, the Fixed Term State Grant and the Certificate of Right) (paragraph 3.12); and (2) gradual acquisition by purchase on a 'willing seller' basis of freehold farms from the colonial era and their conversion to tribal land under the Tribal Land Act (paragraph 2.32) ... The government White Paper, 'National Policy on Land Tenure', issued in April 1985, accepted the recommendations of the Commission, with modest changes ...

The policy adopted is consistent with both the careful and incremental approach to tenure reform adopted by the government of Botswana in the lease terms and in the voluntary mode of conversion to leasehold. It is interesting that government opted for leasehold rather than modification of the residential allocation to make it mortgageable. Such an option had been outlined, together with the leasehold option, in the author's consultancy report to the Ministry of Local Government and Lands in 1980. Two considerations were noted there in favour of the leasehold option; the probable more ready acceptance of leasehold by lenders as security, based on their prior experience with leases of commercial property in the villages as collateral, and the existence of a well-developed body of law governing the use of leases as collateral. The advantage of the residential allocation reform option would have been retention of a legal form with which villages and Land Boards were familiar and comfortable, but this may not have seemed a strong consideration given that the Tribal Land Act had already introduced common law leases into village land administration for commercial uses.

Botswana's approach to tenure reform with respect to residential allocations in the nation's villages can best be described as minimalist: the minimum necessary reform to meet the immediate need. The policy-making process involved extended discussions, was informed by the work of several commissions and appears to have achieved what this author at least considers a very balanced approach: the recognition and addressing of a tenure constraint while avoiding the 'bottleneck' fallacy, in which the tenure constraint is seen as the only obstacle. While the reform clears the legal way for use of residential holdings as collateral, there is clear recognition that there are constraints other than tenurial ones (*e.g.*, land market conditions) on borrowing against such property. The policy documents specifically caution against inflated expectations about credit access in the wake of the reform. The policy-makers have also appreciated that the new need to borrow against such a security applies to only a few of the land holders and so long-term leasehold has been made available on an optional basis. The selection of long-term leasehold as the 'modernising' tenure for residential allocations, when taken together with the 1975 selection of long-term leasehold as the tenure for commercial ranching under Botswana's Tribal Grazing Land Policy, establishes a pattern which will likely affect future tenure choices, as for intensive development of arable land. The obviously high priority given to tenure issues by authorities in Botswana has made it a leader in tenurial innovation in Africa, and the recent tenure reform for residential allocations, together with other tenure reforms, deserves close monitoring and evaluation (Bruce).

Thailand

In terms of the provision of shelter to urban dwellers, the "little tigers" of South East Asia – Korea, Singapore, Hong Kong – have a remarkable record of success. In Korea, for instance, the percentage of the urban population rose from 28% in 1960 to 65% in 1985; in numbers from 7 million to 26.5 million. In the view of many commentators, few countries grew and urbanised as rapidly as Korea since the early 1960s and probably none experienced as little accompanying social distress. The success of Singapore and Hong Kong in developing massive public housing programmes which have raised living standards and all but abolished squatter settlements are well known but for various reasons – principally connected with land policies – are not easily replicable elsewhere. The example of Thailand, however, is worth highlighting for the very rapid way in which in the 1980s it achieved a considerable measure of success in dealing with its urban shelter problem, in part because of its land policies and practices. Two leading practitioners in the field of housing and land development, one from the public and one from the private sector, comment on the position as follows (Tanphiphat and Simapichaicheth, 1990, pp. 11–15). They first summarised the goals of the housing policy developed by a Housing Policy Sub-Committee (HPS) of the National Economic and Social Development Board:

> To enhance the cost-effectiveness and increase supply of housing inputs such as land for housing. The HPS particularly recognizes that the availability of sufficient trunk-infrastructure which would create developable land supplies is a crucial factor. A 'bottle-necked' land market, and the resultant high prices, is the most common barrier preventing the moderate income earners from entering the land and thus the housing market. Although other housing inputs should also be enhanced, HPS has regarded land and financing as the two most urgent goals.
>
> An authoritative study of the land market of Bangkok in 1987 concluded that it is basically sound – with adequate land supply and having relatively few state-imposed land-use restrictions. Land price increases had been generally in line with consumer prices for the most part.
>
> Reduce developers' costs caused by delay in obtaining approvals for land subdivision and building permits. Numerous dialogues between regulators (Lands Department and Bangkok Metropolitan Administration) and developers have been arranged both by HPS and by the developers' associations with the result that each party understands the position of the others. This has enabled compromises to be made, resulting in reduced standards, revised procedures to be more practical for business operations and reduced time delays.
>
> 3. *Housing developers.* Housing developers have become the single most important supplier of housing in the marketplace, whose share of new housing outputs rose rapidly and accounted for almost 70% of the Bangkok housing completions in 1988. To have garnered such a large market share means that developers' products must be targeted at a broadening band of housing consumers.
>
> 4. *Land recording system.* Thailand's land record system and transfer procedures have long been recognised as simple and efficient systems which have contributed to the flexibility with which the private sector responds to the market.

The system adopted is the Torrens system. The key advantage over other systems is that all relevant information is recorded on the land title certificate, and it could be used to record any subsequent changes of ownership, rights or obligations (such as mortgages and liens) without the need to create a new title certificate. With this system all information relating to a particular land parcel is held at the lands offices of the Lands Department (Ministry of Interior), including the official copy of the land title certificate, any land sales or transfer contracts, alteration of rights or obligations, transfer fees and income tax payment receipts. There is, therefore, no need for title searches or title insurance which could be very costly and time consuming. Better still, because the Lands Department requires the use of standardised land sales contract and other documents, most transactions do not require lawyers, which helps to lower transaction costs.

Because of the use of standardised documents and relatively well-organised lands offices and competent personnel, ownership transfers and recording of changes of rights or obligations could be completed quickly and must be completed by the end of the day of the applications being made. Indeed, it is typical for one Government Housing Bank officer to effect the mortgage registrations (including the transfers of ownership from sellers to buyers) of 15 borrowers in one day.

5. *Land-sharing projects*. Land-sharing is a solution that helps prevent the breaking-up and displacement of existing low-income slum communities through eviction. Slums under eviction are usually located in highly central and advantageous locations whose land-owners deemed the lands ripe for higher-yield development – thus terminating the rental arrangements with the tenants. Many slum communities are broken up (and spring up elsewhere) without much fuss; generally, they are offered compensation to cover costs of removal of their homes or any losses arising thereof. However, in some cases, tenants resist, either to dispute inadequate compensation or simply to go on living there for economic reasons such as to be near their workplaces. Even though the land-owners have the legal right to retake the land, they could not physically remove the people, their shelters and other belongings against their will. Less scrupulous landlords have resorted to arson in the past, but normally it would end up in protracted impasse which could be extremely damaging for both sides: loss of business opportunities for the land-owners and for the communities' physical deterioration due to neglect and lack of upkeep in anticipation of their disbandment.

Land-sharing basically involves the tenants giving up some of the land – usually the portions with commercial or high-yield use potential – and rebuilding their houses, usually more densely but in more regular arrangements, on the rest of the site.

Some pre-conditions for successful land-sharing projects are:

- Land-owners who do not want to taint their public image or who genuinely want humanitarian solutions.
- Residents who could present united fronts for expressing their demands and for negotiations.
- Availability of agents who will act as the intermediaries and to contribute or locate resource inputs: manpower, subsidies, long-term loans, etc.
- Land-sharing is still a relatively novel concept. Land-sharing is, as far as we are aware, unique in Thailand. The following are some reasons for its success:

  There is a strong group of slum advocates in Thailand – academics, housing officials, professionals and community activists – that keep the plights of slum communities in the public's consciousness and help foster the view that slums do not house evil people.

  Government agencies that have to deal with slum communities – whether in law enforcement or local government – have been, by and large, benevolent and rarely resort to harsh measures.

  The government, through its housing policy, recognizes the need for slum housing in the economy and has been actively supporting the slum upgrading programmes of the NHA and BMA since 1979.

  Slum dwellers, on the whole, behave responsibly. Squatting or taking of land illegally is usually restricted to government lands which are left unused such as right-of-way of public utilities and water-ways and never on private land.

An important part of this successful development of a legal private housing market is the existence of "a well established and accepted Civil and Commercial Code and a Land Code which collectively lay down the rights and duties of individual land owners. These land laws are now part of Thai culture to a large degree ... As a country, Thailand has never been colonised. As a consequence the country has always been able to select the most appropriate systems and laws for the operation of government without having them imposed from an outside authority. Such is the case with the laws and systems applying to land administration". These laws and systems date back to the nineteenth century with land title registration making its first appearance in 1901. Throughout the twentieth century, there has been a willingness to modernise and amend the land laws and administration when this was perceived to be necessary; to employ sufficient people in the system for it to be a reasonably efficient system; and to ensure an adequacy of trained staff. In addition, "The Royal Thai Government and the Department of Lands ... recognised the importance of taking a broad view of cadastral reform as part of the overall land administration and land management process".

Peru

During the 1980s, an NGO in Peru, the Institute for Liberty and Democracy, founded by Hernando de Soto, was instrumental in developing new laws, procedures and practices on land rights for the urban poor. The story is told in the lead article in *Urban Perspectives* (USAID/RHUDO, Nairobi, 1991, pp. 2–5). ILD began its work in the mid-1980s and such was the grassroots support for action to be taken to correct perceived inequities in urban land rights that within three years, its proposed law on Property Rights was enacted in November 1988 with "full support from all parties across the entire Peruvian political spectrum". Detailed regulation followed in 1989 and the Property Registry constituted by the law was inaugurated in 1990:

> The problem was in the existing, inefficient and cumbersome Public Registry for Real Estate. This Public Registry, created 100 years ago based on an 1861 Spanish model, was designed for another era – certainly not that of today's Peru, with its continuing urban migration and vast informal settlements.
>
> The number of properties registered speaks eloquently of the Public Registry's inefficiency: in more than 100 years of operation, the Public Registry has recorded only 40% of formal properties. The ILD calculated that it takes informal owners 48 months to obtain title using the Public Registry, at a cost of more than seventy times the minimum wage.
>
> This cumbersome registration system excludes the vast majority of informals who continue to live with the uncertainty of insecure property rights. This uncertainty results in various types of economic loss. One example is the loss of economies of scale in developing the land. Rather than following the normal sequence of events in acquiring property (in which the owner first purchases the land, then installs water, sewage and electricity, then builds his house and finally moves in with his furniture and his personal belongings), informals follow exactly the reverse sequence. An informal settler first takes possession of his land, then moves in with his furniture and personal belongings, then builds a house and later tears down a portion of the house to install water, sewage and electricity. The informals' backwards approach to land development involves loss of the economics of scale which are possible

when large tracts of land are developed rationally prior to constructing houses on them.

Since the old Public Registry obviously could not respond to the needs of the informal sector (there are more than 600,000 informal sector houses in Lima alone), the ILD decided that a new, simple and easily-accessible property registration system was required.

This new system, which is called simply the Property Registry, is designed to answer three key questions on the property: Who is the owner? Where is the property located? What encumbrances exist on the property? The system is not designed to deal with issues which the ILD considers extraneous to the functions of a property registry, such as whether property taxes have been paid.

Three basic design principles were adopted: *simplification, deregulation* and *decentralization.*

The ILD sought to simplify the system by facilitating and reducing the cost of the procedure, eliminating overlap and relying on readily available documentation for validating information. For example, notarized public deeds have been replaced by easy-to-compete, printed forms; notarized building certificates have been replaced by printed forms and photographs.

To regulate the system, decision-making powers over certain matters previously controlled by the Public Registry have been transferred to private parties – to users of the system themselves. For example, in many cases government bureaucrats have been replaced by private inspectors; through their elected board members, users participate in the management of the registry.

To decentralize the system, decision making powers were delegated to local registration offices, physically located in the areas covered by the registry. Eleven independent property registries will be created throughout the country. The Public Registry had only one central office in the capital city of Lima. Decentralization will considerably reduce the cost of the service to those living outside the Lima area.

The registration process itself has also been changed. Usually property registries are conceived as a service window where users present their documents. The new Property Registry allows the registry to be taken to the user to obtain the necessary information. In this field system, teams composed of a lawyer, an engineer or architect and a member of the neighbourhood association work with the informal settlers to collect and register the required information on their property.

The results achieved with this new Property Registry speak for themselves: since the new system was inaugurated on January 20, 1990 more than 10,000 titles have been registered at 1% of the previous cost. It is projected that more than 25,000 titles will be registered by the end of July 1990. (Only 30,000 informal settlement properties had been registered by the old Public Registry since informal settlements began 60 years ago.)

The major innovation of the new registry is to provide, for the first time under Peruvian law, for the legal recognition of common law property rights in informal settlements. (The municipalities in which these settlements are located must have first recognized the existence of the settlements.)

The new Property Registry grants registered 'possessors' of property in informal settlements the same property rights as those enjoyed by owners of formal property as collateral for a loan. The new registry cuts the time to obtain these rights from four years to less than one month and reduces the cost by 99%.

In the registration process, the property is first identified according to its physical location. Also, the basic characteristics of any buildings on the land are recorded using a standard printed form. (In order to be registered houses must be constructed of permanent materials and must measure at least 25 square metres. Their basic characteristics are checked by either an architect or an engineer, acting as a private inspector.)

Once the property is registered its common law ownership by a given individual is then validated which establishes the owner's rights over the asset.

Common law ownership is validated by one or two means: (1) presentation of a certificate of possession from the municipality; or (2) by written certification from the informal's housing association, or, if no housing association exists, by signed statements from six neighbours. In the latter case to avoid the possibility of fraud, the owner of the property must also present two additional documents which prove his occupancy, *e.g.* receipts of payments of water or electricity bills.

Once the lot and property have been registered and common law ownership has been validated, a certificate of registry is issued to the owner which gives him the same rights to that property as those enjoyed by any formal sector property owner. According to Peruvian law, these include the right to build or demolish structures on the property (through sale, gift, exchange, etc.), the right to lease or rent the property to a third party, and the right to place a mortgage on the property.

All of the above information is managed through a customized computer system using a series of inter-connected data bases.

The ILD worked very closely with the leaders of the local neighbourhood residents' association in the implementation of the pilot programmes. A member of the association was part of every field registration team. This individual plays a key role in making the system work since he knows the layout of the informal settlement and has the trust of the residents.

General themes running through successful urban land systems

These case studies have deliberately been set out at some length so that a fair understanding can be obtained of the evolution and operation of these successful systems. What general themes seem to run through them? First, there is a clear move away from the centralised state-dominated systems to the development of more effective and equitable systems of land allocations and use. Political factors in the decision-making process over land are, if not eliminated – it would be unrealistic to suppose that that would be achieved over-night – then greatly reduced.

Second, in place of politico-bureaucratic decisions about land taken in secret, greater reliance is placed on open and market-orientated decisions. By market-orientated is meant not just decisions determined by price, by money, though that is the driving force in Thailand, but decisions determined by criteria such as the facilitation of transactions, the perception of land as being an economic no less than a social asset, the desirability, perhaps the normality of attempting to meet demand, *i.e.* to pay attention to the wishes of consumers and the irrelevance of personal factors – political, clientelism, favours, etc. in determining who gets what. Equally important, and more evident in Thailand and Peru than Botswana, though the trends may be in place even there, is the decentralised nature of the land allocation and management process. This too is an aspect of a more market-orientated approach to land where decisions are made by many individuals and organisations and not just by one centralised agency. Decentralisation also helps bring the decision-making process closer to the people, and assists in its accountability.

Third, a notable feature of all the case studies is the care taken by governments to consult with and take account of the views of the users of the system – land developers, residents' associations, customary title holders, squatters, etc. It is abundantly clear that these consultative processes were not a mere formality. Governments were not "consulting" some hand-picked group of sycophants or organisations dependent on a government licence to continue in existence, who could be relied upon to produce the answers the government wanted to hear. In Thailand, the land developers were and are an independent economic force. In Peru, indeed, the NGO, the Institute for Liberty and Democracy, took over the process of preparing the basic legislation and consulting the consumers with the government happy to follow in its wake. In Botswana, great attention was paid both to traditional concerns and the views of modern economic entities.

In a chapter focusing on the role of law in urban land reform, it seems worthwhile to devote a little more space to this issue of consultation. In considering legal frameworks for public action – and at least in the initial stages of land reform, public action is required – probably the single most significant difference between authoritarian administration and democratic governance is the willingness of public officials to listen and respond in their actions to the uncensored and uninhibited views of the people – the electorate, the consumers and producers of national wealth. Thus in constructing new or reforming old legal frameworks, in developing new policies, or implementing existing ones, lawyers should be prepared to focus on the process of consultation and ensure that that is a reality in the administrative process.

Some examples of this may be given. In Tanzania, a Presidential Commission on Land Matters was charged with conducting an inquiry into all land matters – disputes, administration, laws, policies – and coming up with recommendations. The Commission, chaired by a lawyer, visited every district in Tanzania and took evidence from anyone who wanted to appear before it. Only after that process was completed did the Commission get down to formulating its recommendations which were submitted to the President.

Two examples from the realm of compulsory purchase and relocation are especially revealing, for governments too often adopt a high handed attitude towards these issues especially where those people due for relocation or to have their land and houses compulsorily acquired are, as they usually are, the urban poor. The following two examples, however, demonstrate both how consultation can improve the acceptability of what are otherwise likely to be traumatic decisions from the point of view of those being dispossessed and how forces external to the administrative process are sometimes needed to push that process to meaningful consultation.

Resettlement in Emmerton, Barbados

What follows draws on Alleyne, Archer and Walters (1990). Emmerton is an area of land immediately adjacent to Bridgetown, the capital of Barbados. The country's Physical Development Plan of 1971 deemed Emmerton as the city's worst slum area, and as a high priority for clearance and renewal. "It was thus not surprising that after exhaustive design development and economic considerations, the decision was taken to use five acres of the Emmerton area for the construction of the sewage (waste water) treatment facility for the city's first sewerage system." There were at the time some 560 people living in the Emmerton area, predominantly in chattel houses, many of them in a dilapidated condition. Social surveys showed that a majority of the residents did not wish to leave Emmerton but "in general, the persons to be removed accepted it as a measure which the government had to take, but were insistent that uprooting them from their leisurely happy way of life should have its compensation in better standards of living and the minimum dislocation from their livelihoods".

A loan for the construction of the sewerage system was to be provided by the Inter-American Development Bank, one of the conditions of which was that before any disbursement of the loan, a programme and schedule for the relocation of persons from the site would be provided. The government selected a site two-and-a-half-miles from Emmerton and formed an inter-departmental committee of senior officials to plan the logistics of the clearing and the compensation "of landlords who may have suffered any loss as a result of clearance". The National Housing Corporation was designated as the agency to execute the relocation. This early planning for clearance and "rumours of crude methods to be employed by government in the implementation of the removal of residents brought very sharp resentful and hostile reaction from the persons concerned in the removal as well as from several sectors of the Barbadian community".

Government recognised the need for a different approach. The Community Development Division was brought in, and a citizens' committee representing residents to be removed from Emmerton was established. The functions of the committee were to mobilise the entire community, learn their problems, needs and concerns, discuss government's plans with them and represent their views to Government. The Community Development Division's function was to "obtain the active and positive participation of the people of the Emmerton Community ...." and, via in depth interviews, become familiar with their concerns about moving. Government responded to the views and concerns expressed by the citizens' Committee and *inter alia*, agreed to provide improved amenities and utilities at the relocation site rather than, as had been initially determined, the same standards as existed at Emmerton. The conclusion of the commentators on the whole operation was that it "cannot be otherwise described but as a successful coordinated operation ..." even though surveys after the move showed some dissatisfaction with some aspects of it. However, overall, "the early recognition by the Government of Barbados that the people of Emmerton should become actively involved in the matters of resettlement which concerned and influenced their lives and welfare, contributed to the establishment of a harmonious relationship with widespread cooperation and the willingness by most to sacrifice some of their prejudged suspicions and recalcitrance".

The establishment of the Citizens' Committee helped to engender that feeling of belonging and participation in the sewerage-cum-resettlement project which helped both the Government and the residents affected in clarifying roles, solving problems and to prevent the spread of unfounded rumour and faulty beliefs among the residents. The interchange of ideas and goals led to more effective decision-making by government.

Compensation provisions in the Lesotho Highlands Water Project

The Lesotho Highlands Water Project reverses the flow of the Senqu/Orange River in the Lesotho Highlands, creates dams to store the water and redirects its flow in measured quantities into South Africa to provide irrigation for farmland in the Orange Free State and to develop hydro-electric power for Lesotho. Many highland people – predominantly cattle farmers – stood to lose their land and their livelihoods as a result of the project. The legal framework for the execution of this massive World Bank and other international agencies funded project – a treaty between Lesotho and the Republic of South Africa and the Lesotho Highlands Development Authority Order – was gravely deficient in making proper provision for compensation for the highland people or for consulting them about their future. The provisions were subjected to sharp public criticism which had an effect in the World Bank and in turn on the policies and actions of the Lesotho Highlands Development Authority which developed, after widespread consultations with the highland people, realistic and novel forms of compensation set out in a policy document of the Authority (LHDA, 1990):

> Where a field is acquired by the project, LHDA should replace the income thus lost by the affected household and its descendants. Such compensation for the loss of land rights must be directed to both the individual and the community. Compensation should take the form of replacement income rather than

replacement land ... During a transitional period while these alternative forms of income are being introduced, there should be direct replacement of the agricultural income which has been lost. This direct replacement income should be provided to the head of the household, annually for not more than 15 years from the time the field is lost ... The Government of Lesotho should make an explicit long term commitment to devote a major portion of its revenues from the sale of water from LSWP to the welfare and economic development of the communities affected by the project ... Where it is necessary for LHDA to acquire residential property, it should, where possible, arrange with the chief of the affected village for a new residential site or sites to be allocated to the household in question within the same chief's area of jurisdiction ... Where LHDA acquires residential property comprising one or more single room dwellings it should build a new house or houses, totalling the same internal service area as those acquired, on the new site ... Any person aggrieved by compensation arrangements made or not made by LHDA in connection with his loss of land, income or other assets or rights because of the LHWP should be permitted to appeal to the land tribunal established by s.64 of the Land Act 1979 ... if his representations to the LHDA do not satisfy him.

In both these examples, it was administrative practice, adopted as a result of political pressure, which produced fairer practices and procedures. In Lesotho in fact the compensation scheme was at the time it was first introduced outside the law and technically therefore the Authority and the Government of Lesotho were vulnerable to challenge by the Republic of South Africa for non-compliance with the Treaty. This reinforces the point that a legal framework for consultation is preferable to relying on administrative goodwill.

Reverting now back to the lessons from the three success story case studies, a fourth general theme is that of flexibility in implementation. This covers a variety of matters. In Botswana it refers to the willingness to develop new, and adapt old forms of, tenure to suit the new urban needs of the Botswana. In Thailand it refers to the willingness to adjust regulations to facilitate the better operation of the market; to the whole concept of land sharing and negotiated settlements of land disputes; and to the eclectic mixture of laws that make up the Thai legal framework of land management. In Peru, it refers to the willingness of government to allow an NGO to take the lead in law reform and to accept an alternative, simpler system of title registration to that which had existed for 100 years.

What a contrast there is to the overly rigid adherence to planning standards, building regulation standards, centralised and complex systems of title registration and musty old land laws which so many lawyers and bureaucrats insist on in so many of the countries of the developing world which base themselves on the common law and traditions of British colonial public administration. What is it about those two facets of the British colonial experience which generate such conservatism? Is it purely that maintenance of long-standing standards, rules and laws benefit those who urge their retention, or is there something more fundamental – fear of the unknown, especially a home-grown unknown – or is it the philosophy of top-down administration, which is the real legacy of British colonialism, that impedes urban land reform in much of the common law Third World?

It seems worthwhile pursuing the theme of "illegality" a little further. This is in fact the fifth theme of the case studies. A striking characteristic of the Thai and Peruvian examples – the matter did not arise in Botswana – is the clear acceptance of the desirability of addressing the issues as they exist without getting hung up on the legality or illegality of the presence of citizens on urban land. Peru in fact had been down that particular road as described by de Soto in *The Other Path* and had found it led nowhere. It seems the Thai culture of non-confrontation has avoided the worst excesses of approaches to urban land issues that are based on rigid notions of legality and illegality. Too many countries, particularly, it must be said, in Africa, still approach issues of urban land management in these terms and it is distinctly unhelpful. As noted earlier, use of these terms and action taken in pursuance of them is much more of a socio-political than a legal matter – it benefits the urban elite who wield the law – but the point needs to be made that policies and their implementations which are predicated on the basis that the majority of urban dwellers are in some way living "illegally" have not succeeded in dealing with the problems of urban land in the past and are very unlikely to succeed in the future.

There are in fact two intellectual problems to overcome in respect of notions of "illegal" land occupation and use. The first which is the more obvious one is the basic principle, seized on by lawyers, administrators and landowners, that to tolerate the illegal occupation and use of land is contrary to all precepts of good government – adherence to the rule of law, protection of property, compliance with lawful authority – and it really should make no difference whether the illegality is being perpetrated by a few people or by many, perhaps the majority of urban dwellers. The counter-argument to this formalistic position is that the social context of the "illegality" must be considered. For the vast majority of "illegal" occupants and users of land in the cities of the developing world, there is no alternative; the official legal system of land allocation and use is beyond their reach, either because they cannot afford it, or because they lack the political influence and connections to obtain access to it. As has been noted, those with the power to alter that state of affairs too often find it is in interests not to do so. There is nothing contrary to the principles of good government or the rule of law to address the issues giving rise to illegality rather than attempting to "put an end" to the illegality by such means as forcible removal, demolition, criminal charges, etc.

The second intellectual problem is this. Characterisation of popular or informal settlements as "illegal" or "unauthorised" or "slum" leads those who use such terms to assume that the inhabitants of such settlements are, if not all criminals, then certainly living a pretty inferior lawless kind of existence which needs to be contained rather than encouraged.

Nothing could be further from the truth as increasing numbers of research studies have shown. First, informal settlements, even those which start as wholly illegal, do not exist in a Hobbesian state of nature; some system of ordering inter-personal relations in respect of tenurial issues and other matters quickly comes into being. Second, the institutions which are involved in such a system come from both inside and outside the informal settlement; those outside the settlement being part of the official formal system of governance. In practice, they may be local government institutions as was shown to be the case in a study of *barrios* in Caracas, and as occurs in land sharing operations in Bangkok; party officials as is the case in informal settlements in Lusaka and Dar es Salaam and in many Indian cities; organisations of lawyers either official as in Caracas, quasi-official, *i.e.* a legal aid society formally registered in accordance with governmental regulations *e.g.* the Legal Advice Centre in Nairobi, or unofficial – groups of lawyers willing to give their time free or for a fee to persons within the informal settlements – *e.g.* in Bangalore; NGOs; or, in areas where customary law applies, those with authority over land and people within the customary system, *e.g.* in Douala, Bamako, Accra.

Third, while there may be some, perhaps inevitable, reference to formal legal terminology, concepts, forms, etc. within the informal systems, their development and operation is eclectic and consumer-orientated; they aim to satisfy their clientele, keep the peace and uphold legitimate claims and interests to land and housing – legitimate within the informal settlement that is. Fourth, assuming that some official involvement in ordering informal tenurial relations betoken official tolerance of the informal settlement, for whatever reason, a fair degree of security of tenure from external forces – *i.e.* eviction, demolition – is or may be obtained. Even security of tenure from internal forces – *i.e.* landlords – may be strengthened by the existence of official involvement.

These factors reinforce points made already; acceptance of the reality of life in the informal settlements is a necessary prelude to addressing the problems arising therefrom. Concepts of legality and illegality obfuscate rather than illuminate.

What is the way forward?

In coming to the last part of this chapter, there is a need to expand the scope of its coverage. At the level of urban land reform, the way forward has in effect been pointed out in the two preceding parts; follow the general principles derived from the case studies discussed in the case studies: decentralisation of administration; more reliance on open market-orientated systems; more consultations; greater flexibility; and an acceptance of the facts of and in informal settlements. But to enunciate the principles does not of itself deal with the issue of "how": how do we proceed from where we are not to where we ultimately want to get to? Nor does an enunciation of principles of urban land reform deal with the wider question of governance which also has to be faced: can we really discuss urban land reform, its principles, techniques and tools as if it could proceed in a political and governmental vacuum? These wider issues will be dealt with here; the narrower but equally important issue of "how" is discussed at some length in Part V of *Reforming Urban Land Policies and Institutions in Developing Countries* (Farvacque and McAuslan, 1992) and need not be repeated here.

The wider issue of the context of governance within which urban land reform will have to proceed necessitates a brief historical overview.

As a broad generalisation, it may be suggested that the trend of governance world-wide in the four decades from the ending of World War Two in 1945 was that of centralisation of power: the use of the power and authority of central governments to achieve economic growth, social welfare, and national cohesion. Powerful and apparently successful models from both the capitalist world (West) and the socialist world (East) were on offer to the developing world: the New Deal from the USA, and a seminal institution, the Tennessee Valley Authority; the Welfare State from the UK and the plethora of public corporations established in that country in the 1940s; the establishment of a strong executive presidency in France by the Fifth Republic in 1958 after a succession of weak parliamentary governments in the Fourth Republic; the centralised systems of economic development being established in Eastern Europe. Above all, there was the model closest to home for many countries, the colonial government where power resided in a strong central executive with direct lines of control leading back to the central executive in the metropolitan government. These models of governance did not seem to leave much room for decentralised or local government.

The developing world built their structures of government and administration on the basis of these models. Political, economic and social developments then moved in such a way that central power was constantly added to at the expense of local power. For reasons which need not be reviewed here, political development in many countries took the form of military or civil oligarchies seizing power and concentrating all resources at the centre so that they could retain power through the judicious use of those resources to reward supporters. Resources included, in many countries, urban land. Economic development likewise was centralised partly as a corollary of political development, partly as a result of international aid which flowed from central governments and lending agencies to central governments which were required to guarantee repayments and be accountable for how the aid monies and loans were spent. Finally, social developments impelled or were thought to impel centralisation; rapid urbanisation required major programmes of construction; of food security and subsidies; posed major national security and public health problems and demanded rational planning and control of land use. The desire to build a nation required for many countries a programme of unification and modernisation of legal and administrative systems and a reduction in the powers of local and traditional rulers. Land was often a source of such local power and regulated by local norms, so its administration and regulation needed to be centralised.

Emphasis has so far been laid on practice; the practice which provided the basic model; the practice which built on the basic model. But behind the practice was the theory or at least the underlying assumptions about governance which provided the justification for central control and in particular central control over land. Two theories are of relevance here. The first derives from development economics:

> ... When development economics emerged as a sub-discipline in the 1940s and early 1950s there was a pervasive view among economists that the late industrializing countries required strong authoritarian state institutions in order to mobilize the resources required for growth. Democracy was a 'luxury' that could not be afforded by poor states ...
>
> The belief that authoritarian regimes are conducive to economic growth was pervasive not only among students of economic and political development but also among the political elites and enterprise managers in developing countries, as well as among the officers and technocrats in the international financial institutions and assistance agencies (Ruttan, 1991, p. 268).

The second theory or assumption about power derives from the colonial experience and has already been alluded to. Many of the states which have become independent since 1945 are the creation of executive power exercised by colonial authorities. Similarly, rather than the organs of the governance of the state emerging from the cultural and historical experiences of the people, they were imposed from outside and in many respects were designed to render otiose any traditional forms of governance. In respect of specific areas of governance, *e.g.* powers over land, it has already been noted that interests in land, their existence, content, holders, modes of transactions, etc. were explicitly and clearly made to derive from the power of the new colonial authorities rather than from the traditional or existing indigenous authorities which reflected and applied the customs of the people. So power in a new state was seen to come exclusively from the centre, from the top. Indeed the new constitutions with which all states started their independent life, although designed to limit, share and control power, in fact emphasised the locus and the origin of power in the new state: it derived from the centre.

Thus, the assumption about where the power to govern came from, and the assumption about where the power needed to be located to achieve economic development together provided the justification for the practice not merely of centralisation of power but for the robust and not-participative use of power. In the area of urban land management this in turn provided the rationale of land nationalisation, the substitution of parastatal land development authorities for local government, central controls over land transactions and land use, top-down management of sites and services and squatter upgrading programmes, the use of the bulldozer as a tool of land management, and other manifestations of over-centralised bureaucratic systems of management. Such systems of management are antipathetic not only to working with unofficial groups and individuals who are not part of the urban elites, who exercise the powers of management, but, more importantly, to the development of forms and processes of governance which would facilitate such "working with", and indeed regard it as one of the primary purposes of government.

In short, the approaches being argued for in this paper – the creation of flexible consumer-oriented systems of urban land allocation and use, the commitment to consultation, transparency, probity and equity in administrative processes connected with land – cannot be divorced from, indeed may be seen as a paradigm of, the wider issues of good governance now on the agenda of many states and the international aid community; participation and decentralisation in government, transparency and accountability in administration, an enabling rather than a controlling function for the public sector generally. Adoption of the philosophy and approach to governance as a whole will make much easier the development of a system of urban land management which aims to facilitate the operation of efficient and equitable land delivery systems and to contain the externalities of such systems with a flexible, modest and implementable set of regulatory instruments.

There remains the need to take up a matter which has in a sense been left in the air: why should the urban elite bother with urban land reform when they are the winners in the present situation? What incentives can be offered them to give up, as they will see it, some of their benefits? It is important too to understand that politicians, large landowners and senior public servants are not the only persons who have a major interest in the status quo of the existing legal and administrative complexities of urban land management. Armies of lower and middle civil servants and thousands of middle persons who make a living by guiding both the poor and the middle-class through the mazes that exist at present all have a substantial stake in the confused inequitable and irrational systems that now exist. Experience with attempted reforms in many countries has shown that all of these groups will resist simplifications and reforms no matter how sensible they may be: devising incentives that will defuse the opposition of these groups will be necessary for the political viability of reform.

The key issue, however, will be: what can be offered to the gatekeepers to induce their cooperation? To be specific, what can be offered to senior officials who effectively control access to urban land throughout the country, and have in that capacity built up networks of contacts and "banks" of favours owed for past services rendered? Why should such officials cooperate in any programme designed to make access to urban land more simple, more transparent, and more free since this would undermine their own positions and powers?

Doebele has suggested that the best occasions to try to bring about changes in land management practices are in what he calls "moments of transition" – occasions when some specific change in the status of land is about to take place: the sub-division of rural land into urban-sized plots; the provision of infrastructure; the commencement of actual construction; and the re-assembly of lands for re-development. To this may be added the fact that external events may also trigger a moment of transition, for example, the impact of falling foreign remittances on people's propensity to invest in land, which in the specific case of Jordan led to a willingness to contemplate reducing plot sizes so as to maintain land development, albeit with lower profits for developers. This is a useful approach and can be developed in this context.

Just as there are moments of transition in land management, so there are moments of transition in the wider context of governance, either exogenous (*i.e.* structural adjustment programmes) or endogenous (*i.e.* a fundamental change of government from military to elected civilian or from one party to multiparty or from a command-economy government to one committed to introducing market forces). These moments of transition can be used to explain the advantages of more equitable and efficient urban land policies and management practices to the incoming gatekeepers – sometimes even to some of the outgoing gatekeepers who hope to hang on in the new government. There will be, and have been, occasions when the ready availability of such new policies and programmes – which seem likely to provide an immediate and positive political return to a new government or an existing government having to implement a series of policies imposing heavy costs on the usual losers – will be taken up and acted upon.

This indeed seems to have been what happened in Peru where the government or more specifically the president, elected in 1985 and initially very popular, had by 1988 become very unpopular because of failing economic policies and the need to turn to the IMF and adopt its orthodox economic policies. Again in Zambia, shortly after the election won by the MMD which ended over 30-years' rule by President Kaunda, the new minister responsible for lands was calling for international assistance to develop new land policies; he presumably did not know that a blueprint developed along the lines argued for here had been available in Zambia since 1989 but had not been acted upon by the preceding government. Two further examples where a government newly arrived in power focused on the need for changes in urban land policies are Trinidad and Tobago in 1986 where the newly elected government gave support to the Sou Sou land movement which focused on speedy and cheap land allocation to the urban poor, and the Philippines in the same year. There, however, while land reform both rural and urban was on the agenda, powerful vested interests of landowners blunted its effectiveness and the urban land reform law was considerably altered by the legislature before it was passed. In Eastern and Central Europe too, urban land reform has been high on the political agenda.

Thus while moments of transition will not always result in action on urban land reform, their existence is more frequent than might be supposed and gives added weight to the point made earlier on the wider governmental context of urban land reform, for good governance embraces the possibility of changing governments and that, as the examples above show, is probably the most important moments of transition.

A further conclusion may be noted. Given the existence of moments of transition it is important to be ready with new ideas, new policies and draft laws. NGOs have a vital role to play here as the Institute for Liberty and Democracy in Peru and the Sou Sou land movement in Trinidad and Tobago demonstrate. Lawyers have an obvious role to play in such NGOs in turning ideas and policies into practical realities via draft laws.

Conclusion

This chapter began with a quotation from the UNDP's paper: *Cities, People and Poverty*. It will end with a paraphrase from the final paragraph of the Farvacque and McAuslan paper noted earlier.

This chapter has argued for the need for urban land reform and indicated via examples from several countries what can be done and what principles should inform what needs to be done. In conclusion then the overall message may be spelt out; the aim should be to bring about a major re-orientation of urban land management as it operates in most countries. There will be changes in the legal and administrative superstructure; in their day-to-day operations, in the roles the various actors perform in the process of management and in land markets, and in the philosophical basis that provides the intellectual justification for the approach to land management. Instead of the public sector having the dominant controlling role, which is the present official position in too many countries, it will move to a residual enabling role. Instead of the private sector operating at the margins, especially in areas of low-income settlements where its activities may be technically illegal, it will develop into the primary mode of land delivery and development, and will be facilitated to do this. The effect of this will be that fewer public officials will be needed and there will be or should be fewer opportunities to manipulate land delivery systems and actions for political ends. A move towards greater reliance on markets for land delivery and development is designed to benefit the general population by making it easier for them to obtain and develop land, but it may disadvantage those in the political and administrative hierarchies for whom existing secretive and inefficient administrative discretionary systems provide opportunities for illicit private gain and political influence. This in turn will likely mean that the chief obstacles to change in the direction being proposed here will be at the wider political level, which in turn reinforces the point made earlier in this chapter: reforms in urban land management cannot be divorced from reforms in political administrative processes designed to bring about more open, accountable and participative governance.

---

*First published in Vyas, Y. Kibwana, K. Owiti, O. and Wanjala, S. (1994) *Law and Development in the Third World*, Nairobi.

Appendix

Basic information on statutory Land Laws in mainland Commonwealth Africa

Country	**Reception date (RD)**[1] **(English law unless otherwise stated)**	**Basic pre-independence statutory land law on tenure**	**Principal current post-independence tenure laws**	**Replace/ modify (a) col 3/ rec'd, (b) cust, law by col 4 law**[2]	**Texts (T) or other (O) books on land law**[3]
Botswana	10 June 1891 Roman-Dutch from Cape of Good Hope (CGH)	Crown Lands O-in-C 1904	Tribal Land Act, 1968	Modified (a) and (b)	O[4]
Cameroon; (i) East & (ii) West	1924 French civil code 1 Jan 1900	(i) Décret du 21/7/32 (ii) Land and Native Rights Ord. 1927	Land Ordinances, 1974	Replaced (a) and modified (b) and received law	
The Gambia	1 Nov 1888	Land (Banjul and Kombo St Mary) Ord. 1945 Protectorate Lands Ord. 1945	State Lands Act, 1990	Replaced land law in colony and modified received law	None
Ghana	24 Jul 1874 for statutes of gen applic; no date otherwise	*South*: Concessions Ord. 1939; *North*: Land and Native Rights Ord. 1927; Land Registry Ord. 1895	Land Title Registration Law, 1986	Modified (a) and (b)	T and O
Kenya	12 Aug 1897	Crown Lands Ord. 1915 Transfer of Property Act, 1882 (Indian)	Registered Land Act, 1962[5] Land Adjudication Act, 1968	Modified (a) including received law. Replaced (b)	T and O
Lesotho	29 Sept 1884 Roman-Dutch (CGH)	Laws of Lerotholi; Proclamation No.65 of 1922	Land Act, 1979[6]	Modified (a) & (b). Received law still applies	O

Malawi	11 Aug 1902	Public (ne Crown) Land Ordinance 1951 Land Registration Ordinance 1916	Land Act, 1965 Customary Land Development Act; Registered Land Act, 1967[7]	Modified (a) and (b). Received land law still applies.	None
Mozam-bique	Portuguese common law;[8] Decree-Law 43.983/61	Law of 9/5/1901 Decree of 1918 Art. 38, Native Statute for Angola and Mozambique 1955	Land Law, 1997	Replaced (a) Modified (b)	
Namibia	1 Jan 1920 Roman-Dutch (CGH)	Many RSA land laws applied. Crown Lands Disposal Proclam. 1920	None[9]	N/a. All col.3 land laws still apply in Namibia	O
Nigeria	1 Jan 1900; some states have no date for reception of common law and equity	(i) South: Native Lands Acquisition Ord. 1900 & Crown Lands Ord. 1906;(ii) North: Land and Native Rights Ord.1910; Land Registration Ord. 1924	Land Use Decree, 1978	Replaced colonial land laws (other than LRO '24); modified received and customary law	T and O
Sierra Leone	1 Jan 1880	(i) Crown Lands Ord. (ii) Protectorate Lands Ord. 1927; Concessions Ord. 1931[10]		N/a	None
South Africa	1652 Roman-Dutch[11]	***Not applicable.*** Restitution of Land Rights Act, 1994 Extension of Security of Tenure Act, 1997	***Listed in this column are post-1994 Acts.*** Interim Protection of Informal Land Rights Act, 1996	Modified (a) and (b)	T and O
Swaziland	15 Oct 1904 Roman-Dutch (CGH)	Crown Lands O-in-C 1907; Concessions Partition Act, 1907; Crown Lands Disposal Act, 1911	None [12]	Basic land laws not changed.	O

Tanzania:[13] (i) Mainland (ii) Zanzibar	(i) 1 Jan 1922 (ii) 7 Jul 1897	(i) Land Ord 1922 (ii) Public Land Decree, 1921 and 1951; Alienation of Land Decree, 1934	(i) Land Act, 1998; Village Land Act, 1998 (both enacted in 1999) (ii) Commission for Land & Environment Act, 1989; Land Adjudication Act; Registered Land Act, 1990; Land Tenure Act, 1992; Land Transfer Act, 1994	(i) repld (a) incl received law & modified (b) (ii) modified both (a) & (b)	(i) T and O (ii) none
Uganda	11 August 1902	Crown Lands Ord. 1903 Registration of Titles Ord. 1922	Land Act, 1998	Modified (a) and (b). Received law still applies	O
Zambia	17 Aug 1911	Land and Deeds Registry Ord. 1914 and 1944	Land Act, 1995	No.	None
Zimbabwe	10 June 1891 Roman-Dutch (CGH)	Racial segregation in land tenure until formally removed in 1977	Communal Land Act, 1981 The Land Acquisition Acts of 1985 , 1992 and 2000 have not altered or reformed land tenure.	N/a	O

Notes

[1] The reception date is the date on which English (or other) law as it was on that date was "received into" (in reality, imposed upon) the new colonial territory. The terms of each specific statutory provision differed from country to country, both before and since independence. In most cases, this reception date has been confirmed by post-independence legislation but some countries have provided that English law applies as the residual law without reference to any specific date. In the table these are characterised by the words "no date".

The specific date refers to the date on which "statutes of general application" in force in England at that date were to apply to the colonial dependency. Much judicial and academic learning has gone into the question as to whether the date also applies to the rules of the common law and the doctrines of equity which were to be in force from the reception date so that later evolution of those rules and doctrines in England could or could not be applied.

This issue is of less importance in respect of land law than most other branches of the law since land law was fundamentally reformed by statute in England in 1925 so that judicial decisions thereon are less likely to be applicable in countries with pre-1925 reception dates than is the case with other parts of the common law and doctrines of equity.

In all cases where English law is the received law, the received land law is a hotch-potch of statutory laws stretching back from the reforming property statutes of the 1880s to the sixteenth century or earlier. In one or two countries, all or part of the Conveyancing Act, 1911 has been applied.

[2] Modification means any significant alteration of or addition to col.3 law or the received law.

[3] "Textbook" means a book wholly about the land law which is appropriate for use in legal education and practice; "other book" means a social science orientated book of which not less than 60% is about land law.

[4] In respect of Botswana, Lesotho, Namibia, Swaziland and Zimbabwe, basic textbooks on statutory land law are those in use in South Africa.

[5] Kenya became independent in December 1963. Its principal tenure transformation law however was enacted in 1962 and has remained in place since independence.

[6] A new national land policy is being developed which may suggest changes to this Act.

[7] A National Land Policy for Malawi, adopted in December 2001, heralds changes in the basic land laws of the country.

[8] Portuguese law applied in Portuguese possessions from the time the Portuguese first invaded the particular possession; there is no specific reception date. Such law applied to Portuguese settlers and certain categories of Africans and as time went on, to their land relations as well, especially in urban areas. See on this, Narana Coissoro, African Customary Law in the Former Portuguese Territories, 1954–1974 (1984) 28 *Journal of African Law* p. 72.

[9] The Agriculture (Commercial) Land Reform Act, 1995 deals with land redistribution. It leaves untouched both customary and Roman-Dutch land law.

[10] As in The Gambia, so in Sierra Leone: different legal regimes applied to land in the former colony – now the Western Province – and the former protectorate. In the former colony, the Imperial Statutes (Law of Property) Adoption Ordinance applied much English land law of the 1880s and 1890s to land.

[11] This date is the year when Roman-Dutch law was first applied to any part of the area which is now a part of the Republic of South Africa.

[12] There has been a good deal of land legislation since independence but these have been concerned to vest non-freehold land in the king and control speculation in land by non-Swazis; they have not changed the basic laws on tenure. A national land policy is in the process of being developed which may lead to legislative changes.

[13] The two parts of the United Republic retain their own legal system with different reception dates and different land laws. The reception date for the basic received land law in Tanzania Mainland is different to the general reception date which is 22 July 1920. Islamic law is also and always has been part of the basic land law of Zanzibar.

Bibliography

Abrams, C. (1964) *Man's Struggle for Shelter in an Urbanising World*, MIT Press, Cambridge, Mass.

Acharya, B.P. (1987) The Indian Urban Land Ceiling Act: a critique of the 1976 legislation, *Habitat International*, Vol. 11, pp. 39–51.

Acharya, B.P. (1987) The transferability of land pooling/land readjustment techniques, *Habitat International*, Vol. 12(4), pp. 103–17.

Adeniyi, E.N. (1981) Administrative framework for physical planning in Nigeria, in Sada, P.O. and Oguntoyinbo J.S. (eds) *op. cit.*

Agbosu, L.K. (1990) Land Registration in Ghana: Past, Present and the Future, *Journal of African Law*, Vol. 34, pp. 104–27.

Agrawal, P.K. (1993) *Land Reforms in India: Constitutional and Legal Approach*, New Delhi.

Ahmad, I. and Sihombing, J. (1989) (eds) *The Centenary of the Torrens System in Malaysia*, Malayan Law Journal, Kuala Lumpur.

Ajani, G. and Mattei, U. (1995) Codifying property law in the process of transition: some suggestions from comparative law and economics, *Hastings International and Comparative Law Review* (19), pp. 117–37.

Alden Wily, L. (1998) Implications of the Uganda Land Bill for Customary Tenure, Parliamentarians' Workshop on the Land Bill, 1998, Forum for Women in Democracy (FOWODE), Kampala.

Alden Wily, L. (1998) Implications of the Uganda Land Bill for Women, Parliamentarians' Workshop on the Land Bill, 1998, Forum for Women in Democracy (FOWODE), Kampala.

Alleyne, M., Archer, A.B., and Walters, G. (1990) The resettlement of residents from Emmerton, Bridgetown, Barbados, *Environments*, Vol. 16, pp. 90–104.

Amsden, A. (1989) *Asia's Next Giant*, Oxford UP, New York.

Anderson, D. and Grove, R. (1987) *Conservation in Africa: People, Policies and Practice*, Cambridge UP, Cambridge.

Anderson, J.S. (1992) *Lawyers and the Making of English Land Law 1832–1940*, Oxford UP, Oxford, UK.

André, C. and Platteau, J-P. (1996) Land Relations under Unbearable Stress: Rwanda caught in the Malthusian Trap, paper presented at the Third Alistair Berkley Memorial Workshop, London School of Economics.

Angel, S., Archer, R., Tanphiphat, S. and Wegelin, E. (eds) (1983) *Land for Housing the Poor*, Select Books, Singapore.

Arnold, H.J.P. (1962) *Aid for Developing Countries*, Bodley Head, London.

Asante, S.K.B. (1975) *Property Law and Social Goals in Ghana*, Ghana UP, Accra.

Ashworth, W. (1954) *The Genesis of Modern British Town Planning*, Routledge & Kegan Paul, London.

Bangladesh Flood Action Plan FAP – 15 (1992) *Land Acquisition and Resettlement Study*, HIFAB International and Multidisciplinary Action Research Team (MARC) for Ministry of Irrigation, Water Development and Flood Control.

Barker, R. (ed) (1994) *Agricultural Policy Analysis for Transition to a Market-oriented Economy in Viet Nam*, FAO, Rome.

Barua, D.C. (1996) Housing for the Rural Poor: The Grameen Bank Experience, International Workshop on Housing and Hazards, Dhaka, December.

Beckinsale, E.P. and Houston, J.M. (1973) *Urbanisation and its Problems*, Blackwell, Oxford.

Bell, R. (1987) Conservation with a human face: conflict and reconciliation in African land use planning, in Anderson, D. and Grove, R. *op. cit.*

Bentsi-Enchill, K. (1975) The Traditional Legal Systems of Africa, in Lawson, F.H. (Chief Editor) *Property and Trust, International Encyclopaedia of Comparative Law*, Vol. VI, Chapter 2, Section IV, pp. 68–101, The Hague.

Besterman, C. and Cassanelli, L.V. (1996) *The Struggle for Land in Southern Somalia: the war behind the war*, Haan, London.

Bhargava, G. (1983) *Socio-Economic and Legal Implications of Urban Land (Ceiling and Regulation) Act 1976*, Abhinav Publications, New Delhi.

Blaikie, T. (1985) *Political Economy of Soil Erosion*, London.

Bomani, M. (1996) Report of the Legal Task Force, *Change*, Vol. 4 (1&2), pp. 83–99.

Botswana (1983) *Presidential Commission on Land Tenure*, Gaborone.

Bruce, J.W. and Migot-Adholla, S.E. (1994) *Searching for Land Tenure Security in Africa*, Kendall-Hunt Publishing Co, Dubuque, Iowa.

Bruce, J.W. (1988) Residential land and housing development in the major villages of Botswana, *African Urban Quarterly*, Vol. 3, p. 100, Nairobi.

Buch, M.N. (1984) Land Policy and the Urban Poor, *Nagarlok*, Vol. 16, p. 1, New Delhi.

Budlender, G., Latsky, J. and Roux, T. (1997) *Juta's New Land Law*, Kenwyn.

Burgess, R., Carmona, M. and Kolstee, T. (1997) *The Challenge of Sustainable Cities: Neoliberalism and urban strategies in developing countries*, Zed Books, London.

Calvino, I. (1997) *Invisible Cities*, Vintage, London.

Capital Development Authority (1977) *Kikuyu Development Plan, Dodoma*, Dodoma.

Chandrasekhara, C.S. (1969) Zoning law, in Indian Law Institute, *op. cit.*

Chandrasekhara, C.S. (1980) Development control: built-up areas and mixed land use zoning, in D.D. Malhotra (ed), *op. cit.* pp. 52–64.

Charnock, M. (1991) Paradigms, policies and property: a review of the customary law of land tenure, in Mann, K. and Roberts, R. (eds), *op. cit.* pp. 61–84.

CASSAD (1991) *Women in Urban Land Development in Africa: Case studies from Nigeria and Ghana*, Ibadan.

Chowdhury, A.I. (1992) Urban Land Market in Bangladesh, in Islam and Chowdhury, *op. cit.*

Chowdhury, O.H. (1991) *Transfer of Property Act*, 2nd edition, Dhaka Law Reports, Dhaka.

Coulter, R.T. and Tullberg, S.M. (1985) Indian Land Rights, *Antioch Law Journal*, Vol. 3, p. 153.

Dale, P. and McLaughlin, J. (1988) *Land Information Management*, Clarendon Press, Oxford.

Das Gupta, S.K. (ed) (1974) The Calcutta Improvement Trust 1912–1945, in *The Calcutta Improvement Act 1911 and Allied Matters*, Calcutta Improvement Trust, Calcutta.

Development and Planning Commission Document DPC 4/99 (1999) Department of Land Affairs, Pretoria.

Debusmann, R. and Arnold, S. (eds) (1996) *Land Law and Land Ownership in Africa*, Bayreuth.

Dowall, D.E. (1991) *The Land Market Assessment; A new tool for urban management*, UMP Paper No. 4, Washington DC.

Dowall, D.E. and Clarke, G. (1991) *A Framework for Reforming Urban Land Policies in Developing Countries*, UMP Paper No. 7, Washington DC.

Dunkerley, H.B. (ed) (1978) *Urban Land Policy: Issues and opportunities*, World Bank Staff Working Paper 283, Washington DC.

Durrand-Lasserve, A. (1989) *La Situation Fonciere Urbaine en Algerie*, unpublished UMP Discussion Paper, World Bank, Washington DC.
Durrand-Lasserve, A., assisted by Clerc, V. (1996) *Regularization and Integration of Irregular Settlements: Lessons from experience*, Urban Management Programme Working Paper Series, No. 6, Nairobi.
Ega, L.A. (1987) Land policy and land administration in Nigeria: some conceptual and practical issues affecting implementation, *Urban Law and Policy*, Vol. 8, p. 423.
Evenson, N. (1989) *The Indian Metropolis: A view towards the west*, Yale UP, New Haven.
Faizullah, M. (1997) Urban Land Issues and Government in Bangladesh in Islam and Khan, *op. cit.*
Falloux, F. (1987) *Land Management, Titling, Tenancy in Sustainability Issues in Agriculture*, World Bank, Washington DC.
Farooque, M. and Hasan, S.R. (eds) (1996) *Laws Regulating the Environment in Bangladesh*, Bangladesh Environmental Lawyers Association, Dhaka.
Farvacque, C. (1989) *Madagascar: Towards the formulation of a land development strategy*, unpublished UMP Discussion Paper, World Bank, Washington, DC.
Farvacque, C. and McAuslan, P. (1992) *Reforming Urban Land Policies and Institutions in Developing Countries*, UMP Policy Paper No. 5, World Bank, Washington, DC.
Fernandes, E. and Varley, A. (1998) *Illegal Cities: Law and Urban Change in Developing Countries*, Zed Books, London.
Franklin, A.S. (1995) *Land Law in Lesotho: The politics of the 1979 Land Act*, Ashgate, Aldershot.
Franklin, G. (1979) Physical planning in the Third World, *Third World Planning Review*, Vol. 1(1), pp. 7–22.
Frimpong, K. (1986) The administration of tribal lands in Botswana, *Journal of African Law*, Vol. 30, pp. 51–74.
Frimpong, K. (1993) Post-independence land legislation and the process of land tenure reform in Botswana, *Comparative and International Law Journal of South Africa*, Vol. XXVI, pp. 385–95.
Ghai, Y.P. and McAuslan, P. (1970) *Public Law and Political Change in Kenya*, OUP, Nairobi (Chapter III, The development of agrarian administration).

Ghai, Y.P. (1985) Land regimes and paradigms of development: reflections on Melanesian constitutions, *International Journal of the Sociology of Law*, Vol. 13, p. 393.

Ghai, Y.P., Luckham, R. and Snyder, F.G. (eds) (1987) *The Political Economy of Law: a Third World reader*, Oxford UP, New Delhi.

Gihring, T.A. (1976) From elitism to accountability: towards a reformulation of Nigerian town planning law, *Quarterly Journal of Administration*, Vol. X(4), p. 72.

Government of Bangladesh (1993) *National Housing Policy*, Ministry of Housing and Public Works, Dhaka.

Government of Bangladesh (1996) *National Report to the United Nations Conference on Human Settlements*, Dhaka.

Government of India/USAID (1992) *Report of the Regional Policy Seminars on Urban Land Issues in India*, National Housing Bank/Ministry of Urban Development, New Delhi.

Government of the Republic of South Africa (1996) *Green Paper on South African Land Policy*, Department of Land Affairs, Pretoria.

Government of the Republic of South Africa (1997) *White Paper on South African Land Policy*, Department of Land Affairs, Pretoria.

Government of Republic of South Africa, (1999) *Resource Document on the Chapter 1 Principles of the Development Facilitation Act, 1995*, National Development and Planning Commission, Pretoria.

Government of Tanzania. (1994) *Report of the Presidential Commission of Inquiry into Land Matters, Vol I; Land Policy and Land Tenure Structure*, Ministry of Lands, Housing and Urban Development, Tanzania and Scandinavian Institute of African Studies, Dar es Salaam and Uppsala.

Government of Tanzania (1995) *National Land Policy*, Ministry of Lands, Housing and Urban Development, Dar es Salaam.

Government of Tanzania (1997) *Preparation of the Strategic Plan for the Restructuring of the City Council of Dar es Salaam*, Prime Minister's Office Civil Service Reform Programme/Dar es Salaam City Commission/Danida, Dar es Salaam.

Grindle, M.S. (1996) *Challenging the State; Crisis and innovation in Latin America and Africa*, Cambridge UP, Cambridge.

Grindle, M.S. (ed) (1997) *Getting Good Government: Capacity building in the public sectors of developing countries*, Harvard UP, Cambridge, Mass.

Haar, C.M. (ed) (1964) *Law and Land: Anglo-American planning practice*, Harvard UP, Cambridge, Mass.
Hai, A. (1981) The Third World view: planning consultancy in the developing world, *Third World Planning Review*, Vol. 3(2), pp. 133–40.
Hailey (Lord) (1957) *An African Survey Revised*, Oxford UP, Oxford.
Halcrow Fox (1989) *Zambia Land Delivery System Report*, Halcrow Fox and Associates, London.
Hall, P., Thomas, R., Gracey, H. and Drewett, R. (1973) *The Containment of Urban England, Vol. 2: The Planning System: Objectives, Operations, Impacts*, George Allen & Unwin, London.
Hart, W.O. (1964) Land planning and land ownership, in Haar, C.M. *op. cit*.
Haque, M.M. (1992) An overview of urban land management in Bangladesh, in Islam and Chowdhury. *op. cit.*
Hoek-Smit, M.C. (2000) Housing finance in Bangladesh: improving access to housing finance by middle and lower income groups, in Islam (ed) *op. cit.*
Home, R. (1997) *Of Planting and Planning: The Making of British Colonial Cities*, E & FN Spon, London.
Hussain, T. (1995) *Land Rights in Bangladesh*, University Press, Dhaka.
Ibrahim, A. and Sihombing, J. (1989) *The Centenary of the Torrens System in Malaysia*, Malayan Law Journal Pte Ltd, Kuala Lumpur.
ILO (1989) *Women and Land*, Rome.
Indian Law Institute (1969) *Law and Urbanisation in India*, Tripathi, Bombay.
Islam, N. and Khan, M.A. (1992) Land use dynamics in the urban fringe with special reference to land and residential development in the fringe of Dhaka City, in Islam and Chowdhury, *op. cit.*
Islam, N. (1998) *Human Settlements and Urban Development in Bangladesh*, University of Dhaka Press, Dhaka.
Islam, N. and Khan, M.M. (eds) (1997) *Urban Governance in Bangladesh and Pakistan*, Centre for Urban Studies (CUS), Dhaka.
Islam, N. (ed) (1999) *Urban Land and Housing*, CUS, Dhaka.
Islam, N. (1997) *Dhaka: From City to Megacity*, CUS, Dhaka.
Islam, N. (1996) *The Urban Poor in Bangladesh*, CUS, Dhaka.
Islam, N. (ed) (2000) *Urban Land Tenure and Housing Finance in Bangladesh*, CUS, Dhaka.
Islam, N. and Chowdhury, A. I. (eds) (1992) *Urban Land Management in Bangladesh*, Ministry of Land, Dhaka.

Islam, N., Huda, N., Narayan F.B. and Rana, P.B. (eds) (1997) *Addressing the Urban Poverty Agenda in Bangladesh*, University Press, Dhaka.

James, R.W. (1971) *Land Tenure and Policy in Tanzania*, East Africa Literature Bureau, Dar es Salaam.

James, R.W. (1987) *Nigerian Land Use Act: Policy and Principles*, Ile-Ife.

Jones, C. (1996) Plus ça change, plus ça reste le même? The New Zanzibar Land Law Project, *Journal of African Law*, Vol. 40, pp. 19–42.

Jones, G.A. and Ward, P.M. (1998) Privatising the commons: reforming the *ejido* and urban development in Mexico, *International Journal of Urban and Regional Research*, Vol. 22(1), pp. 76–93.

Kanyeihamba, G.W. (1973) Urban planning law in East Africa, *Progress in Planning*, Vol. 2(1), pp. 1–82.

Kanyeihamba, G.W. and McAuslan, P. (eds) (1978) *Urban Legal Problems in Eastern Africa*, Scandinavian Institute of African Studies, Uppsala.

Kaunda, M. (1986–92) Ownership of property rights in land in the first two Republics of Zambia: an evaluation of restrictions on free alienation and some lessons for the future, *Zambian Law Journal*, pp. 61–73.

Kawamara, S. (1999) Parliament to revisit the 1998 Land Act, *The Other Voice*, Vol. 2(1).

Khan, A.A. (ed) (n.d.) *Land Laws of Bangladesh*, Khoshroz Kitan Mahal, Dhaka.

King, A.D. (1976) *Colonial Urban Development: Culture, Social Power and Environment*, Routledge & Kegan Paul, London.

King, K. (1996) *Jua Kali in Kenya*, James Currey, London.

Kitay, M.G. (1985) *Land Acquisition in Developing Countries*, Oelgeschlager, Gunn & Hain/Lincoln Institute of Land Policy, Boston.

Kludze, A.K.P. (1974) The modern Ghanaian law of mortgages, *University of Ghana Law Journal*, Vol. XI, pp. 1–19.

Lamont, J. (1996) Water project told to clean up its act, *Star* (12/9/96), Johannesburg.

Lawal, H. (1984) *Land and Administration in Urban Development with Special Reference to Capital Development Authorities in Nigeria and Tanzania.* Unpublished PhD thesis, University of Warwick.

Lee, M. (1994) *The Cost of the Second Best: The Price of Land Regulation in Asia*, DPU Working Paper, No. 62.

Leshy, J.D. (1985) Indigenous people, land claims and control of mineral development: Australian and US legal systems compared, *University of New South Wales Law Journal*, Vol. 8, p. 271.

Lesotho Highlands Development Authority (1989) *Memorandum on Compensation Policy*, Maseru.

Lim, W.S.W. (1983) Land acquisition for housing with Singapore as a case study, in Angel, S., Archer. R.W., Tanphihpat, S. and Wegelin, E.A. (eds) *op. cit.*

Lugard, F. (1922) *The Dual Mandate in Tropical Africa*, Frank Cass, London (1965) (reprint).

Lysyk, K. (1973) The Indian Title Question in Canada: an appraisal in the light of Calder, *Canadian Bar Review*, Vol. 50, p. 450.

Maddock, K. (1983) *Your Land is Our Land*, Ringwood, Victoria.

Mahmood, Z.H. (1994) Towards effective protection of the housing rights of urban slum dwellers: a view from Bangladesh, *Bangladesh Urban Studies*, Vol. 3(1), pp. 71–86.

Malhotra, D.D. (ed) (1980) *Control of Urban Building Activity*, Centre for Urban Studies, IIPA, New Delhi.

Mann, K. and Roberts, R. (eds) (1991) *Law in Colonial Africa*, James Currey, London.

MacAndrews, C. (1986) *Land Policy in Modern Indonesia, A Study of Land Issues in the New Order Period*, Oelgasehlager, Gunn & Hain in association with the Lincoln Institute of Land Policy, Boston, Mass.

McAuslan, P. (1967) Control of land and agricultural development in Kenya and Tanzania, in Sawyerr, *op. cit*.

McAuslan, P. (1978) Law, housing and the city in Africa, in Kanyeihamba and McAuslan, *op. cit.*

McAuslan, P. (1980) *The Ideologies of Planning Law*, Pergamon, Oxford.

McAuslan, P. (1981) Planning legislation, *A Spatial Planning System for Zimbabwe*, Vol. 2, UNCHS (Habitat) Nairobi, Part III, pp. 149–240.

McAuslan, P. (1985) *Urban Land and Shelter for the Poor*, IIED, London.

McAuslan, P. (1986) Integrated urban development: the way forward, *Third World Affairs*, p. 265.

McAuslan, P. (1987) The Lesotho Highlands Water Project and environmental law: a case study in the light of 'Our Common Future', *Lesotho Law Journal*, Vol. 3, pp. 41–65.

McAuslan, P. (1989) *Town and Country Planning Act for Trinidad and Tobago*, case study for the Urban Management Programme, UNCHS (Habitat), Nairobi.

McAuslan, P. (1991) The Objectives of Planning Legislation in Africa, Swedeplan First International Conference on Planning Legislation in Africa (ICPLA 1), Maseru.

McAuslan, P. (1995 and 1998) Urbanisation, law and development: a record of research, in Stren with Bell, and Fernandes and Varley, *op. cit.*
McAuslan, P. (1998) How workable and accountable is the land management system proposed by the Land Bill?, Parliamentarians' Workshop on the Land Bill 1998, Forum for Women in Democracy (FOWODE), Kampala.
McCoubrey, H. (1988) The English model of planning legislation, *Third World Planning Review*, Vol. 10(4), pp. 371–88.
McMaster, D.N. (1973) The colonial district town in Uganda, in Beckinsale E.P., and Houston, J.M., *op. cit.*
von Mehren, P. and Sawers, T. (1992) Revitalising the law and development movement: a case study of title in Thailand, *Harvard International Law Review*, Vol. 33, pp. 67–94.
Mendiola, E. (1983) Urban land reform in the Philippines, in Angel, S. Archer, R.W., Tanphihpat, S. and Wegelin, E.A. (eds), *op. cit.*
Meriallat, H. (1970) *Land and the Constitution in India*, New Delhi.
Miller, J. Carey (1998) New Wine? The Reform of South African Land Law in its Roman-Dutch Context, Conference Paper, Contemporary Issues of Property Law Centre for the Study of Property Law, University of Reading.
Mohammed, A. (1997) Problems in translating NGO successes into government settlement policy: illustrations from Trinidad and Tobago and Jamaica, *Environment and Urbanisation*, Vol. 9(2), pp. 233–46.
Morse, B. (ed) (1985): *Aboriginal People and the Law: Indian Metis and Inuit Rights in Canada*, Ottawa.
Motha, P. with Yuen, B.K.P. (1989) *Singapore Real Property Guide*, Singapore UP.
Mukoko, S. (1996) On sustainable urban development in sub-Saharan Africa, *Cities*, Vol. 13, p. 265.
National Law School of India University (1992) *Role and Rights of Women in Land Development*, NLSIU, Bangalore.
Nerfin, M. (1965) Towards a housing policy, *Journal of Modern African Studies*, Vol. 3(4), pp. 543–66.
New Zealand Law Commission (1994) *A New Property Law Act*, Report No. 29, Wellington.
Ng'ong'ola, C. (1992) Land problems in some peri-urban villages in Botswana and problems of conception, description and transformation of "tribal" land tenure, *Journal of African Law*, Vol. 36, pp. 140–67.

Njoh, A.J. (1995) Building and urban land use controls in developing countries: a critical appraisal of the Kumba (Cameroon) Zoning Ordinance, *Third World Planning Review*, Vol. 17, pp. 337–56.

North, D. (1990) *Institutions, Institutional Change and Economic Performance*, Cambridge UP, Cambridge.

No named author (1985) Registration Act, 2nd edition, Dhaka Law Reports, Dhaka.

OECD (1986) *Urban Policies in Japan*, Paris.

OECD (1992) *Urban Land Markets: Policies for the 1990s*, Paris.

Ofner, A. (1981) *Property and Politics 1870–1914*, Oxford UP, Oxford.

Ola, C.S. (1986) *Town and Country Planning Law in Nigeria*, Oxford UP, Ibadan.

Omotola, J.A. (1984) *Essays on the Land Use Act*, Lagos.

Omotola, J.A. (1982) The Land Use Act and customary system of tenure, in Omotola (ed) *op. cit*.

Omotola, J.A. (ed) (1982) *The Land Use Act: Report of a National Workshop*, Lagos.

Omotola, J.A. (1985) *Cases on the Land Use Act*, Lagos UP, Lagos.

Onalo, P.L. (1986) *Land Law and Conveyancing in Kenya*, Heinemann, Nairobi.

Ovonji-Odida, I. (1999) Land Law Reform: Challenges and Opportunities for Securing Women's Land Rights in Uganda, DFID Workshop on Land Rights and Sustainable Development in Sub-Saharan Africa: Lessons and Ways Forward in Land Tenure Policy.

Paul-Majumder, P., Mahmud, S. and Afsar, R. (1996) *The Squatters of Dhaka City*, University Press Ltd, Dhaka.

Peterson, N. (ed) (1981) *Aboriginal Land Rights: A Handbook*, Australian Institute of Aboriginal Studies, Canberra.

Perez-Perdomo, R. and Nikken, P. (1980) Law and housing ownership in the Barrios of Caracas, *Urban Law and Policy*, Vol. 3, p. 365, Amsterdam.

Platteau, J-P. (1992) *Land Reform and Structural Adjustment in Sub-Saharan Africa: Controversies and Guidelines*, FAO, Rome.

Platteau, J-P. (1994) Behind the market stage where real societies exist: Part I. The role of public and private order institutions, *Journal of Development Studies*, Vol. 30(2), pp. 533–77; Part II. The role of moral norms, *Journal of Development Studies*, Vol. 30(3), pp. 753–817.

Potts, D. with Mutambirwa, C.C. (1991) High-density housing in Harare: commodification and overcrowding, *Third World Planning Review*, Vol. 13(1), pp. 1–25.

Pugh, R.D.J. (1982) Are northern lands reserved for Indians, *Canadian Bar Review*, Vol. 60, p. 36.

Rahman, M.M. (1994) Housing for the low income households in Dhaka: an exploration for suitable land, *Bangladesh Urban Studies*, Vol. 2(2), pp. 31–43.

Rajagopal, B. (1981) Planning legislation and Administration, *Nargarlok*, Vol. XIII(1), pp. 11–17.

Rakodi, C. (1990) Urban development planning in Tanzania, Zambia and Zimbabwe in the late 80s: a review and research agenda, *Review of Rural and Urban Planning in Southern and Eastern Africa*, Vol. 1(1), pp. 78–110.

Ratten, V.W. (1991) Whatever happened to political development? *Economic Development and Cultural Change*, p. 265.

Redclift, M. (1984) *Development and the Environmental Crisis*, London.

Ricquier, J.M. (1985) *Land Law*, Butterworths, Singapore.

Rodda, A. (ed) (1994) *Women and the Environment,* for the UN Non-Governmental Liaison Service, Zed Books, London.

Rosberg, C.G. and Nottingham, J. (1966) *The Myth of Mau Mau*, Pall Mall Press, London.

Royal Tropical Institute (1990) *Women and Habitat, Urban Management, Empowerment and Women's Strategies*, Amsterdam.

Sachs, A. and Welch, G. (1990) *Liberating the Law: Creating Popular Justice in Mozambique*, Zed Books, London.

Sada, P.O. and Oguntoyinbo J.S. (eds) (1981) *Urbanisation Processes and Problems in Nigeria*, Ibadan UP, Ibadan.

Salter, D.R. (1982) The Land Control Act 1967, some legal and practical shortcomings, *Ardhi*, Vol. 2(1), p. 2.

Santos, M. (1979) *The Shared Space*, Unwin, London.

Sawyerr, A. (ed) (1967) *East African Law and Social Change*, EAPH, Nairobi.

Selvarajah, E. (1983) The impact of the ceiling on housing property law on the slum and shanty improvement program in Sri Lanka, in Angel, S., Archer, R.W., Tanphihpat, S. and Wegelin, E.A. (eds) *op. cit.*

Shafi, S. (c.1986) A case study of government low cost housing scheme, Bastuhara Housing, Mirpur, Dhaka.

Shivji, I. (1997) Implications of the Draft Land Bill, paper presented at a Consultative Conference of NGOs and Interested Persons on Land Tenure Reform, Dar es Salaam.
Shivji, I.G. (1998) *Not Yet Democracy: Reforming Land Tenure in Tanzania*, International Institute for Environment and Development, London.
Siddiqui, Kamal (1997) *Land Management in South Asia, A Comparative Study*, University Press Ltd, Dhaka.
Simpson, S.R. (1976) *Land Law and Registration*, Cambridge UP, Cambridge.
Stevens, R.M. (1955) Planning legislation in the colonies, *Colonial Building Notes*, p. 31.
Stren, R. with Bell, J.K. (1995) *Urban Research in the Developing World Vol.4: Perspectives on the City*, University of Toronto Press, Toronto.
Tanphiphat, S. and Simapichaicheth, P. (1991) Private sector housing in Thailand, *Housing Finance International*, p.10.
Thornton White, L.W., Silberman, L. and Anderson, P.R. (1948) *Nairobi: Master Plan for a Colonial Capital*, Report prepared for the Municipal Council of Nairobi, HSMO, London.
Toulmin, C. and Quan, J. (eds) (2000) *Evolving Land Rights, Policy and Tenure in Africa*, IIED, London.
Tripp, A.M. (1997) *Changing the Rules: The Politics of Liberalisation and the Urban Informal Sector in Tanzania*, University of California Press, Berkeley.
Twaib, F. (1996) The dilemma of the customary landholder: the conflict between customary and statutory rights of occupancy in Tanzania, in Debusmann, R. and Arnold, S. (eds) *op. cit.* pp. 81–112.
Uganda Government (1993) *Report of the Technical Committee on Land Tenure Reform*, Kampala.
United Kingdom Government (1958) *Annual Report on the Colonial Territories for 1956–57*, HMSO, London.
United Kingdom Government (1923) *Indians in Kenya Memorandum*, Cmd 1922, HMSO, London.
United Kingdom Government (1940) *Report of the Royal Commission on the Distribution of the Industrial Population* (Chairman: Montague Barlow) Cmd. 6153, HMSO, London.
United Kingdom Government (1942) *Report of the Committee on Land Utilisation in Rural Areas* (Chairman: Leslie Scott) Cmd. 6378, HMSO, London.

United Kingdom Government (1942) *Final Report of the Expert Committee on Compensation and Betterment* (Chairman: Augustus Uthwatt) Cmd. 6386, HMSO, London.

United Kingdom Government (1971) *Survey of the Land Law of Northern Ireland; Report to the Director of Law Reform for Northern Ireland*, HM Stationery Office, Belfast.

United Kingdom Government (1998) *DFID Project Memorandum for the project: Securing Sustainable Livelihoods through Land Tenure Reform*, Kampala.

UNCHS (Habitat) (1993) *Managing the Access of the Poor to Urban Land: New Approaches for Regularisation Policies in the Developing Countries*, UMP/UNCHS (Habitat)/IFAL/UNAM International Seminar Conclusions and Recommendations, Mexico City.

UNCHS (Habitat) (1989) *Women and Human Settlements Development*, Nairobi.

UNCHS (Habitat) (1994) *Bangladesh Urban and Shelter Sector Review 1993*, Nairobi.

UNCHS (Habitat) (1994) *Working Party Conclusions*, International Conference on Re-appraising the Urban Planning Process as an Instrument of Sustainable Urban Development and Management.

UNCHS (Habitat) (1997) *The Istanbul Declaration and the Habitat Agenda*, Nairobi.

UNCHS (Habitat) (1999) *Guidelines on Practical Aspects in the Realization of the Human Right to Adequate Housing, Including the Formulation of the United Nations Housing Rights Programme*. Progress Report of the Executive Director to the 17th Session of the Human Settlements Commission, Nairobi.

UNCHS (Habitat) (1999) *Communication Development and Women's Participation in Human Settlements Management*, Nairobi.

UNDP (1991) *Cities, People and Poverty*, New York.

USAID/RHUDO (1991) *Urban Perspectives*, Vol. 2, Nairobi.

Wade, R. (1990) *Governing the Market*, Princeton University Press, Princeton, NJ.

Wadhva, K. (1987) NCU, housing legislation and the urban poor, *Nagarlok*, Vol.19, p. 28, New Delhi.

Walsh, A.H. (1969) *The Urban Challenge to Government*, Praeger, New York.

van der Walt, A.J. (1995) Tradition on trial: a critical analysis of the civil-law tradition in South African property law, *South African Journal of Human Rights*, Vol. 11, pp. 169–206.
van der Walt, A.J. (1997) *The Constitutional Property Clause*, Juta, Cape Town.
Werlin, H.H. (1974) *Governing an African City, A Case Study of Nairobi*, Holmes and Meier, London.
West, H. (1972) *Land Policy in Buganda*, Cambridge UP, Cambridge.
Williamson, I. (1989) Placing the improvements and achievements of a National Land Information Project in perspective, a case study of the Thailand Land Titling Project unpublished, World Bank, Washington, DC.
Woodman, G. (1988) Land title registration without prejudice: the Ghana Land Title Registration Law 1986, *Journal of African Law*, Vol. 30, pp. 119–35.
World Bank (1999) *Towards an Urban Strategy for Bangladesh*, Infrastructure Sector Division, South Asia Region.
World Bank (1989) *Sub-Saharan Africa: From Crisis to Sustainable Growth*, Washington DC.
World Bank (1993) *Options for Land Reform and Rural Restructuring in South Africa*, Washington DC.
World Bank (1995) *The World Bank and Legal Technical Assistance*, PRWP 414, Washington DC.
World Bank (1994) *Governance: The World Bank's Experience*, Washington DC.
World Bank (1998) *Assessing Aid; What Works, What Doesn't and Why*, Washington, DC.
World Commission on Environment and Development (1987) *Our Common Future*, Oxford.
Wylie, J.C.W. (1986) *The Land Laws of Trinidad and Tobago*, Government of Trinidad and Tobago, Port-of-Spain.
Yaron, G., Janssen, G. and Maamberua, U. (1992) *Rural Development in the Okavango Region of Namibia: an Assessment of Needs, Opportunties and Constraints*, Gamsberg Macmillan, Windhoek.
Young, C. (1994) *The African Colonial State in Comparative Perspective*, Yale UP, New Haven.

Index

FSC
www.fsc.org
MIX
Papier | Fördert
gute Waldnutzung
FSC® C083411

Kolibri 360 GmbH
Ferdinand-Jühlke-Straße 7
99095 Erfurt, Deutschland
produktsicherheit@kolibri360.de